W9-CMC-668

BYZANTIUM AND THE CRUSADES

CRUSADER WORLDS

General Editor: Jonathan Phillips

Published

Hospitallers – Jonathan Riley-Smith
Unknown Crusader Castles – Kristian Molin

Forthcoming

Crusader Kings and Queens – Deborah Gerish
Crusader Warfare – David Nicolle
Crusaders in the Holy Land – Andrew Jotischky
Crusading and the Wider World – Bernard Hamilton
Egypt and the Crusades – Jonathan Phillips
Heresy and the Crusades – Christoph Maier
The Teutonic Knights – Kristian Molin
Women and the Crusades – Jessalyn Bird

Byzantium and the Crusades

Jonathan Harris

Hambledon and London
London and New York

Hambledon and London

102 Gloucester Avenue
London, NW1 8HX

175 Fifth Avenue
New York, NY 10010
USA

First Published 2003

ISBN 1 85285 298 4

A description of this book is available from the
British Library and from the Library of Congress.

Typeset by Carnegie Publishing, Lancaster,
and printed and bound in Great Britain
by The Bath Press.

Distributed in the United States and Canada
exclusively by Palgrave Macmillan,
a division of St Martin's Press.

Contents

Illustrations

Between Pages 78 and 79

Maps

For Catalina and Simon

Acknowledgements

While yet another book on the crusades may require explanation or even an apology, one on the Byzantine empire does not. Although Byzantium played a crucial role in the western European crusading venture between 1095 and 1291, and although its religion and culture have exercised a deep and lasting influence on eastern Europe and Russia, it remains one of the least known and little studied of past human civilisations. While this book is mainly concerned with the relations between the empire and western Europe in the period of the crusades, it is also an exploration of Byzantine mentality and outlook which, it is hoped, will stimulate readers to deepen their acquaintance with a society as fascinating as it is occasionally bizarre or even repellent. For this reason, wherever possible I have cited the contemporary sources on which I base my analysis in English translation, even when those translations are not necessarily the best or most accurate.

I would like to thank Bernard Hamilton, Eirene Harvalia-Crook, Tia Kolbaba, Tony Morris, Jonathan Phillips and Martin Sheppard who provided information, criticism and corrections on earlier drafts of this book. My debt to the formidable scholarship of Michael Angold, Ralph-Johannes Lilie, Paul Magdalino and Jonathan Shepard will be apparent from the footnotes and bibliography. My thanks are also due to my colleagues at the Hellenic Institute, Julian Chrysostomides and Charalambos Dendrinos, who understood my elusiveness while this book was being written, and the students who have taken my MA course option on Byzantium and the Crusades over the past few years for curbing some of my less convincing ideas. Finally, the research and teaching which are encapsulated here would not have been possible without the support of the Minister of Culture of Greece, Mr Evangelos Venizelos and the encouragement and understanding of Dr Alkestis Soulogianni.

Abbreviations

Anna Comnena	Anna Comnena, *Alexiad*, trans. E. R. A. Sewter (Harmondsworth, 1969)
Choniates	Niketas Choniates, *O City of Byzantium: Annals of Niketas Choniates*, trans. H. J. Magoulias (Detroit, 1984)
Kinnamos	John Kinnamos, *Deeds of Manuel and John Comnenus*, trans. C. M. Brand (New York, 1976)
Fulcher of Chartres	Fulcher of Chartres, *Chronicle*, trans. M. E. McGinty, in *The First Crusade: The Chronicle of Fulcher of Chartres and Other Source Material*, ed. Edward Peters (2nd edn, Philadelphia, 1998), pp. 47–101
Gesta Francorum	*Gesta Francorum et aliorum Hierosolimitanorum*, ed. and trans. Rosalind Hill (London, 1962)
Gunther of Pairis	Gunther of Pairis, *The Capture of Constantinople*, trans. A. J. Andrea (Philadelphia, 1997)
Liudprand	Liudprand of Cremona, *The Embassy to Constantinople and Other Writings*, trans. F. A. Wright (London, 1993)
MGH	Monumenta Germaniae Historica
Odo of Deuil	Odo of Deuil, *De profectione Ludovici VII in orientem*, ed. and trans. V. Berry (New York, 1948)
Orderic Vitalis	Orderic Vitalis, *The Ecclesiastical History*, ed. and trans. Marjorie Chibnall, 6 vols (Oxford, 1969–80)
Pachymeres	George Pachymeres, *Relations historiques*, ed. A. Failler, 5 vols (Paris, 1984–2000)
Psellos	Michael Psellos, *Fourteen Byzantine Rulers*, trans. E. R. A. Sewter (2nd edn, Harmondsworth, 1966)
RHC Oc	*Recueil des historiens des croisades: historiens occidentaux*, 5 vols (Paris, 1844–96)
RHC Or	*Recueil des historiens des croisades: historiens orientaux*, 5 vols (Paris, 1872–1906)

Robert of Clari	Robert of Clari, *The Conquest of Constantinople*, trans. E. H. McNeal (Toronto, 1936)
Villehardouin	Geoffrey of Villehardouin, *The Conquest of Constantinople*, in *Chronicles of the Crusades*, trans. M. R. B. Shaw (Harmondsworth, 1963), pp. 29–160
William of Tyre	William of Tyre, *A History of Deeds Done Beyond the Sea*, trans. E. A. Babcock and A. C. Krey, 2 vols (New York, 1943)

A Note on Spelling

As regards the spelling of Byzantine names in the text and footnotes, I have used those versions which seem to me to be most natural and familiar. While, in general, I have tried to transliterate them as closely as possible to the original Greek, Tornikios, rather than Tornicius, and Eustathios rather than Eustathius, I cannot claim complete consistency. Where there is a recognised English equivalent of a Greek Christian name, I have used it, hence Isaac rather than Isaakios, George rather than Georgios. Similarly, with surnames, where a Latinised version has become standard, it has been used: Anna Comnena rather than Anna Komnene, Comnenus rather than Komnenos, Palaeologus rather than Palaiologos, Cantacuzenus rather than Kantakouzenos.

Introduction

In May 1204, the newly crowned emperor of Constantinople, Baldwin of Flanders, wrote a letter to the pope, Innocent III. It was not an easy task, for Baldwin was one of the leaders of the Fourth Crusade, which had been launched by Innocent in August 1198. The crusaders had originally planned to conquer first Egypt and then Jerusalem, which had been in Muslim hands since its capture by Saladin in 1187, but, instead of fighting the infidel, they had turned their weapons on Christians. They had not only attacked and captured Constantinople, the capital of the Christian Byzantine empire, they had systematically looted its palaces and churches, expelled its rulers and crowned Baldwin as a new emperor of their own. Innocent might well have been expected to be furious at this deviation from the ideals of the crusade and to have excommunicated the entire army. That was exactly what he had done two years earlier when it had perpetrated a similar outrage on another Christian city, that of Zara in Dalmatia.

Surprisingly, in spite of this inconvenient background, Baldwin's justification of the army's actions worked. When Innocent replied in November 1204, he accepted Baldwin's version of events and did not even threaten excommunication. On the contrary, he placed the new emperor, his lands and his people under his protection, and commanded that the crusading army, rather than going on to Egypt, should stay to protect Constantinople from any attempt by the Byzantines to retake the city.[1] Nor did he do so grudgingly, but waxed lyrical on what appeared to be a clear indication of divine favour:

> Surely, this was done by the Lord and is wondrous in our eyes. This is truly a change done by the right hand of the Most High, in which the right hand of the Lord manifested power so that he might exalt the most holy Roman Church while He returns the daughter to the mother, the part to the whole and the member to the head.[2]

Baldwin's letter, and the readiness of the pope to respond favourably to it, pose an obvious and fundamental question. The First Crusade had been launched in 1095 by Innocent III's predecessor, Urban II, ostensibly with a view to helping the Byzantine empire against its Muslim enemies. Just over a century later, events had come full circle. The soldiers of the Fourth Crusade and the pope himself now considered themselves entirely justified in attacking and annexing the empire's capital city. How had this extraordinary reversal come about?

Many minds have pondered this problem and a multiplicity of theories have come and gone over the years. Some sought to identify one individual or group who had deliberately plotted to divert the Fourth Crusade to Constantinople. During the later nineteenth century, for example, Count Louis de Mas Latrie and Charles Hopf placed the entire blame on the Italian maritime republic of Venice and its aged but formidable doge, Enrico Dandolo. Dandolo, so the argument ran, wished to prevent the crusade from attacking Egypt, because Venice had concluded a commercial treaty with the Ayyubid regime there in 1202. The republic's commercial interest dictated an attack on Constantinople instead, because the emperors there had been obstructing Venetian trading activities. The doge therefore cunningly manipulated the crusaders into deviating from their original destination, by allowing them to run up an enormous debt for the hire of Venetian shipping. The theory was discredited when the treaty with Egypt, which Hopf dated to 1202, was shown by Gabriel Hanotaux to belong, in fact, to 1208 or 1212, long after the Fourth Crusade had captured Constantinople.[3] Other theories have sought to blame the German imperial claimant, Philip of Swabia, the crusade leader, Boniface of Montferrat, and even Innocent III himself, only to come up against similarly cogent objections.[4]

With the conspiracy theories out of favour, there remain two primary schools of thought in the voluminous literature on the subject in English. The first argues that this was a classic case of the clash of civilisations. The capture and sack of Constantinople was the culmination of mounting incomprehension, intolerance and hostility between the two halves of the Christian world, the Catholic, western European Latins on the one hand, and the Orthodox, Greek-speaking, eastern Byzantines on the other. The theory was best expressed in 1955 by Sir Steven Runciman, who argued that the crusades had the unfortunate effect of bringing the two societies, which had had little to do with each other in the past, into much closer contact. It was this very contact which opened the way for mutual misunderstanding and mistrust:

> There are idealists who fondly believe that if only the peoples of the world could get to know each other there would be peace and goodwill forever. This is a tragic delusion. It is indeed possible for men and women of education to enjoy the company and customs of foreigners and to feel sympathy for them. But simpler folk who find themselves in a country whose language and habits are unintelligible to them are apt to feel at a loss and resentful.[5]

Proponents of the clash of civilisations theory had only to cite the words of contemporaries to uncover what appeared to be indisputable evidence of this deep mutual antagonism. Byzantine writers, such as Anna Comnena, John Kinnamos or Niketas Choniates, often described western European crusaders as uncouth barbarians, while their western counterparts, Guibert of Nogent, Odo of Deuil or Gunther of Pairis, fulminated against the effeminate and treacherous Byzantines, their schism with the church of Rome and their supposed collusion with Muslim powers.[6] The massacre of Latins in Constantinople in 1182, and the Norman capture and sack of the Byzantine city of Thessalonica in 1185, seemed to be the inevitable outcome of this growing tension and to stand as milestones on a straight road which led to the catastrophe of 1204.

So compelling was the clash of civilisations theory that it seemed all there was left to discuss was when the tension began, and who was to blame. Some historians saw the process as starting as far back as 1054, when some papal legates had excommunicated the patriarch of Constantinople and opened up the schism between the Byzantine and western churches. Others saw the arrival of the First Crusade at Constantinople in 1096 as the beginning of the trouble, as thousands of western knights descended on the Byzantine empire on their way to conquer Jerusalem, raising apprehensions among the Byzantines that these armies might in fact be aiming to conquer Constantinople or other parts of imperial territory. Still others claimed that the accession of the supposedly anti-Latin Andronicus I as Byzantine emperor in 1183 was the real beginning of the mutual antagonism.[7]

There was a similar disparity when it came to apportioning the blame. Some saw the wanton aggression of the crusaders towards the sophisticated and cultured Byzantines as the root of the trouble, others the xenophobia and snobbery of the Byzantines towards people whom they considered to be somehow inferior.[8] Regardless of the precise starting point chosen, or the exact apportionment of blame, the basic theory remains the same.

Compelling though the clash of civilisations theory is, it suffers from at least three serious flaws. The first is that it claims that there was a general and escalating estrangement between Byzantine east and Latin west during the twelfth century. In spite of the frequent harsh words and occasional ugly incidents, the two societies were in fact closely intertwined. Not only did Byzantine emperors of the period of the crusades regularly intermarry with their counterparts in western Europe and the Holy Land, their empire depended on western European manpower. As the Byzantines themselves were quite prepared to admit, Latins made up the most effective and loyal part of the imperial army, and they also served the emperor as ambassadors, translators and counsellors. The notion of two completely divided societies coming into final conflict in 1204 is therefore unconvincing. When the soldiers of the Fourth Crusade first attacked the walls of Constantinople in the summer of 1203, they did so at the behest of a Byzantine prince, Alexios Angelos, while the stiffest resistance that they encountered came not from the Byzantines themselves but from the western European troops in imperial service.[9]

A second flaw in the clash of civilisations theory is that it assumes not only that a complete east-west hostility had developed during the twelfth century, but also that there was a causal link between that hostility and the sack of Constantinople. Yet when the western strike against Constantinople came, in the shape of the Fourth Crusade, there was no premeditated plan to attack the Byzantine capital. On the way to Egypt, the crusade diverted to the Byzantine capital at the request of a prince of the ruling Angelos family who needed help to restore his father to the throne. While individual leaders of the army, including Boniface of Montferrat and the doge of Venice, Enrico Dandolo, may have welcomed the change of objective, most of the rank and file were bitterly opposed to it. A sizeable proportion left the army and made their own way to the Holy Land. Those who remained only agreed very reluctantly to the diversion when subjected to a mixture of financial and emotional blackmail. Even then, many hesitated before the final attack in April 1204, and had serious doubts as to whether it was legitimate to attack a Christian city in this way.[10]

The third and final weakness in the clash of civilisations theory is what happened after 1204. If the mutual antagonism was as sharp as supposed, why was it that so few westerners were prepared to heed the pope's summons and to fight to maintain Constantinople under Latin rule? Because only small numbers of volunteers went out to help Baldwin of Flanders and his successors to defend the city, the Latin emperors suffered from a constant shortage of manpower and their hold on Constantinople lasted only fifty-seven years. By 1261 the Byzantines had recaptured Constantinople and recovered a sizeable part of their empire, as it had been before 1204.

In view of these flaws in the clash of civilisations theory, it is hardly surprising therefore that many scholars have discarded the idea that the Fourth Crusade's sack of Constantinople was the culmination of mounting hostility and have come to the conclusion that it came about as a kind of accident. Proponents of this view lay stress on the unforeseen events which prevented the crusade from going on to Egypt as planned: the massive debt which was owed to the Venetians because not enough crusaders came forward to fill the ships that had been hired; the attack on Zara which the crusade undertook to secure a postponement of that debt; and the proposal made by Alexios Angelos that the crusade should accompany him to Constantinople. The sweeping notion of mounting hostility or indeed any overall thesis as to why relations broke down so completely is largely ignored by this school of thought.[11]

To the question of why a movement originally launched to help the Byzantines ultimately stormed their capital city and divided up their empire, the existing literature on Byzantium and the Crusades yields therefore only either an answer which is unsatisfactory or one which simply avoids the problem and provides no answer at all. Both theories are, moreover, profoundly unpalatable in their implications. If different cultures are bound to come into conflict whenever they interact closely, there is little hope for the modern world of global communication and multi-racial societies. If, on the other hand, the Fourth Crusade came about simply as an accident, it leaves open the question as to whether the whole of history can be understood in this way and whether human beings have any control at all over their own destiny.

This book aims to advance another view of Byzantine interaction with western Europe, the crusades, and the crusader states. It argues that the key, or at least a key, lies not in generalised hostility between peoples or impersonal chance theory, but in the nature of the Byzantine empire and the ideology which underpinned it. That ideology will be examined by looking at the influential group who ran the empire, and the methods and principles they employed in dealing with the world beyond their borders. It will be argued that the disaster of 1204 was the result of an attempt on the part of the Byzantines to implement and sustain their ideology and foreign policy in circumstances which left their actions open to misinterpretation. By pursuing very different ends to those of the reformed papacy and the leaders of crusade armies, and by employing methods that were often considered by western Europeans to be dishonourable, the Byzantines succeeded in giving the impression that the empire was failing to participate in the pious cause of defending Jerusalem and the Holy Land from the common Muslim foe. Western attempts after 1187 to extort what they considered to be the rightful Byzantine financial contribution to the enterprise led directly to the events of April 1204.

By a curious irony, the very same ideology and foreign policy which brought the empire into conflict with western Europe up to 1204 afterwards proved to be its salvation. They enabled it not only to survive the catastrophe of the loss of Constantinople and to recover the city in 1261, but ultimately to outlive the crusader states of Syria and Palestine that fell to Islam in 1291.

1

The Empire of Christ

In about the year 1050, the Byzantine empire, known also as 'Byzantium', was the largest and most prosperous political entity in the Christian world. On its eastern side, it consisted of Asia Minor or Anatolia, that is to say what is now Turkey and part of Armenia, and the island of Cyprus. In the west it covered Greece and the Balkans south of the Danube, the Aegean and Ionian islands, and Crete. The empire also retained two isolated outposts: the cities of Cherson and Bosporos across the Black Sea in the Crimea, and part of southern Italy, the provinces of Calabria and Apulia. Its capital city was Constantinople, the modern Istanbul, strategically situated at the crossing between the empire's European and Asiatic provinces, and founded in the year 330 by the Emperor Constantine I (306–37) on the site of an earlier city named Byzantium.

Since the heartland of the empire was in Greek-speaking areas, its official language was Greek, but it would be wrong to see medieval Byzantium solely as a Greek empire. Armenian and Slavonic languages were also widely spoken, especially in the frontier districts. There were also pockets of Slavs in Asia Minor, and of Armenians in the Balkans, as a result of the policy of forced resettlement pursued by the emperors over the centuries.[1]

The borders of the empire in 1050 were the result of a considerable expansion which had taken place over the previous hundred years, especially during the reigns of the emperors Nikephoros II Phokas (963–69), John I Tzimiskes (969–76) and Basil II (976–1025). In the east, the Byzantines had taken advantage of the increasing weakness of their traditional Muslim enemy, the Abbasid Caliphate in Baghdad. Crete had been taken from the Arabs in 961, Cyprus in 965, Antioch in 969, Edessa in 1032 and Ani in 1045. The empire had also extended its borders on its western side as it settled old scores with its long-time rival, Bulgaria. In 1018 Basil II had completed the conquest of the country and incorporated it into the empire.

One by-product of the period of expansion was that, after 1025, the provinces of the empire enjoyed a period of relative peace and prosperity as the threat of foreign invasion, ever present in previous centuries, now diminished. While frontier cities like Antioch or Belgrade continued to be geared to the needs of defence, other towns, particularly in what is now

Greece, flourished as centres of industry and commerce. Archaeological excavations reveal that areas of Corinth and Athens, which had been deserted for centuries, were now reoccupied and built over, and important industries began to grow up. Corinth produced textiles, cotton, linen and silk, as well as possessing an important glass factory. Athens concentrated on dyes and soap. Thebes was renowned for its high quality silks, prized above all others for the quality of their workmanship. Thessalonica, the second city of the empire, hosted an annual fair which attracted merchants from all parts of the Mediterranean world, as well as being a centre for the production of silk and metalwork.[2] In Asia Minor, wealth lay in agriculture rather than in commerce or manufactures, as peaceful conditions allowed more land to be brought back under cultivation. Here too there were signs of expansion and renewal in the towns. Sardis and Pergamon, inland from the Aegean coast, grew noticeably during the eleventh century, while Ikonion, on the flat Anatolian plain, and Euchaita, to the north in the region of Pontos, flourished as market towns. In north-west Asia Minor, the chief regional centre was Nicaea, of historic importance as the site of two ecumenical councils of the church in 325 and 787, but also a staging post on the road east, and a market for agricultural produce and fish from its lake.[3]

Alongside the economic revival, the more settled conditions that prevailed during the tenth and eleventh centuries had permitted the expansion of monastic life. Barren and uncultivated areas, particularly mountains, were taken over by monasteries and by solitary hermits, who no longer had to fear attack from the Arabs of Crete. At Mount Athos, a rocky peninsula in northern Greece, St Athanasius the Athonite founded the Great Lavra in 963, and several other monasteries were established in the years that followed. An imperial decree of 1046 made Athos into a kind of republic, with each monastery sending representatives to a ruling council based in the town of Karyes. Other monastic centres were in Asia Minor: in Cappadocia, where the monasteries were built by hollowing out the soft volcanic rock, and on the 'holy' mountains of Ida, Latros, Kyminas, Mykale, Auxentios and Olympus.[4]

The new-found wealth of the provinces is reflected in the survival of many more examples of ecclesiastical art than from previous centuries. Many are in styles that were no longer slavish imitations of those used in Constantinople, such as the eleventh-century frescoes in the churches of Kastoria in north-west Greece or in the cave churches of Cappadocia. The rich mosaics and interior decoration of the monasteries of Daphni near Athens and Hosios Loukas in Central Greece bear witness to the availability of wealthy patrons and their readiness to make pious donations to the monasteries.[5]

1. The Byzantine empire, *c.* 1050.

Impressive though the expansion of the empire and the economic development of the provinces had been, what really set the Byzantine empire apart from other Christian states in the eyes of contemporaries was its capital city of Constantinople. The Byzantines themselves took enormous pride in it: so important a place was it in their eyes that they seldom needed to refer to it by name, preferring to use epithets such as the 'Queen of Cities', the 'Great City', or 'the Eye of All Cities'.[6] Nor was the esteem in which Constantinople held restricted to its own citizens. An Arab writer described the Byzantine capital as 'a great and important city, which none can surpass', and the French cleric Fulcher of Chartres, who arrived with the First Crusade in 1097, gushed enthusiastically about the 'excellent and beautiful city'. Geoffrey of Villehardouin observed that the soldiers of the Fourth Crusade who arrived in the summer of 1203 'never imagined that there could be so fine a place in all the world'. Its fame had spread far beyond the borders of the empire. To the Scandinavians, it was known as Micklagard, the great city, and among the Russians as Tsargrad, the imperial city.[7]

There were a number of reasons for the pride which Constantinople inspired on the part of its citizens, and the awe and astonishment on the part of foreigners. One was its impregnability. It enjoyed a natural defensive position, placed on a narrow promontory that was bounded by water on two sides, the Golden Horn and the Bosporos to the north and the Sea of Marmara to the south. On the landward side, previous emperors had constructed a massive, fortified wall stretching from the Golden Horn to the Sea of Marmara, about nine metres high and four and a half metres thick. It was punctuated at intervals by ninety-six towers, providing broad platforms for ballistae and catapults. In front of the walls was a wide ditch, which any assailant had to cross while exposed to withering fire from the walls. The fortifications continued along the seaward sides, making assault by sea equally daunting. Further defence was provided by a heavy iron chain strung from a tower within the city to another in the suburb of Galata on the other side of the water, thus preventing hostile vessels from entering the Golden Horn.[8]

Thanks to these defences, Constantinople had never been captured by a foreign force and had withstood numerous sieges over the centuries. One of the most serious had been mounted by the Persians and Avars in 626, when they had blockaded the city simultaneously from east and west. The Arabs had tried for four years between 674 and 678, with the support of a powerful fleet. Both sieges had to be broken off in the face of the unyielding defences. In later years, the Russians and the Bulgars were also to make the attempt, with similar lack of success. After the last Russian attack, a naval assault in 1043, some fifteen thousand enemy corpses were counted, washed up on the shores of the Bosporos. The towering defences of Constantinople were the first thing a visitor would have seen when arriving by land or sea. The French cleric Odo of Deuil, who travelled with the Second Crusade in 1147 and who had little good to say about the Byzantines, poured scorn on the walls, claiming that they were in poor repair. The soldiers of the Fourth Crusade, however, shuddered when they saw them.[9]

The second aspect of Constantinople that marked it out was its size, for by medieval standards it was a enormous city, and certainly the largest in the Christian world. Rome, which had once been so vast and powerful, had declined by the eleventh century to a shadow of its former self, with large areas within its walls desolate or uninhabited. Paris and London had not yet begun to grow, and by the early twelfth century were still only towns of moderate size with populations of about twenty thousand at most. Constantinople, by contrast, is believed to have had at least 375,000 inhabitants, making it nearly twenty times the size of London, and it has even been estimated that more people lived within in its walls in 1050 than in the whole of the kingdom of England. The closest cities of comparable size were to be found in the Islamic world. Cordova in Spain was probably roughly the same size, while Baghdad was considerably larger.

Like many large cities today, Constantinople's population was multiracial, reflecting both the ethnic composition of the empire as a whole and the world around it. While the majority was composed of Greek-speakers, there were large numbers of Armenians, Russians and Georgians. There was a sizeable Jewish community, concentrated mainly in the suburb of Galata on the other side of the Golden Horn, Italian merchants from the trading cities of Venice, Genoa and Pisa, and mercenaries from western Europe and Scandinavia. There was even a small Arab community in Constantinople, mostly merchants, for whose use a mosque was provided.[10]

Another aspect of Constantinople frequently commented on by natives and visitors alike was its wealth. It was the boast of Constantinople's citizens that two thirds of the riches of the world were concentrated in their city, and visitors like Fulcher of Chartres were astonished by the sheer opulence that they saw around them, especially the abundance of gold, silver and silk.[11] The main reason for this wealth was trade. Thanks to its geographical position between Europe and Asia, Constantinople was an obvious entrepôt where goods from one part of the world could be exchanged for those of another. Merchants gathered in the commercial quarter, along the Golden Horn. The Arabs brought spices, porcelain and jewels, the Italians tin and wool, the Russians wax, amber, honey and fur. These were then sold on or exchanged for products to ship back to their home markets. Although much of this activity was in the hands of foreign merchants, the Byzantine authorities benefited by charging a customs duty, the *kommerkion*, of 10 per cent on all imports and exports, and the city as a whole grew rich on the commercial opportunities presented by the influx of merchants, goods and raw materials.[12]

Constantinople was also, like Athens, Thebes and Corinth, a centre for manufacture, and was particularly well known for its metalwork. The silversmiths were so numerous that they had their own area around the Augousteion, Constantinople's central square, where in 1162 they annoyed the emperor by shouting coarse comments at a visiting Turkish delegation.[13] Most of the high-quality metalwork produced in Constantinople was no doubt made for patrons within the city or the wider empire, but some of it went for export, especially to Italy. The altarpiece known at the Pala d'Oro in St Mark's church in Venice was created in Constantinople during the eleventh century and shipped out around that time. Bronze doors of Constantinopolitan manufacture found their way to the basilica of St Paul's-without-the-walls in Rome, and to the cathedrals of Amalfi, Trani and Salerno in the same period.[14] Other industries based in the imperial capital were silk dressing and dyeing, manufacture of silk garments, and soap, perfume and candle making. Banking and money lending were also tolerated, though strictly regulated.[15]

The wealth of Constantinople was most visible in its buildings, whether public, private or ecclesiastical. It was unusual among medieval cities in being a deliberately planned city, rather than a random jumble of buildings, with space set aside for public events and ceremonies. Most of this space was concentrated at the eastern end, but it was linked to the walls in the west by the long main street known as the Mese. The Mese began at the far south of the Land Walls, at the Golden Gate, an imposing entrance surmounted by four large bronze elephants, and traditionally used to enter the city by emperors returning from a successful campaign.[16] From there the Mese ran east through a series of public squares or forums: the Forum of Arcadius, with its column topped by a statue of the Emperor Arcadius (395–408), the Forum Bovis, named for the large bronze head of an ox which stood there, the Forum of Theodosius and the Forum of Constantine. The long street terminated at the Augousteion, which was dominated by the cathedral of Hagia Sophia and by a huge bronze equestrian statue of the Emperor Justinian (527–65). The figure of the emperor faced east, holding in one hand an orb surrounded by a cross, and his other raised in warning to his enemies. The statue's imperial dignity, however, might have been rather tarnished by the nests regularly built by herons on the emperor's

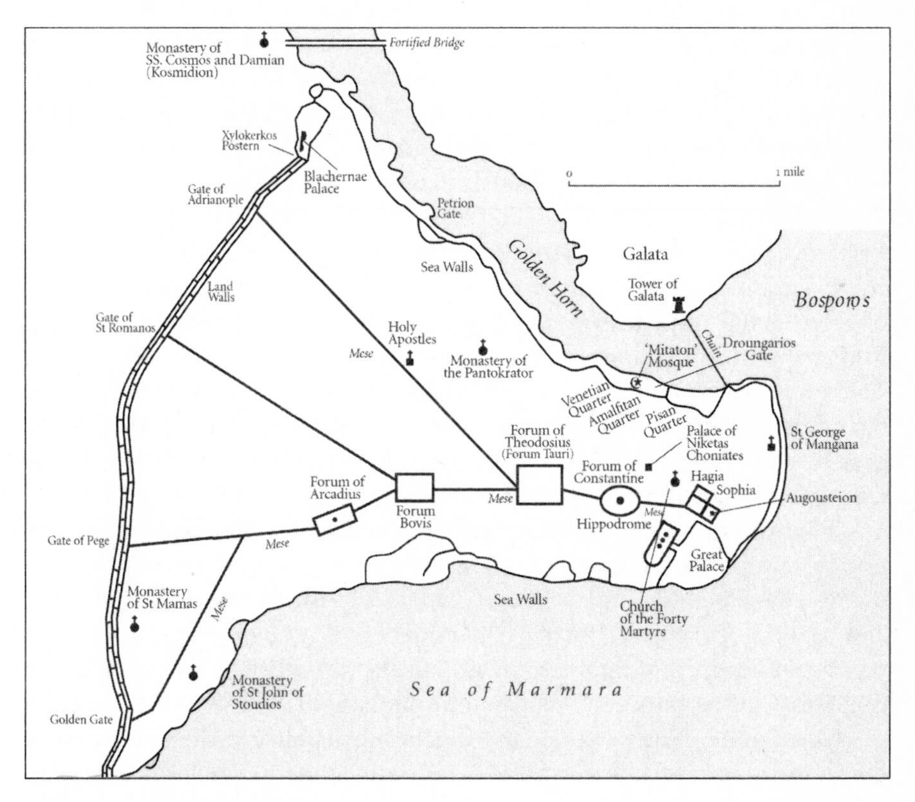

2. The city of Constantinople.

head and along the horse's back. Also in the Augousteion were the Horologion, a mechanical clock one of whose twenty-four doors flew open at the appropriate hour of the day, and the Milion, a milestone from which all distances were measured.[17]

To the south of the Augousteion stood the four hundred metre long Hippodrome, which could seat up to seat up to 100,000 people. It had originally been designed for the staging of chariot races, but provided the venue for any public happening, from executions to displays of tightrope walking. The emperor himself watched these spectacles from the imperial box or *Kathisma*, receiving the acclamations of the crowd before the proceedings commenced. Like a modern football stadium, however, the Hippodrome was prone to accidents. During a horse race in 1184 part of the imperial box collapsed, killing six people in the seats below. The central spine of the Hippodrome was decorated with trophies brought by earlier emperors from all over the Mediterranean world. From Karnak in Egypt had come a granite obelisk dating from 1471 BC, from Greece a bronze column of intertwined serpents, originally set up at Delphi in 478 BC, and from Rome, four bronze horses, made some time in the second century AD. There was a rich profusion of ancient statues and sculptures scattered around the place, serving no other purpose than adornment. Among them were bronze statues of the mythical Calydonian boar, and a pensive Hercules by Lysippos of Sikyon, the famous sculptor of the fourth century BC.[18]

Within this public setting of open squares and spaces there were numerous fine private houses and palaces, the homes of its more prosperous citizens, mainly along the Mese and to either side of it. The thirteenth-century courtier and historian Niketas Choniates had a house which he described as 'incomparable in beauty and immense in size' in the district of Sphorakion, to the north-east of the Forum of Constantine, and another close to the cathedral of Hagia Sophia. The palace of the Botaneiates family, in the area between the Golden Horn and the forum of Constantine, was a complex of buildings containing two private churches and a bath house. Although one observer claimed that mansions such as these overshadowed the street, leaving the poor to live in dirt and darkness, most visitors were favourably impressed and were struck both by their size and their number.[19]

As for the emperors, they possessed two large palaces within Constantinople itself. The older was the Great Palace or Boukoleon, named for a classical statue of a lion attacking an ox which stood within its precincts. It was a complex of buildings rather than a single structure, extending alongside the Hippodrome down to a small harbour, where the imperial galley was moored. The palace also possessed the *Porphyra* or Purple Chamber which overlooked the harbour and which was set aside as the place where children of the reigning emperor were born. Successive emperors had added buildings to it over the years. Theophilos (829–42) had ordered the construction of a series of chambers known as the Kamilas, Basil I (867–86) a five-storied hall known as the Mangana or Magnavra, both of which must have helped to give the palace a rather rambling external appearance. Great care was, however, taken with the gardens, which were mainly given over to wide lawns and terraces. The internal decoration of the palace, especially those parts that were likely to be seen by visiting ambassadors, was particularly lavish. The walls were faced with marble of various colours, and the upper walls and ceilings with mosaics, depicting everything from the triumphs of emperors to birds and animals, both natural and mythological.[20]

During the later eleventh century, the Boukoleon fell out of favour and the emperors of the Comnenus dynasty increasingly resided at the 'lower' palace of Blachernae at the opposite end of the city, by the northern extremity of the Land Walls. Blachernae enjoyed excellent views over the city, the Golden Horn and the countryside beyond the walls. Inside, it was as impressive as Boukoleon, largely thanks to Manuel I Comnenus (1143–80) who extended it, installed long galleries and had them decorated with gold mosaics.[21]

As far as ecclesiastical buildings are concerned, Constantinople was equally well provided. Among its many monasteries, the most famous was that of St John of Stoudios, which had been in existence for some five hundred years, and which on occasion played an important political role as a haven for hard-pressed emperors. Michael V (1041–42) and his uncle sought sanctuary there from the wrath of the Constantinopolitan mob, and Isaac I Comnenus (1057–59) retired there as a monk in the face of opposition to his rule. More recently, St Mamas had gained fame as a result of the reputation of its mystical abbot, Symeon the New Theologian (949–1022). There were other monasteries outside the walls, such as that of SS. Cosmas and Damian, usually referred to as the Kosmidion, close to the Blachernae palace, and the Theotokos Evergetes, some three kilometres away. Both in and around the city were the tall columns on which the bizarre ascetics known as Stylites spent their lives, protected from the elements by small shelters.[22]

While monasteries were remarkable for their number, Constantinople's churches were noted for their size and beauty. Foremost among them was the great cathedral of Hagia Sophia, or the Holy Wisdom, which stood to the north of the Augousteion and the Hippodrome. Built in the sixth century, on the orders of Justinian I, on a rectangular base and topped with an enormous dome thirty-two metres across, it would have towered above the city, the top of the dome still visible from ships far out to sea.

In the interior, the mosaic decoration covered the entire space of the dome, and the galleries were supported by columns of different coloured marble, creating an extraordinary effect when suffused by sunlight shining in from the upper windows. The Byzantines themselves were justifiably proud of the cathedral, which they tended to refer to simply as 'the Great Church'. It seldom failed to excite comment from visitors, who were unlikely to have ever seen a building of that size and who were awestruck by the beauty of the liturgical ceremonies performed there.[23]

There were many other churches almost as impressive. The Holy Apostles, consecrated in 550, was situated on a hill at the very heart of Constantinople. It boasted the tombs of many previous emperors, including Constantine the Great and Justinian, and some superb mosaic decoration. Rather than the wide dome used in Hagia Sophia, the square body of the Holy Apostles was surmounted by five smaller domes, a design which was to prove extremely influential on Byzantine ecclesiastical architecture.[24] St George of Mangana, inside the palace complex of Boukoleon, evoked a lyrical description from the courtier Michael Psellos, who extolled 'the size of the church, its beautiful symmetry, the harmony of its parts, the variety and rhythm of its loveliness'. Niketas Choniates spoke of the 'beauteous form' of the church of the Forty Martyrs.[25]

Thus strength, size, wealth and buildings were all elements in the prestige which Constantinople enjoyed both at home and abroad. Yet its significance in the eyes of contemporaries went much deeper, for Constantinople was regarded as a holy city. Along with Rome, Jerusalem, Antioch and Alexandria, it was one of five which were regarded as the most important in the Christian world and whose bishops had traditionally carried the title of patriarch. It could not, of course, claim that Christ or the Apostles Peter and Paul had ever been physically present within its walls, as could Jerusalem and Rome, although by the eleventh century it had come to be believed, on rather scanty evidence, that the church of Constantinople had been founded by St Andrew.[26] The spiritual aura of Constantinople rested not so much on any direct connection with the events reported in the New Testament but on what had happened since then.

For example, the success with which sieges, often by numerically superior pagan or infidel forces, had been beaten off against all the odds in the past had been interpreted as clear evidence of divine favour. The 'God-Guarded City' became another of the epithets used to describe Constantinople, and it was regarded as enjoying the special protection of the Virgin Mary. Chroniclers recorded how her personal intervention had often saved the day. A visible token of her protection, her wonder-working icon of the *Hodegetria* ('She who Shows the Way'), supposedly painted from the life by St Luke the Evangelist, was housed in one of the city's monasteries. It was brought out in times of danger and paraded on the walls, invariably being credited with the subsequent discomfiture of the enemy.[27]

Constantinople's survival over the centuries, when so many other prominent Christian cities had suffered capture and sack, allowed it to preserve within its walls things which would otherwise have been lost or destroyed, especially relics, items that were supposed in some way to be connected with Jesus Christ and the saints and therefore objects of wonder and veneration. Foremost among these were two sections of the True Cross, on which Christ had hung during the crucifixion on Mount Calvary. The cross allegedly had been discovered by Helena, the mother of Constantine I, while she was on pilgrimage in the Holy Land. She had brought part of it back with her to her son's newly founded city. Another was the Mandylion of Edessa, an image of the face of Christ imprinted on a cloth which, according to legend, had been sent by Christ Himself to the ruler of Edessa. It had been captured by a Byzantine general from the Muslims in 944 and brought back to Constantinople in triumph. By the eleventh century, the True Cross and the Mandylion were housed in a special chapel inside the palace complex of Boukoleon. The same chapel also housed the tunic which Christ had worn at the time of His passion, the Crown of Thorns, the lance which pierced His side, a small phial containing what purported to be some of His blood, part of the robe of the Virgin, and the head of St John the Baptist.[28]

There were other such relics scattered throughout the city. The church of the Holy Apostles possessed the pillar against which Christ had been scourged. In later years, the church of the monastery of the Pantokrator, an imperial foundation of the twelfth century, housed the slab of red marble on which the body of Christ had lain after the crucifixion. The Emperor Manuel I had had it shipped to Constantinople from Ephesus and, when it arrived at the harbour of Boukoleon, had carried up to the palace on his own back.[29] The concentration of so many important relics made Constantinople a goal of pilgrimage in its own right, as well as a stopover on the route east to the Holy Sepulchre in Jerusalem.

Similarly, the antiquity and grandeur of many of the monuments of Constantinople had given them a kind of spiritual aura all of their own and many were attributed with miraculous powers. This was particularly so with Hagia Sophia. Writing only shortly after its construction, Procopius of Caesarea wrote that:

> Whenever anyone enters this church to pray, he understands at once that it is not by any human power or skill, but by the influence of God, that this work has been so finely turned. And so his mind is lifted up toward God and exalted,

> feeling that He cannot be far away, but must especially love to dwell in this place which He has chosen.

As time went by the cathedral had become the subject of numerous myths and legends. Later generations could not believe that such a structure could have been built without divine assistance and asserted that, during construction, the dome had been supported by a golden chain let down from heaven. Every column inside the cathedral was believed to have the power to cure a particular illness when the sufferer rubbed against it.[30]

Quite apart from the specifically Christian sites and relics, many of the ancient statues and columns which were to be found all over Constantinople had acquired mythologies all of their own. One of the statues in the Hippodrome was believed to have the power of determining the true price of goods: the coins were placed in its hand which closed if the sum was correct. Many of the carvings on the bases of columns were reputed to depict future events, although the meaning only became clear after those events had occurred.[31]

All these elements, its strength, its size, its wealth and its holiness, which made up the prestige of Constantinople, were admitted and generally admired by Byzantines and foreigners alike. The Byzantines themselves, however, went further than other Christians, particularly those of western Europe, in believing that Constantinople occupied a supreme place in the Christian world, over and above Rome or Jerusalem. They arrived at that conclusion by the doctrine of *Translatio imperii*, the transfer of empire.

The empire in question was that of Rome, which had a deep spiritual significance in the eyes of the Byzantines. They regarded it as no accident that the reign of the first Roman emperor, Augustus (31 BC–14 AD), had coincided with the birth of the Saviour of the world, Jesus Christ. Both events were part of God's plan for the salvation of mankind. While the souls of believers were to be saved through faith in Christ, their welfare on earth was also provided for, through the *Pax Romana* that had followed Augustus's acquisition of power. God clearly wished that those who believed in Christ should live in one state, ruled by the Roman emperor. Christ himself was seen to have endorsed that belief when he had instructed his questioners to 'Render unto Caesar what is Caesar's, unto God the things that are God's', suggesting that Christians had a duty to obey the emperor, just as they had to obey God. The same message had been preached by the Apostle Peter, who urged Christians to 'Fear God, honour the emperor'.[32] That injunction became even more binding after 313, when Constantine the Great had adopted Christianity as his religion, the first Roman emperor to do so. Theologians living at the time were quick to take advantage of the change and to integrate the office of emperor into the divine scheme of things, arguing that the empire on earth was an image or *mimesis* of the kingdom of Heaven.[33]

Another of Constantine's actions was considered to be almost as important as his conversion to Christianity. Up to the last quarter of the third century AD, the capital city of the Roman empire had, of course, been Rome. As the pressure on the frontiers had increased, however, Rome proved to be an inconvenient base. The later Roman emperors had therefore tended to reside in cities that were closer to the threatened frontiers: Milan, Ravenna or Trier in the west, Nikomedia and Antioch in the east. Constantine had favoured the city of Byzantium, strategically situated as it was on the bridge between Europe and Asia, and in 330 he had inaugurated his new city of Constantinople, the city of Constantine, on the site. Constantine probably had no intention of setting Constantinople up as a new capital city instead of Rome, but later generations of Byzantines saw it in exactly that light. Philotheos, patriarch of Constantinople (1354–55 and 1364–76), writing in 1352, asserted categorically that 'The great and wonderful empire of the Romans was transferred from Italy to the east when Constantine the Great, by divine command, was converted from Hellenism [paganism] to faith in Christ and transformed the city of Byzantium into the present great city, which he called by his own name'. Anna Comnena was convinced that 'power was transferred from Rome to our country and the Queen of Cities'.[34]

As a result of Constantine's decision, therefore, Constantinople was seen to have become the most important city in the Christian world, both a new Rome and a second Jerusalem.[35] The emperors who reigned there were by right the emperors whom Christ and St Peter had commanded that all Christians should obey. The exalted nature of the emperor's position was reflected in his official title of 'Emperor and Autocrat of the Romans' (*Basileus kai Autokrator ton Romaion*). The word used by the Byzantines to describe themselves was *Romaioi* or Romans. The terms 'Byzantine' and 'Byzantines', so familiar today, were applied to them only relatively recently.

Similarly the empire was the Roman empire, the state to which all Christians ought to owe allegiance. It was, however, often referred to by a word which suggested that it was much more than a mere earthly princedom: *Oikoumene*, a virtually untranslatable term but one meaning broadly 'the civilised world'. It made no difference that the empire had contracted drastically since Constantine's day, with the western half of the empire from Italy to Britain lost during the fifth century, and the eastern provinces of Egypt, Syria and Palestine in the seventh. As the monk Cyril unashamedly informed the Khazars in the ninth century: 'Our empire is that of Christ'.[36]

This then was the Byzantine empire as it was in the years before the crusades. A wealthy, powerful state with wide borders but one which did not define itself in terms of those material things. As far as the Byzantines were concerned, what was important was their emperor, their capital city and the spiritual significance which attached to them. This was the decisive influence on the empire's foreign policy and on the people who formulated it.

2

The Rulers of the Empire

The same ideology that gave such a prominent place to Constantinople in the Byzantine mind also attributed an exalted place to the emperor. He was nothing less than the vicegerent of God on earth. Such a position, of course, involved awesome responsibility. The emperor was expected to imitate God, displaying appropriate devoutness (*eulabeia*) and love of mankind (*philanthropeia*), in order to fulfil his allotted task of ensuring the temporal welfare of God's people in His place. The emperor was answerable to no one and received his power directly from God, an idea made visual in Byzantine art through portrayals of Christ or the Virgin Mary crowning a haloed emperor. He alone, as an earlier theorist had put it, 'pilots affairs below'. There was no room for majority decision making for 'anarchy and civil war result from ... polyarchy based on equality'.[1]

Given the theory, it would be reasonable to conclude that the empire was ruled by the emperor and him alone. Yet it is quite clear that in fact this was not the case. A portrait of the Emperor Nikephoros III Botaneiates (1078–81), in a manuscript now in Paris, gives an insight into the real state of affairs. The emperor sits on his throne, attended by allegorical figures representing truth and justice. Nikephoros is not left alone with these manifestations of divine favour, however, for behind him are four smaller, standing figures, dressed in long robes and with turbans on their heads. To his right stands the *Protovestiarios*, who played an important role in government and administration. Next to the *Protovestiarios* stands an imperial secretary, charged with drawing up letters and documents. To the emperor's left stand two more individuals with the title of *Proedros*.[2] These are the emperor's advisers, the members of the imperial civil service.

The existence of a secular bureaucracy was one of many aspects of Byzantine life that marked it out from western Europe in the same period. In the early medieval west, kings relied on priests to fulfil what administrative tasks there were, few laymen at all having the necessary level of literacy. The more complex and developed nature of Byzantine society required rather more than that: a secular, educated elite, trained to the task of administration. Few emperors ruled without their help; Basil II is said to have done so in the later years of his reign, but his attitude was unusual enough to have invited surprised comment as an exception to normal circumstances.[3] As in most human societies, theory and practice were often at variance in Byzantium, and this certainly seems to have been the case as regards the absolute nature of the emperor's power.

This state of affairs had profound repercussions for the way that political policy was formulated in Byzantium. It meant that such policy was not created on the spur of the moment by one individual to meet immediate needs. Rather, it was something that had developed over centuries and was often even committed to writing by a cohesive, administrative group, who preserved, studied and elaborated the fruits of past experience. While emperors came and went, both political aims and methods could be passed from generation to generation, preserving a remarkable continuity.

In discussing the interaction between Byzantium and the crusades, therefore, it is the education and ideology of the imperial civil service, rather than just the characters of individual emperors, that lies at the heart of the question. It is necessary to understand who the members of this political elite were, the ways in which they defined themselves and distinguished themselves from outsiders, the principles they adopted in advising the emperors on foreign policy and the methods they employed to achieve their goals. Only then can any assessment be made as to whether the policies they adopted were sensible and successful or whether they were inherently flawed and ultimately bound to lead to disaster.

A number of factors gave a man entry to the Byzantine political elite and civil service. Strange though it may seem, being castrated as a child was one. Since eunuchs were specifically prohibited from occupying the imperial throne, they were regarded as being more trustworthy. Ten posts at court that involved close contact with the emperor were specifically reserved for them, including that of *Parakoimomenos*, literally 'he who keeps watch alongside' the imperial person.[4]

By no means all Byzantine bureaucrats were eunuchs, however, so in effect entry to the charmed circle came down to two indispensable factors: education and patronage. Both had profound implications for who made up the elite and how they regarded themselves and their office.

Education at a high level had been the key to entry into the higher positions in the imperial civil service throughout empire's history. Back in the year 360, the emperor had specifically commanded that 'by no means shall any person obtain a post of the first order unless it is established that he excels in the practice and training of the liberal studies, and that he is so polished in the use of letters that words proceed from him without the offence of imperfections ...'[5] That meant following a traditional course of higher education, based, at least in theory, on the *Trivium* of poetry, rhetoric and philosophy, and the *Quadrivium* of sciences, geometry, arithmetic, astronomy and music. In practice, however, it consisted of the study of the literature of ancient Greece and especially that of Classical Athens, which the Byzantines regarded as embodying the most perfect examples of Greek poetry and prose. Authors studied included the poets Homer and Hesiod, the philosophers Plato and Aristotle, and the orators Demosthenes and Lysias. It was not merely a question of reading these works but of internalising their language and imitating it. The most common exercise for students, therefore, was to write dialogues in Platonic or Lucianic form, couched in the archaic phraseology of the ancients. This was what the compilers of the Theodosian Code had in mind when they spoke of 'polished use of letters'.[6]

Many Byzantine bureaucrats during the period of the Crusades were therefore men of high culture. This was certainly true of Michael Psellos, who came to dominate the Byzantine court in the mid-eleventh century. As a young man he was reputed to have learned the whole of the *Iliad* by heart and had studied under the learned John Mauropous in Constantinople. The Emperor Constantine IX (1042–54) had been so impressed with his eloquence and fluency that he made him his secretary and one of his closest advisers, thus launching a career that was to last over thirty years.[7] Similarly, Niketas Choniates, who held high office under the emperors of the Angelos family in the period 1185–1204, had been sent as a young man from his home town of Chonai in Asia Minor to Constantinople in order to pursue higher studies and was later to become the author of voluminous theological and historical works.[8] George Akropolites, Maximus Planoudes and Nikephoros Gregoras, advisers to the emperors of the Palaeologus family during the thirteenth and fourteenth centuries, were all products of the same system, both authors and scholars in addition to their role as political advisers.[9]

The higher education in which they had all been schooled was only available in Constantinople and was enjoyed by a tiny minority of the inhabitants of the empire. It has been calculated that no more than two or three hundred individuals were being educated in this way at any one time in the middle Byzantine period (843–1204).[10] As a result, this group formed something of a closed caste, differentiated from the rest of the population by their superior knowledge. That divide is nowhere better illustrated than in a story told by Michael Psellos himself. One day Constantine IX was walking through the palace accompanied by his mistress and a crowd of courtiers. One of the courtiers, wishing to gain favour with the emperor, murmured softly, but audibly, the words 'It were no shame …' That was enough to send a ripple of admiration through his fellow courtiers. They had all been educated and recognised the allusion at once, as coming from the *Iliad*: 'It were no shame that Trojans and well greaved Achaeans should suffer pain long time for woman such as she', a reference to the fabled beauty Helen of Troy. Unfortunately, the act of gallantry fell flat because its object, the emperor's mistress, could not understand what it meant and had to call for a translation, such was the divide between those who were educated and those who were not.[11]

Erudite as these men were, their careers were, in the last analysis, dependent upon patronage. This might come from some relative already ensconced in an influential position. Psellos was able to purchase the title of *Protospatharios* for his future son-in-law, Elpidios, for twenty pounds of gold. The uncle of Symeon the New Theologian no doubt used the same methods to have his nephew appointed as *Spatharokoubicoularios*.[12] The most effective patronage, however, was that of the emperor himself. It allowed the eunuch Basil, chief imperial adviser and *Parakoimomenos*, to obtain his position not by virtue of education but because he was the illegitimate half-brother of Basil II.[13] By the same token, a change of ruler could mean a dramatic reversal of fortune. Psellos embarked on his successful career because he impressed Constantine IX, but the accession of Romanos IV Diogenes (1068–71) saw him sidelined. The coup which brought Alexios V Doukas Mourtzouphlos to power in 1204 was immediately followed by Choniates's dismissal from his post of *Logothete* of the *Sekreta*. One of the first actions of Alexios I Comnenus (1081–1118) as emperor was to purge Psellos's pupil, John Italos, on a charge of heresy.[14]

As a result of the vagaries of imperial patronage, titles were regarded as extremely important by the Byzantine elite, because they marked very clearly the exact point in the hierarchy that an individual had reached and the level of imperial favour that he enjoyed. During the ninth and tenth centuries numerous *taktika*, official lists of titles, offices and the duties that went with them, were lovingly drawn up, such as that compiled by the *Protospatharios* Philotheos in 899. Possibly these *taktika* represented an attempt to codify the whole system. If so, it was labour lost, as titles changed their meaning and importance as often as emperors came and went. The function of a *Protospatharios* had once been military, but by the eleventh century it was a post at court. The *Protovestiarios*, whose office was of the highest importance by the time of the First Crusade, had originated simply as keeper of the wardrobe. The office of *Logothete* conferred control of one of the departments of the administration, but the departments, like the titles, waxed and waned in importance. Alexios I introduced a whole new set of titles with which to honour his supporters, and probably to demote those who held existing ones.[15]

With the titles went an annual pension in gold and some kind of silk garment, both proportionate to the importance of the office. Particular robes were attached to specific court offices. The *Magistros* was entitled to wear a gold embroidered white tunic, the *Kouropalatios* a red tunic mantle and belt. As for the money, a special ceremony was held over seven days during the week before Palm Sunday, when each official appeared before the emperor to receive his due. So lavish were the stipends of some of the higher officials that they brought with them helpers to drag away their heavy sacks of gold.[16]

The importance of education and imperial patronage, expressed through titles and pensions, in bolstering the identity and ethos of the elite is nowhere more apparent than in the outraged scorn which they heaped on rivals whom they believed to lack these prerequisites. Psellos, temporarily thrust aside from his position as adviser to the Empress Theodora (1055–56) by Leo Paraspondylas, questioned his rival's fitness for office on the grounds that he did not have 'long-standing qualifications in the realm of literature or oratory'. Choniates fulminated against the judges appointed by Manuel I because they 'spoke broken Greek and drivelled in their speech'. Akropolites was mortified when John III Vatatzes (1222–54) bestowed impressive titles on 'pitiful men, worth no more than three obols'.[17] The thing that annoyed them more than anything else was the tendency of emperors to try and cut through the system, as Alexios I did, by inventing new offices and titles to bestow on their own creatures, while downgrading traditional ones by granting them to all and sundry. Michael Attaleiates and Michael Psellos were horrified when Constantine IX conferred honours 'indiscriminately on a multitude of persons', and Choniates accused Alexios III Angelos (1195–1203) of selling offices 'as vendors peddle their fruit'.[18]

From this distaste for unqualified outsiders, it followed that the educated elite considered themselves as the people best placed to fulfil the functions of their office. Among the lower ranks these functions included service as tax collectors, governors of provincial cities, as judges, even generals in the field.[19] Embassies to foreign powers were often composed of members of the elite because education and command of archaic language were again considered the quintessential qualifications for the task. John the Grammarian was chosen for a mission to Baghdad in the ninth century because he was 'formidable in debating skills', while, hundreds of years later, Niketas Choniates wrote enthusiastically of how his fellow intellectual Michael Italikos charmed King Conrad III of Germany with his eloquence in 1147. No doubt the same reasoning was behind the choice in 946 of John Anthypatos as ambassador to Damascus, where he impressed his hosts with his knowledge of history and philosophy.[20]

Among the most highly placed at court, however, the main task was to advise the emperor, and to formulate domestic and foreign policy. Of course, some office holders were more influential than others. Psellos implied that Isaac I Comnenus abdicated on his advice and claimed that Constantine X Doukas (1059–67) followed his opinion unhesitatingly. Demetrius Kydones was the personal friend of his master John VI Cantacuzenus (1347–54), remaining at his side both day and night. On the other hand, although Choniates was part of a group which succeeded in persuading Isaac II Angelos (1185–95) to reverse his policy towards the Third Crusade, he does not in general appear to have been an influential voice at court. George Akropolites even claimed that he was beaten up on the orders of Theodore II Laskaris (1254–58) over a disagreement about a treaty with the Bulgarians.[21] Nevertheless, whatever the standing of individual officials with particular emperors, as a group the elite were seen as the people best placed to advise on policy.

To the modern mind, there is something faintly absurd about the conviction of the Byzantine elite that their classical education gave them all the skills they needed to fulfil this weighty responsibility. Psellos went so far as to claim that the experienced general, Romanos IV, had lost the battle of Mantzikert in 1071 because he neglected Psellos's advice. Psellos had probably never been on a battlefield in his life, but he had read up on the subject in the ancient authorities. The same point emerges from a letter sent by Alexios III Angelos to the government of Genoa in 1199. Whoever wrote it could not resist throwing in an allusion to Hesiod, no doubt because such a display of erudition would have been thought likely to impress the recipients.[22]

Literary skills nevertheless played a very important part in the participation of the civil elite in government and foreign policy, since it was they who produced the documents which articulated, defended and sometimes even criticised the policy aims of their imperial masters. For example, they drafted letters and treaties with foreign powers. Psellos, as usual, claimed to excel in this task and was entrusted with drawing up letters to be sent to the Fatimid caliph, in which he exalted the office of his master the emperor. These letters do not survive, but we do have the text of the treaty concluded between Michael VII Doukas (1071–78) and the Norman duke of Apulia and Calabria, Robert Guiscard, in 1074, which was almost certainly drawn up by Psellos. To some extent the text substantiates Psellos's claims, for it is not just a dry enumeration of obligations. It is also a carefully thought out defence of the office and claims of the Byzantine emperor, assuring the duke that 'the word of a pious emperor is truly a seal of gold, for the purity and integrity of his soul is worth more than material gold'.[23]

Much the same can be said about the numerous manuals of military tactics and foreign policy which survive under the names of particular emperors but which were probably ghost-written by members of the elite, such as the *Taktika* of Leo VI (886–912) and the *De administrando imperio* and other treatises associated with Constantine VII (913–59). These preserved the accumulated wisdom of the centuries, on such matters as the reception of foreign envoys or how to bring about the swift surrender of an invested town, and so helped to bring about a certain continuity in imperial policy.[24] Byzantine courtiers also presented and explained that policy in public, by means of panegyrics, delivered in formal and archaic Greek, praising the reigning emperor and his achievements. Nikephoros Chrysoberges delivered one such oration before the Emperor Alexios IV (1203–4), addressing him as 'doer of great deeds ... competitor with Alexander [the Great] in prosperity'. Michael Italikos praised the Syrian campaigns of John II Comnenus (1118–43), Manganeios Prodromos the victories of Manuel I.[25]

Finally, and perhaps most important of all, there was the writing of history. Psellos, Niketas Choniates and George Akropolites all wrote major histories of their own times, in the archaic, classical Greek in which they had been trained. So did Michael Attaleiates, who served the emperors Romanos IV and Nikephoros III, and John Kinnamos, the secretary of Manuel I. There is an almost unbroken succession of historians right down to George Sphrantzes, friend and counsellor of the last emperor, Constantine XI Palaeologus (1449–53). To this list one might add Anna Comnena, who wrote the life of her father, Alexios I, even though as a princess of the blood she was not part of the elite corps of bureaucrats. She shared their educational background, having first taken lessons secretly with the palace eunuchs, before moving on to the traditional *Trivium* and *Quadrivium*, and was well placed to present the aims behind Byzantine policy during the reign of Alexios.[26]

From the point of view of those looking back at Byzantium over the centuries, these histories are particularly important because, unlike panegyrics, they could often be very critical. As Anna Comnena dryly observed, 'all men flatter the current ruler but no one makes the slightest attempt to overpraise the departed'. Most of the histories were written at some remove from the events they describe, giving the authors the freedom and security to say what they wished. This placed Michael Psellos in an embarrassing position when he came to write his history by requiring him to unsay much of the flattery he had once heaped in a panegyric on a now-deceased emperor.[27]

It is these literary productions of the Byzantine elite, whether treaties, letters, manuals, panegyrics or histories, which provide us with the evidence for the principles on which the rulers of Byzantium based their dealings with foreign powers and ultimately with the crusades and the crusader states. We must now look at what those principles were.

In framing foreign policy and advising emperors, the Byzantine political elite were working within the context of a strongly defined political ideology to which all subscribed, whatever their differences in terms of faction or party.[28] The theory, as has already been seen, was that of *Translatio imperii*. The capital of the Roman empire had been moved by Constantine to Constantinople. As a result, the Byzantine emperor was the Roman emperor, the supreme autocrat of the Christian world by divine permission, and it was the duty of all Christians to recognise that.

One can judge how seriously the Byzantine political elite took this ideology by their violent reaction whenever it was challenged by outsiders. In 968 Liudprand, bishop of Cremona, the envoy of the western emperor Otto I (936–73), was present when some hapless papal envoys arrived in Constantinople with a letter describing the emperor as 'emperor of the Greeks' rather than 'of the Romans'. The courtiers present were outraged and threatened that, had they been of higher rank and worthy of notice, the messengers would have been thrown into the sea. As one courtier later explained to Liudprand:

> the sacred Constantine transferred to this city the imperial sceptre, the senate and all the Roman knighthood, and left in Rome nothing but vile slaves, fishermen, confectioners, poulterers, bastards, plebeians, underlings.[29]

John Kinnamos professed himself to be close to tears when he considered those who 'rashly declare that the empire in Byzantium is different from that in Rome'. The patriarch Philotheos railed against 'the short-sightedness and folly' of anyone who refused to accept that the empire ruled from Constantinople was the Roman empire and all the claims to divine favour that that entailed.[30] When, after 800, the western European Carolingians and Ottonians claimed the title of 'emperor of the Romans' for themselves, the Byzantines steadfastly refused to recognise it. A letter sent by the Byzantine emperor to the Frankish emperor Louis the Pious (814–40) addressed him as 'the glorious king of the Franks and Lombards, who is called their emperor'. Liudprand of Cremona reported angrily to his master, Otto I, that the Byzantine chancellor had 'called you not "emperor", which is *Basileus* in his tongue, but "king", which is *Rex* in ours'.[31]

This ideological stance was the key factor in dictating Byzantine foreign policy goals. Those goals were, in fact, enshrined in Byzantine law, which laid down not only that the emperor should ensure the temporal welfare of his people, but also that he should 'guard and secure by his ability the powers which he already possesses [and] to recover by sleepless care those that are lost'. In practice, these ideals were reduced to two overriding concerns. The first was the security of the Roman empire, the *Oikoumene*, which in practice meant that of the all-important city of Constantinople. The second was to secure recognition in the wider world of the claim of the emperor to be the supreme overlord of the Christian world and of the empire to be that unique state endorsed by God.[32]

At first sight the idea that foreign policy could be motivated by a metaphysical ideal appears unlikely: it is sometimes tempting to see Byzantine imperial claims as simply a cloak for 'real concerns' such as the annexation of territory or economic advantage. The very words 'empire' and 'imperial', which are used to describe Byzantium, evoke the implication that the larger such a state is, the better it is, and that its sole aim must be physical aggrandisement. Yet one only has to examine how the Byzantines behaved in the later years of their empire to realise that the ideology was far more potent than the acquisition of land or booty.

During the 1390s, when the Byzantine empire had contracted drastically and Constantinople itself was under siege from the Ottoman sultan Yildirim Bayezid (1389–1402), the patriarch Anthony IV wrote to the grand prince of Moscow, Vasilii I. The Russian ruler had expressed doubts as to the validity of the claims of the Byzantine emperor in view of the almost complete disappearance of his empire, asserting that there was a church but no emperor. The patriarch insisted that, on the contrary, the emperor was still 'autocrat of the Romans, indeed of all Christians. Everywhere the name of the emperor is commemorated by all patriarchs and metropolitans and bishops wherever men are called Christians'. Such insistence on the ideal of the universal emperor in a situation when the emperor ruled little beyond Constantinople itself has been criticised as clinging to an outdated concept in the face of hard reality. The point for the Byzantines, however, was that the ideal was the reality. Just as the loss of territory changed nothing, neither would its acquisition.[33]

The foreign policy aims of Byzantium were therefore essentially defensive and ideological rather than acquisitive, and this was clearly the case in their dealings with the Slav peoples whose lands lay to the north of the empire. While the famous 'Bulgar-Slayer', Basil II, did finally conquer Bulgaria in 1018 and incorporated it into the empire, such drastic action was unusual. The Byzantines were generally content to accept an acknowledgement of the emperor's suzerainty. This they received during the ninth and tenth centuries from the rulers of small Balkan princedoms such as Croatia and Dioclea, and from the grand dukes of Moscow. How it worked in practice is revealed in the case of the Serbs. According to a writer whose name has not come down to us but who was almost certainly an official at the court of Constantine VII:

> The emperor [Basil I], like the humane father who received his senselessly rebellious son who repented and returned to the fold, received and accepted them, and straightaway sent them priests with a diplomatic agent ... when they had all received divine baptism and returned to the Roman allegiance, the emperor's authority was fully restored over their country ... and he wisely determined that they should be governed by princes [of their own nation], chosen by them.[34]

The passage is revealing because, to the Byzantines, acceptance of Christianity from Constantinople also meant an acceptance of the authority of the emperor. This was entirely logical: if the emperor was God's appointed ruler of the Christian world, all Christians owed him allegiance. The fiction was maintained by the emperor 'allowing' the Serbs to be ruled by their own princes. Such rulers were often designated as the 'sons' of the emperor, an unmistakeable indication of the nature of the relationship, which at the same time fitted them into the hierarchical world order, headed by the emperor in Constantinople.[35]

The Byzantines had similar concerns in their dealings with their eastern, Muslim neighbours, who had long ruled over the lost Byzantine provinces of Syria, Palestine and Egypt. There are plenty of instances of the Byzantines fighting aggressive wars against them, and, in some cases, invading and annexing their territory, since it was, after all, part of the perceived role of the Roman emperor to protect Christians by fighting against the infidel. In 975 the Emperor John I Tzimiskes had led a campaign into Syria and Palestine which had reached as far south as Caesarea, within striking distance of Jerusalem itself. This was, however, no crusade, and the Byzantines seem to have given up any idea of capturing the Holy City. John prudently drew back from his advanced position and the Byzantine frontier was stabilised in northern Syria.[36] Both Basil II and Romanos III Argyros (1028–34) mounted further campaigns in Syria, but by the mid eleventh century this expansive drive seems to have come to an end.

Instead, the Byzantines secured their ideological aims by negotiation. In 1027 a treaty was made between the emperor and the Fatimid caliph of Egypt, who then ruled southern Syria and Palestine. It included clauses that provided for the rebuilding of the church of the Holy Sepulchre in Jerusalem and the return to Christianity of those who had been forcibly converted to Islam. It also permitted the emperor to designate the patriarch of Jerusalem. In return the Byzantines released their Muslim prisoners and promised to repair the mosque in Constantinople, which existed for the use of Arab merchants visiting the city. The mosque would have its own muezzin, and Friday prayers there would be said in the name of the Shi'ite Fatimid caliph, rather than his Abbasid rival in Baghdad.[37] The policy was continued and the treaty renewed by successive emperors in 1035 and 1047. In 1063 Constantine X Doukas arranged with the Fatimid caliph, al-Mustansir, the exempt jurisdiction of the patriarch's quarter in Jerusalem and paid for a wall to be built around it.[38] As in the case of Byzantine dealings with the Slavs, these treaties were designed to secure recognition of the Byzantine emperor as the head of the Christian world. In this case, they secured for him the role of Protector of the Holy Places and of the interests of Christians under Muslim rule.

The vindication of an ideology therefore lay at the very heart of Byzantine foreign policy. While that may sound like an illogical basis for foreign policy, it was no more so than the aim of the crusades, which was to seize and hold the strategically useless, but spiritually significant, city of Jerusalem.

While Byzantine aims and ideology were fixed, the means used to achieve them were often infinitely flexible. Military force, or at least the threat of it, was certainly an option. In 864 Michael III (842–67) moved an army up to the Danube frontier and a fleet along the western coast of the Black Sea. His purpose was not to annex the neighbouring khanate of Bulgaria but to force Khan Boris to accept Christianity from Byzantine clergy and to acknowledge the authority of the emperor. When he did this, the troops were withdrawn.[39] Nevertheless, military action tended to be used only as a last resort, Leo VI insisting that war should only be undertaken in defence of one's own country in order to restore peace. As Manuel I confided to the Muslim ruler of Aleppo and Damascus, Nur ed-Din, in 1159, he knew all about 'the evil results to which the effects of war gave rise and the difficulty of attaining the hoped for end'. He therefore negotiated a peace treaty.[40]

Instead, rather more subtle methods were adopted whenever possible. Michael Psellos made clear what he considered them to be:

> Now two things in particular contribute to the hegemony of the Romans, namely our system of honours and our wealth, to which one might add a third: the wise control of the other two and prudence in their distribution.[41]

The second of Psellos's two pillars is easy to comprehend. It has already been shown that the Byzantine emperors commanded an enviable supply of ready money, from the *Kommerkion* which they levied on trade passing through the port of Constantinople. One twelfth-century visitor to Constantinople reckoned that the imperial fisc profited to the tune of some twenty thousand gold pieces a day from these customs dues, and from rents from markets and shops. That was, moreover, by no means their only source of income. Unlike the rulers of western Europe, who drew services in kind from their vassals, the Byzantine emperors presided over a society where coinage circulated widely. They could therefore levy taxes on their own people to fill their treasury. In the provinces, households without land paid a hearth tax, while those with land paid a combined hearth and land tax, all rendered in gold. These sources yielded an estimated annual revenue of some seven million gold pieces and by 1025 the treasury had a huge surplus, the result of prudent management by Basil II.[42]

There was no end to the uses to which this seemingly inexhaustible supply of wealth could be put when it came to dealing with the peoples beyond the empire's borders. In emergencies, it could be used simply to pay them not to attack, as Constantine VIII (1025–28) tended to do during his short reign. Alexios I specifically advised his son John to store up valuable goods for the very purpose of 'stopping the greed' of surrounding nations. This practice was not entirely approved of in all quarters, however, and tended to bring criticism for weakness.[43] Gold could also be used to employ mercenaries from outside the empire to complement the Byzantine armies, often Turkic peoples from central Asia such the Khazars or Hungarians, who are attested in the tenth century, and Uzes and 'Turcopoles', probably Pechenegs or Cumans, reported in the Byzantine armies in the eleventh.[44] It could be used to pay one powerful foreign nation to attack another. In 967, rather than bother to do the job themselves, the Byzantines paid the Russian prince Svjatoslav to attack their troublesome northern neighbour Bulgaria. Or, more economically, the Byzantines could merely threaten to do so. The officials who harangued Liudprand of Cremona warned him that 'With our money, we will rouse the whole world against [Otto I] and we will break him in pieces like a potter's vessel'. An ambassador, sent with an ultimatum to Bohemond of Antioch in about 1100, coolly concluded the interview with the words: 'Our allies have received the money for their gallantry in battle'.[45]

There were, however, more subtle uses of wealth, aimed not so much to purchase the immediate security of Constantinople but to impress 'barbarian' outsiders with the special nature of the emperor, his city and his empire. One tactic was to overwhelm with sheer magnificence. When the Seljuk sultan Kilidj Arslan II (1156–92) visited Constantinople in 1162, he was received by Manuel I who was seated on a throne of gold, covered in jewels and pearls, and wearing an enormous ruby around his neck. Lavish gifts were bestowed on the sultan, in token of the emperor's generosity and patronage.[46] Liudprand of Cremona experienced much the same treatment on his first visit to Constantinople in 949, being received in the Magnavra hall of the Great Palace by the emperor who sat on a throne surrounded by mechanical lions and birds which roared and sang as the envoy approached.[47]

Another use for surplus gold was the diplomatic gift, often with heavy ideological significance attached to it. A gold crown apparently presented by Michael VII Doukas to King Geza I of Hungary (1074–77) carried portraits of Michael and his son Constantine, both bearing the usual nimbus and identified in the inscription as 'emperor of the Romans'. Geza is also depicted, but without a nimbus, his gaze fixed on the emperor, and identified simply as 'king' (*krales*) of Hungary. Thus his place in the order of things was made unambiguously clear. Silks were another common gift and Constantine VII recommended that emperors should also take a good supply of them on campaign for this specific purpose. The rarity of such objects in the lands inhabited by their unsophisticated recipients helped to bolster the empire's reputation as a centre of wealth and power. Sometimes the gift took the form of a golden reliquary, housing portions of relics of the saints. These were, for example, sent to the English king Edward the Confessor (1042–66) and the western emperor Henry IV (1056–1106) during the second half of the eleventh century. Again, there was an ideological significance here: the relics connected their donor, the emperor, with the heavenly kingdom, the source of his power and dignity, and thus were a vital element in achieving the second of the empire's foreign policy aims.[48]

When it came to the second of Psellos's twin pillars – that of honours – it might be thought that he was referring only to internal matters in Constantinople and displaying the typical Byzantine civil servant's obsession with rank. Yet gradations of titles and honours were as vital a part of the Byzantine approach to foreign relations as they were to the structure of the court hierarchy. Thus, hard-pressed by the Pechenegs in the 1050s and wishing to make peace with them, the Byzantines invited the leaders of this troublesome steppe tribe to Constantinople where they were given not only gifts but also imperial titles and offices.[49] Just as was the case with Byzantine officials, foreign office holders could expect to receive an annual pension in gold and an appropriate silk garment, which no doubt greatly added to the lustre of the title. The rulers of Byzantium were well aware that, for the granting of such titles and garments to have full effect, both must have a certain rarity. Accordingly they were very careful to make sure that certain types of silk garment did not circulate too widely. Merchants who sold prohibited silks to foreigners were liable to be flogged, and when Liudprand of Cremona attempted to take some silks home with him in 968 they were confiscated by imperial officials. Cloths of gold and silk, warned the thirteenth-century cleric George Pachymeres, were the 'blood of the Romans'.[50]

The involvement of foreigners in imperial ceremonial was also important. Constantine VII claimed that through ceremonies the power of the empire was made manifest and that the sight of it would incline foreigners to better behaviour. Provision was specifically made for foreign allies and title holders to attend feasts and ceremonies in Constantinople, no doubt to observe and report back the majesty and wealth of the empire. Like the gifts, ceremonies involving foreigners were imbued with a heavy and unmistakable significance. It was standard practice for visiting rulers to be given a seat carefully placed at a lower level than the emperor's throne. Just in case the message was not clear, Liudprand recorded that the Byzantine emperor had a mechanical throne that could raise him up almost to the ceiling from where he could look down on his humble visitor below.[51]

Apart from their twin pillars of money and honours, the Byzantines also excelled at the type of strategies that diplomats over the ages have employed to manipulate their friends and to neutralise their enemies. For example, on occasion they employed the 'carrot and stick' approach to threatening border tribes. Theophylact, bishop of Ochrid, praised Alexios I in a panegyric because he dealt with the Pechenegs in 1087 by first haranguing them 'with words short and shrill, now offering words soft as flakes of winter snow'.[52] There was the 'divide and rule' principle. Constantine VII advised his son to ensure that the Pechenegs were never on friendly terms with the Russians, in case they combined against Constantinople. Manuel I fished in the complex affairs of the city states of northern Italy to prevent them uniting against the Byzantines.[53] Lastly, they were adept at using foreigners' own customs to manipulate them to the advantage of the *Oikoumene.* One such tool was that of the oath, which seems to have had little place in Byzantine society, but which was commonly used to secure the loyalty of foreign allies and mercenaries. Alexios I, for example, required an oath from some Turks who were enrolled in his army, and they duly swore this 'after their own fashion'. When another contingent pledged loyalty to Nikephoros III, they did so by joining their hands on their chest which was presumably what they were used to doing.[54]

These then were some of the methods that the rulers of Byzantium employed with a view to achieving the two all-important aims of their foreign policy. Next it needs to be established how successful or otherwise they were in the pursuit of those aims.

Not only did the Byzantine elite have extremely clear foreign policy goals during the ninth to eleventh centuries, they also enjoyed a high measure of success in achieving them, both in their relations with the Slavs to the north and with the Muslim Arabs to the east. Indeed the success of their diplomacy far excelled the ephemeral gains brought about by the military victories of Basil II and the other 'soldier-emperors'. As far as the Slavs were concerned, the Byzantines succeeded not only in neutralising the threat to Constantinople posed by the Bulgars and the Russians but, by converting them to Christianity, created a 'Byzantine Commonwealth' in eastern Europe, whose peoples looked upon the Byzantine emperor as the head of the Orthodox Christian world.[55] In the case of the Arabs, the Byzantines were dealing with a power that was stronger than their own empire and which had a religion and ideology every bit as compelling as their own. Nevertheless, they succeeded in reversing a situation where the empire was in imminent danger of being overrun in the late seventh century and established a *modus vivendi* with their powerful neighbours. Moreover, while there was not the remotest possibility of the Muslims recognising any authority of the emperor over themselves, they were prepared to accept that his empire had a place in the divine scheme of things and that he had some rights as protector of Christians under their rule.[56]

Yet in spite of these successes in the past, during the eleventh and twelfth centuries the Byzantine elite presided over a situation which ultimately led to disaster for their city and empire in 1204. To account for the difference, some modern commentators have suggested that the very nature of the Byzantine elite was in some way responsible for the disaster, because they were uniquely unqualified for dealing with foreign relations. Their exclusive educational background has led to their being labelled as possessed of 'a pride bordering on conceit'. As regards foreign policy their 'superiority complex' and their tendency to remain in 'the protective shell of their own traditions' made them despise 'all foreigners as brutal and barbarous'.[57] It is certainly true that in their writings they often referred to foreigners as 'barbarians', and often describe them in terms that appear derogatory or contemptuous. Anna Comnena was moved to laughter by the posturing of the Norman Robert Guiscard, and complained that the unpronounceable names of the leaders of the Pechenegs spoiled the tone of her prose. Kinnamos patronisingly noted that 'in prosperity the barbarian is likely to be exalted and boast beyond measure, but in disaster he is downcast more than is suitable and is immoderately humbled'. They appear not even to have known the names of foreign peoples, referring to them by hopelessly outdated terms: the Turks were called 'Persians', the Normans 'Kelts'.[58] If the rulers of the empire really took this line in their everyday dealings with foreign peoples, it may well have been their exclusiveness and narrow-mindedness that caused the breakdown of relations with the west and led to the disaster of 1204.

Yet if this really was the case, the long survival of the empire and its successes in earlier centuries is very difficult to account for. In fact, the apparent attitude to foreigners in the literary histories of Anna Comnena and John Kinnamos is misleading. It was not the result of contempt or ignorance. The classicising literary genre in which these authors wrote demanded that the present be spoken of in the language of the past and that a strict line be drawn between 'them' and 'us', following the ancient Greek division between Greeks and barbarians.[59] There is abundant evidence that in practice members of the elite showed knowledge and understanding of foreign cultures. Manuals like the *De administrando imperio* of Constantine VII are full of carefully compiled information about the lifestyles of peoples that dwelt beyond the empire's borders. Even in literary histories, the classicising masks slips often enough to show that their authors were well informed about particular foreign peoples and sometimes considered them to possess skills superior to those of the Byzantines. Anna Comnena could think of no better way of praising the horsemanship of Nikephoros Katakalon than by saying that one might almost think he was a Norman.[60]

Even in the case of the Muslim Arabs, with whom the empire had been at almost constant war for centuries, educated Byzantines saw the importance of understanding the language and culture of the enemy. Photios, patriarch of Constantinople (858–67 and 878–86), a typical Byzantine scholar and bureaucrat, exchanged friendly letters with the Arab emir of Crete, and John Anthypatos, despatched to Damascus as ambassador in 946, entered into friendly discussions with the intellectuals there. As a result the Byzantines were well informed about the Islamic world and, while they were given to penning fierce polemics against Islam, they seldom made the mistake of westerners of describing it as polytheism or idolatry.[61]

This knowledge and understanding of foreign peoples can be seen at work in Byzantine diplomatic practice. The creation of the Byzantine commonwealth was to a large extent the result of putting that information to good use, allowing the recently Christianised Slavs to have the liturgy and scriptures in their own language, rather than attempting to impose a foreign tongue as western missionaries had done. When an embassy was sent from Constantinople to the court of Saladin in 1189, the Byzantines were able to provide a fluent Arabic speaker to lead it. In selecting a gift to send to the caliph of Cordova, Constantine VII chose not the gold trinkets which would have sufficed for unsophisticated northern tribes but a manuscript of the *Materia medica* of the ancient Greek writer Dioscorides: he was clearly well aware of the esteem in which Greek medicine was held in the Islamic world and the value that would consequently be attached to the gift.[62]

The idea that conflict between the Byzantines and the crusaders arose because of the narrow-mindedness of the Byzantine elite therefore has very little to recommend it. Nevertheless, there are grounds for seeking the causes of the conflict in the nature and ideology of this group, particularly their priorities in making policy, which, as we have seen, were first the security of Constantinople and the *Oikoumene*, and secondly to secure recognition of the claim of their ruler to be the supreme Christian emperor.

These aims were considered to be so high and so pure, that almost any action which advanced them was not only legitimate but positively praiseworthy. Back in the tenth century, Leo VI had remarked that it was sometimes safer and more profitable to master the enemy by stratagems. This principle was still in place by the time of the crusades, when Anna Comnena remarked that 'a general's supreme task is to win, not merely by force of arms, but also by relying on treaties, and there is another way – sometimes when the chance offers itself, an enemy can be beaten by fraud'.[63] Their words have a faintly modern ring, recalling Machiavelli's precept that the ruler 'must not flinch from being blamed for vices which are necessary for safeguarding the state'.[64] Nevertheless, the attitude was a typically Byzantine one, instilled into the ruling classes with their classical education. One insider described how students in higher education were taught 'to weave webs of phrases, and transform the written sense into riddles, saying one thing with their tongues, but hiding something in their minds'. Duplicity was almost a measure of sophistication, a mark of superiority over the uneducated and uncultured.[65]

The practical application of these views can be seen in Byzantine foreign policy. Psellos boasted that he was able to phrase letters to the Fatimid caliph so as to appear to mean one thing, while in fact saying quite another and Anna Comnena praised her father and uncle for having the same ability. Her account of Alexios I's dealings with the Paulician heretics in 1083 is a prime of example of this permissible duplicity in action. The Paulicians were settled on part of imperial territory in Thrace, and, although theoretically subjects of the emperor, were considered to pose a threat to the surrounding area. Unwilling to risk open warfare with them, Alexios summoned them to meet him at Mosynopolis, where he met them personally with a flattering display of friendship, claiming that he wished to register them for military service in his army. Once their suspicions were lulled, the leaders were arrested and the rank and file disarmed. Their property was redistributed among Alexios's own loyal officers and their families driven from their homes. The detail with which Anna Comnena tells the story makes it clear that she considered the ruse in no way dishonourable and simply another valiant deed on the part of her father in defence of the *Oikoumene*.[66]

To those outside the empire, such placing of the interests of the empire before all else could be interpreted in quite a different light. As the French cleric Odo of Deuil remarked bitterly, the Byzantines believed that 'anything which is done for the holy empire cannot be considered perjury'. What was presented by Anna Comnena as smooth resourcefulness looked to outsiders like trickery and duplicity. A disgruntled Russian grumbled that 'the Greeks are crafty even to the present day' and western chronicles from the centuries before the crusades are replete with disparaging remarks about the tendency of the Byzantines to defeat by trickery those whom they could not overcome by force.[67]

There lay the seeds of conflict between the foreign policy of the Byzantine empire and that of the crusades. One ideology saw the highest earthly goal of the pious Christian as the preservation of the *Oikoumene* under the leadership of the emperor and would adopt any means to achieve that aim. The other saw it as making war on the infidel to capture and defend the Holy City of Jerusalem. As time would show, the application of traditional Byzantine diplomatic methods to the papacy, the crusaders and the crusader states was to bring about unforeseen and disastrous consequences.

3

The Search for Security

The interaction between the Byzantine empire and the crusading movement had its origins in the middle of the eleventh century when, after a period of a hundred and fifty years during which they had been on the offensive against their external enemies, the Byzantines suddenly found their borders once more under attack. On the Danube, the steppe tribe known as the Pechenegs began making incursions into the Balkans. In Armenia, the Seljuk Turks were raiding across the border with impunity, while in southern Italy the Normans were slowly conquering the Byzantine provinces of Apulia and Calabria. For Michael Psellos the sudden reversal of the empire's fortunes was nothing less than 'a mighty deluge'.[1]

The situation worsened as the century went on. A treaty made with the Seljuk Turks in 1055 failed to stem the raids which struck ever deeper into Byzantine Asia Minor. In 1058 the city of Melitene was sacked, and Sebasteia suffered the same fate the following year. Six years later, the Seljuk sultan Alp Arslan captured Ani, the old capital of the Armenian kingdom before its annexation by the Byzantines some twenty years before. In 1067 Caesarea, a city far from the frontier that might have considered itself safe, was pillaged and its cathedral of St Basil desecrated. Clearly drastic action needed to be taken and, in August 1071, a large Byzantine army under the personal command of the Emperor Romanos IV Diogenes headed into Armenia in an attempt to put a stop to the raids. Near to the town of Mantzikert, however, Romanos clashed not with isolated Turkish war bands, as he had expected, but with the main army of Alp Arslan, which was travelling through the area on its way south to fight the Fatimids of Egypt. In the ensuing battle, the emperor's troops were scattered, and his own brave stand with his bodyguard only resulted in his being cut off by the victorious Turks and taken prisoner.

Having witnessed the destruction of an entire Byzantine army, Michael Attaleiates, a Byzantine soldier who took part in the battle, could only lament the 'gravity and great shame which marked our defeat, and the intolerable dishonour which adheres to the name of the Romans'.[2] Yet, in spite of Attaleiates's words and although losses had been heavy at Mantzikert, the defeat itself was not a disaster. The terms dictated by the victorious sultan were generous, because his main aim was to resume his march against his most dangerous enemy, the heretical Shi'ite Fatimids. He therefore made no demands for cession of Byzantine territory, and released the captive Romanos, asking only for a moderate ransom in return. The sultan's generosity and preoccupation elsewhere should have allowed the Byzantines a respite to recover from the defeat. Unfortunately, during Romanos's time as a prisoner of the sultan, Michael Psellos and his allies in Constantinople, the Doukas family, had proclaimed Michael VII Doukas as the legitimate emperor there. When Romanos returned from captivity, civil war broke out between the two rival emperors, in which Romanos was defeated and overthrown. Michael VII had little leisure to enjoy the throne. His position was constantly challenged by revolts and attempted usurpations, one of which succeeded in deposing him in 1078. His successor, Nikephoros III Botaneiates, ruled for less than three years before he in turn was toppled by Alexios Comnenus.

In the confusion which resulted from these internal upheavals, independent bands of Turks were able to march into Asia Minor and occupy the land unopposed. At first, the process took place in a piecemeal fashion, but it was given leadership and direction by the arrival of Suleyman ibn Kutlumush, a cousin of Alp Arslan. In 1078, Suleyman took Nicaea, only a hundred kilometres from Constantinople itself, and in 1084 the strategically important city of Antioch, which had once guarded the empire's south-eastern frontier, also fell to the Turks. Adopting the title of sultan, Suleyman made his capital at Ikonion or, in Turkish, Konya. Smyrna, on the Aegean coast, was captured by a semi-independent emir named Tzachas. By 1090, virtually the whole of Asia Minor was in the hands of one Turkish warlord or another, apart from a small area east of Chalcedon, opposite Constantinople, which remained under Byzantine control.[3]

Similar events were taking place in the empire's western provinces. In 1053 the Byzantine government was forced to come to terms with the Pechenegs and to accept their settlement on imperial land south of the Danube. By 1071 the Normans, under their leader Robert Guiscard, had completed their conquest of Byzantine lands with the capture of Bari, putting an end to hundreds of years of imperial rule in southern Italy. Ten years later, Guiscard and his son, Bohemond, launched an attack on the Byzantine Balkan provinces across the Adriatic, and in October 1081 at Dyrrachion inflicted on imperial forces a defeat every bit as severe as that at Mantzikert. This time the emperor, Alexios I Comnenus, 'dusty and bloodstained, bareheaded, with his bright red hair straggling in front his eyes', escaped capture, but only after a high-speed chase on horseback, in which he killed one of his Norman pursuers.[4] There was now a real danger that the Normans would press on to Thessalonica and Constantinople.

The situation was undoubtedly grave, but there were two factors that ensured that the empire had the ability to recover. In the first place, in spite of the bewildering rapidity with which emperors came and went, the civil bureaucracy remained in place and could bring its wealth of accumulated wisdom to bear on the problems of the day. Secondly, that wisdom taught that the situation now faced by the empire was by no means unprecedented. A search through histories and manuals would have revealed, for example, that in August 917, a Byzantine army had been wiped out at Anchialos in Thrace by the khan of the Bulgars, Symeon (893–927), a defeat which delivered most of the Balkans into Symeon's hands and brought his armies to the walls of Constantinople. The empire had recovered from this blow not by overcoming Symeon in battle, but by diplomacy. Symeon's enemies to the north, the Serbs and the Croats, were paid to attack him. A Bulgar embassy returning from north Africa, where it had obtained a promise of help from the Fatimids, was intercepted, and a large bribe sent to the Fatimid caliph to persuade him to keep his fleet at home. These tactics kept Symeon occupied until he suffered a fatal but extremely convenient heart-attack and his khanate fell apart under his ineffectual successor.[5]

Faced with a similar situation in the later eleventh century, the rulers of the *Oikoumene* sought a similar solution, deploying their wealth to pay others to attack their enemies, either as allies or as mercenaries serving in Byzantine armies. There was, however, one crucial difference from Byzantine foreign policy in the past. This time the Byzantines directed their diplomatic efforts towards the Christian west, and particularly the papacy, on an unprecedented scale. In doing so, they were dealing with very different people from the unsophisticated Slavs or the Muslim Arabs, because the papacy, like the Byzantine empire, had claims to the leadership of Christendom. As a result, Byzantine endeavours to save their empire were to have consequences that could not possibly have been foreseen.[6]

That the Pecheneg, Norman and Seljuk incursions presented the rulers of Byzantium with such difficulties was partly the result of policies pursued during the reign of Constantine IX Monomachos (1042–55). Affable and cultured, Constantine had been at the centre of a liberal and relaxed court. He had cheerfully defied conventional morality by installing his mistress in the palace alongside his wife, the empress Zoe, and had surrounded himself with some of the foremost intellectuals of the day, notably Michael Psellos, Constantine Leichoudes and John Xiphilinos. In consultation with these advisers, Constantine IX embarked on a series of reforms to rationalise the administration and defence of the empire. In view of the more peaceful conditions then prevailing on the empire's borders, they had dismantled parts of the static defences. The armies of the *Themata*, military districts where groups of peasants held land in return for some of their number serving in the imperial forces, were run down, being replaced by professional troops based in border fortresses.[7]

The policy had seemed perfectly reasonable at the time, but it meant that there was little standing defence in the interior of the empire, and much less in the way of reserves to be called upon in time of need. As the danger escalated in the second half of the eleventh century, the Byzantines therefore sought to make up the shortfall in their defences by recruiting mercenary soldiers from foreign nations. Faced with the Pecheneg threat in 1090, Alexios I summoned mercenaries 'from all quarters'.[8] This was not a panicky innovation in response to the new and perilous situation. The Byzantines had been employing mercenaries in their armies for centuries. The difference was that they were used in greater numbers as the eleventh century progressed and that a greater proportion of them were western Europeans or 'Latins', as the Byzantines called them.

There were two reasons behind the latter change. First, the threat from the Pechenegs and Turks meant that the Byzantines could not rely entirely on Turkic troops as they had in the past. The danger of employing mercenaries against enemies with whom they were racially akin was revealed all too clearly shortly before the battle of Mantzikert in 1071, when a contingent of Uzes deserted to the Turks.[9] Secondly, western Europeans were suddenly much more visible in Byzantium as a result of the expansion of the pilgrimage traffic to Jerusalem. Byzantine conquests in Syria and the concordat reached with the Fatimid rulers of Jerusalem in 1027 meant that the overland route to Palestine was now much safer, encouraging more western pilgrims to make the journey, and to travel via Constantinople. Western clerics and laymen of the highest rank, such Robert, duke of Normandy and Swein, son of Earl Godwin of Wessex, were thus brought as visitors to the Byzantine capital.[10]

These passing pilgrims received a warm welcome in Constantinople. Western accounts reveal that the more important visitors often departed laden with gifts from the emperor. Ulfric, bishop of Orleans, who was in Constantinople between 1025 and 1028, left with a portion of the True Cross and silk hangings. Pibo of Toul received another piece of True Cross, and Reynald of Langres was presented with the arm of St Mamas. Robert of Normandy was plied with gold and precious cloths.[11]

No doubt part of the motivation behind this largesse was the bolstering of the image of the emperor as the head of the Christian world, the patron and protector of pilgrims and of all Christians. But there was another reason:

Ulfric of Orleans was not only a pilgrim. He was also an ambassador, who brought gifts from King Robert II of France (996–1031). What negotiations took place between the emperor and the bishop is not known but a later incident suggests what they may have been. Around 1090, Robert I the Frisian, count of Flanders (1071–93) was on his way back from a pilgrimage to Jerusalem. Passing through Byzantine territory, he met the emperor Alexios I at Beroea, near Thessalonica. As a result of their discussions, Robert promised to send five hundred horsemen to serve the emperor as allies. These horsemen duly arrived later and served under the emperor's direct command.[12] Clearly, the emperors and their advisers were taking advantage of the passing pilgrim traffic to recruit mercenaries for the Byzantine army.

Such was the need for troops, however, that they were not content to sit and wait for potential western mercenaries to come to them as pilgrims. In 1051, a Byzantine official called Argyros was sent to southern Italy, amply equipped with the usual inducements of gold and silk garments, to recruit Norman knights. Such efforts seem to have spread wider as time went on. Letters were probably sent to William the Conqueror, duke of Normandy, and to Robert of Flanders, inviting them to send knights to Constantinople.[13] The recruiting drive extended as far as England. The discovery in Winchester in 1963 of a leaden seal bearing the name of John Raphael, a Byzantine military commander, suggests that England was being targeted as early as the 1040s. In 1100 a full-scale embassy arrived, armed with gifts of relics, probably on recruiting business.[14]

As a result of the recruiting drive, western mercenaries became a common sight in the Byzantine armies during the eleventh century. Scandinavians made up the famous Varangian guard which was entrusted with the safety of the emperor's person. Normans were particularly numerous in the first part of the century and, after 1066, English volunteers, fleeing from the Norman conquest of their country, were in abundant supply. They made up a sizeable contingent of the force which Alexios I led against Robert Guiscard at Dyrrachion in 1081.[15]

As a policy, the recruitment of foreign troops did not work badly. There were a few instances of mercenaries not serving the emperor as loyally as they might. In 1069, a Norman knight in Byzantine service called Robert Crispin, dissatisfied with his pay, took to robbing local tax collectors. A few years later another Norman, Roussel of Bailleul, attempted to establish a principality for himself on Byzantine land in Asia Minor and had to be brought to heel by imperial forces.[16] In general, however, western mercenaries came to be viewed as some of the most loyal and effective troops in the service of the emperor. The Norman chronicler, Orderic Vitalis, described how the Varangian guard who were entrusted with guarding the emperor and Anna Comnena claimed that they regarded 'loyalty to the emperors and the protection of their persons as a family tradition, a kind of sacred trust and inheritance handed down from generation to generation'. Those who served in the field armies also excited the praise of the Byzantines. Michael Attaleiates recounts with admiration how in 1054 a western soldier single-handedly destroyed a Turkish ballista during the siege of Mantzikert.[17] It was therefore by no means an intrinsic mistake on the part of the Byzantine elite to bring western mercenaries into the empire, but rather the continuation of a strand of foreign policy that had worked very well in the past, and which by and large continued to do so.

Much the same can be said of another traditional part of Byzantine foreign policy, that of alliances cemented by generous subventions. In the eleventh century the rulers of the empire used this method as they had in the past, and with some success. The difference was once more that it was particularly directed towards the west, largely with a view to neutralising the Normans of southern Italy.

With typical pragmatism, the Byzantines' first impulse was to try to come to terms with the Normans themselves. Both Romanos IV and Michael VII Doukas made approaches to Robert Guiscard. In August 1074, with the assistance of Michael Psellos, Michael VII made a treaty with Robert. This was a classic piece of Byzantine diplomacy, which brought Psellos's twin pillars of honours and money to bear: Robert was to receive the title of *Nobelissimos*, one of his sons that of *Kouropalatios* and Robert was given forty-three other titles to dispense among his followers, all of which of course carried an annual pension payable in gold, and appropriate cloths of silk. It is clear too that the objectives of the treaty were in line with the traditional aims of Byzantine foreign policy. It provided for the security of the *Oikoumene*: Robert was to respect Byzantine frontiers and to defend them, suggesting that Michael envisaged recruiting his aid against the Pechenegs and Turks. The treaty also aimed to secure recognition of the emperor's spiritual hegemony. Robert was to confirm the agreement with a solemn oath and was to agree to show the emperor the 'submission and good intentions' that he was due.[18]

In one respect, the treaty did break new ground, perhaps reflecting the gravity of the situation in which the Byzantines found themselves. Michael VII agreed to contract a marriage alliance between Robert's daughter, Helena, and his own son Constantine. Anna Comnena was appalled by this 'extraordinary' concession, claiming that it led to Robert's invasion of the Balkans. Her horror reflected the Byzantine view, articulated by Constantine VII, that members of the imperial family should not marry foreigners, apart from the Franks because of their 'traditional fame and nobility'.[19] Yet Michael's willingness to have a non-Frankish daughter-in-law was not entirely unprecedented. In a treaty concluded in October 927, Romanos I Lekapenos (920–44) had bought off the Bulgarian threat to Constantinople by marrying his granddaughter to Tsar Peter, the son of the recently deceased Symeon. Faced with a similar situation in the late tenth century, when the Russian prince Vladimir was attacking Byzantine possessions in the Crimea, Basil II had purchased security by giving Vladimir the hand of his sister Anna.[20] Michael VII had gone rather further than his predecessors in that he was offering the hand of a *Porphyrogenitos*, the son of a reigning emperor born in the Purple Chamber of the palace of Boukoleon, who was also the heir to the throne. Nevertheless, the treaty of 1074 fitted in with a general pattern of established Byzantine foreign policy.

In the event, Michael VII's deposition in 1078 gave Robert Guiscard the pretext to abrogate the treaty, abandon the marriage alliance and, in 1081, launch his invasion of the Byzantine Balkans over the Adriatic. Alexios I therefore sought alliances elsewhere and despatched the *Protoproedros* Constantine Choerosphaktes to the western emperor, Henry IV, Robert's sworn enemy. The terms offered were not unlike those negotiated with the Normans, although no marriage alliance was offered. The Byzantine envoy came armed with 144,000 pieces of gold, one hundred cloths of purple silk, various relics and other presents. There was also a promise of a further 216,000 gold pieces and the salaries of twenty honorific titles that Henry could confer as he wished. Henry's imperial title meant that Alexios could not be quite so specific in his demand for recognition of his status. Nevertheless, he made it clear in his letter, as preserved by Anna Comnena, that the balance of the money would only be handed over when Henry 'took the oath' according to a formula that Constantine would explain to him. Presumably the oath contained a promise to attack Norman lands in southern Italy and possibly some reference to Alexios's imperial dignity, as that of Robert Guiscard had.[21]

Alexios also made overtures to the maritime republic of Venice, an ideal ally in the circumstances. Situated at the head of the Adriatic, Venice was in a position to use her powerful fleet to cut off Robert's supply of men and supplies from southern Italy to his bridgehead in the Balkans. Many of the terms given by the Byzantines in the treaty, which was concluded in 1082, amounted to much the same mixture of gold and titles that had been dangled before Robert Guiscard and Henry IV. The Byzantine treasury was to pay an annual gift of twenty pounds of gold to be distributed among the churches of Venice. The doge and his successors in perpetuity received the title of *Protosebastos*, a title usually restricted to members of the imperial family. The Venetian patriarch of Grado and his successors received the rank of *Hypertimos*, along with its annual pension of twenty pounds of gold. Moreover, as in the treaty with Robert Guiscard, provision was made to preserve the emperor's rightful dignity. It was specifically laid down that the Venetians should enjoy these rights as long as they 'display a great benevolence and a correct attitude towards Romania [the empire] and toward Our Imperial Majesty'. Other clauses of the treaty, however, reflected Venice's interest in the maritime trade between Constantinople and the west. Venetian merchants were given the right to trade in all manner of merchandise in all parts of the Byzantine empire, free of the *Kommerkion* and other duties and harbour tolls, only the ports on the Black Sea, and on Crete and Cyprus, being placed out of bounds. They were to receive property along the Golden Horn in Constantinople, which was to form the basis of their own commercial quarter.[22]

Alexios, like Michael VII, could be blamed for offering overgenerous concessions in the 1082 treaty. He alienated a significant proportion of the empire's tax revenues in the *Kommerkion* exemption and put the Venetians in a position from which they were able to monopolise the trade between Constantinople and western Europe. Yet, in the context of the situation in the 1080s, the treaty was neither unsuccessful nor unprecedented. It certainly played an important part in the defeat of the Normans. At the Byzantines' request, the Venetians attacked the Norman fleet as it ferried troops between the ports of Apulia and their bridgehead near Dyrrachion. Although they were unable to deny the Normans passage altogether, and at one point suffered a serious reverse, the Venetians inflicted significant damage on Guiscard's fleet and supply lines, enabling Alexios to recover from his defeat at Dyrrachion in October 1081 and to drive the Normans from the Balkans in the two years that followed.[23]

Similarly there were precedents for the grant. The Byzantines had already used trading concessions to gain Venetian military support in the past. An imperial chrysobull, issued in 992, had granted the Venetians a reduced rate of customs duties in return for their agreement to transport Byzantine troops to Italy when required to do so.[24] Even the far-reaching treaty of 1082 was nothing new. In 911, faced with the threat of Russian aggression from the north, the Byzantines had made comparable concessions to Russian merchants: total exemption from customs, their own quarter in the suburb of St Mamas, and a monthly allowance of necessary supplies for a period of six months. Such generous concessions as those of 911 were only made because the Byzantines were in a weak position. The situation changed drastically, however, in 944 when the Byzantine navy inflicted a severe reverse on a Russian fleet. The victorious emperor now negotiated a new treaty. Customs dues were reimposed, settlement at St Mamas was forbidden, and the Russians were no longer allowed to buy silk fabrics costing more than fifty gold pieces. It is clear that the Byzantines regarded the concessions to the Venetians in 1082 in a similar light, as something that it was necessary to grant in the present emergency, but which could be withdrawn at a later date. This is exactly what Alexios's son, John II, later attempted to do.[25]

In the second half of the eleventh century, we therefore find the Byzantine elite pursuing their traditional policies and, within the limitations of the severe challenges they were facing, doing so with some success. But in one all-important instance, the standard procedure went badly wrong and the Byzantines lost control of their policy aims. This was when they sought the assistance of the papacy.

Ruling circles in Byzantium may well have felt that they knew all about the papacy by the middle of the eleventh century. The church of Rome had existed long before Constantine founded the city of Constantinople. The pope presided over one of the five patriarchates of the Christian Church, the one regarded as the most venerable because it had been founded not by one apostle but by two, Saints Peter and Paul. The protection of Rome, like that of Jerusalem, was therefore considered to be an essential part of the role of the *Basileus*, even if, after the eighth century, it lay outside the territory under his effective control. Papal legates were therefore regular visitors to Constantinople and imperial embassies to Rome.

Not that relations had always been cordial in the past. There had been several sharp disagreements on matters of doctrine between the churches of Rome and Constantinople. The most recent had concerned the wording of the Nicene Creed, which had been formulated by the council of Nicaea in 325 and by subsequent councils of the church. During the ninth century, Byzantine churchmen had become aware that the Latin version of the Creed, as used in the western church, had been slightly altered. Whereas the original had stated that the Holy Spirit proceeded from the Father, in the Latin version the word *Filioque* ('and from the Son') had been inserted. The Byzantines objected to the innovation for two reasons. First, it was theologically unsound, as it seemed to subordinate the third person of the Trinity to the other two. Still more important, since the Creed had been made by general or ecumenical councils of the whole church, it could only be altered by another such council, not just by the western church alone.

Disagreement on this issue had led to a state of schism between the eastern and western churches between 863 and 867, when the pope and the patriarch of Constantinople had levelled excommunications at each other and removed each other's names from the diptychs, the list of those who were to be prayed for during divine service. This so-called 'Photian Schism', named for the patriarch of the time, Photios, had eventually been patched up with a compromise formula, but the *Filioque* issue was to return and bedevil relations with the pope in the eleventh and twelfth centuries.

Another issue, which strained relations between Rome and Constantinople, was the support given by the popes to the imperial claims of western monarchs. It had been Pope Leo III (795–816) who had crowned Charlemagne as emperor of the Romans in St Peter's at Christmas 800, in a direct challenge to the position of the Byzantine emperor in Constantinople. Charlemagne's successors made the journey to Rome to have their imperial title confirmed in this way, including Otto I in 962. Hence the remark of a Byzantine civil servant that the pope was 'a silly blockhead' for failing to realise that the only emperor of the Romans was to be found in Constantinople.[26]

In spite of all the disagreements and schisms over the years, however, the papacy could hardly be seen as offering any threat to Constantinople. On the contrary, for most of the tenth and early eleventh century, it was in a lamentable state, prey to aristocratic factions who vied with each other to insert their candidate into the office of pope, and subject to countless scandals which eroded its moral prestige. The Byzantines were given direct proof of the situation in Rome when, in 974, a Roman cardinal arrived in Constantinople claiming that he had been elected as Pope Boniface VII, only to be ejected by a rival, Benedict VII (974–83). Boniface returned to Rome in 984 and overthrew John XIV (983–84), who was subsequently murdered in the Castel Sant' Angelo. Boniface himself then reigned as pope for fifteen months, before he too was murdered, and his corpse dragged through the streets by the Roman mob. It was hardly a state of affairs likely to raise the esteem in which the Byzantines held the successors of St Peter.[27]

Yet although, in the eyes of the Byzantines, the popes held some disagreeable opinions and were given to moral laxity and political faction, they could still be very useful allies in protecting the empire's provinces in southern Italy, given that the papal states lay directly to their north. They had cooperated with the Byzantines against mutual enemies in the past, as in 915 when a joint Byzantine-papal force had had stormed a Saracen stronghold at Garigliano.[28] Consequently, partly because of their potential usefulness but also because of the ancient and apostolic origins of their office, the popes were generally treated with respect. Pope John X (914–28), who was later to be strangled on the orders of his lover's daughter, was addressed in a letter written by the patriarch of Constantinople as 'the most holy pope of the elder Rome'. The popes were often on the receiving end of diplomatic overtures from Constantinople, much like any secular power, although the gifts sent to the pope tended to be gospel books and ecclesiastical vessels, rather than silk garments.[29]

In the search for allies against the Norman threat during the second half of the eleventh century, the pope therefore seemed to be an obvious choice. He had every reason to view the activities of Robert Guiscard with the same alarm that the Byzantines did, and so, in about 1051, the Byzantine envoy, Argyros, was sent to Rome to negotiate an alliance with Pope Leo IX (1048–54). A plan for joint action was worked out but, before he was able to link up with his Byzantine allies, Leo's army was routed by Robert Guiscard and his Normans at Civitate in June 1053 and the pope himself was taken prisoner.[30] The defeat at Civitate was a setback, but the policy of seeking an alliance with the pope was not abandoned. As things turned out, it might have been better if it had been.

What Argyros and those who sent him were probably not aware of was that the papacy of Leo IX and his successors was a very different institution from what it had once been as a result of fundamental changes that were taking place in the papal curia. Following the scandal of the election of three popes in 1045, the western emperor Henry III (1017–56) had intervened and summoned the synod of Sutri in 1046 to restore order. In the years that followed, Leo IX and a number of energetic cardinals, notably Peter Damian of Ostia and Humbert of Silva Candida, had taken it upon themselves to restore the morals of the western church, concentrating on what they considered to be the particularly grave sins of clerical marriage and simony (the purchase of ecclesiastical office). Unlike his predecessors, Leo travelled widely, convening and presiding over church councils in places far removed from Rome, and deposing bishops deemed to be morally unworthy of their sees.

In order the better to equip themselves to root out abuses, Leo IX and his circle laid increasing stress on the doctrine of papal supremacy. In the gospel according to St Matthew, St Peter had been described by Christ as the rock upon which He would build His church and to whom He had entrusted the keys of the keys of the Kingdom of Heaven, promising that 'whatsoever thou shalt bind on earth shall be bound in heaven: and whatsoever thou shalt loose on earth shall be loosed in heaven'.[31] On the basis of this text, Cardinal Humbert and other apologists asserted that the church of Rome, which had been founded by St Peter, was the 'head and mother' church, *caput et mater.* The pope, the successor of St Peter, inherited the powers conferred by Christ and had authority over the whole church. With that power and authority, like those of the Byzantine emperor, came weighty responsibility. The pope was responsible for the spiritual health of the church and therefore of Christendom as a whole. 'Their soundness', wrote Humbert, 'corresponds to the soundness of the Roman church, and they rejoice or languish in union with it.'[32] The doctrine was by no means new, but it was now being stated with greater stridency than ever before.

As a result of these developments the Byzantines were now negotiating with a power which, unlike the Slavs or Arabs, had its own claim to universal leadership within Christendom, a claim which, for reasons entirely unconnected with the Byzantine empire, was fast becoming a central element in the papacy's external relations. Almost immediately, the Byzantine elite received a warning of the change that had taken place.

While still in captivity among the Normans, Leo IX received a copy and translation of a letter written by Leo, archbishop of Ochrid, on the instructions the patriarch of Constantinople, Michael Keroularios (1043–58). The letter was addressed to John, bishop of Trani, a Greek-speaking city in Apulia, and contained an angry accusation that the Normans, apparently with papal approval, were forcing western ecclesiastical customs onto the Greek population of the areas of southern Italy which they now controlled. The letter mounted an impassioned attack on those practices, particularly the use of *azymes* or unleavened bread in communion, and denounced them as unorthodox. In about January 1054, a letter from Keroularios himself reached the pope, in which he signed himself 'Ecumenical Patriarch', a term which was rendered into Latin as 'Universal Patriarch' (*patriarcha universalis*).[33]

These letters had exactly the same effect at the papal court as the arrival of the letter addressed to the 'emperor of the Greeks' in Constantinople in 968: there was outrage.[34] The attack on the validity of western ecclesiastical practices questioned the authority of the pope by suggesting that he was responsible for leading Christians astray. The title of Ecumenical Patriarch seemed to go further and to be a claim on the part of the patriarch of Constantinople to just that universal authority to which only the successor of St Peter was entitled. While it is true that the term simply meant 'patriarch of the *Oikoumene*', that is of the Byzantine empire,[35] it also reflected the all-important Byzantine political theory that their empire was the Christian world, a theory the vindication of which was one of the main aims of the empire's foreign policy. In the atmosphere of Rome under the reformed papacy, Byzantine ideology appeared to be a direct challenge to papal supremacy.

In the light of the offending letters, it was decided during the summer of 1054 to send a legation to Constantinople, under the leadership of no less a person than Cardinal Humbert, to instruct the erring patriarch in the nature of the authority of the Roman see. The legate and his companions went armed with an aggressive letter to Keroularios, reminding him of the biblical basis of papal supremacy:

> How detestable and lamentable indeed is that sacrilegious usurpation, when you pronounce yourself 'Universal Patriarch' everywhere in both writing and speech, when every friend of God would tremble to be honoured by the designation in this way: And who after Christ could be more worthy to be marked with that appellation, than he to whom was said by the divine voice: 'Thou art Peter and upon this rock I will build my Church'? Yet because [St Peter] is not found to have been called 'Universal Apostle', even though he was appointed 'Prince of the Apostles', not a single one of his successors has agreed to be called by such a weighty title ...

To give further weight to the attack, Keroularios was accused in the letter of having obtained his office by improper means, one of the main abuses that the papal reform movement was engaged in rooting out.[36]

Although the legates remained in Constantinople for several weeks after delivering this missive, Keroularios steadfastly refused to retract his criticisms of Latin practices or even to discuss the matter with them. Accordingly, on 16 July, Humbert and his fellow legates walked into the cathedral of Hagia Sophia and, going up to the high altar, placed upon it a bull of excommunication against Michael Keroularios and his associates, including Leo of Ochrid who had written the offending letter to the pope. Hardly surprisingly, Keroularios responded in kind by gathering his synod and issuing an excommunication of the members of the papal legation in turn.[37]

There has been much debate on the significance of the mutual excommunications of 1054. On one level they mark the beginning of a state of schism between the churches of Rome and Constantinople which continues to divide the Orthodox and Catholic churches today. Yet at the time the situation was by no means as serious as it appears with hindsight. In his anathema, Humbert made it clear that his excommunication was aimed solely at Keroularios and his friends, not at the emperor and people of Constantinople, whom he declared to be 'most Christian and orthodox'. The tendency over the past fifty years, therefore, has been to play down the importance of the events of 1054.[38]

The significance, however, lies in the reaction of the Byzantine elite, or rather the complete lack of it. There is no specific mention of the visit of Cardinal Humbert and subsequent excommunications in the extant writings of Michael Psellos or any other contemporary member of the court, even though, as a close adviser to the emperor of the day, Constantine IX, Psellos must have been aware of it. The only discernible reference comes in a funeral oration pronounced by Psellos for Keroularios after the latter's death in 1058, in which he praised the late patriarch's heroic resistance to heretical doctrines.[39]

It therefore seems safe to conclude that Psellos and others did not realise that henceforth there were likely to be problems if they attempted to use the papacy as a means of securing the twin aims of Byzantine foreign policy. Any attempt to use the papacy to advance the first aim, the security of Constantinople, was likely to have repercussions for the second, that of securing recognition of the hegemony of the emperor as the supreme authority in the Christian world.

In spite of the events of 1054, therefore, the emperors and their advisers continued to pursue their policy of seeking an understanding with the papacy. Constantine IX probably had in mind reviving the proposal for an anti-Norman alliance in his discussions with Cardinal Humbert in Constantinople in June 1054. He certainly welcomed the legates very warmly, lodging them in an imperial palace, just outside the Pege gate in the Land Walls. When an overzealous monk of the monastery of St John Stoudios endangered the negotiations by circulating a polemical tract against Latin ecclesiastical practices, Constantine compelled him to make a public retraction before the legates and ordered the offending tract to be burned. He even encouraged Humbert to pen a treatise setting out the western position on the subject of the *Filioque*.[40] In spite of all Constantine's efforts, the subsequent excommunication of Keroularios and the abrupt departure of the legates for Rome brought any negotiations for an alliance to an end.

In the years that followed, the situation in southern Italy changed dramatically. Finding himself having to fight a local faction for possession of Rome, Pope Nicholas II (1058–61) came to terms with the Normans, investing Robert Guiscard with the duchy of Apulia and Calabria in 1059. The investiture was repeated by Nicholas II's successor, Gregory VII (1073–85).[41]

Nevertheless, approaches continued to be made by the Byzantine emperor. In 1073 Michael VII sent two monks to Gregory VII bearing a letter. The precise contents of the letter are not known, and in his reply Gregory contented himself with vague phrases about his desire to see the restoration of the former concord between the churches of Rome and Constantinople, stating that the main matter would be communicated by his messenger.[42] It is unlikely that Michael was hoping to renew the anti-Norman alliance, given that the Normans were now allies and faithful vassals of the papacy and that he himself was now in negotiation with Robert Guiscard. It therefore seems more probable that Michael's embassy was connected with that other preoccupation of Byzantine foreign policy during the eleventh century, the recruitment of mercenaries. We have already seen that the emperors were happy to exploit the passing pilgrimage traffic in an attempt to alleviate the empire's manpower problem, and that embassies were being sent as far afield as England and Flanders for what one assumes to be the same purpose. Michael may well have asked the pope to use his moral authority to urge western knights to enrol in Byzantine service. If that was the case, it would certainly explain Gregory's next move. In March 1074, on receiving news of the deteriorating situation in Asia Minor from returning pilgrims, Gregory issued an encyclical addressed to all the faithful, warning that the Turks were virtually at the walls of Constantinople, and encouraging Christians to go east to help the Byzantine emperor in his struggle against them.[43]

As in the case of his treaty with Robert Guiscard, Michael VII's deposition in 1078 prevented him from developing his strategy towards the papacy further. Gregory VII excommunicated Michael's successors Nikephoros III and Alexios I, regarding them as usurpers, and gave moral support to Robert Guiscard's invasion of the Balkans in 1081.[44] Yet Byzantine efforts to enrol the pope's assistance continued. In 1081 Alexios I is said by Anna Comnena to have tried to woo Gregory away from his support for Robert Guiscard in the usual way, sending to Rome 'moderate gifts, with promises of much largesse and many honours in the future'.[45] Communication was also facilitated by the accession of a new pope, Urban II (1088–99), one of whose first acts was to lift Gregory VII's excommunication of Alexios and to request in return that Latin Christians be allowed to reopen their churches in Constantinople. Alexios responded by gathering a synod in Constantinople to consider ways of restoring amity between the eastern and western churches.[46]

It is not immediately clear why Alexios I and his advisers were so eager to court the pope. By 1095 the crisis facing the Byzantine empire had eased somewhat. In 1083 the Normans had been driven out of the Balkans and in 1091 the Pechenegs had been overwhelmingly defeated at the battle of Mount Levounion. Even Alexios's other principal opponents, the Seljuk Turks in Asia Minor, were not as formidable as they had been, being given over to internal power struggles after the death of Suleyman in 1086. Alexios, however, still faced a manpower shortage if he was to take the offensive against the Seljuk Turks, and to reconquer Asia Minor. This seems to have been the likely reason behind continued contacts with the pope and the embassy despatched to Urban II in the spring of 1095, which met him at a council he was presiding over at Piacenza in northern Italy.[47]

As in the case of Michael VII's contact with Gregory VII, the letter sent by Alexios to Urban II does not survive, nor is the embassy mentioned by Anna Comnena, John Zonaras or by any other contemporary or near-contemporary Byzantine source. Some later commentators have regarded the omission as a deliberate attempt to hide Alexios's role in the genesis of the First Crusade. Yet few of the numerous Byzantine diplomatic dealings with the west in the eleventh century are mentioned by Byzantine historians. Writing in a genre which placed emphasis above all on events in Constantinople and the *Oikoumene*, accounts of happenings further afield are rare and, when they were included, often garbled and unsatisfactory.[48]

The only Byzantine source to mention the embassy at all is the *Synopsis chronike* of Theodore Skoutariotes, a work written some two hundred years after the events of 1095. Skoutariotes stated that Alexios's aim was to obtain soldiers for the empire's armies, but he also claimed that the emperor, desperate to get the Latins as allies, made a cunning and cynical move to secure their compliance. Knowing that western Europeans deeply reverenced the holy places and the city of Jerusalem, and that they were deeply affronted that the Holy Sepulchre was ruled by infidels, he deliberately played on this in his letter to the pope and so succeeded in attracting large numbers of them to the east. The account is clearly anachronistic, dating as it does from a time when the crusades and their preoccupation with Jerusalem were well established and well known in Byzantium.[49] But Skoutariotes's main point, that Alexios approached the pope to secure troops, fits in with the known activity of Byzantine embassies abroad during the eleventh century.

In the absence of contemporary Byzantine accounts, we are thrown back on western chronicles for details about the discussions at Piacenza in 1095. In this case there are two contemporary chronicles, by Ekkehard, abbot of Aura, and Bernold of St Blaise, which mention the embassy. According to these writers, the envoys read a letter from the emperor, drawing a lurid picture of the situation in the east. Alexios claimed, as Gregory VII had done, that the empire's infidel enemies had reached to the very walls of Constantinople and begged help from his fellow Christians against them. Up to this point, Ekkehard and Bernold's accounts are entirely credible, mirroring Alexios's letter to Henry IV of 1081, in which he asked for help against 'the murderous, sinful enemy of God and the Christians'. Also credible is the remark of another chronicler, Guibert of Nogent, that Urban received gifts from Alexios. All these points can be substantiated from other examples of Byzantine diplomatic practice.[50]

In another respect, however, the tone of the embassy, as reported by Bernold and Ekkehard, was very different from that usually employed. Ekkehard claimed that Alexios

> deplored his inability to defend the churches of the east. He beseeched the pope

to call to his aid, if that were possible, the entire west ... He promised to provide for those who should go to fight all that they might need on land and sea.[51]

Not only is Alexios presented as a humble supplicant, but also as one prepared to admit that he was no longer able to fulfil his role of protector of Christians. His request was not for mercenaries to fight under his command but for 'the entire west', with promises to provision them when they arrived, but no indication that he was clearly expecting to lead or to control them in any way.

It is very unlikely that Alexios's letter was couched in these terms. Even the treaties made with Robert Guiscard in 1074 and with the Venetians in 1082, which made far-reaching concessions in response to the desperate situation of the empire in the years immediately after Mantzikert, nevertheless adopted a tone of lordly superiority.[52] Why now, in 1095 when the empire was in a much stronger position, should Alexios suddenly start to complain that he could no longer cope with his imperial role and call upon westerners to emigrate *en masse* to help him?

The answer lies in the outlook of Ekkehard, a participant in the unsuccessful 1101 crusade. He clearly interpreted Alexios's letter in such a way as to reflect papal ideology, which did not recognise Byzantine universalist claims. He was by no means alone in this. Much the same message was placed in a forged version of a letter of Alexios to the count of Flanders, which was circulating in the west at this time, in which Alexios purportedly complained that:

I, albeit I am emperor, can find no remedy or suitable counsel, but am always fleeing in the face of the Turks and Pechenegs, and I remain in a particular city only until I perceive that their arrival is imminent. And I think it is better to be subjected to your Latins than to the abominations of the pagans. Therefore, before Constantinople is captured by them, you most certainly ought to fight with all your strength so that you may joyfully receive in heaven a glorious and ineffable reward.[53]

In interpreting the embassy of Alexios I in this way, Ekkehard and others had turned Byzantine foreign policy on its head. Whereas the Byzantines were apt to insist on the universal claims of their emperor, Alexios was now being presented as willing to give up his empire to the more deserving westerners. While the Byzantines had always drawn in warriors from foreign nations to serve under their banners in return for imperial largesse, they were now portrayed as begging for a rescue mission to retrieve a situation of which they had irrevocably lost control.

It seems that Urban II himself also reinterpreted the tenor of the letter sent in 1095, not with any anti-Byzantine motive, but as a natural reflection of the ideology of his office as it had developed by that time. Under the pressure of events, the popes had gone a great deal beyond the claims being made by Peter Damian and Humbert in the 1040s and 1050s. Gregory VII had found that his attack on lay investiture and simony had brought him into direct conflict with the western emperor, Henry IV, who had no intention of giving up his right to appoint bishops. In 1075 Gregory had therefore promulgated the *Dictatus papae*, a series of statements about the powers of the pope, which included the assertion that he could depose emperors.[54] The statement was obviously put in to strengthen Gregory's hand against Henry IV, but it had an important implication. It meant that the pope was claiming to have authority over secular rulers, even over emperors, and even over Roman emperors. The supreme authority in the Christian world, therefore, was that of the pope, not that of the emperor in Constantinople.

Urban seems to have reflected that view in a sermon which he preached some months after the meeting at Piacenza, in November 1095, at another church council at Clermont in France. Again, there is no definitive, contemporary account of what was said on this occasion and we only have the summaries given by four contemporary, or near contemporary, Latin chroniclers, Fulcher of Chartres, Robert of Rheims, Baldric of Dol and Guibert of Nogent, all of whom give slightly different versions of the sermon. Nevertheless, they all agree on two points. First, that Urban called upon his audience to go to the aid of the eastern Christians against the infidels who had invaded Christian lands in the east. Secondly, that he made no mention whatsoever of the Byzantine emperor.[55]

While missing out Alexios, Urban introduced something else into the picture: the city of Jerusalem and above all the Holy Sepulchre, the cave where the body of Christ was believed to have lain after the crucifixion. While the earliest chronicler, Fulcher, makes no mention of anything beyond an expedition to help Constantinople, all the other accounts agree that, in the words of Guibert of Nogent, Urban urged his audience to consider 'that almighty providence may have destined you for the task of rescuing Jerusalem'. Such an expedition to the holiest shrine in the Christian world, Urban claimed, would be a pilgrimage, carrying with it the benefit of pilgrimage, the remission of penance for sin. Bernold of St Blaise and other chroniclers, writing much closer in time to these events than Guibert, as well as letters written by Urban himself, confirm that the idea that the liberation of Jerusalem, not the defence of Constantinople, had become accepted as the ultimate goal of the expedition within a few months of the council of Clermont.[56]

In presenting the expedition against the Turks as a penitential pilgrimage to the Holy Sepulchre, Urban had changed Alexios's plan to draw in westerners to help defend the *Oikoumene* into something quite different. He had substituted Jerusalem for Constantinople as the Christian city to be snatched from the grasp of the infidel. He had placed the expedition under his leadership, rather than that of the emperor, and in doing so had stated his claim to ultimate authority in the Christian world. In the words of Bernold of St Blaise, 'the lord pope was the principal author of this expedition'. Alexios and his advisers had been left far behind.[57]

Faced with invasion and crisis during the eleventh century the Byzantines had employed the tried and tested tactics of gold and honours to entice western European states and warriors to give them support against their new and dangerous enemies, always ensuring that their largesse elicited a proper respect for the unique place of their empire in the hierarchy of Christian states. In general, their efforts had been rewarded. Mercenaries had enrolled in their armies, Venetian support had enabled them to defeat the Norman invasion. Yet, when it had been applied to the reformed papacy, that policy had been interpreted in a completely different way, in accordance with the papacy's own fast-developing ideology. As a result, the rulers of Byzantium were faced in 1096 with a completely new and unprecedented situation. The question now was how they would react to it.

4

The Passage of the First Crusade

Urban II could hardly have chosen more a more potent formula in his appeal to the western nobility at Clermont. Central authority was weak in western Europe in the eleventh century, and local warfare and sporadic violence were inevitable as the knightly class fought each other to protect and extend their lands. Consequently, many western nobleman were uneasily aware that they had blood on their hands and that in all probability they would pay for it with eternal damnation. It had become increasingly common for them to attempt to atone for their wrongs by making pilgrimages to some sacred shrine, the most important – and most distant – of these being the Holy Sepulchre in Jerusalem. To this warrior elite, obsessed by the consequences of sin, yet compelled by social circumstances to commit it, Urban now proposed an armed pilgrimage, whose participants would not only journey to the Holy Sepulchre, but would liberate it from infidel rule. In the past they had used violence against fellow Christians and had regularly been excommunicated for it. Now they were to unleash their bellicosity on the Muslim world, in an act of war that would attract not damnation, but on the contrary, earn the indulgence issued by the pope: the cancellation of penance due for sins committed in the past. As one clerical apologist for the crusade put it:

> Until now you have waged wrongful wars, often hurling insane spears at each other, driven only by greed and pride, for which you deserved only death and damnation. Now we propose for you battles which offer the gift of glorious martyrdom.[1]

In the months after Urban II's appeal at Clermont in November 1095, the extraordinary success of his appeal became apparent. Immediately after the sermon at Clermont, many of those present took a vow to join the expedition to Jerusalem, wearing crosses of cloth on their shoulders as a sign of their intention. Urban then journeyed across western France during the spring of 1096, repeating his call at towns along his route, and sending written appeals to areas that he could not visit in person. Several important magnates now took the cross, but Urban was careful to ensure that his own leadership of the enterprise was not lost sight of by appointing Adhémar, bishop of Le Puy, as his representative on the expedition. The plan emerged that these volunteers, most of whom came from France and Italy, would be formed into a number of separate armies that would take a different route to arrive at the common assembly point of Constantinople. From there, the combined army would cross the Bosporos to Asia Minor to begin the next stage of the journey towards Jerusalem.

Between 1096 and 1101, the Byzantines came face to face with the unexpected result of the routine embassy to Piacenza as the crusade armies arrived at Constantinople in three waves. The first arrived in the summer of 1096, a diverse, poorly equipped and apparently undisciplined army, sometimes known as the Peasants' or People's Crusade, led by Peter the Hermit and Walter Sansavoir. The second wave was composed of a number of separate armies. It was spearheaded by Hugh, count of Vermandois, the brother of King Philip I of France, who crossed from southern Italy to Dyrrachion. He was followed by a contingent led by Godfrey of Bouillon, duke of Lower Lotharingia, and accompanied by his brothers, Eustace and Baldwin of Boulogne, which crossed into Byzantine territory across the Danube and reached Constantinople by December. Bohemond of Taranto and his followers took the route of Hugh of Vermandois, arriving on 10 April 1097. Finally, Raymond of Saint-Gilles, count of Toulouse, and his army of Provençals reached Constantinople a few days after Bohemond. It was this second wave which later passed through Asia Minor, captured Antioch in 1098, and finally took Jerusalem itself on 15 July 1099. The third wave, composed of contingents from Lombardy, France and Bavaria arrived in the spring and early summer of 1101.[2]

The policy makers in Constantinople, therefore, had very little time to decide how to react before the arrival of the first wave nor would it have been easy to decide what line to take with this unprecedented situation. On the one hand, the crusader armies were supposedly coming east to assist the Byzantines against their Muslim enemies. On the other, they came not under the command of the emperor but under their own leaders, with the nominal authority of the pope represented by the legate, Adhémar. There were, moreover, a frighteningly large number of them: some sixty thousand has been estimated for the first two waves alone. It is hardly surprising, therefore, that Alexios and his advisers were wary of the crusaders and considered that they might constitute a threat to Constantinople itself. Nor is it to be wondered at that the Byzantines fell back on tried and trusted techniques to diffuse the perceived threat. The usual tactics of distributing gifts, exploiting divisions, extracting oaths to respect the rights of the emperor, but using force when absolutely necessary, were all employed. In many ways, these tactics proved to be extremely successful, and they allowed the Byzantines to take advantage of the passage of the crusading armies to reconquer the western half of Asia Minor from the Seljuk Turks. Yet the employment of traditional diplomatic methods towards the First Crusade was also to lead directly to conflict with the crusaders over the city of Antioch and to sow the seeds of the poor reputation that the Byzantines were later to suffer from in western European opinion.[3]

There has been much debate about the exact line of policy pursued by Alexios I towards the First Crusade. The reason is that there is no contemporary Byzantine source of information on these events. They are only described in Greek by two historians writing many years later. One, John Zonaras, should have been well placed to record the crusade from the point of view of the Byzantine elite. He had held office under Alexios I but had been disgraced in 1118 when he had supported Anna Comnena's opposition to the new emperor, John II. His later years were spent in a monastery on an island in the Sea of Marmara, where he occupied his time by writing a history. Yet his account of the crusade, or the 'commotion' as he calls it, is so brief as to be almost useless, and contains demonstrable errors, such as his claim that the crusaders captured Nicaea unaided in 1097 and then sold it to the Byzantines.[4]

It has, therefore, to be left to Anna Comnena, the daughter of Alexios I, to represent the Byzantine view of the crusade. Like Zonaras, Comnena was involved in opposition to the accession of John II in 1118, and had been party to an unsuccessful plot to replace him with her husband, the Caesar Nikephoros Bryennios. Comnena spent her later years in disgrace, living in seclusion in a convent in Constantinople, where she contented herself with compiling a commentary on Aristotle and writing a life of her father, the *Alexiad*.[5] The latter is an extraordinary work. Like that of Psellos, it contains striking descriptive passages and perceptive character sketches. Like Psellos too, Comnena has the engaging habit of personally intruding into the history, confiding to the reader at one point: 'As I write these words, it is nearly time to light the lamps; my pen moves slowly over the paper and I feel myself almost too drowsy to write as the words escape me'. Unlike Zonaras, Comnena gives a lively and detailed account of the First Crusade.[6]

Whatever the literary merits of the *Alexiad*, however, for a number of reasons it has been regarded as a most untrustworthy record of the events of 1095 to 1100. It has been pointed out that Comnena was writing about events which took place when she was a child and which she could not possibly remember. Her account is coloured by hindsight because she was writing in the light of the subsequent Norman seizure of Antioch in 1098. Finally, her work is one of panegyric, designed to boost the posthumous reputation of Alexios I, and by implication to diminish that of his successors.[7]

All these criticisms possess some validity, but they do not diminish the importance of the *Alexiad* as a statement of the attitude of ruling circles in Constantinople to the passage of the First Crusade. While she herself was not part of those circles in 1096, in later years Anna had ample opportunity to talk to those who had been and, by her own account, derived a great deal of information from them. One of them was her uncle, George Palaeologus, who was present when Alexios I discussed future strategy with the crusaders at Pelekanon in June 1097. Another was her husband Bryennios, who had taken part in the clash with the army of Godfrey of Bouillon outside the walls of Constantinople on Maundy Thursday in 1097. Anna claims that she listened to conversations between Palaeologus and Alexios on matters of state, and that she incorporated materials collected by Bryennios into her own history.[8] Thus, however tendentious the *Alexiad* may be in matters of interpretation and tone, it can nevertheless be seen as a reliable guide to the outlook and attitudes of the Byzantine elite and the policy they employed towards the First Crusade.

Anna Comnena is clear from the very beginning what it was that underlay that policy. Alexios and his advisers saw the approaching crusade not as the arrival of long-awaited allies but rather as a potential threat to the *Oikoumene*. Its arrival was 'dreaded' and the declaration of the crusade leadership that they were heading towards Palestine to liberate the Holy Sepulchre was regarded with some scepticism, as a blind to some plan to seize Constantinople itself. Such suspicions were exacerbated by the presence at the head of one of the armies of the south Italian Norman, Bohemond of Taranto, who had played a major part in his father Robert Guiscard's invasion of the empire in 1081. Comnena's claims are substantiated by the Frankish historian, Fulcher of Chartres, who travelled with one of the crusader armies and who later recalled that the emperor 'feared that we might plot some injury to him'.[9]

At the same time, Comnena stressed that the crusade was regarded as presenting an opportunity as well as a threat. Properly organised, these powerful armies could inflict significant damage on the empire's eastern enemies: they 'might destroy the cities of the Ishmaelites or force them to make terms with the Roman sovereigns and thus extend the bounds of Roman territory'.[10] In making preparations for the arrival of the crusading armies, Alexios and his advisers sought to defuse the threat, while turning the situation to their advantage.

How were these two aims to be achieved? Conventional wisdom in Byzantium dictated that, when it was weaker than the empire, a foreign power should be overawed by displays of gold and wealth. If it were stronger, it should be brought to heel by displays of military might and by being reminded of the strength of the walls of Constantinople.[11] The crusading armies may have seemed to fall half way between these two extremes, constituting as they did both a threat and an opportunity. It was, Comnena claims, unprecedented within living memory. Certainly the policy adopted contained elements of reward and threat, a kind of 'carrot and stick' approach. Forces were sent to the Balkan frontiers accompanied by interpreters. They were given instructions to receive the crusading armies in a friendly fashion, and to supply them with provisions. They were, however, to shadow the armies closely as they marched towards Constantinople and to intervene if any attempts were made to pillage the countryside. Everything possible was to be done to keep the various armies and their leaders apart, so that they could not unite against the Byzantines. To prevent them linking up outside Constantinople, each army was to be ferried across the Bosporos to Asia Minor as soon as possible.[12]

In dealing with the first wave, the 'People's Crusade' led by Peter the Hermit and Walter Sansavoir, carrot very soon gave way to stick. Comnena describes how, when Peter and his followers first arrived at Constantinople, Alexios advised him to wait on the European side of the straits until the other contingents arrived. Peter, she says, ignored the advice and crossed the Bosporos. There his force rashly became involved in a confrontation with a Turkish army near Nicaea and was almost annihilated. Alexios sent a force to rescue the survivors, and lectured Peter on his foolishness in ignoring the emperor's advice.[13] Comnena's account is suspect here, in so far as it contradicts her statement elsewhere that Alexios wished above all to prevent the crusader armies from linking up on the European side. Hindsight is evidently at work too, for Comnena is trying to defend Alexios from later accusations that he had betrayed Peter to the Turks. A western chronicle, the *Gesta Francorum*, gives a more convincing version of events. No sooner did Peter reach Constantinople than his followers started looting the suburbs, stripping lead from the roofs in order to sell it. It was therefore Alexios who, not unreasonably, insisted that they be ferried across to the opposite shore of the Bosporos.[14] The safety of Constantinople took precedence over that of Peter and his undisciplined army.

With the second and third waves, Comnena depicts Alexios and his court applying a more sophisticated policy, which sought to draw benefit from the crusaders as well as neutralising the threat they posed. The element of security was certainly there. As they moved through Byzantine territory towards Constantinople, the crusader armies were subjected to close surveillance by bands of Pecheneg mercenaries in Byzantine service. Once they arrived, they were not allowed into the city itself but rather were persuaded to pitch camp near the upper reaches of the Golden Horn around the monastery of Saints Cosmas and Damian, the Kosmidion, outside the walls but close to Alexios's residence in the Blachernae palace.[15] To prevent the armies from linking up, messengers plying between them were intercepted. When Hugh of Vermandois arrived on the Byzantine Adriatic coast with only a few followers, after his fleet had been scattered by a storm, the Byzantine governor of Dyrrachion had him placed under close escort and taken to Constantinople as a virtual prisoner.[16]

At the same time Alexios sought to derive benefit from the new arrivals, particularly as regarded the restoration of imperial rule in Asia Minor. Once at Constantinople, each of the leaders was required to swear an oath, described by Anna Comnena as 'the customary oath of the Latins', consisting of a promise 'that whatever cities, countries or forts he might in future subdue which had in the first place belonged to the Roman empire, he would hand over to the officer appointed by the emperor for this very purpose'.[17] When all had complied with this requirement, the tone of the reception changed dramatically. Alexios handed out generous quantities of gold, silver and costly fabrics as a sign of his approval, filling an entire room of the Kosmidion with presents for Bohemond. In addition, honorary membership of the imperial family appears to have been granted to the leaders of the third wave of the crusade in 1101, who were adopted as Alexios's sons.[18]

None of these methods was new. Strict supervision had always been applied to large groups of foreigners passing through the empire. In their treaties with the Russians in the previous century, the Byzantines had been careful to stipulate that Russians should only enter Constantinople by one particular gate, unarmed and in groups of no more than fifty, and that they were to be kept under surveillance by an imperial officer. The administration of oaths to foreigners was another traditional practice. Michael Attaleiates had done so to the Uze mercenaries in the Byzantine army on the eve of the battle of Mantzikert in 1071 to ensure their loyalty in the coming battle, and oaths had recently been required from Robert of Flanders, Robert Guiscard and the Emperor Henry IV when they entered into agreements with the empire. Gifts of gold, silver and silks had, of course, been poured into the eager hands of 'barbarians' for centuries. Even adoption of the leaders of 1101 was not new. Something similar had been conferred on the Bulgarian Khan Boris in 865.[19] These were standard procedures for neutralising external threats and turning them to the advantage of the *Oikoumene.*

In many ways, to judge by Comnena's account, Alexios and his advisers succeeded in doing just that. When the second wave of crusaders had crossed to Asia Minor in May 1097, their first objective was the city of Nicaea, which had been in Turkish hands since 1078. The Latins invested the city by land, and a squadron of Byzantine ships was launched onto the large lake which borders Nicaea to the west to prevent supplies coming in that way. When a relieving force led by the Turkish sultan, Kilidj Arslan, failed to break through, the garrison surrendered to the Byzantine emperor on 19 June 1097. Later that month, the crusader armies set out across Asia Minor accompanied by a small Byzantine force, and struck a severe blow against the Seljuk Turks at the battle of Dorylaion. The following year Alexios took advantage of the disarray into which the Turks had been thrown by their defeat and sent his brother-in-law, the Grand Duke John Doukas, with an army into western Asia Minor against the independent Turkish emir Tzachas, who was based at Smyrna. Taking with him as a hostage Tzachas's daughter, who had been captured at Nicaea, Doukas fought a successful campaign, taking Smyrna, Ephesus, Sardis and Philadelphia, and restoring Byzantine rule in the area. Further gains followed in the wake of the third wave of crusaders in 1101. One contingent marched into north-eastern Anatolia. Although it enjoyed little success against the Turks, it did capture Ankyra and handed it over to Alexios in accordance with the oaths sworn in Constantinople. As a result, the Byzantines were later able to reassert their control over much of the Black Sea coast.[20]

In some respects, therefore, the handling of the First Crusade by Alexios and his advisers appears to have been another example of the successful application of accumulated wisdom, enabling them not only to prevent any attempt to seize Constantinople, but also to recover a substantial part of Asia Minor. Yet Anna Comnena still lamented that Alexios's toils over the crusade had 'won no advantage for the Roman empire'. From her vantage point in the mid twelfth century, she could see that the crusade had led directly to the Norman seizure of Antioch and to the anti-Byzantine propaganda that was by then circulating in western Europe. She put these setbacks down to a sinister plot harboured by Bohemond from the beginning:

> The truth is that Bohemond was an habitual rogue ... When he left his native land, he was a soured man, for it had no estates at all. Apparently, he left to worship at the Holy Sepulchre, but in reality to seize power for himself – or rather, if possible, to seize the Roman empire itself, as his father [Robert Guiscard] had suggested.[21]

Needless to say, the causes of tension lay much deeper than just Bohemond's supposedly bad character.

Impressive and successful though the methods of Byzantine foreign policy had been in the past, they had been developed for use in dealing with peoples who had no difficulty accepting the assumption of superiority that was integral to the way in which the Byzantines dealt with outsiders. True, modifications had been introduced when dealing with Muslim powers, which were often as wealthy and powerful as the empire and possessed their own religious ideology in Islam. The fact remained, however, that Byzantine foreign policy assumed, and was designed to secure acceptance of, the Byzantine emperor's leadership of the Christian world.

The problem with the crusaders was that they had their own Christian ideology, which was very difficult to reconcile with the Byzantine world view. They regarded themselves as soldiers of Christ, commissioned by Christ himself, through Pope Urban, to liberate the city of Jerusalem from the infidel. There could be no higher or more noble cause for a pious Christian. As Guibert of Nogent put it, the crusaders were the Lord's army, waging a 'most legitimate war' to protect the holy church. God Himself led them and fought through them.[22] The treatment that the crusaders experienced once they arrived in the Byzantine empire, and the behaviour of Alexios in putting the interests of his own empire before the capture of Jerusalem, therefore often aroused deep resentment.

That resentment began almost as soon as they crossed the imperial border. The crusaders discovered that the Byzantine obsession with the security of Constantinople meant that their heels were dogged by bands of Byzantine troops. Before long, clashes occurred. The *Gesta Francorum* relates how Bohemond's contingent of south Italian Normans was attacked by Pecheneg mercenaries without warning as it forded a river. In the ensuing tussle, the Normans captured several Pechenegs who, on being asked why they had attacked, said that they had been ordered to do so by the emperor. Raymond of Aguilers and Peter Tudebode recount how Count Raymond of Toulouse and his Provençal army, having come under attack from the Slavs as they travelled down the Dalmatian coast, believed that they were safely on Christian territory once they arrived at the Byzantine city of Dyrrachion. The harassment continued from the Pechenegs, however, who allegedly attacked and robbed the papal legate, Adhémar of Le Puy, near Pelagonia. When they finally arrived at Constantinople, they found the gates in the Land Walls locked and barred against them. The western chroniclers felt particularly aggrieved by this treatment because it contrasted so starkly with friendly letters from the emperor which arrived at the same time, speaking of peace, brotherhood and alliance.[23]

Such treatment was all the more resented because, on occasion, the emperor seemed to take a friendlier attitude to Muslims, the enemies of the faith, than he did to the soldiers of Christ. Following the capture of Nicaea in June 1097, the crusaders were shocked at the emperor's lenient treatment of the Turks, who were offered the choice of enrolling in the Byzantine army or being given a safe conduct back to their own land. The crusaders felt that they had been robbed of their chance to plunder the city, in spite of the presents distributed by Alexios to make up for it, and suspected that the enrolment of Turks in the Byzantine armies was part of some future plan to do damage to the crusaders.[24]

They were not entirely mistaken here. Although Alexios probably had no particular desire to see the crusade fail, he did not want to be left on bad terms with his Muslim neighbours if, as seemed likely, it did come to grief. Following the victory of the crusaders at Dorylaion in July 1097, the emperor redeemed many of the Turkish prisoners and had them transported to Constantinople. No doubt they were offered the same choice as the garrison of Nicaea. Nor did Alexios see any reason to cease the friendly contacts with the Fatimid regime in Egypt, built up by his predecessors. He even wrote to warn them of the approach of the crusade. He probably also alerted the Danishmend and Seljuk Turks to the approach of the third wave of the First Crusade in 1101.[25] Alexios was, of course, merely pursuing the interests of his empire by all possible means but, measured alongside the standards of the ideology of the crusade, such actions could easily be regarded as treachery.

The insistence of the rulers of the Byzantine empire on securing recognition for their claim to leadership in the Christian world was a further cause for resentment. All the crusader leaders were required to swear the oath to the emperor, which probably involved not only agreeing to hand back captured imperial cities, but also, like that administered to Robert Guiscard in 1074, giving an undertaking to show 'the submission and good intentions' which the emperor was due.[26] This would certainly account for the violent resistance by some, though not all, of the leaders. Godfrey of Bouillon fought a pitched battle on the issue with imperial troops outside the walls of Constantinople on Maundy Thursday 1097 before finally being compelled to give way. Bohemond's nephew, Tancred of Hauteville, protested vigorously that he wanted no other lord than his uncle and ended up in an undignified scuffle with Alexios's brother-in-law, George Palaeologus. The most determined opponent of the oath was Raymond of Toulouse, who insisted that he had taken a vow to God alone, meaning presumably his oath to join the expedition to Jerusalem. He only yielded when he was urgently beseeched to do so by some of the leaders and threatened with violence by Bohemond. Even then he insisted on swearing a modified form of the oath: he only promised either not to sully the life or honour of Alexios, or not to take away the emperor's life or possessions, depending on how the Latin of Raymond of Aguilers and the *Gesta Francorum* is translated.[27]

The whole episode seems to have rankled and to have been seen as an unnecessary humiliation. Anna Comnena's tales of the boastfulness and arrogance of the crusade leaders, though no doubt exaggerated, probably reflect this resentment and the need for self-assertion by people far from home who felt themselves belittled and despised. On one occasion, when Alexios was receiving some of the leaders, probably in the Blachernae palace, one of them, to whom Comnena accords the unlikely name of 'Latinus', had the effrontery to sit himself down on Alexios's throne, in flagrant violation of the custom that all should stand in the presence of the emperor.[28] The crusade leaders clearly felt that they were every bit as good as the Byzantines, and sometimes took a contemptuous attitude to the gifts that their hosts distributed to those who complied with the imperial will. Some complained that they received too little. Raymond of Aguilers grumbled that his master Raymond of Toulouse had his share cut to a minimum because of his obstinacy over the oath. Albert of Aachen felt that Alexios's gifts were not gifts at all because they went straight back into his treasury when they were used to buy food in the emperor's own markets. Even those who were generously treated could be insulted by the very lavishness of the gifts. Bohemond initially sent back the riches brought to him by the emperor's servants, reacting in much the same way as an earlier Norman visitor to Constantinople, Duke Robert, who back in 1035 had refused the emperor's precious gifts.[29]

In one important respect, that of military prowess, the crusaders regarded themselves as distinctly superior. Comnena has 'Latinus' proclaim proudly:

> I am a pure Frank and of noble birth. One thing I know: at a crossroads in the country where I was born is an ancient shrine; to this anyone who wishes to engage in single combat goes, prepared to fight; there he prays to God for help and there he stays awaiting the man who will dare to answer his challenge. At that crossroads I myself have spent time, waiting and longing for the man who would fight – but there was never one who dared.[30]

Yet while the anger of some of the leaders was obviously deeply felt, it would be wrong to accord it too much significance in the long term. In the first place, it appears that not everyone shared the frustration of some of the crusade leaders. As to the harassment by Byzantine troops in the Balkans, many crusaders were well aware that these attacks on their armies were more than balanced by the damage and looting perpetrated by westerners in Byzantine territory. Similar activities by the crusaders in Hungary had elicited a comparable response from the government there.[31] As far as the stay in Constantinople is concerned, there were some who felt that their reception had not been in the least unfriendly or demeaning. Both Stephen, count of Blois, and Fulcher of Chartres, a priest in his army, left glowing accounts, praising Alexios's generosity and asserting that the journey could not have been made without his assistance.[32]

In the case of those who did feel that they had cause for complaint, there was no reason why the misunderstandings and tensions of 1096 and 1097 could not be forgotten later. This was certainly so in the case of Raymond of Toulouse. Although his troops had fought some of the fiercest battles with Byzantine troops in the Balkans, and although he had been the most obstinate opponent of the oath, following the capture of Jerusalem in 1099 Raymond returned to Constantinople and became a staunch ally of Alexios. His change of heart was no doubt motivated by fear of the intentions of his fellow crusaders, Bohemond and Tancred, and by the tensions that had developed after the capture of Antioch in 1098. The Byzantines were always only too happy to exploit such rifts among their enemies.[33]

None of the resentments voiced by some of the leaders over their treatment by the Byzantines should therefore have been anything more than ruffled feathers which would have be smoothed over again in course of time. As it happened, however, within a few years of the capture of Jerusalem, they had come to form the basis of a virulent anti-Byzantine propaganda that was circulating in western Europe. This was a result of the second unforeseen outcome of Byzantine policy towards the First Crusade, the annexation by Bohemond of the city of Antioch.

Both the crusaders and their Byzantine hosts must have known, during the winter and spring of 1096–97, that, if it were to reach Jerusalem, the western army would have to capture Antioch. The city lay astride the main route from Asia Minor into Syria and Palestine, and was strongly fortified. It was not feasible to leave it as a centre for Muslim resistance in the rear. The Byzantines regarded this strategically vital city as being included in the oath sworn by the crusaders to return any cities which had previously belonged to the empire.[34] Although it had been under Muslim rule for a long period between the seventh and tenth centuries, in 969 it had been reconquered by the Emperor Nikephoros II Phokas. It had only been lost again to the Seljuk Turks relatively recently, in 1084.

Given the strategic importance of Antioch, it is not surprising that it should have come up for discussion during the crusaders' stay in the vicinity of Constantinople. What is surprising is that it was to Bohemond, supposedly his deeply mistrusted former foe, that Alexios chose to talk. According to the *Gesta Francorum*, Bohemond was summoned into the emperor's presence and promised that, if he took the required oath, he would be given 'land in extent from Antioch fifteen days journey, and eight in width'. This passage sits very oddly in the text of the *Gesta*, breaking into an account of how regrettable and humiliating it was for Bohemond and his followers to be required to take the oath. It is therefore probably an interpolation, added to the chronicle later for purposes of anti-Byzantine propaganda.[35]

It seems likely, nevertheless, that Alexios did attempt to reach some kind of agreement with Bohemond, possibly involving Antioch, by which the Byzantines would be able to make use of his services. Anna Comnena claims that, when Alexios met Bohemond, the Norman demanded to be invested with the office of Domestic of the East, the commander of the eastern armies, who in the past had operated from frontier bases like Antioch. Alexios, she says, neither granted the request nor denied it, flattering him with hopes and pleading that the time was not ripe at present. Comnena may not be telling the whole story here. Other evidence suggests that Bohemond certainly did regard himself as being in the service of the Byzantines. When Raymond of Toulouse resolutely refused to take the oath, it was Bohemond who threatened to take the emperor's part and to compel Raymond to comply. In May 1097 it was again Bohemond who organised the provisioning of the crusader army, a task which was the responsibility of the emperor but which he had perhaps delegated.[36]

Alexios therefore appears to have been pursuing the familiar policy of recruiting mercenaries for the imperial army. It was not in the least out of the ordinary that he should attempt to recruit a former enemy, for, again, there were precedents. He had incorporated the defeated Pechenegs into his army in 1091. It was not, moreover, only Bohemond whom he was striving to hire: in June 1097 he offered to pay those among the crusader host who did not want to continue to Jerusalem to stay and guard Nicaea. His grandson Manuel I was to make similar offers at the time of the Second Crusade.[37] What is not known are the terms on which Bohemond's services were obtained. Alexios's temporising words, reported by Comnena, may have led the Norman to believe that he was somehow entitled to Antioch.

Another traditional tactic, the administration of oaths, was to cause a similar misunderstanding, and to play a part in the annexation of Antioch. According to Anna Comnena, after the capture of Nicaea in June 1097,

Alexios called a conference of the crusade leaders, to be held at Pelekanon, between Nicaea and Constantinople. The gathering was partly designed to ensure that all those prominent in the crusader host, who had not yet taken the oath, should now do so.[38] For Alexios and his retinue the whole performance was a routine way of ensuring compliance with the terms of an agreement and extracting due recognition of the emperor's status. For the crusaders, on the other hand, it appears to have been regarded as involving much greater mutual commitment. The solemn link between lord and man formed the basis of social obligation in western Europe, so the leaders would certainly have felt themselves bound by it. At the same time, however, they would have expected that their lord, Alexios, would fulfil his part of the bargain, by protecting and aiding his vassals, giving *consilium* and *auxilium* in time of need. The anonymous author of the *Gesta Francorum* expresses this view, asserting that Alexios

> guaranteed good faith and security to all our men, and swore also to come with us, bringing an army and a navy, and faithfully to provide us with provisions by both land and sea, and to take care to restore all those things that we had lost. Moreover he promised that he would not cause or permit anyone to trouble or vex our pilgrims on the way to the Holy Sepulchre.[39]

At the time, however, such a commitment was probably understood, rather than spelt out so succinctly. A letter despatched by the crusade leaders to the pope from Antioch during the first half of 1098, reporting on the agreement made with the emperor, states that Alexios had promised only 'that none of the pilgrims to the Holy Sepulchre would suffer any more injury'.[40] In all probability, the Byzantine courtiers had acted in their accustomed way and employed well-turned but ambiguous phrases to reinforce an impression of support without making any definite commitment.

Alexios certainly displayed considerable evasiveness when the crusaders urged him to march at their head to Jerusalem. As he explained to Raymond of Toulouse, he was worried that his empire would be invaded by foreign enemies if he left its capital. Anna Comnena claimed that it was the vast number of the crusaders that deterred him from joining the enterprise. Whatever the precise excuse, it was agreed instead that, when the crusading host set out for Jerusalem, it would be accompanied only by a small detachment under a Byzantine general called Tatikios, whose task was 'to help and protect them on all occasions and also to take over from them any cities they captured'.[41] Alexios was once more putting his own empire first, and committing as few of its resources as possible to what must have seemed a rather dubious enterprise. In the future, however, the belief cherished by the crusaders that he was under an obligation to help them in time of need was to be an important component in the disagreement over Antioch.

So when the crusader army set out across Asia Minor in the summer of 1097, Alexios and the bulk of his forces remained in the area of Constantinople. The defeat of a Turkish force sent to obstruct their march at Dorylaion in July 1097 was achieved largely without Byzantine help. Nevertheless, the crusaders continued to observe the terms of their oath. When in September they relieved the Armenian city of Comana, which was under siege by the Danishmend Turks, a Provençal knight was installed with a garrison to hold the city for Alexios and the crusade leaders.[42]

It was only at Antioch that the agreement began to break down. The host arrived before the city in October 1097 but found it extremely difficult to capture. The main problem was that the city's walls were so long that it was impossible for the crusaders to blockade every single section of them, which meant that supplies could still be brought in to the besieged Turkish garrison. The crusaders, on the other hand, found themselves constantly short of provisions and were forced to endure great hardship during the winter of 1097–98.

During that time, even the limited Byzantine cooperation with the crusaders on the spot all but disappeared. In about February 1098, Tatikios had abandoned the crusader army and departed for Cyprus. The sources give widely differing reasons for his defection. Anna Comnena, with obvious application of hindsight, claims that the whole thing was engineered by Bohemond, who knew that if Antioch were captured he would be compelled by his oath to hand it over to Alexios. He therefore decided to get rid of Tatikios by telling him that the other leaders were plotting to kill him. The Byzantine general was in any case distressed by the famine and despaired of Antioch ever being taken, so he quietly did as he was advised and left. The Latin sources, taking their cue from the *Gesta Francorum*, assert that Tatikios was afraid when he heard of the approach of a Turkish army and left with the excuse that he was going to Cyprus to collect supplies. Neither version is particularly convincing, though it is perhaps significant that Alexios was not in the least displeased with his general for abandoning his post, appointing him to the command of a Byzantine fleet shortly afterwards.[43] Given Alexios's own actions a few months later, he could hardly have blamed his subordinate for abandoning what appeared to be a hopeless situation.

Antioch finally fell on 3 June 1098, nearly nine months after the siege had begun. The main credit for its capture went to Bohemond. He had made contact with an Armenian renegade inside the city who had lowered a rope from the walls during the night to admit the crusaders. In the ensuing fighting, the Turkish governor, Yaghi Siyan, was killed, along with considerable numbers of Antioch's inhabitants. This triumph did not end the crusaders' plight, however. When the outer city was overrun, the Turkish garrison took refuge in the citadel which towers some three hundred metres above it. There they held out, while the arrival of a large relieving force under the command of Kerbogha, atabeg of Mosul, meant that the westerners were themselves now besieged in Antioch, heavily outnumbered by their Muslim opponents. The shortage of food became desperate, since the crusaders were penned in between the citadel and Kerbogha's army and so could no longer forage in the countryside round about. They were reduced to eating thistles and leaves, and to stewing the skins of horses and asses.[44] There was one hope left: that the Emperor Alexios would come with his army to relieve them.

News of these events reached Constantinople and, according to Anna Comnena, Alexios 'was much concerned to bring help personally' to the crusaders.[45] He said much the same himself in response to a letter from the abbot of Monte Cassino, which had earnestly exhorted him to go to their aid:

> Let your venerable Holiness be assured on that score, for Our Majesty has been placed at their disposal and will aid and advise them on all matters: indeed we have already cooperated with them according to our ability, not as a friend, or relative, but like a father. We have expended among them more than anyone can enumerate. And had not Our Majesty so cooperated with them and aided them, who else would have afforded them help? Nor does it grieve Our Majesty to assist a second time.

This typical production of the Byzantine chancery was accompanied by an equally typical sweetener in the shape of a gift of gold.[46] In spite of the claims in the letter, however, little had been done during the winter of 1097–98. Byzantine ships did attempt to reach Antioch with supplies, but there is no truth in the story that Alexios despatched Edgar the Aethling with a fleet and siege engines to help the crusaders.[47] Nor would it seem that the emperor was in any hurry to rush to Antioch himself. His letter to Monte Cassino was despatched from Constantinople in June 1098, indicating that he had still not yet set out, months after the siege began and at the very time when the crusading army was facing its greatest peril.

It was not a case of callously leaving the crusaders to their fate. What came first was the security of the *Oikoumene.* Anna Comnena says that Alexios was kept at home by the damage being inflicted on the Byzantine coast by Turkish pirates operating on the orders of the Emir Tzachas in

Smyrna. It was decided that Tzachas needed to be dealt with first. When, later in June 1098, Alexios finally did gather his army to head east, he divided it in two. One part was entrusted to the Grand Duke John Doukas and sent to fight Tzachas, the rest followed Alexios in a direct march towards Antioch.

The Byzantine army under Alexios got as far as the town of Philomelion, approximately halfway between Constantinople and Antioch. There he was met by Stephen of Blois and two other western knights, William of Grantmesnil and Peter of Aulps, who, like Tatikios, had despaired of the situation and abandoned the besieged army at Antioch. They now informed the emperor of the desperate straits to which the crusader army had been reduced and swore oaths that it was on the verge of surrender. Moreover, rumours were spreading throughout the Byzantine camp that a huge Turkish army was on its way to prevent the emperor from linking up with his fellow Christians in Antioch.

Given the information put before him, it is unlikely that Alexios hesitated for long, although Comnena gives the impression that he agonised for some time over what decision to make. The main consideration was that he 'might lose Constantinople as well as Antioch'. He cannot have forgotten that Romanos IV had lost the battle of Mantzikert in 1071 by pressing forward, against advice, to engage with a large Turkish force. He therefore decided to retreat, to lead the army back towards Constantinople, taking the evacuated Christian population of the area with him.[48] It was the sensible decision and one which had the interests of the *Oikoumene* at its heart, but in taking it, Alexios had deliberately abandoned the crusaders to their fate.

That fate, however, proved to be rather different from what might have been expected, for events in Antioch now took an extraordinary turn. A soldier in the Provençal army of Raymond of Toulouse, called Peter Bartholomew, claimed that St Andrew had appeared to him in a dream. The apostle had revealed that beneath an altar in Antioch's cathedral of St Peter lay hidden the Holy Lance with which the centurion Longinus had pierced the side of Christ during the Crucifixion and that its discovery would be a sign from God that the crusaders would prevail against all their enemies. Thirteen men were sent to the cathedral to investigate Peter's claims and after a day of toil unearthed the lance. Not everyone was convinced by this miraculous find. Fulcher of Chartres suspected that the relic had been planted. Anna Comnena, who knew that the real Holy Lance was safely in the palace of Boukoleon in Constantinople, referred to Peter Bartholomew's relic as the 'Holy Nail', as if it were something quite different. For most of the crusaders, however, the discovery had a dramatic effect on morale and galvanised them into preparing a desperate counter-attack against the Turks.[49]

On 28 June 1098, after three days of fasting, masses and religious processions, the crusaders moved out of Antioch in six lines of battle and mounted a furious charge against the Turkish army of Kerbogha. Although heavily outnumbered and weak from fasting and privations, the Christian army had a huge advantage in its conviction that God was fighting on their side. Many crusaders afterwards reported that they had seen figures mounted on white horses leading the charge: undoubtedly St George and other soldier saints, dispatched by God to their aid. Even Anna Comnena had to admit that 'a divine power was manifestly aiding the Christians'. Unnerved by the ferocity of the onslaught, Kerbogha's Turks scattered and fled, abandoning their camp and supplies. From his vantage point in the citadel, the commander of the Turkish garrison watched the disaster unfold and realised at once what it meant. He promptly surrendered the citadel, leaving the crusaders in undisputed possession of the entire city.[50] It was an outcome that nobody could possibly have predicted.

The problem now arose of what to do with Antioch. Under the agreement made in Constantinople it should have been handed over to the Byzantines, but that was not possible in the absence of Tatikios. While the siege was still in progress, Bohemond had secured the agreement of some of the leaders, but not Raymond of Toulouse, that the city should be surrendered to him. After the fall of the citadel, in accordance with this agreement, most of the city was therefore handed over to Bohemond, although he had to seize some of the towers in the city walls by force from Raymond of Toulouse's men. The oath to Alexios was not completely forgotten. Hugh of Vermandois was sent to Constantinople in July 1098, to invite the emperor to come and take control of Antioch, but also to suggest that he should keep what the crusaders regarded as his promise to assist them in taking Jerusalem. The crusaders specifically stated that they would regard the agreement as lapsed if the emperor did not come.[51]

Inexplicably, Alexios took time to respond to Hugh's embassy. There is no Byzantine source of information that gives any reason for the long delay. Anna Comnena merely says that Bohemond seized Antioch, without giving any indication that any of the other leaders considered Alexios's rights in the matter.[52] Only in March 1099 was an imperial embassy finally sent. It met the crusade leaders at Arqa in Syria, where they had moved on the next stage of their journey to Jerusalem. Alexios's envoys complained bitterly about Bohemond, who by remaining in occupation of Antioch had broken the agreement to return all captured towns and cities to the emperor. They also stated that the imperial army would arrive by about 1 July. The leaders objected that it had been Alexios who had broken the oath, by failing to follow immediately with a large army and by omitting to send provisions.[53] By this time, Alexios's delay had given Bohemond and Tancred the opportunity that they needed to occupy the towns round about Antioch and carve out a viable principality. Especially important was their capture of the port of Laodicea. By ejecting a Byzantine garrison that had been sent over from Cyprus to occupy the town, they secured themselves access to the sea.[54]

The emperor still had one chance to reassert his authority over the crusade and retrieve the situation in Antioch. In the spring of 1101, the third wave of crusaders arrived in Constantinople, a mixed force of Lombards and Franks, including Stephen, count of Blois, anxious to atone for his earlier flight from Antioch. The newcomers were eager for the fray after receiving news of the capture of Jerusalem, and Alexios sought to turn their bellicosity to his advantage by the same methods: the same oath was required as that sworn by the leaders of the second wave and a Byzantine general, Tzitas, was attached with a small force to the crusader army. There was, however, one slight difference, for Alexios also attached Raymond of Toulouse to the army. Raymond was by now the bitter enemy of Bohemond, and had returned to Constantinople after his humiliation at Antioch, when Bohemond's men had ejected his followers from the city. In all probability, Alexios hoped that once the third wave reached Syria, Raymond would oust the Normans from Antioch and return the city to imperial control. If this was the case, he was to be disappointed. The army marched into northern Asia Minor, capturing Ankyra on the way, but also massacring a group of local Christians who turned out to welcome them. In August, the crusaders ran into heavy Turkish resistance in the area of Gangra and their army was scattered. Tzitas, Raymond and Stephen of Blois managed to escape and return to Constantinople, but many others were killed or taken prisoner. What was left of the army was ingloriously ferried to the Holy Land in Byzantine ships and arrived with neither the strength nor the prestige to dictate terms to the Normans.[55]

The distasteful truth now dawned in Constantinople that the Byzantines had allowed Antioch to slip through their fingers. The strength of their feeling on the issue can be gauged from Comnena's version of a letter which she claims Alexios sent to Bohemond in about 1101. Gone were the flowery phrases. Bohemond was effectively challenged to fight:

> You are aware of the oaths and promises made to the Roman empire, not by you alone, but by all the other counts. Now you are the first to break faith. You

> have seized Antioch and by underhand methods gained possession of certain other fortified places, including Laodicea itself. I bid you withdraw from the city of Antioch and all the other places, thereby doing what is right, and do not try to provoke fresh hostilities and battles against yourself.

Bohemond sent a defiant reply, accusing Alexios of failing to keep to his oath to follow the crusaders to Antioch with a strong force. Both sides were therefore committed to fight and Alexios dispatched an army from Cyprus to capture the ports of Cilicia (the south-eastern coast of Asia Minor) and northern Syria.[56]

Anna Comnena's disappointment at the outcome of the First Crusade from the Byzantine point of view is therefore quite understandable. Although part of Asia Minor had been restored to imperial rule, its most important city had been withheld. Moreover, while Byzantine policy was always to avoid war whenever possible, the empire now found itself embroiled with some of its erstwhile allies. What Comnena did not admit, however, was that the very methods employed by Alexios and his advisers had helped to bring the situation about. It had aroused resentment among the crusader leaders, and that resentment had been used to justify the seizure of Antioch. The future status of Antioch, in turn, was to dictate Byzantine relations with the crusading movement and the crusader states for years afterwards.

5

Jerusalem and Antioch

While the makers of Byzantine foreign policy had dealt with the First Crusade in the only way they knew how, and had achieved mixed success in obtaining their goals, the problems created by the expedition did not disappear after 1101. Although the crusade itself had come and gone, it left a legacy in the shape of four new Christian states in Syria and Palestine, which formed the basis of a western presence that was to endure until 1291.

The first of these states to come into being was the county of Edessa. It was formed by Baldwin of Boulogne who, while the rest of the host was besieging Antioch in late 1097, led his contingent to the city of Edessa at the invitation of its Armenian Christian inhabitants and established himself as ruler of the surrounding area. Edessa was followed by the principality of Antioch, the result of Bohemond's refusal to hand the conquered city over to Alexios I in 1098. To the south, Raymond of Toulouse, disappointed in his attempts to secure first Antioch and later Jerusalem, had conquered most of the coast between Gibelet and Maraclea by 1104 and formed the county of Tripoli.[1]

The largest and most prestigious of the crusader states was the kingdom of Jerusalem and the events surrounding its formation were as tumultuous and violent as those which had brought the principality of Antioch into being. Following the capture of Antioch, the main crusader army moved south, capturing towns and cities as they went. On 7 June 1099 the host reached Jerusalem, which had recently passed under the rule of the Egyptian Fatimids, and immediately mounted a siege. As in the case of Antioch, the campaign soon ran into difficulties. The walls of Jerusalem were too long and the crusaders too few to invest the city completely, food and water were in short supply and ominous reports that a relieving force was marching north from Egypt were circulating in the Christian camp. The leaders therefore sought to reawaken the religious enthusiasm which had proved so effective at Antioch, ordering a solemn procession and fast to implore God's help in taking Jerusalem. In the attack that followed on 15 July 1099, two knights from Tournai who were part of Godfrey of Bouillon's contingent succeeded in gaining a foothold on the walls by leaping across from a wooden siege tower, and opened the way for the crusaders to pour in. Once they were inside, the same fanaticism that had steeled them to face the dangers of battle spurred them to carry out indiscriminate slaughter of the city's Muslim and Jewish inhabitants, many of whom had taken refuge at the Dome of the Rock. So many men, women and children were killed that the streets were said to have run ankle deep in blood. News of the atrocity filtered back to Constantinople and Anna Comnena later recorded it in one disapproving line.[2]

With Jerusalem in Christian hands, Godfrey of Bouillon was elected to rule the city with the title of Advocate of the Holy Sepulchre and, after his death in 1100, his brother, Baldwin of Boulogne, became Baldwin I (1100–18), the first king of Jerusalem. The crusader victory over the Fatimid relieving force at Ascalon in August 1099 and subsequent campaigns created a kingdom which, by the end of Baldwin's reign, extended from Beirut to the Negev desert. The western settlers of the kingdom of Jerusalem and the other crusader states were far outnumbered by their new Muslim and eastern Christian subjects and formed an isolated outpost of Christendom in a part of the world dominated by Islam, but they survived for a number of reasons. The disunity of the Muslims was probably the major one but the concentrated programme of castle building which created a string of impregnable strongholds to hold down the surrounding countryside also undoubtedly played a part. The Templars and Hospitallers, orders of knights who lived under a monastic rule, provided a standing defence force to man the castles and to take the field against Muslim armies. All these factors ensured that the crusader states were no transient phenomenon and that successive Byzantine emperors and their advisers would have to decide what to do about them over a period of almost two hundred years.

Alexios I and his son and successor, John II, might have been expected to have welcomed the establishment of Christian states on the empire's south-eastern flank in opposition to the traditional Muslim enemy. Certainly they never voiced any objection to Baldwin of Boulogne's takeover in Edessa, even though the town had belonged to the empire as recently as 1087 and had a sizeable Greek-speaking population, loyal to the emperor. In the case of Raymond of Toulouse's ambitions towards Tripoli, Alexios actively assisted him in conquering the area, by ordering the Byzantine governor of Cyprus to help the count in building a castle at Pilgrim's Mountain.[3]

Towards the principality of Antioch and the kingdom of Jerusalem, however, the line taken was very different, one dictated by the nature of the Byzantine court in the early years of the twelfth century. Alexios I had come to power in a military coup at a time of national crisis. In order to legitimise his position, he laid stress on his role as the saviour of the empire, the restorer of the traditional values which had been abandoned by his weak and feckless predecessors. One of his first actions on taking over in Constantinople in 1081 had been to bring in his formidable mother, Anna Dalassena, to reform the morals of the imperial palace. According to Anna Comnena, the palace had been 'a scene of utter depravity' since the time of Constantine IX, but under Anna Dalassena's regime it came to resemble a monastery. There also appears to have been a purge of the palace bureaucrats. Whereas the brilliant but unconventional Michael Psellos had dominated imperial policy for most of the 1050s, 1060s and 1070s, his pupil, John Italos, was accused of heresy and disgraced within months of Alexios's accession. Instead, Alexios often chose his advisers from members of his own family, devising new titles and honours in order to promote them above existing officials.[4]

In such an atmosphere, the foreign policy adopted by the first two Comnenian emperors was likely to be at best traditional, and at worst decidedly unimaginative. In their dealings with the crusader states, they were to pursue the same goals, with the same methods, as the empire always had. One aim was, of course, the protection of Constantinople and the *Oikoumene.* In the political testament which he left to guide his son, Alexios warned John of the danger that might be posed by future expeditions to Jerusalem by western armies, 'should these once more, as formerly, be on the move, gaping horribly and trying to devour, in their great numbers, this coveted city'.[5] Yet while crusading expeditions dispatched from the west might be seen in this light, the crusader states in the Levant posed little direct danger to Constantinople. It would therefore appear that it was the second traditional foreign policy aim, the securing of recognition of the status of the emperor, that dictated Byzantine relations with Jerusalem and Antioch.

In the case of Jerusalem, even though they had not ruled the city directly for centuries, the emperors had always been at pains to secure recognition of their status as Protector of the Holy Sepulchre and other holy places there from whoever controlled them. During the eleventh century, the emperors had sought to achieve that aim by negotiation with the Fatimids of Egypt. With the Fatimids now gone, the same recognition would inevitably be sought, sooner or later, from the Frankish kings of Jerusalem, who had taken it for themselves.[6]

As for Antioch, the attitude of the Byzantine authorities was rather more complex. At one level they seem to have seen the city and the surrounding area simply as a part of their territory which had been unjustly seized by Bohemond and which they wanted to regain. After all, unlike Jerusalem, Antioch had been in Byzantine hands within living memory, only falling to the Turks as recently as 1084. Moreover, its strategic position and its location on the trade route between Asia and the Mediterranean made Antioch a particularly important stronghold for the empire. Nevertheless, some modern commentators have been puzzled as to why the Byzantines became so deeply involved in the dispute over Antioch, which led to the diversion of troops and resources from what might be regarded as the main task of reconquering central Anatolia from the Seljuk Turks.[7]

The only way to understand Byzantine policy towards Antioch is to place it within the traditions and outlook of the Byzantine elite, which, as we have seen, valued the vindication of imperial ideology far above acquisition of territory. The reconquest of the barren Anatolian plateau did not necessarily occupy the first place on their agenda. What was important was obtaining recognition of the special place that the empire was believed to occupy in God's plan for the world. In this scheme of things, Antioch had a spiritual significance which far exceeded its military or commercial advantages. Its church, like that of Rome, had been founded by St Peter and it was one of the five patriarchates of the Christian world. The significance of a city like Antioch in Byzantine eyes emerges from two recorded comments of Nikephoros II, the emperor who had conquered it for the empire in 969. Nikephoros described Antioch as the third city of the world, thereby placing only Constantinople and Rome above it in importance. To the western ambassador, Liudprand of Cremona, Nikephoros commented cuttingly that, whereas councils of the church had taken place in Antioch and other places, no councils were recorded in Saxony, the home of Liudprand's master, the western emperor Otto I. Antioch was thus not just a piece of territory like Saxony or Anatolia, but a holy city, similar to Constantinople or Jerusalem.[8]

It is this significance which accounts for the fury with which Alexios I responded to Bohemond's seizure of Antioch. In the years that followed his takeover, Bohemond was to rub salt into the wound. He soon became mistrustful of the patriarch of Antioch, John the Oxite, a Byzantine who had been appointed from Constantinople, and whom Bohemond may well have feared might act as a spy on behalf of Alexios. In 1100 John was forced to leave Antioch, retire to Constantinople, and resign as patriarch. A new patriarch was appointed to replace him by the emperor in Constantinople, but in Antioch Bernard of Valence, a Latin cleric, was appointed to the post. Henceforth there were two claimants to the see, a Latin and a Greek, with the latter remaining in Constantinople under the emperor's protection.[9] In acting in this way, Bohemond was openly challenging the position of the Byzantine emperor as the leader of the Christian world. The aim of Alexios and John, therefore, was to compel Bohemond and his successors

3. The Latin states of Syria and Palestine.

to recognise imperial authority and they were not unsuccessful in their attempts to achieve that aim.

In the later years of his reign, as already seen, Alexios I resorted to military force against Bohemond in Antioch. In about 1100, when negotiations had broken down, an army was despatched to retake the ports of Cilicia and northern Syria from the Latins, no doubt with a view to an attack on Antioch itself.[10] Faced with such unusually direct Byzantine hostility, Bohemond changed tactics. After a period of imprisonment at the hands of the Danishmend Turks in the city of Melitene, he decided in about 1105 to return to western Europe to secure help against the emperor. Having entrusted Antioch to Tancred, he sailed for Apulia. Anna Comnena adds the story that, in order to evade possible pursuit and interception, he faked his own death, and travelled back in a coffin. A dead and putrid cockerel was placed on his chest to deter the curious from taking a look inside.[11]

As soon as he was back, Bohemond embarked on an extensive recruiting tour through France and southern Italy. Tales of his exploits on the First Crusade had gone before him and he received a hero's welcome wherever he went. The king of France was happy to give him his daughter, Constance, in marriage, and volunteers flocked to his banner. In October 1107, when Bohemond set out on his planned expedition, the target was not the Muslim enemies of the crusader states, but the Byzantine empire. His army crossed the Adriatic and landed at Avlona, in imperial territory, and then marched north to lay siege to the port of Dyrrachion. In following in the footsteps of his father in this way, Bohemond may well have been hoping, as Robert Guiscard had done, to seize the Adriatic coast before marching overland to Syria.

For a moment, the threat must have appeared as grave as that of 1081, but in the end it was averted by those useful and time-honoured props of Byzantine foreign policy: avoidance of battle, artful stratagems and judicious use of gold. Alexios did not hurry to confront Bohemond in a pitched battle, as he had in 1081, and his first reaction to the news was calmly to order lunch. He then moved up his forces to surround the western forces as they were besieging Dyrrachion. The old techniques now came into play. An attempt was made to sow discord in the enemy camp by allowing Bohemond to capture some letters supposedly written by Alexios to some of the noblemen in his army, suggesting that they were ready to desert to the emperor. The tactic misfired in so far as Bohemond saw through the letters and did not accuse his followers of treachery. In the weeks that followed, however, as supplies began to run low, deserters began to leave Bohemond's army. William of Clarelès went over to the emperor with fifty

1. The Land Walls of Constantinople. (*Louvre*)

2. Part of the palace of Blachernae. (*Wim Swaan*)

3. Alexios I Comnenus before Christ. Biblioteca Apostolica Vaticana, MS Vat. gr. 666. (*Vatican Library*)

4. Nikephoros III Botaniates and his courtiers, 1078–81. Bibliothèque Nationale, MS Coislin 79, fol. 2r. (*Bibliothèque Nationale*)

5. The siege of Shaizar (1138), with Raymond of Poitiers and Joscelin II playing dice in the tent. Bibliothèque Municipale, Boulogne-sur-Mer, MS 142. (*Bibliothèque Municipale, Boulogne-sur-Mer*)

6. Manuel I Comnenus and Maria of Antioch. Biblioteca Apostolica, Codex Vatican gr. 666, fol. 2r. (*Vatican Library*)

7. Inside the cathedral of Hagia Sophia. (*Dunbarton Oates, Washington DC*)

8. Niketas Choniates, courtier and historian. Österreichische Nationalbibliothek, Vienna, Codex Vindob. hist. gr. 53. (*Österreichiscle Nationalbibliothek*)

followers, to receive the usual gifts and titles. Robert of Montfort and even Bohemond's own half-brother, Guy, were seduced in much the same way.[12] As a result of this haemorrhage of his followers, Bohemond was forced to sue for peace and an agreement was drawn up in September 1108.

Unlike the oaths of 1096 and 1097, the terms of the so-called treaty of Devol are given in their entirety by Anna Comnena, so it is possible to analyse them in detail.[13] The main terms were as follows. The agreement made in Constantinople in 1097, which Bohemond admitted to violating, was declared invalid. One aspect of the earlier agreement was retained, however, in that Bohemond declared himself to be the servant and liege man (*lizios*) of the emperor and of his son John. In return, Bohemond was to be granted the city of Antioch and some of the places nearby for his lifetime, although these could be taken back at any time on demand. He undertook to compel Tancred to return to the emperor all the other towns which he had taken, including Laodicea.[14] In many ways the treaty was a lenient one. Bohemond was left in possession of Antioch as the emperor's vassal, apparently receiving what he had asked for in Constantinople in 1097.

One school of thought asserts that the treaty of Devol represented an advance on the resented oaths extracted during the First Crusade and that it was formulated in the light of western legal practices. That influence has been discerned in the use of a direct Greek translation of the western feudal term *homo ligius* to describe Bohemond's relationship with Alexios, and in the provisions for the relationship between Bohemond's own vassals and the emperor.[15] Whatever western influence there might have been on details in the treaty, in the last analysis it was, like the methods which had brought Bohemond to the negotiating table, a classic piece of Byzantine foreign policy. The clause which provided for Bohemond to give military assistance to the emperor was not so much the obligation of a vassal to a lord but the traditional concern of the Byzantine emperors to sign up their defeated foes as mercenaries, much as Alexios had done with the Turks of Nicaea in 1097. Otherwise there would have been no need for him to agree to pay Bohemond two hundred gold pieces a year, which were probably the wages for the services that the Norman was to render.[16] Similarly, the leniency of the treaty shows that the physical recovery of Antioch was not its main concern. The aim was rather to ensure proper acknowledgement of the emperor's position. Hence a clause was included that the patriarch of Antioch would be appointed by the emperor, not by Bohemond. The text is littered with specific references to the nature of Alexios's office. He was the 'divinely appointed emperor', and the ruler of the Roman empire. In this the treaty of Devol reflected that made by Michael VII with Bohemond's father in 1074, when the Norman duke promised to show the emperor the 'submission and good intentions' that were his due.[17] The securing of this recognition of imperial overlordship was evidently considered quite enough, and there was no need to demand the physical possession of Antioch as well.

There can be no doubt that, at the time, the treaty of Devol would have been regarded as a triumph for Alexios. His old enemy had put his seal to a document which laid out uncompromisingly the exalted nature of the Byzantine imperial office. This may even explain why Bohemond's mausoleum by the cathedral of Canosa in Apulia appears to have been modelled on the church of the Holy Apostles in Constantinople, a visual acceptance of the leading role of the imperial city.[18] The tried and tested methods appeared to have worked once more.

Nevertheless, in spite of the treaty of Devol, the question of Antioch, and of the crusader states in general, was to remain and vex future generations of emperors and bureaucrats in Constantinople. While Bohemond had sworn an oath to serve the emperor, he failed to return to Antioch to enforce the treaty and to compel Tancred to comply, as he had undertaken to. Instead, he went back to Italy, where he died in 1111. The principality which he had established therefore remained in Latin hands and the Latin patriarch of Antioch retained his office.

In his last years, Alexios prepared to take action against Tancred. Ambassadors were sent with threats to Antioch and, when they were rebuffed, approaches were made to the king of Jerusalem and the count of Tripoli. The offer was the usual one: generous amounts of money, in return for military assistance against Tancred. The negotiations dragged on, but no agreement was reached. A similar approach seems to have been made in late 1110 or early 1111 to the Seljuk sultan, though this too yielded no result.[19] The Latins were still left undisturbed in possession of Antioch when Alexios died in 1118.

It was therefore left to John II to force a recognition of imperial authority on the rulers of Antioch and also to revive Byzantine claims to the protectorate of the Holy Places in Jerusalem. During the first part of his reign he seems to have had little opportunity to do either. He had first to face a plot to prevent his succession, orchestrated by his sister, Anna, and mother, Eirene, who wanted Anna's husband, Nikephoros Bryennios, to become emperor. As Alexios lay dying in the monastery of the Mangana, John had to pull the signet ring from his father's finger and show it to the palace guards as proof that he was the chosen successor. The years that followed were plagued by invasion and war with the Venetians, Hungarians, Danishmend Turks and Pechenegs. It was not until the 1130s that the policy makers in Constantinople could turn their attention to the Latin east. By that time, John II was in a much stronger position. He had inflicted defeats on the Pechenegs and Hungarians and made a settlement with the Venetians. The secure financial basis created by his father's fiscal reforms provided him with the wherewithal to field an extremely large army.[20] He was to lead that army on two major expeditions into Syria in 1137–38 and 1142–43.

Inevitably, there has been some difference of opinion as to what John was aiming to achieve with these expeditions. They have often been seen as an attempt to extend the empire's frontiers up to the Euphrates.[21] John's aim, however, like his father's, was the familiar one of securing recognition of the role of the emperor as the supreme autocrat of the Christian world. The methods used were also hardly new, treaties and the threat of force being preferred whenever possible to open warfare and annexation.[22] Seizure of territory was not ruled out entirely. After all the Byzantines had been quick to reconquer western Asia Minor back in 1097–98. John and his advisers, however, may have felt that the occupation of Antioch and the land beyond would have overstretched the empire's resources. A revealing incident later occurred in 1150 when the wife of Count Joscelin II handed over what was left of the county of Edessa to the Byzantines in return for a generous pension. Although garrisons were installed in the remaining fortresses, the new territory was lost to the Muslims within a year.[23] As in the case of the treaty of Devol, John II seems therefore to have been seeking recognition rather than physical domination.

That impression is reinforced by a careful examination of the three main sources of information on John's Syrian expeditions. From the western point of view, there is the *History* of William, archbishop of Tyre (1175–*c.* 1184), and from the Byzantine, the works of John Kinnamos and Niketas Choniates. In some ways, these authors are difficult to interpret. All three were writing many years after the end of John's reign. William of Tyre composed his history after 1170, perhaps some forty years afterwards. The Byzantine historians were at work even later, Kinnamos after 1180 and Choniates, in his final draft, probably after 1204.[24] It is therefore almost certain that errors and distortions crept in over the years, and these may explain why all three differ, sometimes markedly, in their accounts of John's Syrian expeditions and the reasons behind them. There is, however, another explanation for the differences, especially those that separate William of Tyre from the Byzantine writers, and this is the matter of outlook and interpretation.

As a western European, albeit one born in Jerusalem, William of Tyre was the product of a society where status was based on the holding of land. As a result, acquisition of territory was an important end in itself, even for so spiritual enterprise as a crusade. William characterises the outcome of the First Crusade in these terms, remarking how the Latins 'appropriated the Land of Promise and practically the whole of Syria'.[25] Not surprisingly, he consistently presents John's actions in the same way, as aiming at the physical conquest of the city of Antioch and the land around. Kinnamos and Choniates, on the other hand, came from a society where status was based on the position one held at the imperial court, signalled by the holding of titles and honours. Foreign policy was essentially an extension of that hierarchy to the nations on the empire's borders, and conquest of territory was only a means of achieving that end. They present John's expeditions to Syria in exactly that light.

To start with, however, the three writers are broadly in agreement over what lay immediately behind John's decision to go to Antioch in 1137. While Choniates does not given any reason at all and suggests that John was in the area solely to deal with the troublesome Armenians of Cilicia,[26] both William of Tyre and Kinnamos link the expedition to John's fury at a failed marriage alliance. Following the death of Prince Bohemond II in 1130, John had entered into negotiations with the regency for Bohemond's young daughter, Constance. An agreement was reached that Constance should marry John's youngest son, Manuel, but, while John was campaigning against the Armenians in nearby Cilicia, news arrived that the regency had changed their mind and had instead given her hand to a younger son of the duke of Aquitaine, Raymond of Poitiers, who thus became prince of Antioch. Kinnamos stresses that John had wanted the marriage between Manuel and Constance because he wished to have Antioch in his power. When this failed to come about, according to William of Tyre, John 'claimed Antioch with all the adjacent provinces as his own and wished to recall them to his jurisdiction', citing the agreement made between Alexios I and the crusaders in 1096 as a justification. Clearly, John wished to extend his power over Antioch in some way.

The vagueness of William of Tyre and Kinnamos, however, leaves open the question of exactly what kind of sovereignty John had in mind here. Whatever it was, he was prepared to use considerable force to get it. Both historians describe how, when John's army reached Antioch in late August 1137, he used formidable siege engines to batter the walls. Faced with a superior force, Raymond of Poitiers had little choice but to come to terms. On what those terms were, however, the Byzantines differ markedly from William of Tyre. William gives a detailed breakdown of the agreement that was then drawn up. Raymond declared himself to be a liege vassal of the emperor and took a solemn oath that, whenever the emperor should desire, he should be allowed to enter Antioch or its citadel. In return

Raymond would receive the towns of Aleppo, Shaizar, Hama and Homs. These were currently in Muslim hands, but, when they had been captured and given to Raymond, he would in turn hand Antioch over to John 'to hold by right of ownership', while he himself would rule in Aleppo instead.[27]

The Byzantine version of the treaty, on the other hand, is much vaguer. Kinnamos says only that it was agreed that 'the emperor should be and be proclaimed lord but [Raymond] should lawfully be guardian of it by authority'. Choniates is even more succinct, stating only that John regarded Raymond as his liegeman (*lizios*). Most significantly of all, neither makes any mention of any undertaking on the part of Raymond to hand Antioch over to John, an undertaking that was also absent from the treaty of Devol of 1108.[28]

This divergence between the Greek and Latin sources leaves a seemingly intractable problem of who to believe. Most modern accounts have inclined towards William of Tyre, since his version of events is so much more detailed than that of Kinnamos or Choniates.[29] This, however, is where differences of interpretation and outlook need to be considered. William of Tyre presented the agreement as involving the physical handover of Antioch because he would have assumed that this was what the emperor sought above all. Kinnamos and Choniates, on the other hand, imbued with the ideology of the Byzantine court, saw the whole affair in terms of the acknowledgement of the authority of the Byzantine emperor by the prince of Antioch. There is no reason to think that the details given by William are necessarily false. It is merely that the Byzantines would not have interpreted them in that way.

If that point is accepted, it makes John II's conduct during the rest of the expedition of 1137–38 much more understandable. Following the agreement made between John and Raymond, whatever its exact terms were, in May 1138 a joint Byzantine-Frankish army set out for Aleppo and was joined by a contingent led by Count Joscelin II of Edessa. The expedition does not have to be seen as an attempt to grab land to compensate Raymond for the loss of Antioch. Rather John was reasserting another aspect of his role as leader of the *Oikoumene*, a role that had been usurped by the First Crusade. Although it was an article of Byzantine policy to avoid war where possible, part of the role of the emperor to protect the Christian people by waging war against the infidel. John now prepared to do so with all available resources. An Arab eyewitness describes the terror inspired by John's siege engines, which could hurl millstones further than a bow shot and demolish entire houses. Having seen John's impressive army as it passed through Cilicia, a Jewish physician confidently predicted that he would soon be entering Aleppo or Damascus.[30]

The first objective of the Christian army was Aleppo, whose Muslim ruler, Zengi, was presenting an ever-increasing threat to the principality of Antioch and the county of Edessa. When the defences of Aleppo proved too strong, even for John's well-equipped force, the army turned its attention southwards to the town of Shaizar, on the Orontes river. William of Tyre, who presented the campaign as an attempt to provide an alternative principality for Raymond, describes how, while John was noticeable for his energy and courage during the siege of Shaizar, Raymond exerted himself as little as possible, presumably because a victory for John would rob him of Antioch. He spent most of the time 'playing games of chance' with Count Joscelin. John was so incensed by this conduct that he broke off the siege after a month in return for a generous payment from the emir of Shaizar.[31]

Kinnamos and Choniates interpret the episode in an entirely different way. They make no mention of the conduct of Raymond as the reason for John's abandoning the siege. Kinnamos says that John accepted the emir's indemnity because he realised that it would be impossible to take the city. Choniates says that John abandoned Shaizar because he had heard that Edessa was under attack and hastened to its aid. Moreover, since both were imbued with Byzantine ideology, they regarded the emperor as having captured something far more important than the town itself. As part of their payment to induce John to withdraw, the citizens of Shaizar handed over a cross, carved from red marble, supposedly fashioned on the orders of Constantine the Great, and taken by the Turks from Romanos IV after the battle of Mantzikert in 1071.[32] Byzantine emperors had always regarded it as an important part of their role to restore precious objects and relics to Christian hands. The famous Mandylion had been extorted from the Muslims of Edessa in much the same way back in 944. Later the Byzantines were to make efforts to recover the portion of the True Cross lost by the Latins at the battle of Hattin in 1187.[33] Such objects, added to the already impressive collection in Constantinople, enhanced the prestige of the emperor and of the imperial city.

William of Tyre's version of subsequent events follows on from the reason he gave for John's withdrawal from Shaizar. On his return to Antioch, the emperor made a solemn entry, accompanied by processions of clergy and people, and then demanded that the city must still be surrendered to him, even though Aleppo and Shaizar had not been taken. Raymond managed to avoid compliance because Joscelin II stirred up a riot among the Latin inhabitants of the city who did not want it to be handed over to the Byzantines. The emperor, who had left his army outside the walls of the city, found himself besieged in the citadel. He promptly withdrew his demand that the citadel be handed over and left the city. Once he was at a safe distance, Raymond sent envoys to John's camp to appease his anger and even offered to hand over the citadel. John, however, declined and returned to Constantinople.[34]

The Byzantine account is a great deal more laconic. Kinnamos ignores any subsequent stay in Antioch altogether, having John return directly to Constantinople. Choniates, however, does describe John's entry into Antioch, and predictably places great emphasis on its ideological significance. He stresses the warm welcome of the Antiochene population and the splendour of John's reception.[35] Once again, the Greek and Latin accounts are by no means irreconcilable. The difference is one of interpretation not fact. William's version assumes that John was eager for possession of the city, Choniates that he sought recognition of his hegemony.

The same difference of interpretation underlies the Latin and Greek accounts of John's second expedition to Syria in 1142–43. At first sight, the Byzantine historians seem to be suggesting that annexation of Antioch and the surrounding area was the main motive behind the expedition. Kinnamos says that John wanted to make Antioch, along with Cilicia, Attalia and Cyprus, into an appanage for his youngest son Manuel. Choniates says that John had a burning desire 'to unite Antioch to Constantinople' and to extend his dominion over it and that this was the secret purpose behind his campaign.[36] Yet both of these statements fall short of outright conquest. It is unlikely that Kinnamos meant that John planned to detach a part of the empire's territory and give it to Manuel. The idea of doing such a thing would have flown in the face of Byzantine concepts of the indivisibility of imperial power.[37] It is much more likely that John was considering a marriage alliance involving Manuel, as he had before 1137. As for Choniates, his words could just as well be interpreted as a desire to bring Antioch within the orbit of the empire, by forcing an acknowledgement of imperial suzerainty.

William of Tyre, on the other hand, in a much more detailed narrative, is far more specific. He describes how John descended on Syria with a huge army 'which seemingly no kingdom of the world could withstand'. The emperor once again demanded that Raymond surrender Antioch, along with its citadel and fortifications, in accordance with the earlier agreement, so that John could better wage war on neighbouring Muslim cities. Although Raymond on several occasions invited John to come to the city, the nobles and people were adamant that it should not be handed over to the 'effeminate Greeks'. An embassy led by the patriarch was therefore sent to John, to say that Raymond had no power to hand over the city, thus forcing an angry emperor to spend the winter with his army in Cilicia.[38] The divergence is the same: a Latin obsession with physical possession and domination, a Byzantine concern with recognition of the right order of things.

During the second expedition, as the sources make clear, John widened his aims to include the protectorate of the Holy Places in Jerusalem. The key lies in John's stated intention, reported by both William of Tyre and Choniates, to go on pilgrimage to Jerusalem during his second sojourn in the east. Choniates says that John had always wanted to visit the Holy Sepulchre and to adorn it with gifts. William of Tyre reports that the emperor sent letters to the king of Jerusalem announcing his intention to pay that visit, bringing his army with him. The king was perturbed, fearing a Byzantine invasion. He therefore replied that the kingdom of Jerusalem was not rich or large enough to host the emperor's army, and begged that he only bring ten thousand men with him. John thereupon decided not to go because 'he did not regard it as befitting to his imperial glory that he who was ever wont to move attended by many thousands should proceed with such a small escort'.[39] John's insistence on this point suggests that he had his eye on the ideological significance of his visit and on the restoration of the role of Protector of the Holy Places which his eleventh-century predecessors had established by their treaty with the Fatimids, and which Manuel I was later to enjoy over the kingdom of Jerusalem.

John's early and unexpected death put an end to further negotiations with Antioch and Jerusalem. While hunting boar in the Cilician forests, he accidentally cut his hand on one of the arrows in his quiver. The wound turned septic and he died on 8 April 1143. His designated successor was his youngest son Manuel, who at once returned with the army to Constantinople in order to prevent his brother Isaac from seizing the throne. John's body was carried home with the returning columns and was finally interred in the monastery of the Pantokrator, which he himself had founded in 1136.[40]

In spite of this abrupt ending, both John's expeditions to Syria and his general policy towards the crusader states appeared to contemporaries to have been a success. An oration delivered by Michael Italikos, shortly after John returned to Constantinople in 1138, gives an insight into the ideology of those who surrounded his throne. Summing up the achievement of John in the east, Italikos claimed that the prince of Edessa had offered him the help of his lance, the king of Jerusalem had set down his crown and recognised John as the only emperor, and the sovereignty of Constantinople had been extended over Antioch.[41] It might be objected that since this oration was almost certainly given in the presence of the emperor, it would therefore have been at pains to tell him what he wanted to hear. Italikos was merely trying to make the best of a bad job, flattering an emperor who had in fact returned empty-handed, having failed to secure the major prize.

Yet the expedition of 1137 also seems to have been regarded as a success by one of John's political opponents. His sister Anna Comnena wrote that John 'reduced the city of Antioch'. Had John been aiming to conquer the place and failed, Anna would hardly have passed the opportunity for criticism, especially as her husband, Nikephoros Bryennios, had died of an illness contracted while serving with John's army in Syria. Elsewhere she bemoans how many of the achievements of Alexios I were frittered away by 'the stupidity of those who inherited his throne'.[42] John's Syrian campaigns can therefore be compared with that of Michael III against Bulgaria in 864, when the aim was not to annex Bulgaria but to force Khan Boris to acknowledge the sovereignty of the Byzantine emperor.[43] Seen in that light, John had achieved much of what he set out to do.

Even some Latin sources hint at much the same thing. Orderic Vitalis, who was writing only a few years after the expedition of 1137–38, makes no mention of the agreement to hand Antioch over to John. Instead, after an initial clash between John's troops and those of the prince of Antioch, Raymond realised that Byzantine claims to Antioch were true, and so he became the emperor's vassal and received Antioch from him with a promise of help against the infidels of Damascus, a version of events not dissimilar to that of the Byzantine historians.[44] Another Latin writer, Odo of Deuil, gives an insight into John's priorities, recording that, when he took the towns of Tarsus and Mamistra in 1137, John expelled the Latin bishops he found there and replaced them with his own appointees.[45] This action displays John's concern with the ideological significance of his expedition and suggests once more that it was recognition of his authority that he sought.

These contemporary attitudes no doubt provided the starting point for Kinnamos and Choniates in their accounts of an emperor of whom they could have had no personal recollection. Both were almost unreservedly favourable and it is not difficult to see why. John was seen as having fulfilled all the duties of a Roman emperor. He had defended the *Oikoumene*, leading successful campaigns against its enemies east and west, and he had upheld the divinely ordained order of the world by compelling recognition of the authority of the emperor. For Choniates, therefore, John was 'the most royal' of emperors, an image preserved in perpetuity in the mosaic portrait of him in the cathedral of Hagia Sophia.[46]

Yet while Anna Comnena, John Kinnamos and Niketas Choniates might look back with fond nostalgia on the reigns of Alexios I and John II, as emperors who knew how to rule, it is easier, from a more distant perspective, to discern the negative side of their policy towards the crusader states. While those policies enhanced their reputation in the eyes of Byzantines, they did little for the image of their empire in western Europe, particularly at the papal curia. They could all too easily be seen as working against the pious goal of maintaining the Latin presence in the east and so keeping Jerusalem in the hands of Christians. Those whose temporal interests clashed with those of the Byzantines were quick to use this accusation as a way of justifying their conflict with the emperor.

The first to do so was Bohemond. His arrival in the west in 1106 was the signal for the start of a propaganda war, as he toured Italy and France gathering troops for his 'expedition across the sea'. In the course of this recruiting drive, Bohemond wrote a letter to Pope Paschal II (1099–1118), in which he levelled a number of charges at Alexios in order to justify his planned attack.

First, like his father Robert Guiscard before him, Bohemond claimed that Alexios was not the legitimate emperor, but a usurper who had won power by 'horrible plots and treachery', a reference to his overthrow of the previous emperor, Nikephoros III, in 1081. This charge was a grave one to western ears because it meant that Alexios had won his throne by overthrowing his rightful lord, a violation of an oath of fealty that he was assumed by westerners to have taken to the previous emperor. The same charge had been used to justify the Norman invasion of England in 1066. Bohemond clearly meant to make the most of this justification, for when he arrived in France, he had with him a son of the emperor Romanos IV Diogenes and other Byzantine nobles, who had supposedly been deprived of their ancestral dignities, living proof of the iniquity of Alexios.[47] It was not the last time that action against Constantinople was to be undertaken on behalf of some wronged claimant to the Byzantine throne.

Secondly, in his letter to Paschal II, Bohemond asserted that Alexios was responsible for the 'robbing and drowning of pilgrims'.[48] This is presumably a reference to Alexios's reception of the First Crusade. The charge made briefly and obliquely in the letter was made in much more detail in a short, anonymous Latin account of the First Crusade, known as the *Gesta Francorum*, which was circulating in western Europe at the time of Bohemond's recruiting tour and which formed the basis of other accounts, notably those of Robert of Rheims and Guibert of Nogent. It was almost certainly the work of a knight or cleric in Bohemond's army, and presents the Norman leader as a great warrior (*bellipotens*) and a distinguished man (*honestissimus vir*), the undoubted hero of the enterprise. The portrayal of Alexios I, on the other hand, is consistently hostile. He is described as 'the abominable emperor' (*nequissimus imperator*) and his every deed is presented as a sinister machination devised to bring about the destruction of the crusaders. His insistence on an oath is an attempt to 'seize these knights of Christ adroitly and by fraud'. He rejoices when the Turks massacre the followers of Peter the Hermit, and plots with them to bring about the downfall of the crusaders. The *Gesta* also claims that Alexios had promised Bohemond the land around Antioch, thereby removing any justification for Alexios's attempt to get the city back and portraying him as a liar and an oath breaker.[49]

Another anti-Byzantine history circulating in the west in 1106–7 was Ekkehard of Aura's account of the fate of the third wave of the First Crusade. The various contingents that made up this expedition had all, like that accompanied by Tzitas and Raymond of Toulouse, come to grief in Asia Minor in the summer of 1101, a disaster that Ekkehard, an eyewitness and participant, laid at the door of Alexios. One of Ekkehard's accusations was that the emperor had plotted to drown the crusaders as they sailed across the Bosporos to Asia Minor, a tale that Bohemond was apparently referring to in his letter to Paschal II.[50]

Effective and widespread though Bohemond's propaganda was, his expedition against the Byzantine empire was not a success and ended with his humiliation in the treaty of Devol. Nevertheless, his efforts had two important long-term consequences: it was to lead to an overwhelmingly negative portrayal of the Byzantines in western chronicles and it was to create a link between supposed Byzantine opposition to the cause of the crusades and the schism between the churches.

As far as the image of Byzantium in the west was concerned, it was above all the *Gesta Francorum* which was the most influential. Its account of the First Crusade was copied by those who had never travelled to the east, such as William of Malmesbury or Orderic Vitalis. They repeated all the *Gesta*'s horror stories and added new ones. Alexios I was 'wily and smooth-spoken, a prolific and ingenious master of the art of deception', who plotted to poison the crusaders, to set savage lions and leopards on them, and to lead them into Turkish ambushes.[51] As the twelfth century went on, the unflattering descriptions were increasingly extended to all Byzantines, not just Alexios, as feeble and effeminate, yet deceitful and treacherous. They were always referred to as 'Greeks' and never as 'Romans', thereby implicitly denying their claim to continuity with the Roman *Imperium*. Guibert of Nogent questioned the very basis of Byzantine political thought, the office of the emperor, excoriating the foolishness and fickleness of the Greeks who raised a man to power one day, then drove him into exile the next. Some compared these modern Greeks with their ancient forebears, and found in favour of the latter: the Byzantines had lost all the virtues of the ancient Greeks and inherited only their vices, part of a long drawn out decline that had begun after the Trojan war.[52]

It would be wrong to read too much into what was clearly ignorant prejudice. The Byzantines had been on the receiving end of such diatribes from Latin writers before, especially from those who had been outmanoeuvred by slick Byzantine diplomatic practices. Pope Nicholas I (858–67) deeply disapproved of the Bulgarian policy of Michael III and criticised the emperor for subjecting the Bulgars to the empire under the pretext of religion. Liudprand of Cremona, who had failed to secure a marriage alliance between the Ottonians and the Byzantine emperor in the tenth century, raged against the 'soft effeminate creatures, with their long sleeves and hoods and bonnets, idle liars of neither gender ...' whom he had encountered in Constantinople. The chronicler Widukind of Corvey registered his disgust that the Greeks defeated by tricks those whom they could not overcome by force.[53]

Such ruffled feelings and embittered comments were usually provoked by some temporary political difference and had no significance in the long run. That was not the case, however, with another of the charges brought by Bohemond in 1106–7. In his letter to Paschal II, Bohemond claimed that Alexios had 'removed unity in the universal and apostolic church from his people, in so far as was in him, from which it is plain that he and his people dissent from the Roman Church'. This aspect of the anti-Byzantine propaganda circulating at this time was also picked up and repeated by later writers. Tracts on the errors of the Greeks were produced in increasing numbers as the twelfth century progressed, penned by earnest clerics such as Rupert of Deutz, who fulminated against the refusal of the Byzantines to accept the authority of the Apostolic See, against their unsoundness on the *Filioque* issue, and against their use of leavened bread in communion.[54]

Such theological hair-splitting hardly presented a threat in itself. The danger for Byzantium lay in the idea, implicit in Bohemond's letter, that because the Byzantines were in schism with the Roman church, it was legitimate to make war on them. He may well have convinced the papal curia that this was so, for he was accompanied to France on his recruiting tour by a papal legate, Bruno of Segni, suggesting that he had papal blessing for the enterprise. Anna Comnena for one was quite convinced that the invasion of the empire in 1107 had the backing of the pope.[55]

The linkage between the schism, Byzantine failure to support the crusades and the crusader states, and the legitimacy of making war on them was to return. In March 1138, Pope Innocent II issued an edict against John II 'who separates himself from the unity of the church' and called on all Latins serving in the Byzantine armies to desert because John had striven to take Antioch from Raymond of Poitiers. In 1147 a French bishop, Godfrey of Langres, went even further, arguing that John's attack on Antioch showed that the Byzantines were Christians in name only and that it would therefore be legitimate to make an attack on Constantinople itself. Much the same was said by the clergy with the army of the Fourth Crusade in April 1204.[56]

The Byzantines were not unaware of the danger. They do seem to have realised that what for them were legitimate actions in defence of the *Oikoumene*, or of the rightful position of the emperor, could be given a very different construction in the west. Just as standard foreign policy methods, like employment of mercenaries and preference for stratagems rather than open warfare, could be interpreted as effeminacy and duplicity, so the Byzantine treatment of the First Crusade and policy towards the crusader states could easily be seen as a betrayal of the common cause of the Christians. Even during the passage of the First Crusade, Alexios I and his advisers had realised perfectly well the necessity of presenting their actions in such a way as to avoid any implication that they had failed to support the pious enterprise. Anna Comnena recalled that Alexios wished to win some success to enhance his position in the eyes of the crusaders and his letters sent to the abbot of Monte Cassino in 1097 and 1098 display a similar concern.[57]

In the aftermath of the crusade, Alexios worked hard to refute the propaganda circulating in the west. At the time of Bohemond's recruiting tour, he discovered that the Norman leader was denouncing him as 'an enemy of the Christians', prompting the emperor to write to the governments of Pisa, Genoa and Venice warning them not to believe Bohemond's version of events or to join his expedition. To present himself as a pious Christian ruler, he secured the release of some Latin knights who had been captured by the Fatimids, treated them well in Constantinople, then sent them back to Italy, in the hope that they would counteract the impression given by Bohemond.[58] In his last years he was in correspondence with Paschal II, seeking ways by which the schism might be resolved, and the main plank of anti-Byzantine propaganda removed. John II did much the same, sending an embassy to Rome in 1124. He organised a debate in Constantinople in 1136 between representatives of the Roman and Byzantine churches on the issues that divided them.[59]

These initiatives were not entirely unsuccessful and were probably responsible for the positive views of the Byzantine emperors preserved in some western chronicles. Orderic Vitalis, for example, described Alexios I as 'a man of great wisdom, merciful to the poor, a brave and illustrious warrior who was genial to his soldiers, open-handed in giving, and a most diligent servant of the divine law'.[60] Clearly the empire still had friends in the west.

Nevertheless, the problem remained that in pursuing their traditional foreign policy aim the Byzantines were placing themselves on a collision course with western Europe. In vindicating their own ideology, they were inevitably violating that of the reformed papacy and of its creations, the crusades and the Latin states of Syria. When they acted to protect the role of the emperor as the leader of Christendom, they could be accused of being its enemy and the confederates of the infidels. As the twelfth century went on, however, some at the Byzantine court were prepared to learn from their mistakes and to try to present their policies in ways acceptable to western opinion.

6

Innovation and Continuity

The new emperor, Manuel I (1143–80), appears to have been fortunate in inspiring immense personal loyalty in those who served him. He is the hero of a history written by his secretary, John Kinnamos, who attributes every possible virtue to him, not only bravery in combat, but also intellect, humanity and even a good grasp of philosophy and medical skill. John Phokas, who served as a soldier in Manuel's army, spoke of him in later years as the 'world saving' and glorious emperor.[1] What is more surprising is that Manuel also received a good press in western chronicles, presenting a shining exception to the generally unflattering picture of the 'Greeks'. For William of Tyre, he was 'beloved of God ... a great-souled man of incomparable energy', whose 'memory will ever be held in benediction'. Robert of Clari extolled him as a generous and worthy man.[2] Some have therefore seen him as an inspired innovator who substituted cooperation for confrontation in his dealing with the west and the crusader states.[3]

Yet although Manuel undoubtedly used rather more imagination and skill in this area of foreign policy than father and grandfather, the extent of his innovation and cooperation should not be exaggerated. Manuel was not 'pro-Latin': he was – of course – pro-Byzantine. A close examination of his actions shows that he and his advisers were pursuing the same goals as Alexios I and John II. The only difference was that they were more careful to present his policies in the right way, in order to avoid giving offence to the rulers of the crusader states and their backers in the west, particularly the papacy. Moreover, this more careful approach only emerged in the later years of Manuel's reign, when he had learned from earlier mistakes. Nevertheless, sensitivity to western opinion was to ensure that Manuel was largely to achieve the goal of extending Byzantine suzerainty over the crusader states.

In the early years of his reign, Manuel I's approach to the principality of Antioch was indistinguishable from that of his predecessors. When, shortly after his accession, the Antiochenes sent an embassy to him, demanding the return of areas they claimed were illegally occupied by the Byzantines, Manuel's reply, as preserved by Kinnamos, was an uncompromising assertion of Byzantine rights over Antioch.[4] Afterwards, when Raymond of Poitiers began to attack Byzantine-held cities in Cilicia, Manuel despatched an army under Andronicus and John Kontostephanos which advanced to the walls of Antioch. Faced once more with superior force, Raymond was compelled to travel to Constantinople in 1145 and make peace. At first Manuel refused even to receive his visitor and waited for him to grovel sufficiently. It was only when Raymond made a propitiatory visit to the tomb of John II in the Pantokrator monastery that he was allowed to take the now familiar vow to become Manuel's *lizios* or vassal.[5]

The fundamental continuity of Manuel's tactics is even more apparent in his dealing with the Second Crusade. Indeed, the parallels between his actions and Alexios I's treatment of the First Crusade are so strong that some have been tempted to see Anna Comnena's version of the events of 1096–97 as having been modelled on those of 1147–48, which took place around the time she was writing.[6] No such explanation is needed, however. The continuity of the foreign policy pursued by the Byzantine elite is sufficient reason why the two expeditions were handled in almost exactly the same way. Manuel I was simply following the advice of his grandfather to protect the 'coveted city' when the nations of the west were on the move.[7]

The Second Crusade was called by Pope Eugenius III in 1145. Unlike the appeal of Urban II in 1095, Eugenius's crusading bull, *Quantum praedecessores*, was not in any way inspired by diplomatic contact with the Byzantine emperor. It was issued in response to the capture of the city of Edessa in 1144 by Zengi, atabeg of Mosul and Aleppo, and to the threat to the crusader states that the Muslim victory posed. Nevertheless, the Byzantine empire could not avoid involvement. In response to the pope's appeal, two large armies were formed, one headed by the French king Louis VII, the other by the western emperor-elect Conrad III. Both decided to follow the route of the First Crusade through the Balkans to Constantinople on the way to the Holy Land.

The official Byzantine attitude to the Second Crusade is voiced by John Kinnamos. He states right at the beginning of his account that the journey to Jerusalem was only a pretext and that the real aim of the expedition was the conquest of Constantinople.[8] Manuel probably feared that the crusade would once more be exploited by the Normans of southern Italy and his fears were not ill-founded. He may have known that Louis VII's original plan had been to travel via Italy and join up with the Norman ruler, Roger II, there. In the event, Roger did not participate in the expedition, but in the autumn of 1147, at the very time that the Second Crusade was passing through Byzantine territory, he launched an attack on Byzantine Greece, just as Robert Guiscard and Bohemond had done before him. His fleet occupied the island of Corfu, and then sailed up the Gulf of Corinth to raid the prosperous towns of Corinth and Thebes.[9]

Roger's action did much to raise tension in Constantinople and to give the impression that the approaching crusade armies were a threat. Like Alexios I before him, Manuel and his advisers were seeking therefore to protect the *Oikoumene* and extract what advantage they could from the crusade, and they adopted the classic carrot and stick approach that Alexios had used in 1096–97. As another member of the educated elite, Eustathios, archbishop of Thessalonica, put it in an oration written in praise of Manuel:

> [He] was able to deal with his enemies with enviable skill, playing off one against the other with the aim of bringing about peace and tranquillity. He spilt as little of his own subjects' blood as he could, but roused up his enemies against one another. Thus by creating wars among foreign peoples, he hoped to obtain the greatest possible success, increasing the strength of the empire and exhausting that of his opponents.[10]

Others followed Eustathios's line. Manganeios Prodromos celebrated Manuel's saving of Constantinople from 'the wild beast from the west'. Kinnamos reveals, apparently with pride, the familiar stratagems that the emperor used to achieve that end. Like Alexios I, he laid in supplies in the Balkans but clearly also had an army on hand to shadow the crusaders and to intervene if necessary. He demanded oaths, presumably along the lines of those sworn by the crusaders in 1097, to return towns and territory which had formerly belonged to the empire. He deliberately tried to ensure that the two armies did not link up so that the kings could not make common cause against the Byzantines. He attempted to bribe their soldiers to enter his service.[11]

How this was seen by the Byzantine government to work in practice can be seen from Kinnamos's account of the very different receptions accorded to the German contingent of Conrad III and the French under Louis VII. By all accounts, the Germans caused more trouble to the Byzantine authorities. From the moment they entered Byzantine territory, in August 1147, a number of ugly incidents occurred. Rather than paying for supplies, the crusaders seized them by force. Near Philippopolis, a group of inebriated Germans took exception to a display of snake-charming in a tavern, in the belief that it was a cloak for an attempt to poison them, and burned most of the buildings outside the city walls. At Adrianople, when a German lying sick in a monastery was murdered by some vengeful locals, Conrad's nephew, Frederick Barbarossa, took matters into his own hands and promptly burnt the monastery down. In the light of these events, Manuel was understandably unwilling for the Germans to approach the imperial capital. He therefore sent an envoy, Andronicus Opos, to the German camp, to beg them to head for Gallipoli and to cross to Asia Minor by the Dardanelles, rather than the Bosporos. This Conrad refused to do and kept his army on the road to Constantinople.[12]

Manuel therefore made preparations to defend the city, but was reluctant to make an open attack on the Germans because of their 'ostensible purpose' of travelling to the Holy Land. In spite of having lost many men and much equipment when a swollen river flooded their camp, the Germans remained belligerent and a major confrontation took place outside the walls of Constantinople. According to Kinnamos, the Germans were worsted by the smaller imperial army, composed largely of Turkish and Cuman mercenaries, because the Byzantines were 'superior in military science and perseverance in battle'. On receiving news of this reverse, Conrad who had hitherto been boastful and arrogant, became downcast and humbled, accepting Manuel's superior strength and wisdom and allowing himself and his troops to be ferried across to Asia Minor. He did not escape, however, without a lecture on Byzantine political theory, Manuel allegedly reminding Conrad that he was dealing with the Roman empire: 'Consider that they possess this country whose ancestors passed through the whole earth with arms, and became masters of yourselves and every other race under the sun.'[13] The right order of things had been vindicated and the empire saved.

Kinnamos contrasts Conrad's reception to that of Louis VII, who entered Byzantine territory some weeks after Conrad and reached Constantinople on 4 October 1147. The Byzantine historian guessed that Louis had heard about the rough treatment meted out to the Germans, and so behaved himself impeccably. Consequently he received a splendid and cordial welcome, but one which would have left him in no doubt as to his subordinate status. He was given a seat which was deliberately placed at a lower level then that of the emperor and instructed by his host in 'what was proper'. He was given a guided tour of the city, which included the palace of Blachernae and the relics in the chapel of the palace of Boukoleon. Then, having given pledges to be the friend and ally of the emperor, Louis and his army were ferried over the Bosporos.[14] Again, the imperial city had been protected and the crusaders compelled to acknowledge the sovereignty of the emperor. Kinnamos, like Eustathios, clearly regarded Manuel's handling of the episode as a great success.

Needless to say, many crusaders, like their predecessors of the 1090s, were much less impressed by their reception in Constantinople. Their anger was to be all the sharper because the Second Crusade was not a success. Both armies were badly mauled by the Seljuk Turks in Asia Minor and,

4. The Byzantine empire, *c.* 1150.

once they arrived in Syria, they failed in their main objective of capturing Damascus in July 1148. Instead, Damascus was in 1154 brought under the rule of Zengi's son and successor, Nur ed-Din, greatly increasing his resources and his ability to threaten the crusader states. A scapegoat was needed to explain the disaster, and the policies pursued by the Byzantines meant that they were well suited to the role.

The sharpest criticism came not from the camp of Conrad, whom Kinnamos identified as the chief malefactor, but from that of the king of France. His chaplain, Odo of Deuil, wrote a first-hand account of the expedition which, like the *Gesta Francorum* before it, is characterised by its virulent anti-Byzantine bias. Like the *Gesta*, Odo's *De profectione Ludovici VII in orientem* contains all the usual sneers about Greek effeminacy and duplicity, but it cannot be dismissed merely as the expression of personal prejudice. Odo made certain specific accusations against the Byzantines, claiming that they promised to aid and supply the crusade, yet in the event, actively worked against it.

According to Odo, Greek duplicity began at Ratisbon in Germany, where some Byzantine envoys met Louis VII before he arrived in Byzantine territory. Odo commented caustically on the pompous flattery with which they prefaced their speeches before the king and on the long-winded letters which they read out, as they attempted with 'inept humility' to secure the goodwill of the French. The ambassadors requested that the French king would not attack the emperor's territory and that he should restore to the emperor any place captured by the crusaders from the Turks which had previously belonged to the empire. In return for a partial acceptance of these terms, the ambassadors promised that adequate supplies would be provided for the French army.[15]

This undertaking, Odo asserts, was reneged upon. Once the French army had crossed the Danube into Byzantine territory, it discovered that Manuel had failed to provide sufficient food supplies. The local Byzantines made matters worse by offering an unfair rate of exchange for French copper coins, and by defrauding the crusaders when they sold them food: they would remain behind the walls of their cities and let down baskets into which the westerners were instructed to place the purchase money. When this had been hauled up over the battlements, food of inferior quality would be sent down in the baskets to the furious, but impotent, crusaders below.[16]

Such incidents might be dismissed as the dishonesty of a minority, but when the French reached Constantinople they received what they considered proof that the emperor himself was working against them. They discovered that Manuel had made a twelve-year truce with the Seljuk Turks, the very enemy that the crusaders would have to fight if they were to reach

Jerusalem.[17] The subsequent French experience in Asia Minor seemed to suggest that the emperor had agreed not so much a truce with the Turks as a military alliance. The guides provided by Manuel led the army on the wrong road, and then abandoned it to attacks by the Turks.[18] Both Odo and Louis VII himself, by now thoroughly jaundiced by their previous tribulations, assumed that Manuel had encouraged these attacks.[19]

As Odo has to admit, not all these accusations could be successfully pinned on the Byzantines. The shortage of supplies and the harsh line sometimes taken by the Byzantine authorities were mainly the fault of Germans, who had commandeered everything without payment as they preceded the French and had indulged in looting and pillaging along the route.[20] Nevertheless, Odo's charges were an understandable response to traditional Byzantine foreign methods.

Take Odo's account of the prolix but duplicitous ambassadors to the French king at Ratisbon. Judging by the letter written by Manuel to Louis VII in August 1146, one can see his point. It is a flowery missive in which the emperor professed himself at great length to be eager to receive the French king in Constantinople. Nevertheless, almost as an afterthought, Manuel inserted the observation that 'Your Nobility, however, knows that, when the sceptre of empire was held by the noteworthy emperor, my grandfather, a great multitude of armies from those parts came across and agreements were made between both sides', an oblique allusion to the oaths sworn by the leaders of the first crusade to return captured towns and territory to the emperor in 1096–97.[21] The letter was a typical production of the Byzantine imperial chancery, in which the harsh demand for guarantees from the French was buried under mounds of flattery.

Odo's charge that Manuel colluded with the Turks has some substance too. In his letter of August 1146, Manuel posed as a participant in the struggle against the common Muslim enemy. He assured the king that he was currently at war with the Seljuk Turks, and that he had been leading his army against them when news of the plan for the Second Crusade arrived. Yet it is clear from Kinnamos that Manuel made peace with the Seljuks the following year, a pact that the French did not learn about until they reached Constantinople.[22] Manuel, no doubt, wanted his hands free so that he could deal with what he regarded as a more serious threat to Constantinople than the Turks.

Finally even Odo's most serious claim, that Manuel actively encouraged the Turks to attack the crusaders as they passed through Asia Minor, is substantiated by two Syriac writers and by the Byzantine Niketas Choniates.[23] The attacks on the crusaders may have been the result only of cooperation at a local level between Greeks and Turks, but they were not inconsistent with known Byzantine methods. In order to weaken the passing crusade armies so that they would have no opportunity to attack Byzantine territory, Alexios I and Manuel I had ordered attacks on their armies in the Balkans, usually by Pecheneg mercenaries. There was little difference between this and paying the Turks to do the same thing in Asia Minor.

Odo's version of events and extreme anti-Byzantine views were never as widely circulated as the *Gesta Francorum*'s account of the First Crusade. Nevertheless, the tales of the duplicity and treachery of the 'Greek emperor' soon found their way into chronicles and histories, such as those of Henry Huntingdon and William of Newburgh, and it was widely, though by no means universally, believed in the west that the crusade failed at least partly thanks to Byzantine machinations.[24]

As in the early years of the twelfth century, the circulation of such propaganda could be dangerous and provide a justification for western military action against Constantinople, along the lines of Bohemond's invasion in 1107 or Roger II's attack of 1147. The idea had first been mooted, when the army of Louis VII was at Constantinople in October 1147, by Bishop Godfrey of Langres. Such action could be justified, according to Odo of Deuil, partly on the grounds of Byzantine actions against the prince of Antioch, but also because of the heresies of the Byzantines. As well as referring to the matters of leavened and unleavened bread and the *Filioque*, Odo described how the French had discovered that, if a Latin priest celebrated mass at a Greek altar, the Byzantine priests would wash it, as if to purify it from defilement. If a Latin married a Greek, he was expected to be baptised again, as if his original baptism were invalid. 'Because of this', Odo concluded, 'they were judged not to be Christians, and the Franks considered killing them a matter of no importance ...'[25]

Bishop Godfrey's proposal was not accepted at the time, but in the immediate aftermath of the crusade a number of influential figures in western Europe made efforts to forge an alliance against the Byzantine empire. Peter the Venerable, abbot of Cluny, wrote to Roger II urging him to make peace with Conrad III so that together they could wreak revenge on the Greeks and 'their worthless king'. Abbot Suger of St-Denis was also in contact with Roger, in an attempt to draw him into a new crusade, which may have been intended to strike first at Constantinople. The plan, however, received little support either in France or Rome and had petered out by 1150.[26]

Nevertheless, the rulers of Byzantium had been given yet another reminder of the fury that their pursuit of their usual policy could provoke in western opinion. Manuel appears to have appreciated the danger at a very early stage and to have taken steps to counteract it even when the Second Crusade was still within his borders. Mindful of the danger posed by the

Normans of southern Italy and Sicily, he made efforts to arrive at an understanding with Conrad III. In this he was following in the footsteps of Alexios I and John II, both of whom had turned to the western emperor in order to stave off the threat from the Normans.[27] Following the defeat of his army and subsequent illness in Asia Minor in the winter of 1147–48, Conrad returned to Constantinople. There, as Conrad himself declared, Manuel 'showed us more honour than was ever shown to any one of our predecessors'. The following spring, Conrad set out by ship for the Holy Land, where he participated in the unsuccessful attack on Damascus. Returning home in late 1148 or early 1149, Conrad met Manuel once more at Thessalonica and there concluded a treaty of alliance with him. The agreement was cemented with a marriage alliance, Manuel marrying Conrad's sister-in-law, Bertha of Sulzbach. As Conrad remained true to this treaty, even when pressed to join an alliance with Roger II, Manuel's diplomatic efforts can be said to have done much to defuse western hostility in the aftermath of the Second Crusade.[28]

It is after 1150 that the change of tone in Manuel's dealing with the west, which sets him apart from his father and grandfather, becomes apparent. There were probably a number of factors behind the change. As already seen, an awareness of the dangers of provoking western hostility and of providing an excuse for an attack launched from the heel of Italy undoubtedly played a part. That danger seemed even more acute after 1152, when the new western emperor, Frederick I Barbarossa (1152–90), began a campaign to impose his will on Italy. If Frederick succeeded in conquering Italy, he would dominate the natural springboard for attacks on the Balkan provinces of the Byzantine empire. The old trick of playing the emperor off against the Normans, which had worked so well in 1150, would be useless. The change may also have been a response to the growing weakness of the crusader states. Faced by a more united Muslim opposition under Nur ed-Din, after about 1158 their rulers began actively to solicit Byzantine help, and so made it easier for the emperor to assert his hegemony.[29]

There were, however, other, internal, factors behind the change of tone. During the first half of the twelfth century, the Byzantine ruling classes had slowly become much better informed about the claims of the reformed papacy. The change does not seem to have been appreciated in 1126, when John II sent a letter to pope Honorius II propounding the old doctrine of the two swords, the idea that authority in the Christian world was divided between the secular and spiritual powers.[30] Ten years later, the Byzantines were certainly aware that the papacy was claiming much more than that. When a papal legate visited Constantinople in 1136, the archbishop of

Nikomedia told him that the doctrine of papal primacy would turn the Byzantines from sons of the church into its slaves. Anna Comnena, writing in the 1140s, denounced the claim of the pope to preside over the entire *Oikoumene* as typical Latin arrogance, especially as it seemed to be a usurpation of the prerogative of the Byzantine emperor. Basil of Ochrid, archbishop of Thessalonica, writing to the pope in 1154, upheld the traditions of the Byzantine church against Roman claims, insisting that the churches of Constantinople and Rome were of equal standing.[31]

More importantly, however, they were becoming aware of the link between papal claims for universal authority and the ideology of the crusades. This was a more difficult idea for them to grasp, as the Byzantine empire had no concept of holy war. The Byzantines took their teaching on warfare from St Basil of Caesarea (330–79), who, while acknowledging that it was sometimes necessary for Christians to take up arms in defence of their country, advised that those who had done so should abstain from communion for three years. Killing, though sometimes justified, could never be praiseworthy, let alone be the grounds for remission of sin. An attempt by the Emperor Nikephoros II in the tenth century to have those of his soldiers who died fighting against Muslims declared martyrs was firmly resisted by the patriarch of Constantinople and never became the teaching of the Byzantine church.[32]

Given that background, it was only to be expected that educated Byzantines would react with perplexity and disgust to the idea of a cleric preaching war and promising spiritual rewards for participation in it. An imperial ambassador to the western emperor, Lothar III, in 1137 gave him and his court a long lecture on the errors of the papacy, one of which was organising and participating in warfare.[33] Anna Comnena expressed her shock that Gregory VII, the disciple of the Man of Peace, should lead an army against Emperor Henry IV. Distasteful as it was, there was nothing for it but to admit, as Anna Comnena did, that 'the Latin customs with regard to priests differ from ours'.[34] An understanding of this and other aspects of crusade ideology among the policy makers in Constantinople would have helped to make them more careful in the impression they gave to western Europeans.

An arrival at that understanding was all the more possible in the new atmosphere of Manuel's court. The repressive, even monastic, regime instituted by Alexios I and Anna Dalassena appears to have been abandoned. Sexual mores were relaxed, and the palace once again became the scene of imperial love affairs as it had in the days of Constantine IX. Choniates rather primly recorded that Manuel 'being young and passionate, was wholly devoted to a dissolute and voluptuous life and given over to banqueting and revelling; whatever the flower of youth suggested and his vulgar passions prompted, that he did.'[35] The change in atmosphere, however, also had implications for imperial foreign policy. Manuel brought in new men, such as John of Poutze, John Hagiotheodorites and Theodore Styppeiotes, making the court a much more vibrant and innovative place. While Alexios I had recommended the study of Scripture and the Fathers as an ideal leisure pursuit, Manuel's court was the scene of all kinds of intellectual activity, with free discussion of theology and astrology encouraged. That more open environment seems to have led to a more knowledgeable and flexible approach to other cultures. Manuel, for example, attempted to make it easier for Muslims to convert to Christianity by proposing that the section of the catechism which anathematised the 'god of Mohammed' be removed.[36]

That same approach can be detected in the attitude of Manuel's court towards western Europe. The emperor seems to have employed Latins in roles other than their familiar ones of mercenaries, such the Pisans Leo Tuscus and Hugo Eteriano, who acted as interpreters and advisers on western affairs. He took an interest in the customs of western Europe. He was prepared to participate in tournaments, a western institution, hitherto unknown in Byzantium, and is even alleged to have written to the king of England, Henry II (1154–89), to ask about the geography and notable features of his realm.[37] Not only were Manuel and his advisers much better informed about western Europe than their predecessors had been, they also used this knowledge after 1150 to dress up Byzantine policies in a way that would be acceptable, in a well thought out attempt to remove two of the elements of anti-Byzantine propaganda in the west: failure to support the crusading enterprise; and schism from the church of Rome.

As regards the former, they were careful to present Byzantine dealings with the Muslim powers in crusading terms and to stress the emperor's actions on behalf of Christendom as a whole. A letter written by Manuel to Henry II of England in 1176, for example, described Byzantine campaigns against the Seljuk Turks in the following terms:

> From the beginning, Our Imperial Majesty has nourished hatred in the heart against the Persians, the enemies of God, when we have beheld them vaunting over the Christians, triumphing over the name of God, and holding sway over the land of the Christians.[38]

Manuel seems to have written letters to the pope around the same time in a similar tone. The Byzantines themselves were aware of what Manuel was trying to do. Kinnamos recalled how Manuel was particularly eager to score a victory over the Turks in order to impress his German wife, Bertha, no doubt with a view to tales of his great deeds getting back to the west.[39]

The stratagem worked. Gradually, the negative impression given by the Byzantine treatment of the Second Crusade was smoothed away. By 1160 Louis VII appears to have forgotten all about it and wrote to Manuel, referring to the kindly way in which he had been received in Constantinople in 1147. The process of reconciliation was completed in March 1180, when Louis's daughter Agnes was married to Manuel's son Alexios. It is no doubt due to this careful self-presentation and diplomacy that we owe the enthusiastic posthumous accounts of Manuel in Latin chronicles.[40]

Manuel also sought to defuse the issue of the schism with Rome which those who sought to justify attacking the empire had used to such good effect. In 1166 a council was held in Constantinople to discuss the differences between the churches at which Manuel actively encouraged westerners to put forward their point of view. He expressed a willingness to root out those practices which had so shocked Odo of Deuil at the time of the Second Crusade, particularly the washing of altars that had been used by Latin priests and the rebaptism of Latins who married Byzantines. He made efforts to find some compromise on the matter of papal authority, reinterpreting the Donation of Constantine, a document which supported papal claims to universal authority, in such a way as to make it compatible with the claims of the Byzantine emperor.[41]

This type of approach, however, had its limits. Manuel was soon to discover that no amount of repackaging could disguise the fundamental differences that that existed between east and west over the questions of papal authority and the *Filioque*. In an interview with the Pisan, Hugo Eteriano, he lamented that:

> to break the thread of this discord is very difficult or well nigh impossible. For the Greek will never write that the Spirit proceeds from the Son, while the Latin will never delete or pass over what he has written. How will this wound be healed?[42]

He was forced to come to the same conclusion in his attempts to reconcile papal authority with Byzantine imperial claims. According to Kinnamos, when the pope found himself at war with Frederick Barbarossa after 1160, he offered to recognise Manuel as the Roman emperor. The agreement, however, foundered when it became clear that the pope expected Manuel to reside at Rome rather than Constantinople. Manuel could not, of course, accept such a reversal of the all-important doctrine of *Translatio imperii*.[43]

There were, therefore, very firm limits beyond which Manuel would not go in his efforts to present a more acceptable face to the west. Beneath the façade, Byzantine foreign policy goals remained exactly the same, and many of the methods were unchanged too. This is nowhere more apparent than in Manuel's dealings with the principality of Antioch and the kingdom of Jerusalem in the 1150s and 1160s.

An opportunity to interfere in the affairs of Antioch arose as a result of the death of Raymond of Poitiers in June 1149, in a battle fought against the forces of Nur ed-Din. Raymond's son, Bohemond III, was too young to rule, so it was imperative that a regent be appointed to govern the principality during his minority. The king of Jerusalem, Baldwin III (1143–63), occupied the role for a time. When he departed for his own kingdom, Count Joscelin II of Edessa was summoned to take over, but he was ambushed by brigands on his way to Antioch and taken off to Aleppo as a prisoner.[44]

In 1152, Manuel stepped in and sent a Norman in his service, John Roger, to Antioch to seek the hand of Raymond's widow, Constance. The plan came to nothing. The people of Antioch were opposed to the match because they feared that they might become subject to Byzantine taxation, while Constance herself decided that John Roger was too old, and married instead a French nobleman, Reynald of Châtillon, who thus became the new prince of Antioch.[45] Undaunted by this setback, Manuel decided, with impressive pragmatism, to use Reynald as his agent in the east. In 1156, he hired the prince of Antioch's services against the Armenian prince Thoros, who had embarked on attacks on the Byzantine cities of Cilicia.[46] The episode shows the basic continuity between Manuel's policy and his father's and grandfather's. He clearly considered it important that Antioch be brought under imperial suzerainty, but tried to do so not by annexation but by placing some kind of imperial agent in charge of the city. John II had envisaged this role for Manuel himself, proposing him as a suitor for Constance back in 1137. Alexios I, by the treaty of Devol, had appointed Bohemond to the role. Yet it also demonstrates the care with which Manuel sought to make his actions inoffensive to western opinion, by choosing to work through Latin agents rather than intervening militarily.

In the event, Reynald provided Manuel with the perfect opportunity and excuse to do just that. Having driven Thoros's forces back, the prince of Antioch considered that Manuel was too slow in coming up with the promised reward. Reynald therefore allied himself with Thoros, and they launched a joint raid on the Byzantine island of Cyprus, causing great damage in particular to the monasteries of the island, which he did not scruple to plunder. According to William of Tyre, the raiders

> showed no mercy to age or sex, neither did they recognise difference of condition. Finally, laden with a vast amount of riches and spoils of every kind, they returned

> to the sea shore. When the ships were ready, they embarked and set sail for Antioch. There, within a short time, all the wealth which had been so wickedly acquired was dissipated; for, as says the proverb, 'Booty wickedly acquired brings no good results'.[47]

It is clear from the words of this Latin chronicler that opinion in the kingdom of Jerusalem was shocked by this attack on fellow Christians and that the perpetrators richly deserved to be punished. Reynald had, therefore, played into Manuel's hands and provided a pretext for the emperor to take military action against Antioch. Moreover, Manuel's conciliatory attitude towards the papacy and the pope's own preoccupation with the threat from Frederick Barbarossa seem to have ensured that there would be no opposition from that quarter either.[48] Thus when Manuel marched on Antioch in 1158, Reynald could hope for little outside help and he hurried to meet Manuel at Mamistra and to make peace as soon as news of the emperor's approach reached him.

The continuity of Manuel's policy and methods is further demonstrated by the conditions which he imposed on his defeated foe. The supremacy of the Byzantine emperor had to be publicly asserted in a humiliating spectacle, and, since he was in a strong position, Manuel had no need to forego any of the details. Reynald appeared in person at the Byzantine camp, barefoot, dressed in a short woollen tunic and with a rope around his neck. He handed his sword to the emperor and then fell prostrate at his feet where he lay 'till all were disgusted and the glory of the Latins was turned into shame'. A poet at the Byzantine court exploited the episode for all it was worth, recounting how Reynald was forced to 'curl up like a small puppy' at Manuel's 'red-slippered feet'.[49]

Similarly, the detailed stipulations of Manuel's treaty with Reynald reveal the underlying continuity. Reynald agreed that the citadel of Antioch should be surrendered to the Byzantines on demand, that the Latin patriarch of Antioch should be replaced by a Greek one, and that he should provide a contingent to serve in the Byzantine army.[50] The first two demands had been made before, the last was a time-honoured way of treating a defeated enemy. After spending the winter in Cilicia, in April 1159 Manuel made a ceremonial entry into Antioch, just as his father had done before him, to make the point absolutely clear. Manuel entered the city on horseback, wearing a jewelled garment over his armour, while Reynald and the nobles of Antioch walked alongside.[51]

Manuel now prepared to do what John II had done and demonstrate his hegemony by leading an expedition against Nur ed-Din. A joint Frankish-Byzantine army set out against Aleppo but the attack was never pressed home, prompting an Armenian chronicler to conclude sourly that the emperor who had arrived like a powerful eagle had departed like a weak fox. Instead, Manuel entered into negotiations with ambassadors from the sultan. Nur ed-Din agreed to provide the Byzantines with help against the Seljuk Turks of Konya and, more importantly, to release many of the French and German captives taken at the time of the Second Crusade.[52] As in the case of John II's recovery of the marble cross at the end of the siege of Shaizar in 1138, Manuel had succeeded in enhancing imperial prestige without the need for a costly campaign. Restoring Christian prisoners to their families was an important part of the image of the pious Christian emperor. Alexios I had employed it as a way of combating Bohemond's propaganda, and in coming years, Manuel was often to pay the ransoms of Latin knights and nobles who had been captured in battle as a way presenting himself in a favourable light to western opinion. In 1180, he doled out no less than 150,000 Tyrian dinars and released one thousand Muslim prisoners in return for Baldwin of Ibelin.[53] Manuel's dealings with Nur ed-Din were not a retreat but a continuation of policy by other means.

Unlike Alexios and John, Manuel was able to maintain his influence in Antioch after his return to Constantinople in 1159. He achieved this partly by a marriage alliance. In 1162, after the death of his first wife Bertha of Sulzbach, he married Maria, one of the daughters of Raymond of Poitiers and the sister of the young Bohemond III. He also put Bohemond III in his debt by paying his ransom of 100,000 dinars after the prince had been captured by Nur ed-Din at the battle of Harim in 1164. In return, Manuel was able to demand a substantial concession, the reinstatement of the Greek patriarch, Athanasius I Manasses, in accordance with the treaty of Devol and the agreement made in 1158. The Latin patriarch, Aimery of Limoges, was sent off to live in the nearby village of Cursat.[54]

There were, of course, limits to the influence that Manuel could wield in distant Antioch. In 1170 an earthquake brought the sanctuary of the cathedral in Antioch crashing down. The unfortunate Patriarch Athanasius, who happened to be celebrating the liturgy at the time, was buried under the rubble and killed. Prince Bohemond considered the earthquake to be a clear case of divine judgment and at once recalled the exiled Aimery. Manuel appointed a new Greek patriarch, Cyril II, but kept him in Constantinople and made no effort to impose him on the Antiochenes, perhaps because he realised that to do so would cause further ill will.[55]

This setback aside, Manuel could view his achievements in Antioch with some satisfaction by the later years of his reign, especially as it had all been done without incurring western opprobrium. Whether his greater success was due to his more cautious tone in presenting his actions, or the favourable conditions in Syria and western Europe at the time, is difficult to say.

Careful consideration of western sensibility also guided Manuel's policy towards the kingdom of Jerusalem between 1158 and 1171. The old objective of securing recognition of the emperor's hegemony and his guardianship of Jerusalem and the Holy Places was central to Manuel's agenda. Unlike in the case of Antioch, however, Manuel did not have a *casus belli* which justified the overt humiliation of Reynald of Châtillon. The Byzantine emperor had, therefore, to tread even more carefully.

Manuel's dealings with the kingdom of Jerusalem began in 1157 when King Baldwin III sent an embassy to Constantinople to request a Byzantine princess as his wife. It is not difficult to discern the motive behind the request. Baldwin was chronically short of men and resources with which to defend his kingdom and, since little help seemed to be forthcoming from the west, he turned to the fabled wealth of the Byzantine emperor. As William of Tyre put it, Manuel would be able 'to relieve from his own abundance the distress under which our realm was suffering and to change our poverty into superabundance'. The ambassadors returned with Manuel's thirteen-year-old niece, Theodora, along with one hundred thousand gold pieces for her dowry and an extra ten thousand for marriage expenses. Theodora also came equipped with jewels and silk garments which William of Tyre reckoned as being worth a further fourteen thousand gold pieces.[56]

Byzantine money was never distributed without the expectation of something in return. That was exacted when Manuel and his army were encamped near Antioch in 1159, after Reynald of Châtillon had been brought to heel. Baldwin III travelled north to pay his respects and received a warm welcome, liberal gifts of the usual type being lavished on him and his followers. Nevertheless, there were the usual formalities to be followed so that no one should be under any illusions about the right order of things. When the two rulers held court together, Baldwin was seated on a throne placed lower than that of the emperor. When Manuel entered Antioch, the king was required to ride behind him. Baldwin seems also to have consented to that familiar instrument of Byzantine policy, an oath.[57]

A similar process was followed in 1165 when Baldwin's successor, Amalric (1163–74), sent an embassy to Constantinople to ask for a Byzantine bride. Another niece, Maria Comnena, was despatched to Jerusalem, accompanied by a number of Byzantine nobles whose job it was to ensure that 'none of the prescribed ceremonies was omitted'. In return, Amalric renewed the oath of loyalty sworn by his brother Baldwin.[58]

All this was, of course, the stock-in-trade of Byzantine diplomacy. The greater sensitivity employed by Manuel, however, emerges from the carefully stage-managed visit of Amalric himself to Constantinople in March 1171, to request the emperor's aid for the by-now beleaguered kingdom of Jerusalem. As recorded in detail by William of Tyre, the visit was an object lesson in the reception of an obedient monarch of lower status at the Byzantine court. All the usual visual symbols were rolled out. Amalric was presented with lavish gifts, was received by the emperor, who sat on a throne of gold, and was given a slightly lower throne on which to sit. Touchingly, however, William of Tyre reveals that curtains were drawn around the emperor's throne as Amalric approached it, so that the king's retinue would not see how the emperor showed too much condescension in his greeting to the king. It is much more likely that the curtains were drawn to hide the obeisance made by Amalric. Manuel probably had no desire to risk censure by imposing a public humiliation on Amalric as had been meted out to Reynald. If this is so, it is another good example of Manuel's judicious cloaking of traditional Byzantine diplomatic practice.[59]

The visual symbols apart, Manuel needed to demonstrate his overlordship of the kingdom of Jerusalem by leading the war against the common Muslim foe. Distance and preoccupation with other matters made it difficult for Manuel to lead, and he was therefore reduced to participation. He provided ships for two joint attacks with the forces of the kingdom of Jerusalem against Fatimid Egypt in 1169 and 1177. Neither expedition was a success. In 1169 the Byzantines provided a fleet of some three hundred ships, but they only came with provisions for six months. The convoy did not arrive at Damietta until October, by which time the Byzantine provisions were beginning to run out. After a chaotic siege, the Byzantines withdrew, and half their fleet was wrecked in a storm on the way back to Constantinople. Most serious of all, Christian intervention in Egypt played a large part in allowing Nur ed-Din's lieutenant, Saladin, to install himself as vizier to the Fatimid caliph in March 1169.[60] In 1177 another Byzantine fleet was sent to Palestine to join in an invasion of Egypt, but this time the attack never got off the ground, due to the refusal of Count Philip of Flanders and several prominent nobles of the kingdom of Jerusalem to participate.[61]

The failure of these enterprises should not divert attention from Byzantine participation in them as part of the age-old concern to secure recognition of the emperor's role as the leader of the Christian world. That concern is even more apparent in the prerogatives which Manuel obtained within the Holy Land itself. Like his predecessors of the eleventh century in their negotiations with the Fatimids, Manuel secured the right to participate in the rebuilding and decoration of the basilicas and Greek monasteries in the

Holy Land, including the church of the Holy Sepulchre in Jerusalem. From the reign of Amalric, Byzantine clergy were allowed to perform the Greek liturgy every day at the church of the Holy Sepulchre.

A tangible reminder of the influence that Manuel secured in the kingdom of Jerusalem can still be seen in the church of the Holy Nativity in Bethlehem. During the 1160s the nave was redecorated, partly at Manuel's expense, with mosaics depicting the councils of the church. On the south wall of the church an inscription in Greek records that 'the present work was finished by the hand of Ephraim the monk, painter and mosaicist, in the reign of the great emperor Manuel Porphyrogenitos Comnenus and in the time of the great king of Jerusalem, Amalric.' The placing of Manuel's name first was a public recognition and visual symbol of the emperor's overlordship although, as in the case of Antioch, there were limits: the Latin version of the inscription, which is the one which would have been read by westerners, places Amalric's name before that of Manuel.[62]

Nevertheless, by the early 1170s, Manuel could look back on his achievements and those of predecessors with some satisfaction. Tried and tested Byzantine policy had produced the unwanted results of the schism and the First Crusade. Alexios I and John II had nevertheless applied that policy not unsuccessfully to the crusaders states, but had incurred western resentment that had on one occasion coalesced into direct military action against the empire. Manuel had taken this success further and, partly by an intelligent awareness of western sensitivities on certain points, had secured an acceptance of the empire's hegemony over Antioch and Jerusalem. In the last analysis, however, Byzantine success between 1150 and 1180 was dependent on an intelligent and well-informed emperor and courtiers who had the acumen to pursue traditional goals without sparking off western hostility.

7

Andronicus

After the death of Manuel I in 1180, a series of violent political upheavals removed not only his designated successor but also the courtiers who had probably played an important role in framing foreign policy and packaging it for western consumption. As a result, within five years the empire was back where it had been in 1150 in the eyes of western European opinion. Virulent anti-Byzantine propaganda was once more circulating, reviving the old charges of schism with Rome and of collusion with the infidel which Manuel and his advisers had worked so hard to avoid.

Such a rapid unravelling of the careful balance created during Manuel's reign needs to be explained, and the reason usually given is the seizure of power by a supposedly 'anti-Latin' faction in Constantinople, led by Manuel's cousin, Andronicus Comnenus. As well as instituting a reign of terror in Constantinople, Andronicus allegedly exploited the bigoted nationalism of the Byzantine populace to gain power, and then shifted the emphasis in foreign policy away from conciliating western opinion to direct confrontation.[1]

For a number of reasons, however, this picture of the motives behind Andronicus's dealings with the west is inaccurate. In the first place, Andronicus himself was not specifically anti-Latin. His takeover in 1182 was motivated rather by a desire for personal revenge on Manuel I and his supporters. Secondly, the Byzantine population was not gripped by xenophobic hatred of all western Europeans, as is sometimes claimed. Lastly, the policy pursued by Andronicus towards the crusader states was not new and anti-Latin, but rather a continuation of a line of conduct that can be traced back over one hundred and fifty years. Byzantine foreign policy was not, and had never been, formulated in terms of pro- or anti-Latin, but on the doctrine of *Translatio imperii* and the consequent need to defend Constantinople and to ensure recognition of the status of the emperor.

Nevertheless, Andronicus can be blamed for the renewed hostility to Byzantium in western Europe and the crusader states, because, unlike Manuel I, he showed complete indifference to how his actions might be interpreted by western opinion. During his seizure of power in 1182, he permitted a massacre of Italian residents of Constantinople. In the light of that atrocity, it did not matter that Byzantine foreign policy had no specifically anti-Latin motive. Henceforth it would inevitably be seen in that light in the west, so that fairly routine matters, like an agreement with the sultan of Syria and Egypt, Saladin, over the protectorship of the Holy Places, came to be seen as deliberate and sinister machinations against the Holy Land and Jerusalem.

To substantiate these points, it first needs to be considered why Andronicus's coup has been seen, quite wrongly, as anti-Latin. The misconception arose because of developments which took place within the Byzantine empire between the middle of the eleventh century and the end of the reign of Manuel I. During that time, the numbers of western Europeans living in Constantinople increased enormously. They fulfilled a variety of roles, many of them in the service of the emperor. Most were probably mercenary soldiers, from the Scandinavians and Englishmen who made up the Varangian guard in the palace, to the Norman knights who were an important component of the armies led on campaign by the first three emperors of the Comnenus dynasty. They had plenty of other uses, however. For obvious reasons all the emperors of the twelfth century used Latins to lead embassies to western European courts, such as Wilfricus of Lincoln who was sent to England by Alexios I in 1100.[2]

The number of Latins in imperial service and the variety of roles they fulfilled seem to have increased still further under Manuel I. He brought in translators and advisers to his court, and the Latin element there would have been reinforced by his marriage alliances. Both of Manuel's wives, Bertha of Sulzbach and Maria of Antioch, were of Latin origin and during 1180 he arranged marriages for his children with westerners: his daughter Maria the Porphyrogenita to Renier, son of the marquis of Montferrat, and his son Alexios to Agnes, the daughter of Louis VII of France. These wives and husbands would have brought their own retinues and followers with them to Constantinople. Nevertheless, Latins were already playing a central role in the imperial court long before 1143, as is apparent from the text of the treaty of Devol of 1108, where most of those who signed the document from the Byzantine side were western Europeans.[3]

It is sometimes assumed that many Byzantines must have resented the presence of these outsiders at the centre of power. After all, the eleventh-century courtier and soldier, Kekaumenos, had counselled the emperor not to bestow high rank or great offices of states on foreigners because it would not 'please your own officers who are of Roman origin'.[4] Yet that was not necessarily the case. Many writers of the time, including Anna Comnena and Niketas Choniates, paid fulsome tribute to the loyalty and courage of the Latins in Byzantine service.[5] The Byzantine empire was not, after all, a Greek national state. It was only to be expected that Christians of all races should be found in the service of the universal Christian emperor.

Inevitably, there were occasions when some Latins were the object of hostility, in the same way as the Byzantines sometimes were in the west. The Pisan Hugo Eteriano reported that Latins were pointed out in the streets of the Byzantine capital as objects of hatred and detestation. This was, however, as a result of the highly charged atmosphere during the theological debates organised by Manuel I in the 1160s, and was not necessarily a permanent state of affairs.[6]

Similarly, there were occasional rumblings of discontent over the privileged position enjoyed by some westerners. Choniates records that many people felt that Manuel I preferred them in his service over Byzantines. Rather than confining them to military roles, as in the past, he gave them posts in the imperial administration, appointing them as judges and tax collectors when they could not even speak Greek properly. George Tornikios, when trying to secure a post at court for his uncle, found that there was fierce competition from 'those of barbarian tongue', 'taken from the market place to the imperial palace'.[7]

These complaints seem to confirm the reports of western chroniclers that Manuel gave all the best jobs at his court to Latins,[8] but they should be treated with caution for two reasons. First, apart from these vague remarks, there is no evidence for any named individual of Latin origin occupying any of the important administrative posts at court.[9] Secondly, the words of Choniates and Tornikios must been seen in the wider context of the jealousy with which members of the Byzantine ruling elite guarded the right to office that they believed their education gave them. They had always been quick to denigrate rivals in the competition for office, whether Byzantine or foreign, by questioning their education and competence in Greek, as Psellos did in the case of Leo Paraspondylas.[10] Choniates and Tornikios provide evidence not of anti-Latin prejudice but of the usual vigilant guardianship by a small and privileged group of the right of entry to their charmed circle.

It is quite clear that there was not necessarily a widespread dislike of all westerners at all times in Constantinople. That does not mean, however, that there were not groups among western Europeans who were singled out for resentment. One group of Latins was most certainly the cause of deep and long lasting antipathy. These were not those of the crusader states but the representatives of the Italian mercantile republics, especially the Venetians.

The reasons for this hostility go back to 1082, when Alexios I, desperate to find an ally against Robert Guiscard, had made a treaty with Venice. So acute was his need that the emperor had granted the Venetians far-reaching concessions in the maritime trade between Constantinople and the west. Venetian merchants were given the right to trade in nearly all parts of the empire, free of the *Kommerkion* and other dues, and were granted their own commercial quarter, along the Golden Horn in Constantinople.[11] The Byzantine government appears to have regarded these concessions as a temporary measure, which could be withdrawn once the empire was in a stronger position. The moment seemed to have arrived when John II acceded in 1118 and refused to renew the treaty of 1082. Matters did not, however, go according to plan. Venice responded with speed and with force. A fleet was despatched to attack Corfu, Cephallonia, Rhodes and other Byzantine coasts and islands. Based in faraway Constantinople, John was powerless to do anything about these incursions and in 1126 was forced to give way and to restore the original commercial privileges.[12]

Nevertheless, in spite of this unpleasant experience, the Byzantine authorities continued to grant similar trading concessions to other Italian merchant cities. In 1111 a treaty was made with Pisa, giving lesser exemptions from customs dues, and a commercial quarter and a landing stage on the Golden Horn. In 1155 a similar agreement was reached with the Genoese, who also received a wharf in Constantinople. To have made these concessions was not as risky and unwise as it sounds. The same policy was followed by the rulers of the crusader states, who provided the Italian republics with similar concessions and commercial quarters in the ports of Acre, Tyre and Sidon. It may have been that the wealth the Italians generated by their trading activities more than compensated for any concessions in the matter of customs dues, or alternatively the Byzantines may have hoped to play the Venetians off against their commercial rivals.[13]

Whatever the precise considerations of policy behind these treaties, many of the inhabitants of Constantinople deeply resented the intrusion of these foreign merchants into their city and their favoured status as regarded the *Kommerkion*. With some exaggeration, Eustathios, archbishop of Thessalonica, estimated that there were sixty thousand of them by 1180, and both John Kinnamos and Niketas Choniates complained that their favoured status made them arrogant and contemptuous towards native Byzantines.[14] These complaints cannot be dismissed as mere hysterical xenophobia, for negative reactions to Italian merchants were by no means restricted to the Byzantines. A wide body of western opinion regarded the Venetians and Genoese as arrogant and materialistic, probably in response to the single-minded commercial policies they pursued. There was also as much tension between the Italian communities themselves as between Greeks and Italians. In 1162 the Pisans and Venetians banded together with the local Byzantines to mount an attack on the Genoese and drive them from their compound.[15] Although hostility towards Italian merchants was not restricted to the Byzantines, it would seem nevertheless that there was a particularly deep antipathy towards them in Constantinople.

That resentment may have been behind the dramatic action of the supposedly pro-Latin Manuel I. In sharp contrast to his usual practice of conciliating western opinion, in the spring of 1171 Manuel secretly brought troops into Constantinople. On 12 March he suddenly ordered the arrest of all Venetians in the city and the confiscation of their goods. Instructions were also sent to provincial governors to do the same.[16] Various motives have been given for Manuel's action. It may have been a punishment levelled at the Venetians for an attack they had made on the Genoese quarter in Constantinople, when several warehouses were set alight. It may have been connected to Manuel's policy in Italy, where he was playing off the Italian city states against the German emperor, Frederick Barbarossa. It may have been an attempt to court the favour of the people of Constantinople. Niketas Choniates ascribes it to personal motives. Manuel, he says, had never forgiven the Venetians for an insult they had paid him when the Byzantines and Venetians were besieging the forces of Roger II of Sicily on Corfu back in 1149. Some Venetian sailors had stolen the imperial galley and, finding the imperial regalia on board, had staged a mocking burlesque of imperial ceremonial.[17] Whatever it was that prompted Manuel to strike so decisively, one thing is clear: his action was directed against the Venetians, and the Venetians alone.

It was only to be expected that retribution would follow. Inevitably, some Venetians escaped the round-up and sailed back to their own city to raise the alarm. As in 1126, a fleet was despatched to bring the Byzantine emperor to heel. This time the Venetians reached as far as the island of Euboea, but a combination of an energetic Byzantine naval response and disease decimating the Venetian crews forced them to turn back. The Venetians were therefore compelled to resort to long drawn out negotiations in an attempt to extort compensation for their losses in 1171 and to have their trading privileges renewed.[18]

That was the situation when Manuel died in 1180. The Venetians were temporarily excluded from Constantinople but a strong legacy of mistrust remained between the imperial government and Venice as a result of the events of 1171. That mistrust was to play an important part in later events. A later Venetian chronicler even made up a story that Enrico Dandolo, the doge who played so signal a role in the Fourth Crusade, was blinded in a brawl in Constantinople at this time and henceforth harboured a bitter grudge against the Byzantines.[19] Moreover, the Pisans and Genoese, who were as much objects of resentment as the Venetians, remained entrenched in their cantonments on the Golden Horn. It was anti-Italian sentiment, rather than any general hostility to all westerners, that played a part in events in Constantinople in the years 1180–82.

Those events are a striking example of Byzantine internal politics at their most ruthless and cruel. When Manuel I died, he left as his heir his eleven-year-old son, Alexios II. A regency was therefore formed under the boy's mother, Maria of Antioch, with real power in the hands of the *Protosebastos* Alexios Comnenus, nephew of the late emperor. The regency of Maria and Alexios soon proved unpopular in Constantinople. The *Protosebastos* was widely known to be Maria's lover. He was rumoured to be diverting public funds for his own purposes, and was feared to have designs on seizing the throne himself. This opposition to the regency coalesced into a faction which centred on Manuel I's daughter by his first marriage, Maria the Porphyrogenita, and her husband Renier. When, in April 1181, their plot to have the *Protosebastos* murdered was discovered, they barricaded themselves inside the cathedral of Hagia Sophia, and there was fighting in the streets between the supporters of the two sides.[20]

Modern accounts tend to ascribe the outbreak of opposition to a resentment of the 'pro-Latin' stance of the regency. It was, after all, nominally headed by a Latin, Maria of Antioch, and contemporary Latin writers claimed that Alexios II and the *Protosebastos* followed Manuel I's putative policy of preferring the Latins over the Byzantines and giving them the highest honours.[21] That interpretation cannot be sustained. Maria the Porphyrogenita was herself married to, and assisted in her plans by, a Latin, Renier of Montferrat. To defend themselves in their sanctuary of Hagia Sophia, Maria and Renier recruited Italian mercenaries, an odd course of action if the motive behind the revolt was anti-Latin.[22] The fact is that both sides were happy to use Latin help against their opponents in what was essentially a dynastic power struggle within the Comnenus family. The motives of the opposition party were personal hatred of the *Protosebastos* and a desire to eject him from his position of influence, rather than dislike of favouritism to the Latins.

The same motivation can be traced in the next stage of the conflict. When fighting died down, a truce was arranged. Maria the Porphyrogenita and Renier were allowed to emerge from the cathedral and go free, but most of their supporters remained in prison. The opposition therefore decided to appeal for aid from another member of the family outside Constantinople. A message was accordingly sent to the late emperor's cousin, the governor of the province of Pontos, Andronicus Comnenus, at his castle on the Black Sea.

Like Maria the Porphyrogenita, Andronicus had his own, personal reasons for becoming involved in political opposition to the regency, which had nothing to do with anti-Latin prejudice. He had long been something of a maverick outsider in the Comnenus family. The son of John II's younger brother, Isaac, Andronicus was already in his sixties in 1182, with a lifetime of scandal and adventurous exploits behind him. During the 1150s, he had fallen into disfavour at court as a result of his involvement in various plots against Manuel I and of the first of his many illicit affairs with his female relatives, in this case his niece, Eudokia. He was imprisoned for nine years in the dungeons beneath the palace of Boukoleon, before escaping in about 1164 by smuggling a wax impression of the keys out to his supporters. He fled to Russia where he was welcomed at the court of Prince Jaroslav of Galicia. Pardoned and restored to imperial favour, he was sent to Cilicia as governor in 1166. His rehabilitation proved to be short-lived. Andronicus caused outrage in Constantinople by deserting his post and installing himself in the city of Antioch, where he entered into a marriage engagement with Philippa, one of the daughters of Raymond of Poitiers and the sister of Manuel's second wife, Maria. Before long, however, Andronicus realised that Manuel's client state of Antioch was hardly a safe refuge and so he abandoned Philippa and absconded to the kingdom of Jerusalem, taking with him most of the year's tax receipts from Cilicia and Cyprus. King Amalric nevertheless received him amicably enough and granted him Beirut as a fief. Andronicus, who appears to have been incapable of avoiding scandal, then fell in love with Theodora, the niece of Manuel I and the widow of the previous king of Jerusalem, Baldwin III. The couple eloped first to the court of Nur ed-Din, and then to that of Saltuq Ibn Ali, the ruler of Erzerum in eastern Asia Minor. Andronicus did not return to Byzantine territory until July 1180, when he was again forgiven and allowed to live quietly with Theodora and their children in Pontos.[23]

Nevertheless, it would seem that Andronicus had neither forgiven nor forgotten his long period in the wilderness. The appeal from Constantinople was therefore irresistible. In the spring of 1182, he gathered an army and marched on the capital. His following was not large and with determined opposition his revolt would easily have been put down. By the time he reached the Bosporos, however, public opinion in Constantinople had swung firmly behind him and he was hailed as the saviour of the young emperor from the evil influence of the empress and the *Protosebastos*. The commander of the fleet deserted to Andronicus and elements within the city arrested the *Protosebastos* and took him across the straits to the rebel camp. Andronicus was therefore able to ferry his troops across to the city and capture it with virtually no opposition.[24]

This *coup d'état* brought Andronicus Comnenus to power, first as regent, then as Emperor Andronicus I (1183–85). How he saw his takeover emerges from Choniates's account of his triumphant entry into Constantinople in May 1182. Almost at once, Andronicus went to the monastery of the Pantokrator, ostensibly to pay his respects at the marble sarcophagus of the late Emperor Manuel. Some bystanders, however, claimed that he had used the occasion to vow revenge on his cousin, his persecutor and the cause of his many wanderings, and had promised that he would 'fall upon his family like a lion pouncing on a large prey'.[25]

In the months that followed, Andronicus did exactly that. The empire was plunged into to an orgy of political violence as he proceeded to liquidate his political opponents with brutal efficiency. The *Protosebastos* Alexios, who no longer presented a threat, was immured in a monastery. Others were not so lucky. The empress and regent, Maria of Antioch, was strangled, and her memory obliterated. Andronicus had pictures of her in public places replaced with his own portrait. He had no intention of sparing even those members of the imperial family who had opposed the regency and supported his takeover. Maria the Porphyrogenita and Renier of Montferrat were both murdered within a few months, probably poisoned. The young Alexios II was first sidelined when Andronicus was proclaimed emperor in September 1183. Shortly afterwards, he was strangled with a bow string and his body dumped into the Bosporos. His young French wife, Agnes, survived, although her life was purchased at the cost of having to marry Andronicus, fifty years her senior.[26]

At the same time as destroying his relatives, Andronicus carried out a purge of the administration, bringing in his own creatures instead. Men like Andronicus Kontostephanos, who had led troops against Raymond of Poitiers in Antioch at the behest of Manuel I, were now disgraced. Instead Michael Haploucheir and Stephen Hagiochristophorites now held the emperor's confidence. Some who had served under Manuel and the regency, such as Constantine Patrenos and Constantine Makrodoukas, sought to save themselves by casting in their lot with the new regime, but changing sides offered little protection. Makrodoukas ended up being put on trial and condemned: he was dragged off to a hill outside Constantinople and impaled. Andronicus was clearly determined to rid himself of the group who had advised Manuel I and who might retain some loyalty to Alexios II. Hagiochristophorites's voice, recalled Choniates, 'crashed throughout the palace' as he sought out all who were regarded as suspect. Yet in making such a clean sweep, Andronicus must have deprived himself of a great deal of accumulated wisdom and experience.[27]

Andronicus's purges were not restricted to members of the imperial family and the palace bureaucracy. The inhabitants of the cities of Nicaea and Prousa in Asia Minor, which had held out against Andronicus's takeover, suffered for their defiance. Many were impaled *en masse* outside the city's walls where, Choniates recounts, their corpses 'swayed in the wind like scarecrows'.[28]

The main victims of Andronicus's coup were therefore not Latins but the Byzantines themselves. The high-profile Latins who perished, Maria of Antioch and Renier of Montferrat, did so because they were the wife and son-in-law of Manuel I respectively. The only member of Manuel's immediate family to survive was a Latin, his French daughter-in-law, Agnes. Moreover, Andronicus depended on a certain degree of Latin support to carry out his purge. Like all his predecessors, he had plenty of Latin mercenaries in his service and he relied on them to deal with his political opponents. German Varangians guarded the *Protosebastos* Alexios after his arrest in 1182 while Andronicus, like his predecessors, had a personal bodyguard of Latin troops.[29] It was impossible to be 'anti-Latin' in a general sense in twelfth-century Constantinople: western Europeans were simply far too useful.

Even though Andronicus's purges were generally directed against his own family and their supporters, he succeeded in earning himself the reputation as an enemy of the Latins on account of an appalling atrocity which accompanied his seizure of the throne in May 1182. It was not unknown for the armies of victorious usurpers to go on the rampage once they were inside the walls of Constantinople. Alexios I's had done so in 1081 and caused widespread damage.[30] On this occasion, however, Andronicus's troops made common cause with the citizens of Constantinople in an attack on a very specific target: the westerners who lived along the shores of the Golden Horn, the majority of whom were probably Genoese and Pisans. Many of the Italians had got wind of what was going to happen beforehand and had fled in ships, but the aged, the infirm and those left behind were killed without mercy. A hospital run by the knights of St John was attacked, and the sick murdered in their beds. Among the victims were mothers and children and a visiting papal legate, who was allegedly decapitated and his head tied to the tail of a dog. The pretext given by those responsible was that the Italians were likely to support the Empress Maria against Andronicus, but no doubt the general unpopularity of the merchants was an equally important factor. Yet even Eustathios of Thessalonica, who was no friend of the Italian merchant communities, was shocked by the violence and regarded it as indefensible. While Choniates asserted categorically that Andronicus actively set his troops to make the attack, it may well be that they simply got out of hand. Whichever it was, it made no difference to the way the massacre was seen in the west.[31]

Many of the survivors reached Syria, where they recounted their experiences in graphic detail. The patient work of Manuel I over thirty years was undone in a day. 'In such a fashion', wrote William of Tyre, 'did the perfidious Greek nation, a brood of vipers ... requite their guests – those who had not deserved such treatment and were far from anticipating anything of the kind.' For William, the attack on the Genoese and Pisans was an attack on all Latins, motivated by Greek hatred of Latin military prowess and superiority, and of their adhesion to the church of Rome. By the time the story had reached western Europe further refinements had been added, bringing in the old accusations of schism and collusion with the Muslims. It was alleged that the massacre had been carried out with the help of the Saracens and the papal legate had died a martyr when he had proclaimed his obedience to Rome to the bloodthirsty mob.[32]

In the long term, the episode was a disaster for Byzantine relations with western Europe, the papacy and the crusader states. Although anti-Latin sentiment was behind neither Andronicus's coup nor the policy which he pursued thereafter towards the crusader states, such was the outrage caused by the massacre, and so tarnished was the reputation of the Byzantines, that almost anything they did was likely to be interpreted as a sinister plot.

Once in power, Andronicus had to formulate foreign policy, especially because the kings of Hungary and Sicily were threatening to invade the empire's western provinces. The danger of a major attack probably accounts for the conciliatory policy that Andronicus pursued towards Venice, opening negotiations on compensation for the losses incurred in 1171. A Venetian embassy visited Constantinople in 1184 and an agreement was reached that compensation of fifteen hundred gold pieces would be paid in instalments over the next six years. The Venetians appear also to have been given permission to return to their old quarter on the Golden Horn and to resume their commercial activities there.[33]

Given this eirenic approach to Venice, it is all the more odd that, within a few years of his death, a report was circulating in the west that Andronicus had entered into an alliance with Saladin, the sultan of Egypt and Syria, with a view to bringing about the destruction of the crusader states of Antioch and Jerusalem and partitioning their territory between Byzantium and the Ayyubid sultanate. Many modern accounts have taken this report literally and cited it as evidence that Andronicus was pursuing an 'anti-Latin' foreign policy.[34]

There are, however, good grounds for taking a different view. The negotiations between Andronicus and Saladin are not mentioned by any contemporary or near-contemporary Byzantine or Muslim source. Information on them is contained only in a letter supposedly written by an anonymous correspondent from the Latin east in about 1189 and preserved in the chronicle of a German monk, Magnus of Reichersberg (d. 1195). This in itself dictates that the evidence should be treated with some caution, and the contents of the letter reinforce that conclusion.

According to Magnus of Reichersberg's correspondent, Andronicus I was driven to send an embassy to Saladin by his fear of the Latins, particularly the kings of Sicily and Hungary. Andronicus reminded the Muslim ruler of their friendship in the past, presumably referring to the time when Andronicus, on the run from disgrace at home, had been a guest at the court of Nur-ed-Din, and proposed the following terms. The emperor and the sultan were to provide each other with mutual aid against their common enemies, the Seljuk Turks of Konya and the Latin states of Palestine and Syria. If Saladin and the emperor were to make war on the sultan of Konya, the emperor was to receive any land taken up as far east as Antioch and Armenia. On the other hand, if Saladin were to conquer the kingdom of Jerusalem with Byzantine help, then the Byzantines would receive the city of Jerusalem and all the coastal cities except Ascalon. Finally, Saladin was to pay homage (*hominium*) to Andronicus because he was emperor. Saladin responded favourably to the proposal and sent an embassy of his own to Constantinople.[35]

Detailed though this report of the negotiations is, it is very difficult to accept it at face value in view of the many inconsistencies and absurdities that it contains. It claims that Andronicus made his approach to the Ayyubid court because he was seeking help against the Hungarians and the Normans of southern Italy, his enemies in the west. Yet he negotiated a treaty that made no provision whatsoever for Saladin to help the empire against those enemies. Instead it promised major acquisitions of territory in the east, Asia Minor, Jerusalem and the coast of Palestine. It seems incredible that Andronicus should have been dreaming of extending the empire in the east when he was in imminent danger of losing it in the west. Another peculiar feature was the undertaking of Saladin to pay homage to Andronicus. It is hardly credible that Saladin, whose main political platform was that of *jihad* against the infidel, would enter into an agreement whereby he would hold part of his conquests as the vassal of a Christian ruler, and would hand over the rest as a gift.

These unbelievable aspects of the report make it likely that it was another piece of anti-Byzantine propaganda, like the *Gesta Francorum*, circulated in the west to present the Byzantines as the enemies of the crusade against whom military action was justifiable. Yet that does not mean that the report should be dismissed as a tissue of lies. Like so much western anti-Byzantine propaganda, it accurately reflected some aspects of traditional Byzantine foreign policy, albeit overlain with interpretations arising from crusade ideology and feudal notions of the importance of landholding.

There is, for example, no reason to doubt that Andronicus was in contact with Saladin. Byzantine rulers had always been prepared to negotiate with their Muslim counterparts and had maintained very cordial relations with Saladin's predecessors in Egypt, the Fatimids. Alexios I had even taken care to warn them of the approach of the First Crusade.[36] Both Manuel I and the regency, in spite of their concern to avoid alienating western opinion, continued to negotiate with Muslim powers whenever possible. Manuel had made a peace treaty with Nur ed-Din in 1159, and Alexios the *Protosebastos* had sent an embassy to Cairo to make peace with Saladin in 1181. Moreover, one of the terms reported by Magnus of Reicherberg's informant, mutual aid against the Seljuk Turks of Konya, had featured in Manuel's earlier negotiations with Nur ed-Din, suggesting that at least part of the information given by the Latin source was correct.[37]

What is less clear is whether we can believe the most radical of the clauses supposedly contained in the treaty, that the Byzantines and Saladin would take joint action against the kingdom of Jerusalem and, having overthrown it, partition it between themselves. If the treaty had indeed provided for such an action, it would have been unprecedented, a complete departure from traditional Byzantine foreign policy and would vindicate the claim that Andronicus's foreign policy was anti-Latin.[38]

A close examination of the exact terms of the agreement, as reported in the letter from the east, bears up neither of those interpretations. The two rulers allegedly agreed that if

> by the advice and help of that man [Saladin] the emperor were able to occupy the land of the pilgrims, the same Saladin would retain for himself other land, but Jerusalem and the all the places on the sea except Ascalon he would set free, on such condition however that he should hold it (*eam*) from the aforesaid emperor.[39]

These terms are distinctly ambiguous. The pronoun *eam* could refer either to the 'other land' (*aliam terram*) or to 'Jerusalem and all the places on the coast' (*Ierusalem et totam maritimam*), leaving the letter open to two possible interpretations. If it refers to the former, it would indeed mean that Saladin would hand Jerusalem and the coastal cities over to the emperor and that he would hold the rest of Palestine as a fief. If the latter, the meaning would be quite different: Saladin would hold most of Palestine by right of conquest, but Jerusalem and the maritime cities he would hold as a fief of the emperor.

The second interpretation is the more convincing one, as it avoids the implication that Saladin, the leader of the Muslim struggle against the infidel, was prepared to hand over a large portion of his planned conquest to a Christian emperor. Nevertheless, even if this is accepted, the arrangement still seems a peculiar one. It is by no means clear what was meant by the 'homage' that Saladin was supposed to pay to Andronicus for Jerusalem, given that it was a western term that had no validity in Muslim or Byzantine society.

It is here that the nature of the source of information has to be taken into account. Even if Magnus's informant was a Latin living in the east at the time, it is unlikely that he would have been privy to the exact details of the negotiations between two foreign powers or in a position to outline the precise details of the agreement. He was also ignorant of the terms that might have been used in such an agreement and therefore used the inappropriate vocabulary of western feudalism. What in fact he is giving us is therefore a feudal, Latin interpretation of an agreement whose basis was that if Saladin took Jerusalem, he would recognise the Byzantine emperor as Protector of the Holy Places and of the Christians living there.

If that indeed was what was meant, then Andronicus's treaty would have been nothing new, but simply a continuation of the policy that the Byzantines had been employing towards the Holy Land, and whoever ruled it, for centuries past. They had sought that recognition from the Fatimids in the eleventh century and the Latins in the twelfth. Now, possibly as an insurance policy, Andronicus I sought an undertaking from Saladin that, in the event of his coming to control Jerusalem, he would make the same concession. Neither party can have had any idea that Saladin would be in a position to grant the request within three years.[40]

The treaty with Saladin need not therefore necessarily be seen as anti-Latin. It is true that, following the death of Manuel I and the accession of a minor, Byzantium had lost some of the influence which Manuel had established in the principality of Antioch and the kingdom of Jerusalem. That influence had been secured because it brought with it powerful military and financial aid for the crusader states, which the embattled regency in Constantinople was hardly in a position to offer. Consequently, in 1180 the prince of Antioch, Bohemond III, repudiated his Byzantine wife, Theodora, another of Manuel I's apparently inexhaustible supply of nieces. With this tie broken, he started to expand his principality at the expense of Byzantine cities in Cilicia. Relations with Jerusalem worsened as the pro-Byzantine party there lost ground, culminating in the accession as king in 1186 of Guy of Lusignan, who had always been opposed to cooperation with Byzantium. That party would no doubt have been strengthened by the disturbing news from Constantinople in 1182.[41]

It is difficult to know whether Andronicus was aware of these events or not. To judge by the main Greek account of his brief reign, that of Niketas Choniates, his attention was entirely occupied first with imposing his will on his own subjects and then with invasions of his empire by the Hungarians and by the Normans of southern Italy. His negotiations with Saladin were probably not so much an attempt to obtain from the Muslims the influence in the Holy Land that was being denied by the Latins, but rather the old game of playing one side off against another, hoping that whoever came out on top, the Byzantine emperor would preserve his position of protector of the Holy Places. Unfortunately, in the highly charged atmosphere created by the massacre of 1182, which Andronicus had condoned if not orchestrated, any Byzantine dealing with Muslim powers was bound to be interpreted in the worst possible light. This is what seems to have happened here.

How Andronicus's policy might have developed in the long run is impossible to say, for he was never given the chance to take it any further. By September 1185, he was showing distinct signs of megalomania as his purges of his real, potential and imagined political opponents continued unabated. As a warning to his enemies, he had a portrait of himself painted on an outer wall of the church of the Forty Martyrs, depicting him in peasant garb, holding a sickle. There could be no doubt at whom the sickle was aimed: the grandees who had supported the previous regime. Andronicus was on record as boasting to his sons that he would rid them of giants, so that after he was gone they would have only pygmies to rule over.[42]

As the executions of members of the nobility grew ever more frequent, one individual was driven to a desperate act of rebellion. When a group of henchmen led by Stephen Hagiochristophorites was sent to arrest a young nobleman called Isaac Angelos, who was suspected of plotting against Andronicus, Angelos at first hid in his house, while his pursuers prowled around the courtyard outside. Reasoning, however, that he was likely to die anyway, Isaac crept to the stables, leapt onto a horse and charged out, brandishing a sword. Having killed Hagiochristophorites with a single blow to the head, Angelos galloped across the city to Hagia Sophia to take sanctuary. News of his exploit soon spread, and Angelos found himself the centre of popular demonstrations against Andronicus.

Fearing for his life as his troops lost control of the city to the frenzied mob, Andronicus left Constantinople by ship, taking his young wife, Agnes, his mistress and a few attendants with him, in the hope of sailing across the Black Sea to his former refuge in Russia. Unfortunately, a contrary wind prevented the ship from making much progress up the Bosporos before the pursuers arrived. Andronicus was taken prisoner and dragged back to Constantinople. Taken to the Hippodrome, the erstwhile emperor was lynched by the crowd, no doubt composed of many of the people who had welcomed him so enthusiastically four years earlier. For several days, his corpse was left hanging head down amidst the antique statues and columns. It was then taken to a nearby monastery but was not buried. It could still be peered at by the curious for many years after.[43]

As for Angelos, amid scenes of wild jubilation, he was anointed by the patriarch and found himself emperor as Isaac II. Andronicus's reign of terror was over, and the Byzantine ruling classes could now congratulate themselves on having survived his ruthless purges. Isaac II and his advisers, however, were now to inherit an unfortunate legacy from Andronicus's short tenure of office. By giving free reign to his troops in 1182, Andronicus had effectively destroyed the empire's standing in the west and sparked off the type of anti-Byzantine propaganda which could be used to justify western military action against the empire. The test for the new regime was whether it would succeed in retrieving the situation.

8

Iron not Gold

If the news of the massacre in Constantinople in 1182 was a shock to western opinion, it was to be eclipsed five years later by a far worse calamity. In the summer of 1187 Saladin invaded the kingdom of Jerusalem with a force of 20,000 men and laid siege to Tiberias. The king of Jerusalem, Guy of Lusignan, hurried to the rescue and unwisely led his army into the arid lands to the west of Lake Tiberias. When a battle was fought on 4 July on the slopes of the twin peaks known as the Horns of Hattin, the Christian army was suffering acutely from thirst and heat exhaustion and proved no match for Saladin's troops. By the end of the day, not only had King Guy and most of his leading nobles been taken prisoner but the relic of the True Cross which had accompanied the Latin army into battle was also in Muslim hands. Reynald of Châtillon, the old adversary of Manuel I, was among the prisoners, but he was swiftly executed by Saladin himself. All the Templar and Hospitaller prisoners suffered the same fate at the hands of Sufi holy men.

Having wiped out the main opposition, Saladin was able to occupy most of the kingdom of Jerusalem in the months that followed. He easily captured the castles and towns whose garrisons had been with the Christian army at Hattin and occupied the entire coast south of Tripoli. Only the port of Tyre held out, ably defended by Conrad of Montferrat, the brother of the ill-fated Renier. On 2 October Saladin captured Jerusalem itself, bringing to an end the Latin occupation of the holy city that had lasted for eighty-eight years.

The depth of the outrage and grief felt in western Europe can be gauged from the emotive language of the crusading bull *Audita tremendi*, issued by Pope Gregory VIII on 29 October 1187 in response to the arrival of news of the defeat at Hattin. Gregory, much like Urban II before him, portrayed the Muslims as 'savage barbarians thirsting after Christian blood', but he did not place the whole blame on them. Rather the defeat was the result of the sinful lapses of Christians, not just those living in the kingdom of Jerusalem but of all the faithful. The military response to Saladin's victory was therefore to be accompanied by sincere repentance.[1] There was, however, a body of opinion that placed the blame rather differently. According to Magnus of Reichersberg's correspondent, the fall of Jerusalem had been brought about by the new Byzantine emperor, Isaac II Angelos. Once he had overthrown Andronicus I, Isaac allegedly wished to have his elder brother Alexios with him in Constantinople. Alexios was, at the time, a guest at Saladin's court at Damascus, and, on receiving his brother's summons, he travelled to the port of Acre in the kingdom of Jerusalem to take ship. There, however, he was arrested on the orders of Count Raymond of Tripoli and the prince of Antioch, who had got wind of Byzantine negotiations with the Ayyubids. Isaac thereupon appealed to Saladin to attack the Latin states to liberate Alexios, and sent a fleet of eighty galleys in support. Although Isaac's fleet was destroyed off Cyprus by the Sicilian admiral Margaritone, Saladin was successful at Hattin and went on to conquer Jerusalem.[2]

There are a few elements of fact in this account that can be substantiated from other sources. Alexios Angelos does seem to have spent time in the Muslim world, either as a prisoner or as a refugee from the purges of Andronicus I. A Byzantine fleet of seventy ships was dispatched to the eastern Mediterranean in 1186 and was destroyed by Margaritone, although its objective was not the kingdom of Jerusalem but Cyprus, which was in revolt against imperial rule under Isaac Comnenus.[3] Like most of the contents of Magnus of Reichersberg's letter, however, much of this tale is clearly spurious. As the Arab writer Ibn al-Athir recounts, Saladin went to war with the kingdom of Jerusalem not at the behest of Isaac II but because of the provocations offered by Reynald of Châtillon, who preyed on the Muslim caravans that plied between Damascus and Mecca from his fortress of Karak in Transjordan.[4]

Nevertheless, in the highly-charged atmosphere that prevailed after the massacre of 1182 and the loss of Jerusalem in 1187, the story was only too likely to gain credence in some quarters, and before long further rumours were circulating that the Byzantine emperor had entered into a treaty with Saladin to prevent a crusade from reaching the Holy Land and reversing the defeat at Hattin. Many modern commentators, while rejecting the sensational elements, have accepted the general tenor of the western version of events, and have asserted that a military alliance existed between the new emperor, Isaac II Angelos, and Saladin to defeat the Third Crusade and to prevent it from recovering Jerusalem.[5] In fact, no such alliance existed in a formal sense. Isaac II and his advisers were merely pursuing the traditional foreign policy goals by tried and tested means. It was only that in the west, thanks to the events of Andronicus I's reign, these policies were now inevitably interpreted as collusion with the enemy.

It may well have been that, at the beginning of his reign, Isaac II had no idea whatsoever of the damaging rumours that were circulating. Indeed, it is likely that Saladin's victory went almost unnoticed in the empire, since at the time it was only just recovering from a major blow inflicted on it as a result of unprovoked western aggression. In June 1185 the old enemy, the Normans of southern Italy, had taken advantage of the internal disarray of the last months of the reign of Andronicus I to land an army on the Adriatic coast. They quickly captured Dyrrachion, which had successfully withstood Bohemond in 1108, and then advanced across the Balkans towards Thessalonica. After a short siege the city fell on 24 August, and its capture was accompanied by atrocities every bit as savage as those inflicted on the Latins of Constantinople in 1182.[6]

The Norman threat was ultimately contained. During November 1185 the Byzantine general Alexios Branas defeated the Norman army at Mosynopolis and Dimitrika, forcing it to withdraw and ultimately to evacuate Byzantine territory altogether. Nevertheless, the episode might well have increased the perception in the Byzantine court that western Europe presented a threat. It was in the context of the sack of Thessalonica that Choniates wrote his oft-quoted lines that:

> Between us and the Franks is set the widest gulf. We are poles apart. We have not a single thought in common. They are stiff-necked, with a proud affectation of an upright carriage and love to sneer at the modesty and smoothness of our manners. But we look upon their arrogance and boasting and pride as a flux of the snivel which keeps their noses in the air and we tread them down by the might of Christ, who giveth unto us the power to trample upon the adder and upon the scorpion.[7]

It was this fear and hatred of western Europeans in general which, it is argued, drove Isaac II into the arms of Saladin. Although, in general, he set about reversing many aspect of his predecessor's reign, bringing in new advisers, recalling those who had fled into exile and even ordering the demolition of a water tower erected by Andronicus, in one respect there was continuity. Isaac carried on with Andronicus's negotiations with Saladin. According to Magnus of Reichersberg's informant, by the time Saladin's response to Andronicus's embassy reached Constantinople in the autumn of 1185, Isaac II was safely on the throne. 'Out of fear of the Latins', the new emperor decided to ratify the treaty and set his golden seal to it.[8]

The letter of Magnus of Reichersberg's informant, and other letters sent to the west by Conrad of Montferrat, by some French envoys in Constantinople and by Queen Sibylla of Jerusalem provide further details on the negotiations. They describe how, following his capture of Jerusalem in October 1187, Saladin sent an embassy to Constantinople to announce his victory over the kingdom of Jerusalem. Isaac II hastened to respond and sent his own embassy to the sultan at Acre in early 1188 to request a renewal of the alliance and to warn him that a new crusade was being prepared in the west. Receiving confirmation that large western armies were indeed on the way to Palestine, Saladin sent ambassadors back to Constantinople to renew the alliance. This time, the terms of the alliance were as follows: Isaac was to send a hundred galleys to assist Saladin in the siege of Antioch, and he promised that he would impede the progress of any crusading army that crossed his territory. In return, Saladin was to hand the whole of the Holy Land over to the Byzantines and to turn all the churches there over to Greek clergy.

These breathless accounts of Greek perfidy include all the paraphernalia of anti-Byzantine propaganda. Isaac II had agreed to imprison any westerner in Constantinople who took the cross and had sent supplies of corn to Saladin's forces in Jerusalem, actions that were 'the height of iniquity and desolation of Christianity'. In return, Saladin had rich gifts sent to Constantinople. These included a barrel of poisoned wine to use against any passing crusader armies. So powerful was the poison that its very odour alone could kill, its efficacy having been tested on an unfortunate Frankish prisoner. Adding apostasy to treachery, the Byzantines had even allowed the sultan to send an idol to Constantinople so that it could be set up and publicly worshipped there. In return for their cooperation, the Byzantines were promised that they would receive the Holy Land from a grateful Saladin.[9]

As in the case of the alliance supposedly concluded between Saladin and Andronicus I, the account in western writings of the sultan's dealings with Isaac II is less than convincing. Many elements, like the poisoned wine, are obvious fabrications. The assertion that Saladin, who based his leadership on the *jihad* to recover the Holy Land, would be prepared, once he had conquered it, to hand it over to another Christian power is simply unbelievable. Most suspect of all is the claim that Isaac concluded the treaty with Saladin because he hated and feared Latins. In spite of the aggression of the Sicilian Normans, the policies pursued by Isaac and his advisers in the early years of his reign show a desire to conciliate western opinion reminiscent of the reign of Manuel I. Isaac opened negotiations with the Pisans and Genoese to compensate them for their losses in the massacre of 1182 and sent agents to mediate when, in 1187, another assault was mounted by the Constantinopolitans on the Italian quarter. He contracted marriage alliances with western powers, marrying his sister Theodora to Conrad of Montferrat in 1187 and his daughter Eirene to Roger, son of King Tancred of Sicily, in 1193. It is also difficult to see Isaac as anti-Latin when he, just like his predecessors, employed Latins as mercenaries, ambassadors and translators. He relied on Conrad of Montferrat to organise the defence of Constantinople during an attempted military coup in 1187, and sent an Englishman called Peter as his ambassador to Genoa in 1192.[10]

If hatred of Latins was not behind Isaac's alliance with Saladin, it is not at first sight easy to determine what was. The evidence of Latin sources cannot be checked against Byzantine sources, because the latter fail to mention the agreement with Saladin altogether, apart from a brief mention in Choniates that implies that it was a mere rumour.[11] Fortunately, however, there is some information on this later round of negotiations from Arab and Syriac sources. The work of Abu Shama (1203–67) and the biography of Saladin by his younger contemporary, Baha al-Din (1145–1234), both discuss the negotiations with the Byzantines. The only point at issue, they claim, was the mosque in Constantinople and the insistence that Friday prayer there should henceforth be said in the name of the Abbasid Caliph supported by Saladin.[12] A Christian Syriac writer indicates what it was that Isaac wanted in return for his concession over the mosque: Bar Hebraeus recorded that, after Saladin's conquest of Jerusalem, the administration of the church of the Holy Sepulchre was handed over to the Greek Patriarch. This was, of course, tantamount to the Protectorship of the Holy Places, the same concession that Isaac II's predecessors had sought from the kings of Jerusalem before 1187 and from the Fatimids before that.[13] There is no mention whatsoever in either the Arabic or Syriac accounts of any proposed military cooperation against the Third Crusade or any promise by Saladin to hand the Holy Land over to the Byzantines. It therefore seems safe to assume that no such agreement existed. Once again, it appears that the Latin reporters had picked up some genuine information about these negotiations in garbled fashion, mixed in with the horror stories. The 'idol', which Magnus's informant and Conrad of Montferrat say was sent to Constantinople, was probably a mimbar or pulpit, destined to be installed in the Constantinople mosque, which the Arab sources confirm was despatched. Two Latin accounts of the Third Crusade even mention that a mosque had recently been built in Constantinople, quite unaware that it had, in fact, been there for years.[14] The letter of Conrad of Montferrat confirms what it was that Isaac wanted in exchange, recording that once Saladin was in control of the Holy Land he would hand all its churches over to the emperor, so that the Greek rite could be celebrated in them.[15]

Thus it is not difficult to discover what had happened. Inevitably with the massacre of 1182 still fresh in their minds, Latin writers interpreted these rather limited negotiations as a sinister plot against the crusade. Moreover, just as Isaac II's implementation of traditional Byzantine policy towards a Muslim power which controlled the city of Jerusalem aroused western ire, so did his handling of the Third Crusade, which was motivated by that other perennial goal of Byzantine foreign policy, the security of the *Oikoumene* and particularly of Constantinople.

In response to Gregory VIII's appeal of late 1187, three armies were formed to undertake the expedition to recover Jerusalem from Saladin, led by the three most powerful monarchs in the west. Those under Richard I of England and Philip Augustus of France travelled to Palestine by sea and did not venture near Constantinople. The third, under the German emperor Frederick Barbarossa, planned to follow the route of the First and Second Crusades and to travel by land via Constantinople and Asia Minor.

It was widely believed in the Byzantine capital, as it had been about the First and Second Crusades, that the real motive behind the expedition of Frederick Barbarossa was the capture of Constantinople. He was, after all, an old enemy of the Byzantine empire. During the Second Crusade's passage through Byzantine territory in 1147, Barbarossa had been responsible for burning down a monastery near Adrianople in revenge for the murder of a German nobleman. On succeeding Conrad III, Frederick had done what his uncle had not and had himself crowned emperor of the Romans by the pope in 1155. His adoption of this title was a direct challenge to the Byzantine doctrine of *Translatio imperii*, which held that the only true Roman emperor was the one in Constantinople. The two emperors had also been at odds over Italy: Manuel I had supported the Italian city states in their war against Frederick and, during the 1160s, rumours had circulated in Constantinople that Barbarossa was planning an attack on the empire in revenge.[16]

It is hardly surprising that many people in Constantinople therefore viewed the prospect of Frederick marching across the Balkans at the head of a large army with some alarm. The patriarch of Constantinople, Dositheos, delivered a prophecy that Barbarossa would seize the Queen of Cities itself and would enter by the Xylokerkos postern near the Blachernae palace, prompting Isaac II to have the gateway blocked up with bricks and mortar. More seriously, information emerged that Frederick was in negotiation with the Serbs, who had recently obtained their independence from the Byzantines and who were regarded as enemies of the empire. Frederick was therefore, despite his crusading vow to go to Jerusalem, a potential threat to the *Oikoumene.*[17]

To avert the threat Isaac II decided to play the old game, much as Alexios I and Manuel I had done with earlier crusades, of weakening the crusade army to ensure that it was not in a position to attack Constantinople and of playing the crusaders off against the Muslim powers to try and derive maximum benefit for his own empire. Like his predecessors, he outwardly claimed to be giving all possible support to the enterprise. Before Frederick set out Isaac despatched the logothete of the drome, John Doukas Kamateros, with an embassy to meet the German emperor at Nuremberg in the autumn of 1188, much as Manuel I done to Louis VII at Ratisbon. An agreement was duly arrived at by which Isaac promised to give Frederick's army free passage through his empire and to provide markets, while Frederick swore to keep the peace while passing through Byzantine territory.[18]

In spite of these undertakings, Isaac was clearly determined to obstruct the German army's progress to ensure that it did not endanger the Byzantine capital. No sooner had the German army crossed the Danube into Byzantine territory in June 1189 and moved south towards Nish than clashes began to occur, first with local peasants and then with imperial troops. Prisoners taken during these skirmishes admitted that they were acting on the orders of the Byzantine authorities, much as the Pechenegs who had attacked the First Crusade had done. The promised supplies also failed to materialise, forcing the Germans to forage for food. When the German army reached Philippopolis on 24 August 1189, news arrived that Isaac II had arrested and imprisoned the ambassadors that Frederick had sent on ahead to Constantinople.[19]

The western response was predictable. As in the case of Odo of Deuil's description of the Second Crusade, Latin accounts accuse the Byzantines of having reneged on the agreement at Nuremberg. The final provocation came when Byzantine ambassadors arrived at the German camp with letters from Isaac, summarised as follows by Dietpold, bishop of Passau:

> This said king [Isaac] proudly and arrogantly referred to himself as an angel of God, the origin of our faith and emperor of the Romans. He sent to our lord emperor his greeting and said that he had heard from the kings of France and England ... that the lord emperor intended to enter Greece and that he wished, when he had overthrown and ejected the Greeks, to transfer the empire to his son, the duke of Swabia. Moreover, he said that the friendship which he had heard had been established between the lord emperor and the great kral [of Serbia] seemed to him to be very sinister and suspicious. For the rest, he added, that the lord emperor should send him hostages from his army as a mark of good faith, and having crossed the arm of St George, he should withdraw in accordance with the oath he had sworn. He added that half of the land, which our army was going to conquer from the Saracens, he wished to be assigned to his use.[20]

The letter contained nothing new. The demand for guarantees of the empire's security and for the return of any captured land were, of course, exactly those made of earlier crusading armies. Like Odo of Deuil before them, however, the Germans were deeply offended by the grandiloquent tone of these letters, in which Isaac naturally described himself as 'emperor of the Romans' but referred to Frederick as 'king of the Germans'. Even Isaac's surname of Angelos was resented because the German clerks who translated the letter took it to mean that the Byzantine emperor considered himself to be an angel.[21]

To Frederick and his followers, the Byzantines appeared to be doing everything they possibly could to provoke their fellow Christians and to prevent them from reaching the Holy Land. The apparent explanation for such conduct emerged from a tearful letter which reached the German camp from Sibylla, the former queen of Jerusalem, warning that:

> the emperor of Constantinople, the persecutor of the church of God, has entered into a conspiracy with Saladin, the seducer and destroyer of the Holy Name, against the name of our lord Jesus Christ ... I tell you truthfully that you ought to believe the most faithful bearer of this letter. For he himself witnesses what he has seen with his own eyes and heard with his own ears. This is the reason that with my head bowed to the ground and with bent knees, I ask your Magnificence that, inasmuch as you are the head of the world and the wall of the house of Israel, you should never believe the Grecian emperor.[22]

Chroniclers in the German camp were quick to see the supposed alliance with Saladin as the key to Isaac's actions. The Austrian chronicler known as Ansbert declared that the Byzantine emperor had imprisoned the German ambassadors because 'he wished to please his friend and ally the Saracen Saladin, the enemy of the cross and of all Christians'. He had even given the German envoys' best horses to some visiting ambassadors from Egypt.[23] Once the Germans believed that such a plot was afoot, their paranoia knew no bounds. Stories circulated that the patriarch of Constantinople had promised a plenary indulgence to anyone who killed a crusader, and the tale of the poisoned wine, supposedly sent by Saladin to Isaac, spread like wildfire. On one occasion, it was reported, some treacherous Greeks had left some barrels of the deadly brew in a captured town, in the hope that the Germans would drink it, but their gleeful cachinnations gave the game away. One group of Germans became convinced that some wall paintings in a church contained an incitement to the congregation to kill crusaders, and they proceeded to burn the church and lay waste the area round about.[24]

Isaac, who of course had no agreement with Saladin to molest the Third Crusade or to poison the crusaders, was only employing the standard Byzantine tactic of attempting to neutralise any potential threat to Constantinople. This time, however, the policy misfired badly, largely because the Byzantine army proved unable to fulfil the task of wearing the Germans down. Whereas Anna Comnena and John Kinnamos had been able to boast that the Byzantine forces had worsted the armies of Godfrey of Bouillon and Conrad III by superior tactics, the roles were now reversed. This time the Byzantines were not dealing with a number of contingents under their own leaders, whose disunity they could exploit, but one very large and experienced army under a leader to whom it was intensely loyal. The difference became apparent when Frederick's army clashed with a Byzantine force led by Manuel Kamytzes outside Philippopolis on 29 August 1189. Most of the Byzantine troops fled in the face of the German attack, and only the Alan mercenaries from the Caucasus put up any sustained resistance.[25] Encouraged by this proof of Byzantine weakness, Barbarossa went over to the offensive during the autumn of 1189, allowing his army to plunder the countryside of Thrace at will. On 22 November he occupied Adrianople to act as his base for the winter.[26]

Barbarossa's plans at this stage are revealed in the angry letters which he wrote to his son Henry and to Duke Leopold of Austria, complaining of what he regarded as a Byzantine breach of faith. Isaac had violated the oaths that had been sworn by his ambassador at Nuremberg and it was therefore plain that, in order to cross the straits, the Germans would have first to conquer Constantinople. Barbarossa instructed his son to contact Venice, Genoa, Ancona and Pisa to collect the necessary ships for the task. Henry was also to write to the pope and to ask him to rouse the Christian people against the Greeks, the enemies of the cross.[27]

As it happened, Frederick did not have to carry out his threat. Faced with overwhelming force, Isaac had little option but to back down. He released the imprisoned ambassadors, and, after protracted negotiations, a treaty was concluded at Adrianople in February 1190. Isaac had to agree to reverse his previous obstructionism and to facilitate the passage of the German army to Asia Minor with all the resources at his disposal. Ships were to be sent to Gallipoli to ferry the troops across the straits and markets were to be provided to supply them. He also handed over hostages and a large indemnity in the form of gold and silver coin and silk cloths.[28]

Isaac II still attempted to make capital out of the situation. As Alexios I had done, Isaac saw no reason to sacrifice his good relations with Muslim powers just because a crusade was passing through his territory. He sent letters to Saladin, warning him that a new crusade to recover Jerusalem was gathering in the west. In late 1189, while Barbarossa was still in Thrace, Isaac wrote to Saladin again. This time he gave an account of Frederick's progress through the Balkans and claimed that the Germans had been so mauled by the Byzantine army that they no longer posed a threat to the Ayyubid regime. He even implied that he had done this in accordance with an agreement with Saladin. The letter has been interpreted as a feeble attempt by Isaac to persuade Saladin to fulfil his supposed side of the bargain, as recounted by the Latin sources, and hand over the Holy Land, even though Isaac had failed, on his side, to stop Frederick Barbarossa from passing through his empire.[29] There was, however, no such agreement. What the letter was trying to do was to play Saladin off against Frederick, by claiming that the attempt to harass Frederick's army (which the Byzantines would have done anyway) was done to oblige Saladin. The ploy had been used before. Alexios I had written to the Turks of Damascus in 1110 telling them that he had tried to block the passage of the First Crusade, no doubt with the same end in view.[30]

Unfortunately for Isaac, his dealings with Saladin were ultimately no more successful than those with Barbarossa. The sultan and his advisers were not in the least taken in. They had received a much more realistic report of Frederick's passage through the Byzantine empire from the katholikos of Armenia, and dryly concluded that Isaac 'fears the Franks because of his empire and he wants to repel them; if he succeeds completely, he will claim that it is in our interest; in the opposite case, he will claim that he is far from the aim that we are both pursuing'.[31] Isaac's attempt to play Frederick off against Saladin had failed miserably. As he himself was compelled to admit, all he had obtained as a result was 'the enmity of the Franks and their kin'.[32]

That was all the more the case because Frederick Barbarossa's crusade, like that of Conrad III, was not a success. The Germans faced further difficulties once they were across the Dardanelles and on the march through Asia Minor during the spring of 1190. There were further ambushes and skirmishes, which Ansbert ascribes to the faithlessness of the Greeks, who breached the treaty once again. The might of Frederick's army, however, once more prevailed. Local resistance was swept aside, and when the Seljuk Turks offered battle Frederick captured their capital of Konya, a feat that Manuel I had never been able to achieve.[33] Saladin's recent conquests would have been put in grave jeopardy if Barbarossa had ever reached the Holy Land. In the event, the German emperor was drowned on 10 June 1190 while attempting to swim across a river in Cilicia. Thereafter his army fell victim to low morale and sickness, and only a severely reduced force finally arrived in Palestine in early 1191. As in 1148, it was not difficult to find a scapegoat for the disaster.

At the time, court circles in Byzantium probably did not realise how disastrous Isaac's handling of Frederick Barbarossa's crusade had been. Isaac himself was still riding high on his reputation for overthrowing the tyrant Andronicus and defeating the Normans of southern Italy. Eustathios of Thessalonica declared that Isaac's accession had brought 'benefit and good fortune' to the *Oikoumene*. Choniates, in one of the laudatory orations that members of the Byzantine elite were expected to produce in honour of the reigning emperor, described him in Homeric terms as the 'godlike' emperor and praised him for dealing effectively with the threat to Constantinople posed by Barbarossa.[34]

In later years, however, Choniates was to change his mind, probably as a result of the disastrous role played by Isaac in the Fourth Crusade. In his *History*, which was written or revised after 1204, Choniates portrayed Isaac as someone who was so convinced that his miraculous accession to the throne was a sign of God's favour that he believed that he could simply sit back and allow God to see to the affairs of the empire.[35] Choniates also changed his mind on the effectiveness of Isaac's dealings with Frederick Barbarossa, and the wisdom of applying traditional Byzantine foreign policy methods to passing crusades.

Choniates's attitude towards the crusades and western Europeans in general has been badly misunderstood in the past. He has been described as a 'fervent Greek patriot' who regarded all Latins as 'one hostile block', universally dedicated to the overthrow of the empire and the seizure of its riches. His failure to mention the treaty with Saladin, other than very obliquely, has been interpreted as deliberate concealment of something which he would have regarded as highly discreditable to the empire.[36]

Yet Choniates was neither a bigoted nationalist nor a deliberate liar. His *History* shows a remarkable even-handedness towards the Latins. Although he denounced the perpetrators of atrocities, such the Normans who sacked Thessalonica in 1185, he wrote enthusiastically of the bravery of other Latins such as Conrad of Montferrat, whom he compares favourably to the Byzantines. Moreover, Choniates was also prepared to criticise both the rulers and the people of his own empire and bring to light incidents which discredited them vis-à-vis the west. He admitted that the sufferings of Thessalonica at the hands of the Normans had come about partly as Latin revenge for the massacre of 1182, and he condemned the deliberate mistreatment of Norman prisoners of war captured in the victories of Alexios Branas.[37]

The importance of Choniates's *History*, however, goes far beyond its basic balance. It is from Choniates that we first discern doubts being raised inside Byzantium as to the wisdom of applying traditional Byzantine foreign policy aims and methods to crusading expeditions and to the crusader states. Those doubts can already be found in Choniates's account of the events which took place under John II and Manuel I. In 1142, he wrote, John II saw no point in entering Antioch to be 'properly venerated and honoured, only to leave without having achieved anything innovative in the public affairs of the city or having altered anything in the established customs of the city'. Choniates's words suggest that he was unconvinced of the worth of the public spectacles with which the Byzantines loved to make manifest the supremacy of their emperor. Similarly, in his account of the passage of the Second Crusade in 1147–48, he questioned some of the stratagems employed by Manuel I to turn the situation to his advantage. In stark contrast to Anna Comnena and John Kinnamos, he declared that the crusaders were absolutely sincere in their declaration that their aim was to bring assistance to the kingdom of Jerusalem, rather than to seize Constantinople, and he even showed some awareness of crusading ideology in a heroic speech placed in the mouth of Louis VII. At the same time, Choniates offered criticisms of the Byzantine treatment of the crusaders, confirming stories in the Latin accounts that the local Byzantine population joined with the Turks in attacks on the crusaders, and that they cheated them and sold them poisoned food. These 'iniquitous and unholy' deeds were not merely the work of local, rogue elements, Choniates implied, but were deliberate imperial policy designed as 'indelible memorials for posterity, deterrents against attacking the Romans'.[38] The whole passage suggests that Choniates felt that the interests of the *Oikoumene* were not well served by arousing the resentment of those who had the power to do it a great deal of harm.

That criticism rose to a crescendo in his account of the Third Crusade, which, unlike his description of the Second Crusade, was written from first-hand experience. At the time that Frederick was passing through the Balkans, Choniates was governor of Philippopolis, which lay on the route of the German army, so that he was both an eyewitness and a participant in events.[39] While the western sources portray Isaac's handling of the crusade as a sinister plot in alliance with Saladin, Choniates describes it as a fiasco, the result of a policy that was inconsistent, badly thought out and ultimately profitless. He presents Isaac's response as a hopeless mixture of bluster and indecision, largely prompted by the 'worthless' prophecies of the Patriarch Dositheos. At first, Isaac took an aggressive line. He detained Frederick's envoys in Constantinople, ordered his troops to block the mountain passes with boulders and fallen trees, and told Choniates to rebuild the walls of Philippopolis, which the Germans were fast approaching. Almost immediately, however, he countermanded his orders and commanded that the walls be pulled down, in case they provided Frederick with a place of refuge. Shifting his ground again, the emperor ordered Manuel Kamytzes to attack the Germans in August 1189, leading to the humiliating defeat of the Byzantine army near Philippopolis. Choniates describes how he and others then went to Isaac and relayed the news to him, adding that the policy of obstructing the Germans was giving rise to a rumour that Isaac was in league with Saladin and that the two rulers had sealed their pact by drinking each other's blood. Isaac was persuaded, and swung round to doing precisely the opposite of his earlier efforts. He now tried to expedite Barbarossa's passage, releasing the imprisoned envoys, handing over hostages, and promising to provide provisions and supplies for the German army. Even then, Isaac's efforts were attended by a farcical atmosphere. He had selected a number of high officials to act as hostages, but when the time came for them to go to Frederick's camp, none could be found. Humble secretaries had to be sent instead.[40]

Frederick, on the other hand, is portrayed by Choniates as a model of moderation and fidelity to his purpose, a genuine crusader whose sole aim was to aid the Christians of Palestine and who had no plans whatsoever to attack Constantinople until he was provoked. The western emperor acted properly from the beginning, sending an embassy to Constantinople to request free passage through the empire for his troops on their way to Palestine and the provision of markets. Choniates blames the Byzantines for the subsequent breakdown of the agreement. The imperial envoys, John Doukas Kamateros and Andronicus Cantacuzenus, who had been sent to facilitate Frederick's passage, 'through ignorance of their obligations and unmanliness' succeeded in provoking him and making him see the Byzantines as enemies. As a result, the oaths were broken. The Germans found themselves short of food, and were forced to forage in the countryside as they passed. Later, in April 1190, when Frederick reached Laodicea in Asia Minor, the last outpost of Byzantine territory, he proclaimed that, had he been received in the empire in peace, 'the Germans would have crossed the Roman borders long before, their lances at rest in their sheaths, without tasting the blood of Christians'. Reporting Frederick's tragic end, Choniates paid tribute to him in fulsome terms:

> He was a man who deserved to enjoy a blessed and perpetual memory and justly to be deemed fortunate in his end by prudent men, not only because he was well-born and ruled over many nations as an heir of the third generation but also because his burning passion for Christ was greater than that of any other Christian monarch of his time. Setting aside fatherland, royal luxury and repose, the worldly happiness of enjoying the company of his loved ones at home, and his sumptuous way of life, he chose instead to suffer affliction with the Christians of Palestine for the name of Christ and due regard for his life-giving tomb.[41]

Choniates's account of the Third Crusade is startling in its contrast to those of Anna Comnena on the First and Kinnamos on the Second. While they praise the actions of the Byzantine emperors and portray the crusaders as a potential threat to the *Oikoumene*, Choniates does precisely the opposite, making the western ruler the hero of the episode and the Byzantine emperor an incompetent fool. The differences, however, go even deeper than that. It was not simply that the earlier authors had admired the emperors of whom they wrote, while Choniates despised Isaac II. Choniates goes beyond criticism of an individual emperor to call into question the very diplomatic practices which had regulated Byzantium's relations with its neighbours for so long.

To take just one example, he criticises the Byzantine custom of making envoys stand in the presence of the emperor, a practice which was patently designed to reflect the right order of things but which inevitably aroused resentment from westerners. According to Choniates, when the German envoys were finally released and returned to Frederick at his camp, the western emperor was furious to hear that they had been made to stand in Isaac's presence. He made a point of having them sit down with him, even the cooks and grooms, 'to mock the Romans and to show that there was no distinction among them in virtue and family'. How different from the self-assurance of Anna Comnena in her scandalised account of the arrogant Latinus, who broke the rules and sat down on the emperor's throne while Alexios I himself was still on his feet.[42]

Such critical passages recur as the *History* proceeds, another instance being the description of the reception of a German embassy during the 1190s. The Byzantine emperor, by this time Isaac II's brother Alexios III (1195–1203), resorted to the tried and tested technique of overawing the barbarian with wealth and magnificence. Meeting the German envoys on Christmas day 1196, he and his courtiers donned their finest robes and jewels. The tactic proved a mistake and quite inappropriate for the circumstances. The envoys were unimpressed and announced dryly:

> The Germans have neither need of such spectacles, nor do they wish to become worshippers of ornaments and garments secured by brooches suited only for women whose painted faces, headdresses and glittering earrings are especially pleasing to men ... The time has now come to take off effeminate garments and brooches, and to put on iron instead of gold.[43]

For Choniates, the message was clear. Byzantine diplomacy was a fatal mix of swaggering arrogance and abject submission, and completely unsuited to the situation in which the empire now found itself.

In all probability, as has been said, Choniates arrived at that conclusion after having witnessed the sack of Constantinople in April 1204. Yet already, during the Third Crusade, an incident occurred which provided a stark warning of how Byzantine foreign policy was providing western Europeans with all the justification they needed for aggression towards the empire.

Shortly after the death of Barbarossa, in July 1190, the English and French fleets carrying the armies of Richard the Lionheart and Philip Augustus joined up at Marseilles, and set out on their sea journey to Palestine. After wintering at Messina, the French contingent reached Acre in April 1191, while the English fleet followed on behind. The reason for Richard's delay was a detour made to the island of Cyprus.

Officially, Cyprus formed part of the Byzantine empire, but since 1184 it had been under the rule of Isaac Comnenus, a renegade member of the previous imperial dynasty, who had proclaimed himself emperor in opposition to Andronicus I. On 6 May Richard landed with his troops at Limassol, and, after a short and easy campaign, defeated Isaac Comnenus's army and occupied the island. Isaac took refuge in a castle, but is said to have agreed to surrender provided that Richard would promise not to put him in chains of iron. Once he had Isaac in his hands, Richard had special silver chains made and locked him up in those.

This was no mere raid like that of Reynald of Châtillon in 1156. Although Richard himself left for the Holy Land within a few weeks, he clearly intended that the island should remain in western hands. Shortly after his departure, he sold all his rights in Cyprus to the Knights Templar for 100,000 Saracen bezants. The Templars then governed the island until April 1192 but they were not effective rulers. They did not send enough troops and the people of Nicosia rose up against them. The master of the Templars thereupon realised that his order was not up to the task, and surrendered the island back to Richard. Richard now sold the island again, this time to Guy of Lusignan, the former king of Jerusalem, whose family were to rule the island until 1489.[44]

This was the first time that a crusading army had seized territory directly from the Byzantines and held onto it. Such an action had to be justified somehow, since knights who had taken the cross were supposed to fight against infidels and not against their fellow Christians. The immediate *casus belli* was apparently the result of a storm which drove some of the ships in Richard's fleet onto the coast of Cyprus. Isaac Comnenus had the crews imprisoned and maltreated, and also made attempts to capture a ship carrying Richard's sister, Joanna, and his bride-to-be Berengaria of Navarre. In a letter of August 1191 to his justiciar in England, Richard cited this as his justification for landing on Cyprus and overthrowing the usurper.[45]

The western chroniclers who record these events, however, clearly felt that further justification was needed. They therefore availed themselves of all the stock in trade of anti-Byzantine propaganda of the crusading period. In the first place, Isaac Comnenus hated the Latins and was always on the look out for some way of doing them harm. He had killed his own wife and son because the latter had confessed to liking westerners. He was an enemy of the Christian faith: he would stand at the altar on Good Friday and expect people to bow down and worship him. He mistreated pilgrims to the Holy Land, having those who were unfortunate enough to land on his island rounded up and beheaded. Like his counterpart in Constantinople, he had failed to assist the crusade and had withheld supplies from crusaders fighting in the Holy Land. Finally, he was friendly with Saladin, and the two rulers had undergone a ceremony of drinking each other's blood as a sign that they were allies.[46]

Alongside these familiar and ludicrous slurs, a new justification for action against the Greeks during a crusade appears for the first time. The chroniclers often commented that Cyprus was a wealthy island, 'stuffed with much treasure and various riches'. Lest their master Richard be accused of wanting to take the place out of greed, however, they were at pains to point out that this wealth was of immense value to the crusade. Cyprus was close to the Syrian coast and in the past Jerusalem 'used to receive no little benefit each year' from Cyprus. Moreover, although Richard kept the gold, silk and jewels that he captured for himself, he passed on the silver and food supplies to his men. Attacking Byzantine territory was therefore justified if it provided financial or strategic advantages for the crusaders.[47]

It is unlikely that Choniates or any other Byzantine saw the significance of conquest of Cyprus at the time. The two surviving Byzantine accounts of Richard's invasion are both strongly prejudiced against Isaac Comnenus and show no sympathy to him in his downfall. The monk Neophytos (1134–*c.* 1214), a recluse who spent most of his life living in a cave on Cyprus, called the seizure of the island by Isaac Comnenus a disaster and describes how Isaac plundered and mistreated his own people. Choniates spoke of the 'horrors wickedly inflicted on the Cypriots' by their 'master and destroyer'. Neither takes the opportunity to vent their spleen on Richard, though Neophytos describes him as a wretch and a sinner.[48] The government in Constantinople reacted to the seizure of Cyprus in much the same way as it had to the occupation of Antioch by Bohemond in 1098. Diplomatic efforts were launched to find allies who would help to get it back. As usual the Byzantines cast their net widely in their attempt to defend the *Oikoumene.* Embassies were sent to both Saladin and the pope in Rome, though neither showed any interest in helping to recover the island.[49]

It is likely from the western point of view, too, that the significance of the capture of Cyprus was not immediately appreciated. After his victory,

Richard departed for the Holy Land and to the siege of Acre, which surrendered to the crusaders on 12 July 1191. The subsequent campaign did not succeed in retaking Jerusalem itself, but it did re-establish Latin control of the coast and save the kingdom of Jerusalem from the extinction with which it had been threatened at the end of 1187. Until Jerusalem was retaken, however, the task could not be regarded as complete. Thus after the departure of Richard I from Acre, in September 1192, further plans were soon afoot for another expedition to finish the job. In all those plans the wealth and resources of the Byzantine empire, like those of Cyprus, were seen by many in the west as providing vital support for the enterprise. It can, therefore, hardly be maintained that what happened next was merely a series of accidents.

9

The Fall of Constantinople

The Byzantines knew that their diplomacy had backfired on them. That much is obvious from the plaintive remark of Isaac II in his letter to Saladin that his action had earned him 'the enmity of the Franks and their kin.'[1] The sophisticated game that they had played had created a strong impression in western Europe that Byzantium was working against efforts to recover Jerusalem and was guilty of collusion with the Muslims. Unfortunately, while the Byzantine elite had realised that the old policy had not worked, they had nothing with which to replace it. In the years leading up to the sack of Constantinople in April 1204, they appear to have been increasingly gripped by a collective paralysis, sometimes sticking to traditional methods, sometimes attempting to revive the conciliatory tone of Manuel I, and often doing nothing whatsoever. They simply seem to have run out of ideas as their empire and ideology crumbled before their eyes.

Attempts were made to stave off the threat. In the aftermath of the Third Crusade, Isaac II and his advisers tried to repair the damage caused by the treaty with Saladin and the bungled attempt to block the passage of Frederick Barbarossa's army. In a letter to the pope, drawn up by the courtier Demetrius Tornikios between 1191 and 1195, Isaac returned to the tone of Manuel I and attempted to present himself in a guise acceptable to western opinion, maintaining earnestly that the fate of the Holy Places touched him most deeply and afflicted him with constant sadness.[2]

Isaac had, however, run out of time to make up for his disastrous dealings with Frederick Barbarossa. In April 1195, while he was hunting at Kypsella in Thrace, his elder brother Alexios and a group of conspirators seized the imperial regalia which had been left behind in a tent. Isaac returned from his exertions to discover that his brother had been proclaimed emperor. In an attempt to ride his way out of trouble, as he had ten years before, Isaac tried to lead a charge on the camp but none of his servants would follow him, compelling him to make an ignominious flight on horseback. Overtaken by Alexios's supporters and taken to a monastery close by, he suffered the fate of so many deposed Byzantine emperors and was blinded, such mutilation being deemed a disqualification for imperial office. He was then taken back to Constantinople to be imprisoned first in the dungeons beneath the palace of Boukoleon, and then at Diplokionion on the Bosporos. Isaac was less than forty years old at the time of his overthrow and, in spite of his blinding, was still destined to play an important part in events leading up to the sack of Constantinople in 1204.[3]

Once in power Alexios III pursued much the same line of policy as his brother had and went even further in his efforts to build bridges with the west, perhaps because his position was weaker. To the usual charges of collusion with infidels and schism with Rome, Alexios had added a third by making himself emperor 'by treason'. Consequently, all three elements which had been used by Bohemond to justify his attack on the empire in 1107, that the emperor was a usurper, that he was a schismatic, and that he had worked against the cause of the crusade, were once more in place, and Alexios III, like Alexios I Comnenus before him, had to do something to defuse the anti-Byzantine propaganda that was circulating in the west.[4] He did this by contacting the pope, sending ambassadors to Rome in February 1199 bearing precious gifts for the newly-elected Innocent III (1198–1216). The ambassadors carried letters from the patriarch of Constantinople, John X Kamateros, and one from Alexios himself in which, like his brother Isaac, he expressed pious concern at the fate of the Holy Sepulchre and sincere hopes for its recovery. Alexios was, however, careful not to commit Byzantium to any crusading enterprise. The precise moment when Jerusalem would be recovered for Christianity was, he hastened to say, in the hands of God and he took the opportunity to complain about the behaviour of Frederick Barbarossa's army when it traversed the empire in 1189–90. No doubt with a view to removing the charge of schism, Alexios also raised the question of a reunion of the churches and asked the pope to call a council for this purpose.[5]

These initiatives were hardly original, but at least they showed some appreciation of the situation. Choniates, however, was not impressed. He later condemned the emperors of the Angelos family and their advisers as supine, because they failed to do anything to deal with the threat from the west. He was particularly scathing about Alexios III. According to Choniates, once Alexios was safely in power, he completely neglected affairs of state, like a steersman who lets go of the ship's tiller.[6] These jaundiced comments should be treated with some caution, since Choniates was writing at the court of Alexios's son-in-law and rival for power, Theodore Laskaris. Nevertheless, even if Choniates's political bias and bureaucratic prejudices are discounted, the impression remains of inactivity as the storm gathered.

The driving force behind the storm was the problem of financing the effort being put together to retake Jerusalem. The famous story that Richard the

Lionheart would have sold London to pay for his crusade, if he could have found a buyer, may be apocryphal but it highlights the sheer difficulty faced by the primitive economies of western Europe in providing the money to equip and transport large armies to a field of action far from home. Taxes, like the 'Saladin tithe' levied in England and France in 1188, were unpopular and sometimes impossible to collect. Most crusaders simply paid their own way, but that often meant that they ran short of funds and experienced considerable privation and hardship during the campaign. They were also vulnerable to natural disasters, like the sudden downpour which soaked and ruined the food supply of Richard I's army in the Holy Land. No wonder that in his letters, sent back to the west in 1191–92, Richard had complained that many of his vassals would not be able to stay on the campaign, unless further supplies of money were sent.[7]

In the years after the Third Crusade, however, a solution to the problem seemed to present itself. In the light of the spurious stories of Byzantium's dealings with Saladin, the perception had arisen in the west that the empire should atone for its previous conduct by making its immense resources freely available for the purposes of a crusade. That conclusion was made all the more attractive by the empire's obvious weakness by 1195, in stark contrast to the position under John II and Manuel I. The first signs of the decline in Byzantine power had appeared in the last years of Manuel's reign. In 1176 Manuel had suffered a serious defeat by the Seljuk Turks at the battle of Myriokephalon, a setback which greatly diminished the empire's military prestige. Internal political instability followed Manuel's death, with no less than six emperors acceding and subsequently being deposed in the period 1180–1204. In addition there were numerous military revolts as generals and noblemen attempted to seize Constantinople and usurp the throne.

Instability at the centre was matched by separatism in the provinces. The large army amassed by the Comnenian emperors had to be paid for by ever more stringent tax demands. These inevitably aroused resentment. In 1185 the attempt to impose a new tax caused Bulgaria to rise in revolt and ultimately to break away from imperial rule. In other areas, local magnates seized power from the imperial authority, as did Isaac Comnenus on the island of Cyprus in 1184 and Theodore Mangaphas in the city of Philadelphia in Asia Minor in 1188.[8]

The internal disarray of the empire played into the hands of western aggressors, providing an excuse for military intervention. This was amply demonstrated during the Norman invasion of the Balkan provinces in 1185. The irony was that to some extent the Normans were invited in by the Byzantines themselves. During Andronicus I's reign of terror in 1183–85, many of his potential victims had fled from Constantinople to Rome, Konya, Antioch, Jerusalem or any court that would receive them. Two of them, Alexios Comnenus and Maleinos of Philippopolis, went to King William II of Sicily and begged for his help in overthrowing Andronicus, thus providing him with the perfect cloak for his invasion of the Byzantine empire in June 1185. Even after Andronicus's overthrow in September of that year, a number of young men claiming to be the murdered Alexios II were moving around Asia Minor, attempting to incite local Muslim rulers to intervene in the empire on their behalf.[9]

Those who did lead armies into Byzantine territory soon discovered that the empire was in no position to defend itself. The Normans enjoyed striking initial success in their 1185 invasion. Meeting little resistance, they were able to march straight to Thessalonica, the empire's second city, and to capture it after only a short siege, a feat that neither Bohemond nor Roger II had come close to. Frederick Barbarossa's army swept aside the ill-judged resistance of Isaac II's army four years later. These events were carefully noted by outside observers and it was concluded at the court of Saladin that nothing was to be gained from the emperor's friendship and nothing to be feared from his enmity.[10] Nor was it lost on the west. While Byzantium's disastrous diplomacy and reputation for collusion with the enemy had provided a justification for aggression, its weakness furnished an opportunity, and its wealth an incentive.

The first to avail himself of the opportunity was the son and successor of Frederick Barbarossa, Henry VI (1190–97), who was not only western emperor but, from 1194, was also master of the Norman kingdom of Sicily. On Good Friday 1195 Henry had assumed the cross at Bari, taking advantage of the favourable situation presented by the death of Saladin in 1193 and the disunity among the late sultan's heirs. Almost immediately, Henry sent envoys to Constantinople to deliver what amounted to an ultimatum. The envoys laid formal claim to all the land between Dyrrachion and Thessalonica that had briefly been occupied by the forces of William II in 1185. It appears, however, that Henry's main aim was not the conquest of the Byzantine empire but the threat of doing so in order to extort Byzantine help for his proposed crusade. His envoys called for Byzantine ports to be put in readiness to receive Henry's fleet and for Byzantine ships to join the expedition, as well as the payment of five thousand pounds of gold. If the Byzantines failed to deliver, the envoys grimly warned, Henry would 'come and pay you a visit in your empire'.[11]

Alexios III and his advisers were well aware that they would not be able to resist Henry VI if he invaded to enforce his demands. An attempt was made to negotiate and a Byzantine envoy, Eumathios Philokales, succeeded in getting the tribute reduced to one thousand pounds of gold. This small success apart, Alexios III now had no option but to give way and to raise the tribute demanded. A special tax, the *Alamanikon* or German tax, was levied on the provinces to meet the demand, and the gold and silver ornaments on the tombs of long dead emperors were plundered to provide further funds, only that of Constantine the Great in the church of the Holy Apostles being spared by imperial decree.[12]

In the event, the gathered treasure never had to be despatched because, on 28 September 1197, Henry VI suddenly died at the age of only thirty-three. The precedent had, however, been set. Byzantium was expected to demonstrate its commitment to the cause of Christendom by putting its hand in its pocket, and was to be threatened with force if it failed to comply.

The example of Henry VI was followed by another great western potentate, Pope Innocent III. At the very beginning of his pontificate, on 15 August 1198, Innocent preached a new crusade as another attempt to recapture Jerusalem. From the first, Innocent appears to have wanted to keep the new crusade, known to posterity as the Fourth Crusade, under his own overall command. He therefore had far more to do with mundane matters of supply than most previous popes.

That involvement emerges from a letter sent by Innocent to Alexios III in November 1199. In many respects, the pope's letter was most restrained and conciliatory. He made no mention of the pact with Saladin or even the supposed complicity of the emperor in the loss of Jerusalem, perhaps because he was suspicious of some of the ludicrous stories that were circulating. He even allowed the version of the clash with Frederick I given by Alexios in a previous letter, which accused the western emperor of breaking the agreement, to go by uncorrected, no doubt because, as a Staufer and frequent enemy of the papacy, Frederick was hardly entitled to Innocent's sympathy. But in other respects Innocent's letter was uncompromising. After briefly congratulating Alexios on his dutiful approach to the Apostolic See, Innocent sternly warned him that the Byzantines must put an end to the schism, by bringing the Byzantine church back to Rome 'like a limb to the head and a daughter to the mother'. As regards the recovery of Jerusalem, Innocent had little time for the suggestion made by Alexios that the matter should be left in the hands of God:

> If you wish to wait, because the time of the redemption of that same land is unknown to men, and do nothing by yourself, leaving all things to divine disposition, the Holy Sepulchre may be delivered from the hands of the Saracens without the help of your aid. Therefore through negligence your Imperial

> Magnificence will incur divine wrath, when through solicitude you could have merited the gratitude of the Lord.[13]

Precisely what kind of assistance Innocent had in mind that Alexios would provide for the forthcoming crusade is not spelt out specifically, but the use of the word *subventio* seems to suggest that financial aid was meant. As Innocent had already told Alexios in an earlier letter, a pious Byzantine emperor would use his ample resources to assist the cause of the crusade. Any hope that the Byzantine emperor might have had that he could lie low and not become involved in the preparations for another assault on the Holy Land was dispelled once and for all. His financial contribution was expected and demanded with the full authority of the successor of St Peter.[14]

There remained, however, the question of what was to be done if the emperor failed to do his Christian duty. As a priest, Innocent could hardly express himself in the same brutal terms as those used by Henry VI. Nevertheless, in November 1202 he issued to Alexios III what amounted to a thinly veiled threat:

> Even though, from the time of Manuel, your predecessor of honoured memory, the empire of Constantinople has not deserved such as we ought [otherwise] to have effected because it has always answered us and our predecessors with words and not backed them up with deeds, nevertheless we have set a policy of proceeding in a spirit of mildness and gentleness, believing that, when you have considered the favour of how much we have done for you, you ought all the more quickly to correct what has thus far been less prudently neglected by you and your predecessors. For you ought most zealously to attend to this as human energy allows so that you might be able to extinguish or feed the fire in distant regions lest it be able in some measure to reach all the way to your territories.[15]

The threat is perfectly clear under the verbiage. If Byzantium failed to cooperate, it could expect to meet force. What kind of force Innocent had in mind was discussed in the instructions which he sent to the leaders of the Fourth Crusade in June 1203. Anticipating that the army might run short of food, Innocent undertook to write to the Byzantine emperor and to ask him to make the necessary supplies available. If, however, the emperor, like his predecessors, failed to perform his Christian duty in this respect, Innocent had his response ready: 'Necessity, especially when one is occupied in necessary work, excuses much in many situations'. If the emperor attempted to impede the crusaders' journey, as had his predecessors, military action would be justified.[16]

Innocent was not urging a full-scale assault on Constantinople. He insisted that he was not countenancing rapine but 'tolerating what, in the face of grave necessity, cannot be avoided without serious loss'. His aim was clearly to extract assistance and church union from Alexios III, and he probably believed that this could be done without resort to force. That would certainly explain why, in June 1203, Innocent warned the crusade leaders that neither the schism nor the usurpation of Alexios III gave them any justification for intervening in the Byzantine empire. Their task was to liberate Jerusalem and they were not to allow themselves to be deviated from it.[17]

In spite of this specific prohibition, it is not difficult to imagine how Innocent's earlier words were interpreted in the crusade army. Gunther of Pairis was convinced that the pope had permitted the crusaders to take 'half a year's supply of free food' from the Byzantine coast, that Innocent III hated Constantinople, and that he wanted the city to be captured, provided that this could be achieved without bloodshed.[18] Innocent's letters therefore contained an ambivalence which allowed the crusade leadership, and the clergy who were travelling with the army, to argue that an attack on the Byzantine capital was not only justified, but laudable. All these justifications were to be brought to bear in April 1204, when the Fourth Crusade captured and sacked Constantinople.

In addition to Henry VI and Innocent III, there was a third western ruler who saw the Byzantine empire as a way of financing the reconquest of Jerusalem. This was Boniface, marquis of Montferrat, who, following the death of Count Thibaut III of Champagne in May 1201, was elected as leader of the gathering crusade in September.[19] The Montferrat family had long-standing connections with Constantinople. Boniface's younger brother, Renier, had married the daughter of Manuel I in 1180 and had perished in the purges which followed the usurpation of Andronicus I. Another brother, Conrad, had gone out to Constantinople in 1187, married the sister of Isaac II and saved his brother-in-law from an attempted coup by Alexios Branas. Conrad, however had not remained long in Constantinople. He departed for Palestine in high dudgeon because he considered that his talents had not been sufficiently rewarded. There he saved Tyre from Saladin's army and was eventually chosen to succeed as king of Jerusalem. Before he could be crowned, however, he fell victim to an assassin's knife on 28 April 1192.

Given those connections, Boniface has always been seen as one of the prime movers behind the diversion of the Fourth Crusade to Constantinople. A contemporary chronicler and participant in the crusade, the Picard knight Robert of Clari, asserted that Boniface's motive in going to Constantinople was that he bore a grudge against the Byzantine emperor because of the ungrateful treatment of Conrad. Another chronicler, the monk Robert of Torigny (d. 1186), recorded another motive. When Renier had married the Porphyrogenita Maria, the Emperor Manuel had granted his new son-in-law the city of Thessalonica, probably as some kind of *pronoia* or fief. In view of the fact that, after the Fourth Crusade, Boniface did indeed end up as king of Thessalonica, both opinion in the papal curia in the early thirteenth century and more recent commentators have seen a desire to cash in on his family's eastern inheritance behind Boniface's support for the diversion.[20]

Neither personal vendetta nor territorial ambition, however, is a convincing explanation. The emperor who had slighted Conrad, Isaac II, was now languishing in prison, and the diversion of the Fourth Crusade, rather than wreaking vengeance on him, rescued him and restored him to his throne. As for territorial ambitions, it is quite clear that Boniface received Thessalonica after 1204 not as a long desired prize, but as a consolation after he had been outmanoeuvred by Baldwin of Flanders and the Venetians in the election for the new Latin emperor of Constantinople.[21] It is far more likely that Boniface, who was after all in a very good position to appreciate the wealth and resources of Constantinople, saw the diversion as a means of financing the crusade and of ensuring that it would reach the Holy Land. In a letter to Innocent III of August 1203, Boniface explained the decision to go to Constantinople in exactly those terms.[22] Like Henry VI and Innocent III, however, Boniface no doubt also believed that resort to force would be justified if the sought-after supplies were not forthcoming. Moreover, like William II of Sicily, he had a pretext for his intervention.

At the time that the Fourth Crusade was being planned in the west, not only was the former Isaac II still a prisoner, but so was his young son Alexios. For some inexplicable reason, Alexios III decided to release his nephew and to allow him to accompany the imperial army on a campaign to put down a rebellion in Thrace. This proved to be a great mistake. Prince Alexios succeeded in escaping from the army and persuading the captain of a Pisan ship to hide him on the vessel as it set sail for Italy from the port of Athyra on the Sea of Marmara. By one account, Alexios was hidden in a barrel with a false bottom. After an anxious moment, when the ship was stopped by an imperial warship and searched, Alexios arrived safely at the Italian port of Ancona in the early autumn of 1201.[23]

Like so many of the losers in Byzantine political upheavals had done before him, Prince Alexios now sought help from foreign powers. At some point, he went to Rome, but he was unable to interest Innocent III in his cause.[24] He had more luck when he travelled into northern Italy, where the army of the Fourth Crusade was assembling at Venice under its recently elected leader Boniface of Montferrat. Stopping at Verona, Prince Alexios met members of the army en route for Venice and his companions advised him that this force might be able to help him against his uncle. Alexios therefore made an approach to Boniface and the other leaders, who were extremely interested in what he had to say. The message was sent back: 'If your young lord will agree to help us reconquer Jerusalem, we in our turn will help him regain his empire.' The leaders then sent envoys with him on the next stage of his journey, which was north to the court of Philip of Swabia, brother of the late Emperor Henry VI, and claimant to the western empire, at Hagenau on the Rhine. Alexios no doubt chose this destination because Philip was the second husband of his sister, Eirene. At Christmas 1201, Alexios was joined at Hagenau by Boniface of Montferrat.[25]

It is impossible to know exactly what was said during the discussions at Hagenau, but it is not difficult to guess. The two children of Isaac II would have been anxious to secure his restoration, while Philip of Swabia, the son and brother of prominent crusade leaders, and Boniface of Montferrat, the elected leader of the new crusade, would have wanted supplies for the expedition. Subsequent events certainly bear out this interpretation.

The need for Byzantine wealth was all the greater because the Fourth Crusade had been plagued by shortage of finance from the very beginning. Unlike the Third Crusade and the expedition organised by Henry VI, both of which mounted a direct assault on the Holy Land, the plan now was that the army would sail to the Nile Delta in Egypt where it would disembark, conquer the country, and use it as a base from which to march on Jerusalem.[26] The plan naturally necessitated a large fleet which was likely to cost a great deal.

The only western power which possessed ships in the required numbers was Venice. In April 1201, Geoffrey of Villehardouin, marshal of Champagne and author of an account of the crusade, and five other envoys therefore negotiated a treaty with the doge, Enrico Dandolo. In return for the sum of eighty-five thousand marks, Venice would provide transport for four thousand five hundred knights and their horses, nine thousand squires and twenty thousand foot soldiers to Egypt. The problem was that, when the crusading army arrived in Venice and was quartered nearby, its numbers amounted to only a third of the projected force. Since it had been agreed that each soldier would pay for his own passage, the crusaders found themselves thirty-five thousand marks short of the sum they had promised.[27] The Venetians reluctantly allowed the crusaders to postpone their payment if they would assist in the capture of the town of Zara (Zadar) on the Dalmatian coast, which had defected from Venetian allegiance in 1186. Zara was taken by the combined Venetian and crusader force on 24 November 1202, but the financial problem remained. The debt to the Venetians had only been postponed, while during the winter of 1202–3, when the army was quartered at Zara, supplies began to run dangerously low. According to Robert of Clari, many men on the expedition had 'neither money nor provisions to maintain themselves'.[28]

It was at this point that the proposal to divert to Constantinople first emerged publicly. In January 1203, some envoys sent by Philip of Swabia arrived in Zara, bringing a message on behalf of Alexios Angelos. Through the envoys, Prince Alexios promised that, if the crusaders' fleet would accompany him to Constantinople and restore Isaac II to the throne, Alexios would see to it that the schism was brought to an end and the Byzantine church placed under the authority of the pope. Of more immediate interest, he promised that he would relieve the current financial crisis by handing over two hundred thousand silver marks and providing ample supplies for every man in the army. He also undertook to go with the crusader host to Egypt, at the head of a contingent of ten thousand men. Once that campaign was over, he would maintain a corps of five hundred knights in the Holy Land to assist in its defence.[29] In short, the Byzantine prince was promising to turn the Byzantine empire from obstructing the crusades, as it was perceived to have done in the past, to being an active participant in them.

Yet Alexios's proposal by no means met with unanimous approval. One of the prime motives for participation in a crusade was to obtain remission of sin through the indulgence offered by the pope to those who fought to defend the Holy Land. Many feared that by going elsewhere they would miss out on this spiritual benefit. Even the plan to attack Muslim Egypt had been controversial, so that the leaders had initially kept it secret.[30] The news that it was now planned to go to a Christian city therefore aroused vociferous opposition, led by the Cistercian abbot Guy of Vaux. The debate raged on for several months. When the fleet moved on from Zara to Corfu, a large group staged a kind of sit-down protest, declaring that they would remain on the island until ships could be found to take them to Brindisi, from where they could make their own way to the Holy Land. Between January and April, a considerable number of crusaders, including the prominent noblemen Simon of Montfort and Enguerrand of Boves, carried out their threat and left the army.[31]

On the other hand, Alexios's proposal had the support of all the leaders, that is the doge, Enrico Dandolo, Baldwin of Flanders, Louis of Blois, Hugh of Saint-Pol and, of course, Boniface of Montferrat, and they employed every resource at their disposal in order to convince the rank and file. Their argument was in part a strategic one. Earlier crusaders had gone directly to Syria but had achieved nothing: only by going via Constantinople could success be ensured. The latter option was presented as a roundabout route to Jerusalem similar to that originally planned via Egypt. More telling for most of the soldiers, however, was the argument that it was better to go to Constantinople than to die of hunger. Spiritual doubts were addressed by the abbot of Loos and the bishops with the army who urged that it would not be sinful to go to Constantinople but a righteous deed because it would be the best way to win back Jerusalem. When all else failed, the leaders resorted to emotional blackmail. Boniface went down on his knees before the recalcitrants and begged them not to abandon the enterprise, causing them to burst into tears and to agree to stay with the army until Michaelmas, provided that afterwards ships were then provided to take them to Syria.[32] The principle that Byzantium should supply the crusade therefore won the day, albeit with some difficulty. It remained to be seen whether the army could be persuaded to take the next step and resort to force if the emperor failed to deliver.

Villehardouin and Robert of Clari record the voyage of the crusading fleet to Constantinople as a stirring event. The ships departed from Corfu on a fine and sunny day, propelled by a favourable wind, 'so fine a sight that had never been seen before'. So impressive did they look that, when they passed two ships returning from Syria, a sergeant on board one of them deserted his companions and rowed across to the larger fleet, announcing 'I'm going with these people, for it certainly seems to me they'll win some land for themselves'. Meanwhile, Prince Alexios had set out from Germany and had reached Zara, where he was met by the doge and Boniface. He was conveyed from there to Dyrrachion, in Byzantine territory, where he was joyfully recognised by the local people as the lawful emperor, and on then to join the main army. Over the next few weeks the fleet sailed up the Aegean and into the Sea of Marmara. On 23 June the ships dropped anchor at St Stephen's abbey, seven miles south-west of Constantinople, but still affording a good view of the imposing Sea Walls and the sheer size of the city.[33]

In spite of the appearance of this formidable force, however, Choniates says that nobody inside the walls took any notice of their arrival. Rather than making any preparations, Alexios III 'sat back like a spectator'.[34] When his response finally came, it was entirely predictable. An envoy was despatched to Boniface of Montferrat and the other leaders at their newly established base in a palace at Chalcedon, on the opposite side of the Bosporos from Constantinople. To undertake the mission, Alexios chose one of the many Latins in his service, a Lombard named Nicholas Roux, who delivered the following message:

> My lords, the Emperor Alexios has sent me to say he is well aware that, next to kings, you are the noblest men alive, and come from the best country in the world. He therefore seriously wonders why, and for what purpose, you have

> entered this land over which he rules. For you are Christians just as he is, and he knows very well that you have left your own country to deliver the Holy Land oversea, and the Holy Cross and Sepulchre. If you are poor and in want of supplies, he will give you a share of his provisions and his money, provided you withdraw from his land. If you refuse to leave, he would be reluctant to do you harm, yet it is in his power to do so.[35]

With its mixture of flattery, bribery and threat, the message delivered by Roux was classic Byzantine diplomacy. He came armed with gifts and promises of gold and silver, although these were refused, because 'we did not want the Greeks to solicit or soften us with their gifts'.[36] Roux was sent away with the uncompromising message that Alexios must yield the throne to his nephew. The leaders knew now that they could extort much more than the usual baubles.

With this overture repulsed, Alexios III had no other plan to fall back on. He now sat behind the walls of Constantinople and waited for the crusaders to take the initiative. His forces around the city made little attempt to interfere with the western fleet or the troops who had landed and they withdrew precipitately when attacked themselves. The Latins were therefore able to occupy the north shore of the Golden Horn. After an attempt to persuade the citizens of Constantinople to open their gates voluntarily to Prince Alexios evoked no response, the crusaders mounted an attack. The first objective was to bring the fleet into the Golden Horn, where it could mount an assault on the weaker Sea Walls along that side of the city. Entrance to the Golden Horn was sealed off by a chain strung between two towers on either side of the strait. The crusaders captured the tower on the Galata side, when the garrison ill-advisedly sallied out to attack them. The chain was then uncoupled, allowing the Venetian ships to sail in unopposed. Choniates, full of indignation at Alexios III's inaction, described the chaotic rout that ensued as the Byzantine ships in the Golden Horn were either captured or grounded themselves on the beaches.[37]

Similarly incompetent resistance was offered when, on 17 July 1203, the fleet attacked the city in earnest for the first time, directing the main offensive against the walls along the Golden Horn, with scaling ladders mounted on the turrets over the prows of the ships. Choniates claims that Alexios III, who had already decided on flight, took no part in resisting the onslaught. As far as Choniates was concerned, by allowing the Venetian fleet to reach the Sea Walls at all, Alexios had brought matters to a pass where remedy was fast becoming impossible. These events were also having a serious effect on Byzantine morale. Villehardouin describes how the people of Constantinople were deeply depressed by the victories of the Latin troops. Morale was further damaged by the fires, which were started by the Latin soldiers who had gained a foothold on the Sea Walls. These spread rapidly in the area of the Blachernae palace, causing extensive damage. The fires at last spurred Alexios to action, but, although he led his troops out against the crusaders on the far side of the Land Walls, he failed to press home his attack in spite of his numerical superiority. On the night of 17–18 July he simply gave up and fled from the city, taking with him as much in treasure as he could carry.[38]

With Alexios III gone, the courtiers in the palace, of whom Choniates was one, had themselves to decide what to do next. Alexios had left behind his wife Euphrosyne and many of his relatives and close friends, but it was decided not to choose a new emperor from this group, as they were all regarded as tainted with the treason of the departed emperor. Another faction in the court therefore decided to turn to the former Emperor Isaac II. One of the courtiers, the eunuch Constantine Philoxenites, gained the support of the Varangian guard who seized and imprisoned Euphrosyne and her relatives, and brought Isaac back to the palace. Though blind and broken in health after his long incarceration, Isaac was brought up from his prison, placed on the throne and proclaimed emperor. His first move was to send messengers to the Latin camp, to summon his son, Prince Alexios, to join him in Constantinople so that he could be crowned as co-emperor.[39] The withdrawal of Alexios III and the restoration of Isaac II was an open admission that the rulers of Byzantium had reached the end of their options, but they had at least kept the crusade army outside the walls of Constantinople.

The Byzantine empire was now ruled by two supposedly compliant emperors, and the crusade leaders therefore could begin the task of extracting the *subventio* for the expedition to Egypt. Almost at once, a delegation was sent by the crusade leaders to remind Isaac II and Alexios IV of the promise made at Zara to put the empire under the ecclesiastical jurisdiction of Rome, to pay two hundred thousand silver marks to the army along with a year's supply of provisions to men of all ranks, and to provide troops to garrison the Holy Land. The Emperor Isaac, who presumably now learned of the terms for the first time, admitted that they were heavy, but no more than the crusaders deserved. He therefore ratified the treaty and thereafter seems to have been largely sidelined by his son and fellow emperor.[40]

Villehardouin portrays the period which immediately followed as one of happy Graeco-Latin cooperation. Small groups from the crusader army were allowed into the city to admire its churches and relics, while a friendly trade was carried on between the two sides. In a report sent to his vassals in the west, Hugh of Saint-Pol wrote enthusiastically that Alexios IV was faithfully fulfilling his promises. He had sent challenging letters to the sultan of Egypt, threatening to make war on him. The patriarch of Constantinople was petitioning for submission to Rome.[41] Inside Constantinople, the official line was also that all was going well. The court orator, Nikephoros Chrysoberges, praised Alexios because he was able to 'draw forth the foreign-tongued Italians' and instruct them that they would prosper only as long as they sided with him.[42] Chrysoberges clearly wanted to suggest that Alexios IV was following in the footsteps of Alexios I and Manuel I Comnenus, in exploiting the crusade for the good of the *Oikoumene.*

Many among the Byzantine elite, however, must have had serious doubts about Alexios's ability to control his dangerous friends and have regarded his favours to them as undermining everything that was sacred in Byzantine eyes, not least Michael Psellos's twin pillars of honours and money. Choniates, writing some years later, gave voice to these feelings, presenting an ironic picture of Isaac and Alexios hastening to provide feasts and entertainments in the palace for the crusade leaders, who heard themselves acclaimed 'benefactors and saviours, and receiving every other noble appellation for having honoured the power-loving Alexios in his childish actions'.[43] It was, however, the second of the two pillars, money, that Alexios IV seemed to be undermining the fastest. According to Choniates, he had now to resort to desperate measures to gather the immense sums that he had promised to his allies. Byzantine wealth, that time-honoured weapon for dealing with dangerous enemies, was not, it turned out, inexhaustible. When conventional sources dried up, Alexios was forced to seize church plate and to hack the frames off icons in order to melt them down into coin. Even then he still could not muster the vast sums demanded of him, so he decided to play for time. He asked the crusade leaders whether they could remain for another year while he gathered the rest of the promised sum, and requested help in subduing the European provinces of the empire, which were largely still loyal to Alexios III, so that he could start collecting taxes there. Accompanied by Boniface of Montferrat, Alexios IV led an army out into Thrace. During the late summer and autumn of 1203, he forced his uncle Alexios to flee from Adrianople and had some success in establishing his authority in the hinterland.[44]

In spite of this success, in Alexios IV's absence the deep resentment aroused by his taxation and conciliatory policy towards the crusade army had reached boiling point in Constantinople. As Alexios confided to the crusade leaders, his own people hated him because of his relations with the Latins, and, if the army ever left, he would undoubtedly be killed.[45] During his absence in Thrace, the Constantinopolitan populace became increasingly restive and a number of clashes took place between crusaders and locals.

One began when some Franks tried to burn down the Mitaton mosque which stood near the Golden Horn, and a crowd of Byzantines went to the rescue. A fire broke out in the section of the city along the Golden Horn where the Italian communities lived, causing their residents to flee to the crusader camp in the belief that it had been started by the Byzantines. One group, whom Choniates scornfully describes as 'the wine-bibbing portion of the vulgar masses', attacked and smashed a colossal ancient bronze statue of the goddess Athena which stood in the Forum of Constantine, because they believed that its outstretched arm was beckoning the crusaders to attack the city.[46]

However much Alexios IV relied on the crusade army to protect him from his own people and to assist him against Alexios III, by December 1203 his payments of treasure had dwindled and then ceased altogether. Alexios may have been pressurised by his courtiers or the populace into taking this step, or he may actually have run out of money. As far as the crusaders were concerned, however, the Greeks had once more reneged on their promises.[47] The attempt to secure their cooperation in the crusade by peaceful means had failed. It was therefore legitimate to secure their wealth by force of arms.

The first step of the crusader leaders was to send an embassy, consisting of three Frenchmen, Conon of Béthune, Miles of Brabant and Geoffrey of Villehardouin, and three Venetians across to the imperial city. Alexios IV and Isaac II received them in the midst of their courtiers at the palace of Blachernae, and were faced with a blunt demand that they fulfil the covenant as agreed at Zara: 'If you do this, [the leaders of the crusade] will be extremely pleased; but if not, they will no longer regard you as their lord and their friend, but will use every means in their power to obtain their due.' The ultimatum elicited the type of outraged reaction which the Byzantine elite reserved for those who failed to respect the position of the emperor of the Romans, as Villehardouin recalled:

> The Greeks were much amazed and deeply shocked by this openly defiant message, and declared that no one had ever yet been so bold as to dare to issue such a challenge to an emperor of Constantinople in his own hall. The Emperor Alexios himself, and all the other Greeks, who so often in the past had greeted them with smiling faces, now scowled fiercely at the envoys. The noise of angry voices filled the hall. The envoys turned to go: they made their way to the gate and mounted their horses. There was not a man among them who was not extremely glad to find himself outside ... Thus the war began ...[48]

In spite of their bellicose tone on this occasion, in the desultory warfare that followed the Byzantines displayed the same lack of policy and leadership as they had the previous summer. Fire ships were launched over the Golden Horn towards the Venetian fleet, but Alexios IV was unwilling to lead the army into a full-scale battle with the Latins, clearly believing that an accommodation could still be reached.[49] Internal opposition to Alexios reached a head in January 1204, when a great crowd gathered in Hagia Sophia to elect a new emperor, but irresolution still dominated. When Choniates was pressed to nominate a candidate for the imperial office, he declined to do so on the grounds that 'whoever was proposed for election would be led out the very next day like a sheep to slaughter, and that the chiefs of the Latin hosts would wrap their arms around Alexios and defend him'. The assembly was reduced to endless bickering as to who the new emperor should be. It was only after three days that a reluctant youth, Nicholas Kannavos, was chosen. In spite of everything that had passed, the only response that Alexios IV could think of was to contact Boniface of Montferrat and ask for help against the usurper.

Amidst the confusion, it seemed for a moment that a strong man had stepped forward to seize the initiative. The *Protovestiarios* Alexios Doukas Mourtzouphlos had gained popularity by engaging a Latin force outside the walls on 7 January, in defiance of specific orders from Alexios IV not to do so. In February 1204, he led a palace coup and had both Alexios IV and his rival Kannavos flung into prison. Alexios IV was strangled after he foiled two attempted poisonings by taking antidotes. The shock of these events was all too much for the enfeebled Isaac II, who expired around the same time.[50]

The way was thus cleared for Mourtzouphlos to be crowned emperor as Alexios V. He immediately made a number of attempts to placate Byzantine public opinion and to take on the Latins in open battle. Unfortunately, he had little success. A sally against the foraging force led by Henry of Flanders ended in disaster when Alexios V found himself deserted by his troops. In a further blow to morale and to Byzantine imperial ideology, Henry's troops captured a richly adorned icon of the Mother of God that Alexios's army had carried with it. The Virgin Mary was considered to be the special protector of the city of Constantinople. The emperors had always carried her image into battle as what Choniates called 'their fellow general' and Psellos 'the surest protection against [their] opponent's terrific onslaught'. Although this icon was probably not the famous *Hodegetria*, its loss seemed to suggest that divine protection had now been withdrawn and the favour of the Virgin had been transferred to the enemies of the empire. The victors were not slow to exploit their prize, taking the icon in a galley to be rowed up and down before the walls of Constantinople.[51]

While the Byzantines were failing to mount an effective opposition to the Latin army, their actions had provided the Latins with all the justification they needed to make a full-scale assault of Constantinople. The long-standing grievances of the schism and the failure to advance the cause of the crusades were now once more appealed to justify the forthcoming assault and to overcome the scruples of those unwilling to attack a Christian city. The Byzantines had reneged on the agreement sworn at Zara and they had murdered their rightful lord and emperor, Alexios IV. 'Have you ever heard of any people', asked Villehardouin, 'guilty of such atrocious treachery?' 'An idle cowardly rabble', fulminated Gunther of Pairis, 'an unfaithful burden to its kings.' The Latin clergy present assured the soldiers that fighting to bring Constantinople under the authority of Rome was a just cause, and that they would therefore benefit from an indulgence, just as if they were fighting to liberate Jerusalem.[52]

When the attack on the Sea Walls began early on Friday 9 April, the Byzantines were once more unable to mount effective resistance. At first, they were saved by contrary winds, but a second assault on 13 April was assisted by a strong breeze which drove the crusaders' ships onto the southern shore of the Golden Horn and allowed their crews to push scaling ladders against the Sea Walls and clamber over into the city. Far from saving the city, Alexios V followed in the footsteps of Alexios III and fled.

Once the defences had been breached, the fighting seems to have come to an abrupt end. The leaders had expected at least a month of street fighting to give them control of the city, but they soon realised, to their amazement, that no resistance at all was to be offered. The crusade army suffered only one casualty inside the walls, a knight who plunged with his horse into a pit while charging after the retreating enemy.[53]

Given the events of the past months, when the crusade leaders had been trying so hard to extort as much as they could from Constantinople, it is hardly surprising what happened next. After months of hardship bordering on starvation, the soldiery found themselves among the opulent palaces and churches of Constantinople and ran riot as each individual rushed to secure what he considered to be his by right. The imperial palaces of Boukoleon and Blachernae escaped unscathed, because Boniface of Montferrat and Henry of Flanders moved swiftly to place them under their protection. Niketas Choniates's house close to Hagia Sophia was also spared because a Venetian friend of his, a long-term resident of Constantinople, positioned himself at the door and pretended that he was a soldier with the army who had appropriated the house as his share of the spoils. Most of the other houses and palaces of the wealthy, however, were systematically ransacked for anything of value. Villehardouin enthused that 'so much booty had never been gained in any city since the creation of the world'; Robert of Clari estimated only that it was the greatest haul since the time of Alexander the Great, but grumbled because most of it found its way into the hands of the wealthy and powerful rather than of ordinary soldiers like himself. Various estimates put the value of the loot at nine hundred thousand silver marks.[54]

A significant section of the city, however, was not looted, either because it was burned out or because it was still on fire. During the presence of the crusader fleet, Constantinople was ravaged by three fires. The first took place between 17 and 18 July 1203, during the first assault which put Alexios IV on the throne. The second, and most damaging, raged between 19 and 20 August, following the attack on the Mitaton mosque. Finally, in April 1204, shortly after the crusaders had captured the Sea Walls, a few of them, fearing a Byzantine counter-attack, had set fire to the houses round about. The flames spread rapidly, as far as the Droungarios gate in the Sea Walls opposite Galata. As a result of the three conflagrations, about a sixth of the city was burned down.[55]

There could be no more obvious demonstration of the complete defeat of Byzantine ideology and foreign policy. The city of Constantinople, which was so central to both, had fallen and was in the hands of those who subscribed to an entirely different set of values, the crusading ideal dictated from Rome. In their attempt to protect Constantinople and the *Oikoumene*, the rulers of Byzantium had first provoked western aggression and then proved themselves incapable of withstanding it. The events of April 1204 should, therefore, have spelt the end of the empire.

10

Recovery

In 1204, the Latin west and its spiritual leader, Pope Innocent III, seemed to have triumphed. While the Fourth Crusade had failed to bring help to the beleaguered Latin states of the Levant, it appeared, at a stroke, to have ended the schism with the church of Constantinople and had delivered the strategically important city and its wealth into the hands of the crusaders. The outcome appeared to be a manifest indication of divine favour towards western Christians and a chastisement of the Byzantines for their failure to accept papal authority and to cooperate in the defence of Jerusalem.[1] Yet in the years that followed, the Byzantine empire was to revive and to recover Constantinople. It was the crusader states, which the Fourth Crusade had been launched to assist, that were ultimately to succumb. The irony was that the empire survived partly thanks the reassertion of the very same ideology and diplomatic methods which had brought it into conflict with the west and had led to the disaster of 1204.

With Constantinople under Latin occupation, the victors implemented a pact which had been made between the Venetians and the crusaders in March 1204, shortly before the final attack, which provided for the replacement of the Byzantine ruling hierarchy with a Latin one. An electoral council of six Venetians and six Franks was to elect a new emperor from among the crusade leadership.[2] Contrary to expectations, they chose not Boniface of Montferrat but Baldwin, count of Flanders, who was duly crowned in Hagia Sophia by the bishop of Soissons on 16 May 1204. The Venetians were awarded control over the office of patriarch of Constantinople, and, hardly surprisingly, appointed Tommaso Morosini, a Venetian, to the post. This takeover of the upper echelons of the empire was completed when Boniface of Montferrat married Margaret of Hungary, the widow of Isaac II.[3]

The pact made in March also provided for the partition of the empire among the victors. Constantinople itself was divided between the new emperor Baldwin and the Venetians. Baldwin received the greater part, including the imperial palaces of Blachernae and Boukoleon, but the Venetians took Hagia Sophia and a vastly increased commercial quarter along the Golden Horn. They also secured the exclusion of their Genoese and

Pisan rivals from the commerce of the empire. Of the provinces, the emperor was to take Asia Minor, Thrace, and the islands of Lesbos, Chios and Samos, to form what has become known as the Latin empire of Constantinople. The rest was to be divided among the Venetians, the Roman Church and the emperor's vassals. The agreement was implemented over the next few years, and although it did not always work out entirely as planned, a number of Frankish states on former Byzantine territory came into being, not unlike those formed in the Levant after the First Crusade. In Thessaly and Macedonia, Boniface of Montferrat formed the kingdom of Thessalonica. In the Peloponnese, the Latin principality of Achaia was set up by William of Champlitte. Athens became the centre of another Latin feudatory, the duchy of Athens. Lesser figures received one of some six hundred smaller parcels of land, held either from the emperor in Constantinople or from the king of Thessalonica. The Venetians, who were not interested in controlling large tracts of territory, seized islands and harbours which could serve as bases for their maritime trade. These included the towns of Methone and Corone in the Peloponnese; Dyrrachion and Ragusa on the Adriatic coast, the Ionian islands; Crete, Euboea (or Negroponte), Naxos; and the ports of Gallipoli and Rhadestos on the Sea of Marmara.[4]

Faced with what appeared to be the invincible strength and power of the western Europeans who now ruled them, many of the inhabitants of Constantinople seem to have been prepared at first to throw in their lot with the new order. Their own leaders, Alexios III Angelos, Alexios V Doukas, the patriarch John X Kamateros, and most of the nobility and bureaucracy had, in any case, fled the city, leaving it largely to the poor, the aged and the infirm. When it was clear that the Latins were in control, some Byzantines openly hailed Boniface of Montferrat as the new *Basileus*, and when Baldwin of Flanders was crowned in Hagia Sophia a crowd of locals gathered to cheer. Shortly afterwards, when Alexios V was betrayed to the crusaders by his rival Alexios III and brought as a prisoner to Constantinople, he was jeered and taunted by his former subjects as he passed through the streets, on his way to execution by being hurled from the column of Theodosius.[5]

There was a similar reaction in the provinces. Choniates recorded that when he and his fellow bureaucrats fled from Constantinople to the countryside of Thrace, they found themselves the object of scorn and derision from the local people, who rejoiced that those who had once lorded it over them and collected their taxes were now reduced to poverty and misery. When, in the summer of 1204, the Emperor Baldwin moved towards Thessalonica with his army, the population streamed out to welcome him and acknowledged him as emperor. Boniface of Montferrat experienced a similar reception in Thessaly, thanks to some Byzantines who accompanied him and carefully arranged matters. As the new Latin overlords established themselves, many local landowners adjusted quite easily to the change. The lands which they had held as *pronoia* from the emperor, they now kept as fiefs from their new lords. In matters of religion, although the Byzantine bishops were replaced with Latin ones, and Greeks were compelled to pay a tax to support the Latin church, at parish level no changes were made and the local Greeks carried on worshipping in their own churches much as they had always done.[6] In the months immediately following the sack of Constantinople, it might well have appeared that the ideology that had sustained Byzantium for so long had been destroyed along with so much else, and that all the lands of the empire would be integrated into a wider, western Christendom.

While in some areas Latin rule was accepted passively, in others there was open defiance. These were the places where members of the Byzantine ruling classes had taken refuge, particularly the three so-called successor states. The first to be set up was at Trebizond on the Black Sea. Two grandsons of Andronicus I, Alexios and David Comnenus, captured Trebizond in April 1204, a few days before Constantinople fell to the crusaders, and conquered the territory around it, including Pontos, which had once been governed by their grandfather. The second emerged in Epiros, in western Greece. This area had originally been assigned to Venice in the partition treaty of March 1204, but Venice only took control of the coastal cities of Dyrrachion and Ragusa. The gap was filled by Michael Angelos, a cousin of the emperors Isaac II and Alexios III, who set himself up as ruler of the area in the town of Arta. Finally, Theodore Laskaris, a son-in-law of Alexios III, established himself at Nicaea in Asia Minor.[7]

All three states were formed in conscious continuation of the empire. They modelled their courts on that of Constantinople in every detail of administration, civil service and imperial household. Their rulers were surrounded and advised by members of the elite, defined by high-sounding titles and schooled in the traditional course of higher education. At Arta, officials rejoiced in the titles of *Megalepifanestatos* ('Great, Most High Appearing') and *Paneutychestatos* ('All Most Fortunate'). At Nicaea, the refugees who had streamed out of Constantinople in 1204 re-established the higher schools to turn out the next generation of the ruling elite, and produced elegant orations in archaic Greek, extolling their new home as a second Athens, though not, of course, a second Constantinople.[8]

Similarly, the rulers of all three states inherited the pretensions of their predecessors in Constantinople to be the universal Christian emperor. The first independent ruler of Trebizond, Alexios I (1204–22), adopted the imperial title from the beginning. Theodore Laskaris of Nicaea waited until 1208, when he was crowned 'Emperor and Autocrat of the Romans' by a new, Greek, patriarch of Constantinople, appointed in opposition to the Latin patriarch, Morosini. Theodore Angelos of Epiros took the same step at Thessalonica in 1224, with the archbishop of Ochrid performing the ceremony. All three now considered themselves the legitimate successor of the Byzantine emperors who had reigned in Constantinople before 1204. The clergy of Arta hailed their ruler as 'the descendant of various emperors', and the Nicaean emperor told the pope in 1237 that 'the ancestors of our majesty ... for many centuries held sway over Constantinople'.[9]

Given the inglorious collapse of the empire in 1203–4 and the craven behaviour of its rulers, it is at first sight surprising that these governments in exile should be so eager to revive a system that appeared to have been so discredited. Indeed critics of the system were to be found among the exiles at Nicaea. Nikephoros Blemmydes (1197–1272) blamed the 'culpable conduct of those who were on the throne' for delivering Constantinople into the hands of the Latins. Niketas Choniates, who revised and completed his *History* at the court of Theodore I Laskaris at Nicaea, said much the same. Choniates even went so far as to compare the Byzantine political system unfavourably with that of the Latins, contrasting the ritualistic Byzantine court, where all were made to stand in the presence of the emperor, with the more egalitarian practice among the Germans, where even the servants were allowed to sit. Choniates's brother Michael, archbishop of Athens, wrote despairingly that, while the Latins could debate matters among themselves in an orderly fashion, the Byzantines were incapable of restraining their anger. Doubts were even expressed about the exclusivity of the Byzantine empire. Some Byzantine intellectuals now described themselves and their fellow countrymen as 'Hellenes', rather than 'Romans', as if defining themselves as a race like any other rather than as inheritors of the Roman political tradition.[10]

Yet while Byzantine intellectuals might criticise their former rulers and even aspects of imperial ideology, there was one factor that made them determined to cling to their religion and ideology, and to reject that of western Europe. This was the memory of what had taken place in Constantinople during April 1204. As the refugees reached Arta and Nicaea, they had a very disturbing tale to tell. Naturally, there were reports of atrocities. Nicholas Mesarites, the future archbishop of Ephesus, recounted how new-born babes had been murdered, monks had been tortured and women indecently assaulted. Choniates was an eyewitness to an attempted rape, which he succeeded in preventing, as he and his family were escaping from Constantinople.[11]

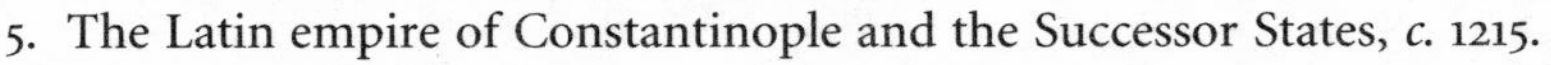
5. The Latin empire of Constantinople and the Successor States, *c.* 1215.

What really kindled the fury of the Byzantines, however, was the yawning gap between the professed pious intention of the crusaders and their conduct towards the churches and holy places in Constantinople. It was reported that a crowd of them had entered Hagia Sophia and started to remove the gold and silver candlesticks and ecclesiastical vessels, including a huge ciborium that weighed thousands of pounds. So numerous and heavy were these objects that they had brought donkeys and mules into the cathedral to carry them away. Hardly surprisingly, these creatures had left their dung and urine within the hallowed precincts. One of them had lost its footing on the slippery marble pavement and, as it went crashing down, had impaled itself on the metal objects with which it was loaded and its blood had spread in a pool over the floor. It was also claimed that the looters had brought in a prostitute who performed a dance on the *synthronon*, the most sacred part of the church, behind the iconostasis.

Another group was reported to have burst into the church of the Holy Apostles, where many emperors of the past lay buried. They opened the tomb of the Emperor Justinian. Finding that his corpse was uncorrupted after over six hundred years, they left it alone but stripped off anything of value from the sarcophagus. At other shrines and churches, they destroyed icons and turned a marble altar screen into a latrine.[12] In short, they had desecrated and profaned everything that the Byzantines held sacred.

No doubt there was exaggeration, but the Byzantine account is confirmed by western sources, in spite of the Latin claim that before the attack in April 1204 the crusaders took a vow not to harm any ecclesiastical building.[13] Innocent III was outraged when news of these events reached his ears:

> It was not enough for them to empty the imperial treasuries and to plunder the spoils of princes and lesser folk, but rather they extended their hands to church treasuries and, what was more serious, to their possessions, even ripping away silver tablets from altars and breaking them into pieces among themselves ...[14]

A Latin writer reported that the church and monastery of Christ Pantokrator, which had been founded by John II Comnenus and which contained both John's tomb and that of his son Manuel I, suffered a similar fate to that of Hagia Sophia and the Holy Apostles. The crusaders had received reports that the church was being used as a repository for valuables brought in from the countryside for safety. The looters were accompanied by an abbot, Martin of Pairis, and two priests, who were determined to seize any holy relics that the church might contain. Finding an elderly Greek priest, Abbot Martin threatened to kill him unless he revealed where the relics were, and departed with part of the True Cross, a trace of the blood of Christ and other items hidden in his cassock.[15]

Events such as these confirmed the suspicions the Byzantines had always had about the crusading ideal. Taking the teaching of St Basil as their starting point, they could not understand how a priest like the pope could organise and despatch armies, even for as worthy a cause as the liberation of Jerusalem. Here now was the proof of their fears. Choniates and Mesarites dwelt on the disparity between the crusading ideal and the conduct of the crusaders in Constantinople. They poured scorn on those who had taken the cross and had vowed to fight Muslims, yet had turned aside and despoiled a Christian city instead. Saladin, when he had taken Jerusalem in 1187, had dealt magnanimously with his defeated enemies. 'How differently', complained Choniates, 'the Latins treated us who love Christ and are their fellow believers, guiltless of any wrong against them.' As for their ransacking of churches: 'Such was the reverence for holy things of those who bore the Lord's cross on their shoulders'. To make matters worse, their own priests had urged them to act in this way.[16] In the very moment when it appeared to have been overthrown, the ideology of the Byzantine empire had therefore been vindicated and that of the Latin west shown to be a hypocritical sham. No wonder that the rulers of the successor states felt a sense of mission and purpose in fighting to recover Constantinople.

They were helped in achieving this aim by three factors. In the first place, the people of Constantinople, who seem at the beginning to have regarded the Latin takeover as just another change of ruler, soon became disillusioned. The newly installed ecclesiastical authorities demanded the recognition of the authority of the pope and of the Venetian patriarch, Tommaso Morosini. During the second half of 1206, a number of meetings took place between the Greek clergy, led by John and Nicholas Mesarites, and Morosini and the papal legate, Cardinal Benedict of Santa Susanna. No agreement was reached and the discussions ended with Morosini shouting angrily: 'You should accept me. You are disobedient and we shall treat you for what you are!'[17] The Greeks of Constantinople then wrote to the pope, requesting that they should be allowed to have a patriarch of their own. No answer was received and in 1213 a new legate, Pelagius, carried out Morosini's threat. He closed the Orthodox churches in Constantinople, prompting many among the Greek clergy to leave for Nicaea. From this point, the people of Constantinople, who could not hope to accommodate themselves to the new regime, now longed for liberation by their Orthodox brethren.[18]

A second factor, which made the liberation of Constantinople a distinct possibility, was the manifest weakness of the Latin empire which revealed itself only a short time after it was established. Within a year of his coronation, the Emperor Baldwin was defeated and captured by the Bulgarians at Adrianople. After a brief revival under Baldwin's brother, Henry (1206–16), the Latin empire declined into a state of terminal weakness. The pact of March 1204 had only assigned to the Latin emperor a fraction of the territories that his Byzantine predecessor had enjoyed and he had not succeeded even in subduing all of these. As a result, he was unable to bring in the substantial tax receipts which had been such a strength to the Byzantine empire and was constantly short of money.[19]

Starved of tax income, the Latin emperors resorted to milking the city of Constantinople of anything of value. When the gold and silver was gone, they turned to the bronze. The colossal statue of the goddess Hera in the Forum of Constantine was pulled down and broken up, a team of eight oxen being called in to drag away the enormous head. One by one, the ancient Greek statues that lined the Hippodrome were removed and melted down, such as the Calydonian boar and Lysippos of Sicyon's Hercules. Some were spared destruction to be taken away as trophies. The four bronze horses, symbols of the chariot races that had taken place in the Hippodrome over the centuries, were appropriated by the Venetians and shipped off to become ornaments on the façade of Saint Mark's church. Only the serpent column from Delphi was left in place, perhaps because of its historical associations. When the bronze was gone, they turned to the lead. The Latin emperor Baldwin II (1228–61) had the lead stripped from the roofs of the imperial palaces and sold for scrap.[20]

Another source of revenue was the sale of relics. Many of these were stolen before the Latin emperor could draw any profit from them. Conrad, bishop of Halberstadt, and Martin, abbot of Pairis, both carried substantial numbers of items back for the benefit of their home churches. In the chaos that followed the defeat at Adrianople in 1205, an English priest who had charge of the relic collection in the palace of Boukoleon allegedly stole a piece of the True Cross and took it back to the priory of Bromholm in Norfolk.[21] Nevertheless, enough remained to provide some benefit for the Latin regime. The head of John the Baptist and other items were taken by Nivelon, bishop of Soissons, to give authority to an appeal for help for the beleaguered defenders of Constantinople. In 1237, Baldwin II pawned the Crown of Thorns to a Venetian merchant for 13,134 gold pieces. When it was clear that the debt could not be redeemed, the relic was taken over by agents of Louis IX of France, who paid the debt and took the relic to Paris, where the Sainte-Chapelle was specially built to house it.[22] Needless to say, such wholesale despoliation of the Queen of Cities was hardly likely to endear its Latin rulers to its inhabitants.

While the Latin empire tottered, none of the other Frankish states of Greece achieved a powerful enough position to come to its rescue. In 1207 Boniface of Montferrat perished in battle against the Bulgarians, leaving the kingdom of Thessalonica in grave danger. In the Peloponnese, by dint of assiduous castle-building, Latin rule was more enduring, but the princes of Achaia were never able to extend their rule northwards.

Finally, the successor states also profited from the extreme reluctance of many western Europeans to go to the assistance of the Latin empire. This had not been a problem in the early days, because in November 1204 Innocent III had assured the Emperor Baldwin that defending the city against any Byzantine attempt to retake it would earn exactly the same remission of penance as fighting the Muslims in Egypt or Palestine would have done.[23] As a result, many western knights who would have gone to the Holy Land migrated to Constantinople. As late as 1237, a call by Pope Gregory IX (1227–41) for a crusade to defend the Latin position in Greece received a good response.[24]

As the thirteenth century progressed, however, it became clear that not everyone in Europe was convinced that defending the Latin empire would really attract the same spiritual reward as fighting for Jerusalem. The change was largely the result of the propensity of Innocent III and his successors to call for crusades not against the Muslims, for the defence of Jerusalem, but against Christians in western Europe. Notorious examples were the Albigensian crusade of 1208 and the crusade preached in 1240 by Pope Gregory IX against the German emperor, Frederick II, which offered a full indulgence to those who took part and commutation of the vows of those who had undertaken to go to the Holy Land if they would take part in the war against Frederick instead.

In the light of these developments, many western knights refused to answer the pope's call to fight for any other purpose than the defence of the Holy Land. In 1239, when Richard, duke of Cornwall, was planning a crusade, the pope suggested he and his followers should commute their crusading vow by making a money payment which could be used for the defence of Constantinople. The would-be crusaders responded by taking a solemn oath at Northampton to go only to the Holy Land 'lest their honest vow be hindered by the objections of the Roman Church and diverted to shedding Christian blood in Greece or in Italy'. Even the foremost crusading monarch of the thirteenth century, Louis IX of France, showed a similar reluctance to get involved, pleading poverty to avoid sending a promised contingent of three hundred knights to assist the Latin empire.[25] The inability of the Latin emperors to pay for their own defence was therefore compounded by a lack of willing volunteers coming to help them from the west.

At first, it looked as if Epiros among the three successor states would take advantage of these three factors and would win the race to recapture

Constantinople. From the moment of his accession to power in 1215, its ruler Theodore Angelos was determined to expand his territory eastwards, and set himself, as a first objective, the capture of Thessalonica. This he achieved in 1224, bringing to an abrupt end the short-lived Latin kingdom which had been established by Boniface of Montferrat. In the years that followed, the now Emperor Theodore led his forces to the very walls of Constantinople and it looked as if he would soon achieve his ultimate ambition. In 1230, however, Theodore quarrelled with the Bulgarian ruler, John Asen II, and his invasion of Bulgaria ended in his defeat and capture at the battle of Klokotnitsa. In the aftermath, most of Epiros was overrun by the Bulgarians, and the ambitions of its rulers to retake Constantinople evaporated.[26]

Since Trebizond was too far away to launch an effective assault on Constantinople, it was left to the Byzantines of Nicaea to lead the resistance. During the reign of Theodore I Laskaris (1208–22), the small principality was fighting for survival. The territory it occupied had been allocated to the Latin empire in the pact of March 1204, and Theodore I had to fight off a number of attempts by Henry of Flanders to implement the pact. On his eastern frontier, Theodore had to contend with the Seljuk Turks, who invaded Nicaean territory in the spring 1211, ostensibly acting on behalf of the former emperor Alexios III Angelos, who was a guest at the sultan's court in Konya. Theodore's victory at Antioch on the Meander ended the threat, and delivered Alexios III as a prisoner into his hands. He showed no mercy to his father-in-law, who was incarcerated for the rest of his life. It is unlikely that Alexios III's role in handing Constantinople over to the Latins was either forgiven or forgotten.

The real architect of Nicaean success was Theodore's son-in-law and successor, John III Vatatzes (1222–54), a remarkable ruler who was later canonised as a saint of the Orthodox Church and whose feast day is still celebrated on 4 November. Unusually for a Byzantine monarch, John took particular interest in increasing the agricultural production of his estates, and he even had a rudimentary economic policy. He forbade his subjects from purchasing luxury goods from foreign merchants. This policy might have been ethical in origin, but it was no doubt directed against the Venetians, the chief prop of the Latin empire of Constantinople, who monopolised the trade of the region.[27] John also pursued an astute diplomacy towards the west, marrying the illegitimate daughter of the German emperor Frederick II in the 1240s. Many in the west and the crusader states were shocked at Frederick's alliance with a Greek ruler who was out of communion with the church of Rome, but by this time Frederick was himself an excommunicate and in conflict with the papacy. He was therefore perfectly happy to associate himself with a ruler branded by the pope as a schismatic.[28]

Careful husbanding of resources and intelligent diplomacy enabled John III to make serious inroads into the territory of the Latin empire. A final showdown in Asia Minor came with John's victory at the battle of Poimamenon in 1225. Nicaean forces were then able to occupy those few areas of Asia Minor that were still in Latin hands and to take over the islands of Lesbos, Chios and Samos. Before long John III had expanded Nicaean power beyond Asia Minor. By making an alliance with the Bulgarians in 1235, he was able to lead his forces across the Dardanelles into Europe to take part in a joint siege of Constantinople. The alliance soon broke down, but it left John in possession of the strategically vital town of Gallipoli and a bridgehead into Europe. By 1246 he had conquered Thessalonica and a large part of the southern Balkans.[29]

John III did not enjoy the final triumph of recapturing Constantinople. That was left to one of his generals, Michael Palaeologus, a man who never had the remotest chance of being considered for canonisation. Ruthless and pragmatic, Michael's rise to power had many similarities to that of Andronicus I. In 1258, he was appointed regent for John III's grandson, the seven-year-old John IV Laskaris, having probably had the previous regent, George Mouzalon, murdered during a church service. Once he was secure in power, the regent had himself crowned emperor as Michael VIII (1259–82). His young charge was first sidelined, then imprisoned and blinded. Many Byzantines were prepared to forgive Michael this atrocity, in view of his later recovery of Constantinople. They were to be less forbearing over his actions after 1274.

By 1259, the Latin empire consisted solely of Constantinople and a few miles of land round about, and it must have been obvious that the empire of Nicaea was poised to take it over. Other powers in the region therefore hastily made common cause to defeat Michael VIII, and a coalition came into being consisting of the ruler of Epiros, Michael II, the king of Sicily, Manfred, and the prince of Achaia, William of Villehardouin. In autumn 1259 Michael's brother, John Palaeologus, met the combined army of the coalition at Pelagonia, in Epiros, and won a complete victory. Every single one of the four hundred knights sent by the king of Sicily was killed. The prince of Achaia tried to escape when he saw what was happening, and hid under a bush, but was found and recognised because of his unusually protruding teeth. The victory at Pelagonia ensured that there was no land-based power which could stop the Nicaeans from recovering Constantinople.[30]

The only obstacle to the recovery of Constantinople was now the maritime power of Venice, whose fleet guarded the waters around the city. Michael VIII therefore turned to Genoa and on 13 March 1261, he concluded the treaty of Nymphaion, by which the Genoese promised to aid him in time of war. In return, they were granted extensive privileges, notably tax and customs concessions throughout the empire, and their own commercial quarters in the chief ports of the empire, including Constantinople, once it was recovered. In short, the treaty granted to Genoa the commercial hegemony in the Levant that Venice had enjoyed since the eleventh century.[31]

Genoese help was not needed in the end. In July 1261 one of Michael's generals, Alexios Strategopoulos, was in the area of the Land Walls of Constantinople with his army when he received information that the city was virtually undefended. Much of the Latin garrison had gone off to attack the Nicaean island of Daphnousia. News also came that one of the gates in the walls had been left open by a sympathiser on the inside. The chance was seized and the army entered Constantinople on the night of 25 July 1261. There was virtually no resistance and by daybreak the city was in Strategopoulos's hands.

Michael VIII was on the Asian side of the Bosporos with his part of the army when the news of the capture of Constantinople arrived. It was very early in the morning and the emperor was still asleep in his tent. The news was given to Michael's sister Eulogia, who went into the emperor's tent and tickled his feet with a feather. At first Michael did not believe the news, but then a messenger arrived bringing the crown and sceptre of the Latin emperor, which Baldwin II had left behind in his rush to escape. Michael then led his army over the Sea of Marmara to Constantinople, arriving on 14 August. He did not enter immediately, however, spending the night outside the Land Walls, so that he could enter on 15 August, the Feast of the Dormition of the Virgin. The historian George Akropolites describes Michael's triumphant entry into Constantinople. The emperor entered through the Golden Gate and processed the Mese, towards Hagia Sophia. At the head of the procession was an icon of the Virgin Mary, in recognition that the triumph was the result of her intervention, not of any human strength. Once he entered Hagia Sophia, Michael was met by the patriarch of Constantinople, who solemnly crowned him for a second time. Michael then took up residence in the palace of Boukoleon, so recently vacated by the hapless Baldwin. In later years, he looked back on this as one of his finest achievements, boasting that Constantinople 'returned to the Romans, when God delivered her through ourselves'.[32]

Given the continuity of so many aspects of Byzantine ideology and court culture in Nicaea and the apparent reconstitution in 1261 of the empire as it had been before 1204, one might have expected that the foreign policy pursued by Michael VIII to have had much the same aims as before, not only the protection of the *Oikoumene* and the city of Constantinople but also the securing of recognition of the emperor's claim to be the supreme Christian ruler. Elements of continuity can certainly be found. In 1282 Michael VIII summoned the emperor of Trebizond, John II (1280–97), to Constantinople and insisted that he renounce the imperial title. In return John received the hand of the emperor's daughter in marriage and the title of Despot. It was a classic piece of Byzantine diplomacy, titles and honours being used as a way of bringing a less powerful foreign ruler into the Byzantine 'family' of princes, under the emperor's overlordship.[33]

It is possible to see this concern for recognition being pursued in Michael's dealings with western powers. In a treaty concluded with the Genoese, for example, the honours that the *podestà* sent from Genoa to govern the Genoese colony in Constantinople was to pay to the emperor, a double prostration and kissing of the emperor's hand and foot, were specifically laid down as visible symbols of the emperor's status. The treaty which Michael VIII made with William, prince of Achaia, which secured the prince's release after the battle of Pelagonia, bestowed on William the title of Grand Domestic and the privilege of standing as godfather to one of the emperor's sons. As in the case of the crusaders in 1096, the pact with William was confirmed by an oath.[34]

There is evidence that Michael VIII was also concerned to secure recognition of his role as protector of the Holy Places from the crusader states of Syria and other powers in the region. In the early years of the thirteenth century there had been little opportunity for his predecessors to do so. While the nascent empire of Nicaea was fighting for survival, the kingdom of Jerusalem and the principality of Antioch were undergoing something of a resurgence. Efforts had continued to be made to recover Jerusalem. The Fifth Crusade revived the plan of the Fourth and invaded Egypt in 1217, only to be forced to withdraw in 1221. In 1228, however, the German emperor Frederick II sailed to the Holy Land and, by the treaty of Jaffa, which he concluded with the sultan of Egypt in 1229, secured the return of Jerusalem to Christian rule. There was also good news from the east where the Mongols overran Persia during the 1230s and seemed to offer the promise of a powerful ally in the war against Islam.

The favourable situation was, however, not to last. On 23 August 1244 Jerusalem was recaptured by Khwarismian mercenaries, Persians who had moved west as refugees from the Mongols. Worse was to come on 17 October in the same year, when the Latins, who had joined forces with one faction in a feud among the Ayyubids, were heavily defeated at the battle of La Forbie. The Templars and Hospitallers who took part were almost wiped out and the defeat marked the collapse of the gradual reconstruction of the kingdom of Jerusalem that had been taking place since 1191. In 1249 Louis IX led the Seventh Crusade in an attack on Egypt in the hope of destroying Ayyubid power at its source. The expedition enjoyed initial success but ended in disaster when Louis's army was forced to retreat from Mansourah and finally to surrender. The crusade was also indirectly responsible for the *coup d'état* of May 1250 when Turanshah, the last Ayyubid ruler, was assassinated and replaced by a series of militaristic and aggressive Mamluk sultans. By the time that the Mamluks defeated a Mongol army at Ain Jalut in 1260, the crusader states were in a very vulnerable position indeed, since the new Mamluk sultan, Baibars (1260–77), was determined to eradicate them. In 1268 Baibars achieved a spectacular victory when he captured Antioch from the successors of Bohemond.[35]

John III Vatatzes may have attempted to take advantage of the situation. While Louis IX was residing in Acre between 1250 and 1254, John sent an embassy to him which may have been connected with Byzantine claims to the protectorship of the Holy Places. He also initiated contact with the Mongols and sent an embassy to the court of the Khan Mongka in 1253.[36] This last initiative paid off handsomely. When, in 1260, the Mongol ilkhan of Persia, Hulagu, received the submission of the prince of Antioch, Bohemond VI, he insisted that a Greek patriarch be restored in the city, possibly in response to a direct request from Nicaea.[37]

Once he was re-established in Constantinople, Michael VIII seems to have sought a similar favour from the Mamluk sultan, Baibars. In 1261 he received some ambassadors from Egypt and through them he made a request to Baibars that his nominee for the patriarchate of Jerusalem be appointed. In return, Michael promised that the Constantinople mosque would be restored and even arranged for Cuman mercenaries to be shipped from the Crimea to Egypt.[38] Michael also made agreements with Mongol leaders. Michael's illegitimate daughter, Maria, was sent to marry Hulagu, but since he died before she arrived she was given to his son, Abaka, instead. Another, legitimate daughter, Euphrosyne, went to Nogai, ruler of the Golden Horde in south Russia in 1266.[39]

In general, however, Byzantine foreign policy during the thirteenth century was more concerned with security than with recognition. A treaty made between Michael VIII and Baibars's successor, Khalawun, in 1281 was primarily a non-aggression pact, with clauses providing for the mutual good treatment of merchants. Michael's aim in making these alliances seems to have been to protect the empire's eastern flank by playing off the Mamluks against the Ilkhanids of Persia and the Golden Horde, and the two groups of Mongols against each other. At the same time, this would leave him free to deal with the threat from western Europe.[40]

This preference for security over recognition was a matter of necessity rather than choice. Although Michael VIII may have wanted to pursue the old policy with the old methods, he was well aware that he did not have the resources to do so. The empire as reconstituted in 1261 was a great deal smaller than that ruled over by the Comneni and Angeloi, consisting of about a third of Asia Minor, a strip of territory across the Balkans, part of the Peloponnese and some of the Aegean islands. It was not for another century and a half that the rest of the Peloponnese was reconquered from the principality of Achaia. Crete, Cyprus and the Ionian islands were never recovered. This shrinkage of territory meant that the emperors in Constantinople received only a fraction of the tax receipts that their predecessors had enjoyed. The other source of revenue, customs duties, was also in decline, as much of Constantinople's trade was diverted through the Genoese colony of Galata on the opposite side of the Golden Horn. The Byzantine courtier Nikephoros Gregoras estimated that by the mid fourteenth century the Genoese earned two hundred thousand gold pieces in duties a year, while the Byzantine treasury received a mere thirty thousand.[41] For Michael VIII and his successors the security of their empire was usually all they could hope for; recognition of imperial status often had to be left unclaimed.

There was another factor that ensured that Michael VIII and his advisers could not pursue traditional Byzantine foreign policy in the way Manuel I had done. Byzantine relations with western Europe were now on a very different footing. When he had placed the new Latin empire of Constantinople under the protection of the Holy See in November 1204, Innocent III had equated any Byzantine attempt to recapture the city with an assault on the Roman Church.[42] When news of the recapture of Constantinople by Michael VIII reached Rome, Pope Urban IV (1261–64) had therefore no hesitation in preaching a crusade specifically against Michael VIII and his followers, promising that those who joined the expedition would have the same remission of sins granted to those who went to the Holy Land. Justification was given partly on the grounds that the Greeks were schismatics who had fallen away from Rome, but also because, if they succeeded in re-establishing the old Byzantine borders, the way to Jerusalem and the Holy Land would be barred.[43]

At first the empire was protected from such calls to arms by the reluctance of western Europeans to get involved in crusades against Christians. It only needed a powerful and ambitious western ruler to decide that taking part in an expedition to Constantinople would be in his interests, however, for a very serious threat to be presented to the empire. This was exactly what occurred in 1266, when Charles of Anjou, the brother of King Louis IX of France, succeeded in establishing himself, with papal blessing, as king of Sicily and southern Italy, and inheritor of the old ambitions of the Norman rulers of the region to seize the opposite shore of the Adriatic. In 1277 Charles also obtained the title of king of Jerusalem, and with it leadership of the defence of the Holy Land. The recapture of Constantinople now became an integral part of Charles's plans to dominate the eastern Mediterranean. On 27 May 1267 he made a treaty at Viterbo with Baldwin II, the exiled Latin emperor of Constantinople. The agreement was that Charles was to send a fleet to take Constantinople, restore Baldwin to his throne and provide a force of two thousand cavalrymen to defend the Latin empire for a year thereafter. In return he would receive one third of the lands conquered from the Byzantine empire in the Balkans. The agreement had the active blessing of the pope and was couched in terms that gave the proposed expedition all the aura of a crusade, 'the pious task of restoring the noble limb severed by the schismatics from the body of our common mother, the Holy Roman Church'.[44]

Faced with so powerful an enemy, Michael VIII and his advisers had to find some way of defusing the situation. The empire's straitened resources meant that they did not have a large army or fleet at their disposal to defend Constantinople, so they fell back on the policy adopted by Manuel I Comnenus of seeking to defuse western hostility by opening negotiations to remove the schism between the churches. There had already been extensive negotiations under John III Vatatzes, and Michael might have been deterred by their lack of success.[45] He seems, however, to have made the approach in a slightly different way, playing on the crisis that was facing the Latin east and presenting Byzantium as a potential active partner in the defence of the Holy Land.

The pope at the time was Gregory X (1272–76). Originally, Tedaldo Visconti of Piacenza, archdeacon of Liège, Gregory had been at Acre at the time of his election, and was known for his passionate attachment to the defence of the Holy Land. On his return to Rome, probably during 1273, Gregory received a letter from Michael VIII, who claimed to be devoted to the Apostolic See and eager to work for the union of the churches. Gregory had already called a council of the church to meet at Lyons in May 1274, which was to discuss a new crusade to rescue the embattled Holy Land. Michael was therefore invited to send a delegation to the council.[46]

The Byzantine delegation, led by George Akropolites, arrived at Lyons in June 1274. It was now that the difference between the situation of the

Byzantine empire in 1274 and that before 1204 made itself felt. Whereas, in the past, Byzantine emperors had been able to prolong negotiations for union without actually coming to an agreement, so pressing was the threat from Charles of Anjou that Michael's envoys had to come to terms. On 6 July 1274, apparently without having entered into any debate on the issue, Akropolites read out a letter from Michael in the cathedral of St John at Lyons agreeing to end the schism on Roman terms. The letter contained a formal acceptance of the *Filioque* clause, an acknowledgement of the church of Rome's authority over the whole church, and an acceptance of the western position on minor matters such as the doctrine of purgatory and the use of unleavened bread in communion. A mass was then celebrated in which the priests with the Byzantine delegation openly used the *Filioque* during the creed, not once but three times just to make sure that they were heard.[47] When Akropolites and the delegation returned to Constantinople, the ceremony was re-enacted in the presence of the emperor on 16 January 1275. A compliant cleric, John Bekkos, formerly the archivist of Hagia Sophia, was raised to the patriarchate, with the job of implementing the newly agreed union.[48]

The submission had the desired effect. The Byzantines were now once more in communion with Rome and Michael announced his intention of cooperating with a crusade to recover Jerusalem which would march east via Constantinople. He would supply the expedition with supplies, money and anything else it needed. All justification for an assault on the Byzantine empire by Charles of Anjou as a 'pious enterprise' was removed at a stroke. Papal legates were sent to Constantinople to arrange a truce between Charles and Michael.[49]

Michael VIII's dealings with the papacy at the council of Lyons might therefore seem to have been both sensible and successful. In the context of what had gone before, however, they were risky, to say the least. The rulers of Nicaea had recovered Constantinople partly by taking advantage of the deep hostility that had developed among its population against its Latin occupiers. As a papal envoy to Constantinople later advised the pope, the memory of the sack of April 1204, and the attempt to force western ecclesiastical hierarchy and dogmas on the city, made the Byzantines utterly opposed to any agreement with Rome. So deep were such feelings that, as one Dominican monk living in Galata complained, the locals would even break a cup out of which a Latin had drunk as if it were something contaminated.[50]

The unprecedented concession made by Akropolites at Lyons, therefore, opened up a deep rift within Byzantine society. A large number of people in Constantinople simply refused to accept the union of Lyons, and those who had supported and implemented imperial policy found themselves branded as traitors. George Metochites, who had conducted negotiations with the pope on the emperor's behalf during 1275, was told by the anti-unionists on his return that he had 'become a Latin'. Among the ringleaders of the opposition were Michael's own sister Eulogia, who defiantly insisted that 'Better that my brother's empire should perish, than the purity of the Orthodox faith'. Most vociferous of all were the monks, particularly those of Mount Athos, who disseminated tracts attacking the union as a surrender to heresy.[51]

Determined to crush the opposition, Michael meted out severe punishments to those who raised their voices against the union. Eulogia was imprisoned, although she later succeeded in escaping to Bulgaria. A monk called Meletios had his tongue cut out; another, Galaktion, was blinded.[52] Neither the opposition nor the penalties attached to it were restricted to the ranks of fanatical monks, the sort of people whom the courtier Gregoras disdainfully described as wearing hair shirts like theatrical costumes.[53] Many highly educated courtiers were equally dismayed at what they regarded as the betrayal of their ancestral faith and suffered from the emperor's retribution in due measure. Manuel Holobolos and Theodore Mouzalon, who refused to undertake an embassy to Rome, were flogged. The *Protostrator* Andronicus Palaeologus died in prison.[54]

As a result of this opposition, Michael's policy towards Charles of Anjou and the papacy began to unravel. Rumours of the state of affairs in Constantinople drifted back to Rome and gave rise to accusations that Michael VIII had reneged on the agreement made at Lyons. In 1281 Pope Martin IV, a Frenchman sympathetic to Charles of Anjou, repudiated the union of Lyons, excommunicated Michael VIII, and urged Charles of Anjou to launch a crusade against the Greeks.[55] Charles was only too happy to comply and began to build a fleet in the harbour of Palermo in Sicily.

Michael's unprecedented attempt to save the empire by making a major concession to western ideology had failed, but in the hour of crisis the empire's salvation was provided by two of the time-honoured tactics of Byzantine diplomacy: that of paying another power to attack the enemy; and that of stirring up discord in the enemy camp. Ambassadors were despatched to the king of Aragon, Peter III, who was promised the sum of sixty thousand gold pieces if he would invade Sicily. At the same time, *agents provocateurs* were circulating in Sicily, stirring up discontent with French rule among the local population. These tactics worked well. On 30 March 1282 the population of Sicily rose up in revolt against their French rulers and King Peter of Aragon invaded the island a few months later. Charles of Anjou was forced to divert his attention from the attack on

Constantinople to defending his own kingdom. Both tactics had been used by Alexios I against Robert Guiscard two hundred years before, though with not nearly such spectacular success.[56] Where innovation had failed, tradition won the day.

Michael VIII did not live to enjoy his victory for long. In December 1282, while campaigning with his troops in Thrace, he fell ill and died, aged fifty-eight. With him at the time of his death was his son Andronicus, who was immediately proclaimed emperor Andronicus II Palaeologus (1282–1328). On his return to Constantinople, Andronicus's first official act was to abrogate the union of Lyons and to proclaim the restoration of Orthodoxy. After all, the miraculous frustration of the plans of Charles of Anjou seemed to confirm that the Byzantine view of the world had been right all along and that Constantinople really was the centre of the *Oikoumene.* Andronicus therefore deposed the patriarch John Bekkos and restored the previous incumbent, Joseph, to office. Bishops who had supported Michael were deposed and replaced with anti-unionists. All those who had been thrown into prison for opposing Michael were now released, and were greeted as they emerged by cheering crowds and ringing church bells.[57]

As for his father, the body of Michael VIII was not brought back to Constantinople for burial in one of the great churches of the city. On the orders of Andronicus, his corpse was buried in unconsecrated ground close to the village where he had died. Not until the following spring was it moved to a monastery in Selymbria. It was held by the church that he had died as a heretic and so could not be buried according to the rites of the Orthodox church. He was not to be forgiven for his betrayal of Byzantine faith and ideology.

It might have been expected that hordes of crusaders would have swept down on Andronicus II to exact retribution for his flouting of papal authority, but none came. In due course the pope excommunicated him. Various crusade propagandists, such as Ramon Lull and Peter Dubois, wrote tracts asserting that the best way to recover Jerusalem would be by first capturing Constantinople from the schismatic Greeks. The pope wrote to Andronicus II urging him to accept baptism into the Roman church so that the Holy Land might be liberated more easily. The emperor does not seem to have replied. Therefore, as late as 1322, three years absolution was being granted to anyone who would fight for the principality of Achaia against 'Greeks, schismatics and other infidels'.[58] By that time, however, the crusading agenda had changed radically as a result of cataclysmic events in Latin Syria.

A few years after the accession of Andronicus II, reports spread through Constantinople of terrifying portents. In Hagia Sophia, an image of the

Virgin Mary painted on a wall had started to shed tears. Blood had flowed from an icon of St George. Many predicted that a terrible disaster was about to strike the empire. The chronicler of the events, the deacon George Pachymeres, however, realised with hindsight that the portents had not related to Constantinople at all but to the Christians of Syria. On 26 April 1289 a Mamluk army captured Tripoli, massacred or enslaved the inhabitants and razed the entire city to the ground. In May 1291 it was the turn of Acre to suffer the same fate. The remaining towns in Christian hands were captured or were evacuated before the year was out, bringing the Latin presence in the east to an end. The account of these events takes up very little space in the history of Pachymeres. He and his fellow Byzantines were much more interested in what was going on inside their own empire. Indeed, throughout the entire period of the crusades, they always had been.[59]

11

Survival

The Byzantine empire not only survived the severe blow inflicted on it by the Fourth Crusade, but outlived those creations of the crusade ideal, the Latin states of Syria. By 1291, however, the empire itself was entering on a period of sustained decline. During the reign of Andronicus II, it proved incapable of defending its eastern frontier in Asia Minor against the independent Turkish emirs who were the successors to the old Seljuk sultanate. By the time that Andronicus was deposed in 1328, most of Asia Minor had been lost for ever. In 1354, the Osmanli or Ottoman Turks succeeded in establishing a bridgehead at Gallipoli, on the European side of the Bosporos, from which they launched their conquest of the Balkans. The Byzantine empire lingered on for another century, until 29 May 1453, when Constantinople was finally captured by the Ottoman sultan Mehmed II.

Byzantium today is numbered among the ranks of lost civilisations, one whose material remains are generally much less well known and less impressive than those ancient Egypt or Rome. While the cathedral of Hagia Sophia still stands out on the skyline of modern Istanbul, the nearby Hippodrome is merely an open space, its high banks of seating having long since disappeared. John II's monastery of the Pantokrator, where Andronicus Comnenus once breathed his murderous threats against the family of his hated cousin, is little more than a shell. To the west, the Land Walls still guard the city among the apartment blocks and dual carriageways, but of the great palaces of Boukoleon and Blachernae only a few scattered fragments remain. The church of the Holy Apostles, with its tombs of past emperors, the monastery of Kosmidion, where Alexios I tried to bribe Bohemond with a room full of gold, and the houses and palaces of the wealthy that once elicited the admiration of Fulcher of Chartres have all vanished without trace.

Such a complete and utter annihilation of an empire which had once been so formidable a power in the eastern Mediterranean must have some rational explanation, and the crusades have to be considered as a major factor. Although the Ottoman Turks delivered the final blow, the seizure of Constantinople and the dismemberment of the provinces by the Fourth Crusade in 1204 undoubtedly contributed to the empire's downfall. In spite of the recapture of Constantinople in 1261, the empire as reconstituted by Michael VIII Palaeologus was a smaller, impoverished shadow of its former self. Subsequent western hostility and attempts to retake Constantinople weakened it still further and left it open to attack by its Muslim enemies in the east. Michael VIII's preoccupation with defence against the threat of Charles of Anjou, and his draining of the treasury to pay the enormous bribe to the king of Aragon, meant that little could be spared to defend the eastern provinces against the Turks.

Any assessment of why the Byzantine empire disappeared has therefore to consider why the Fourth Crusade attacked and captured Constantinople. As we have seen, the theory that the events of 1204 were the culmination of a century of misunderstanding between two very different civilisations is unconvincing. Far from being alien to Byzantine culture, many western Europeans active in the Latin east were deeply involved in it. Such differences as there were, over theology, ecclesiastical hierarchy, and liturgical practice, gave rise to plenty of harsh words but were not in themselves the cause of armed conflict.

Equally flimsy is the argument that the Fourth Crusade was an accident, the fortuitous outcome of a random and unpredictable sequence of events. The pronouncements of the German emperor Henry VI and Pope Innocent III make it quite clear that, by the 1190s, western European leaders held the opinion that the Byzantine empire was under an obligation to assist the crusading effort and that it was quite legitimate to use force if the emperor failed to do his duty. Such a failure occurred in January 1204 and was followed by retribution only a few months later.

The sack of Constantinople should be seen instead as the outcome of the failure of a human institution: the codified foreign policy aims and methods preserved over the centuries by the Byzantine ruling elite. The policy was not inherently flawed. It had achieved great successes in the ninth and tenth centuries when it had helped to spread Byzantine influence in the Slav lands to the north. It was to be successful again in the thirteenth century, helping to recover Constantinople in 1261, and to frustrate the plans of Charles of Anjou in 1282. Yet, when these aims and methods were applied to the reformed papacy, the crusades and the crusader states between 1054 and 1204, they were to prove a liability. By being seen to put their own empire before the struggle for Jerusalem, and by using any method to achieve their goals, the rulers of Byzantium appeared to be betraying the cause of the crusade and colluding with the infidel. That perception prompted crusade leaders first to demand Byzantine money to supply their armies, then to attack and occupy Byzantine territory when it was not forthcoming.

That is not to say that the Byzantine imperial system somehow brought about its own ruin. On the contrary, the empire was one of the most successful and long-lived bodies politic, lasting for over a thousand years from Constantine's foundation of Constantinople in 330 until the fall of the city in 1453. The very ideology that brought the empire into conflict with western Europe undoubtedly played a role in its amazing longevity. The empire ultimately disappeared because no human institution can survive indefinitely as conditions change and new challenges arise. This was the opinion of at least one of the Byzantines themselves, Michael Kritoboulos, a nobleman of the generation which witnessed Mehmed II's capture of Constantinople:

> Who does not know that since men have existed, the kingly or ruling power has not always remained in the same people, nor has it been limited to one race or nation? Like the planets, rule has gone from nation to nation and from place to place in succession, always changing and passing, now to the Assyrians, the Medes, the Persians, and then to the Greeks and Romans, according to the times and epochs establishing itself in a place and never returning to the same.[1]

Yet even though the empire disappeared as a political entity in 1453, other aspects of Byzantine civilisation survived. Its religious tradition, so fiercely defended by the opponents of Michael VIII in the 1270s, is perpetuated in the Orthodox churches of eastern Europe. Its literary tradition, based on the ancient Greek classics, so beloved of Michael Psellos and Niketas Choniates, passed to Italy at the time of the Renaissance, where émigrés from Constantinople taught, copied and translated the key texts which formed their inheritance.[2] While the crusades are now nothing more than a slightly embarrassing spectre which haunts the conscience of liberal Europe and America, the legacy of Byzantium lives on.

Notes

Notes to Introduction

1. *Die Register Innocenz III*, ed. O. Hageneder et al., 7 vols (Graz and Cologne, 1964–99), vii, pp. 253–62, 262–63; trans. Alfred J. Andrea, *Contemporary Sources for the Fourth Crusade* (Leiden, 2000), pp. 100–112, 112–15.
2. *Die Register Innocenz III*, vii, p. 264; Andrea, *Contemporary Sources*, p. 117.
3. Gabriel Hanotaux, 'Les Vénitiens ont-ils trahi la chrétienté en 1202?', *Revue Historique*, 4 (1877), pp. 74–102, Nevertheless, the theory of Venetian duplicity has persisted: Edwin Pears, *The Fall of Constantinople: Being the Story of the Fourth Crusade* (London, 1885), pp. 263–67; John Godfrey, *1204: The Unholy Crusade* (Oxford, 1980), p. 74; D. M. Nicol, *Byzantium and Venice: A Study in Diplomatic and Cultural Relations* (Cambridge, 1988), pp. 124–26.
4. For a summary of these and other theories see Donald E. Queller, *The Latin Conquest of Constantinople* (New York, 1971); Donald E. Queller and S. J. Stratton, 'A Century of Controversy on the Fourth Crusade', *Studies in Medieval and Renaissance History*, 6 (1969), pp. 235–77; C. M. Brand, 'The Fourth Crusade: Some Recent Interpretations', *Medievalia et Humanistica*, 12 (1984), pp. 33–45; Michael Angold, 'The Road to 1204: The Byzantine Background to the Fourth Crusade', *Journal of Medieval History*, 25 (1999), pp. 257–78.
5. Steven Runciman, *The Eastern Schism* (Cambridge, 1955), pp. 79–80.
6. Choniates, p. 167; Guibert of Nogent, *The Deeds of God through the Franks*, trans. Robert Levine (Woodbridge, 1997), p. 38.
7. On 1054 as the beginning of mutual hostility, see Edward Gibbon, *The History of the Decline and Fall of the Roman Empire*, ed. J. B. Bury, 7 vols (London, 1926–27), vi, pp. 385–86; A. A. Vasiliev, *History of the Byzantine Empire, 324–1453* (2nd edn, Madison, Wisconsin, 1952), pp. 338–39; George Ostrogorsky, *History of the Byzantine State*, trans. J. M. Hussey (2nd edn, Oxford, 1968), pp. 334–37. On 1096, see Runciman, *Eastern Schism*, pp. 79–80; D. M. Nicol, 'Byzantium and the Papacy in the Eleventh Century', *Journal of Ecclesiastical History*, 13 (1962), pp. 1–20, at 19; H. E. J. Cowdrey, 'The Gregorian Papacy, Byzantium, and the First Crusade', *Byzantinische Forschungen*, 13 (1988), pp. 145–69, at 167; D. M. Nicol, 'The Byzantine View of Western Europe', *Greek, Roman and Byzantine Studies*, 8 (1967), pp. 315–39, at 329–30; Michael Angold, *The Byzantine Empire, 1025–1204: A Political History* (2nd edn, Harlow, 1997), pp. 233–40. On 1180, see Charles M. Brand, *Byzantium Confronts the West, 1180–1204* (Cambridge, Massachusetts, 1968), pp. 41, 175, 188.

8. On western barbarity see Steven Runciman, *A History of the Crusades*, 3 vols (Cambridge, 1951–54), iii, p. 131. Byzantine snobbery: D. M. Nicol, 'The Byzantine View of Western Europe', *Greek, Roman and Byzantine Studies*, 8 (1967), pp. 315–39, at 329; A. A. M. Bryer, 'The First Encounter with the West, AD 1050–1204', *Byzantium: An Introduction*, ed. Philip Whitting (2nd edn, London, 1981), pp. 85–110, at 103.
9. Choniates, pp. 210, 212–13; Robert of Clari, p. 95.
10. Villehardouin, pp. 51–56; Robert of Clari, pp. 59, 93–94; D. E. Queller, T. K. Compton and D. A. Campbell, 'The Fourth Crusade: The Neglected Majority', *Speculum*, 49 (1974), pp. 441–65.
11. Among proponents of this theory are Jonathan Riley-Smith, *The Crusades: A Short History* (New Haven and London, 1987), p. 130; Warren Treadgold, *A History of the Byzantine State and Society* (Stanford, California, 1997), p. 666; Donald E. Queller and Thomas F. Madden, *The Fourth Crusade: The Conquest of Constantinople* (2nd edn, Philadelphia, 1997).

Notes to Chapter 1: The Empire of Christ

1. Anna Comnena, p. 463; Choniates, pp. 11, 222; Nina G. Garsoïan, 'The Problem of Armenian Integration into the Byzantine Empire', in *Studies on the Internal Diaspora of the Byzantine Empire*, ed. H. Ahrweiler and A. E. Laiou (Washington, DC, 1998), pp. 53–124, at 56–61; Cyril Mango, *Byzantium: The Empire of New Rome* (London, 1980), pp. 13–31.
2. Gladys R. Davidson, 'A Mediaeval Glass Factory at Corinth', *American Journal of Archaeology*, 44 (1940), pp. 297–324; R. S. Lopez, 'Silk Industry in the Byzantine Empire', *Speculum*, 20 (1945), pp. 1–42; Alan Harvey, *Economic Expansion in the Byzantine Empire, 900–1200* (Cambridge, 1990), pp. 213–37; Robert Browning, 'Byzantine Thessalonike: A Unique City?', *Dialogos: Hellenic Studies Review*, 2 (1995), pp. 91–104, at 93.
3. Harvey, *Economic Expansion*, pp. 208–13; Clive Foss, *Byzantine and Turkish Sardis* (Cambridge, Massachusetts, 1976), pp. 70–71; Michael Angold, *The Byzantine Empire, 1025–1204: A Political History* (2nd edn, Harlow, 1997), pp. 86–87; Clive Foss, *Nicaea: A Byzantine Capital and its Praises* (Brookline, Massachusetts, 1996), pp. 29–39.
4. Rosemary Morris, *Monks and Laymen in Byzantium, 843–1118* (Cambridge, 1995), pp. 19–29.
5. Ann Wharton Epstein, 'Middle Byzantine Churches of Kastoria: Dates and Implications', *Art Bulletin*, 62 (1980), pp. 190–207; Robin Cormack, *Byzantine Art* (Oxford, 2000), pp. 145–50, 163–70.
6. Choniates, p. 317; Psellos, p. 114; Anna Comnena, p. 63.
7. Dean A. Miller, *Imperial Constantinople* (New York, 1969), p. 1; Fulcher of Chartres, pp. 58–59; Villehardouin, p. 59; Robert of Clari, p. 67; Krijnie N. Ciggaar, *Western Travellers to Constantinople: The West and Byzantium, 962–1204. Cultural and Political Relations* (Leiden, 1996), pp. 102–3; Dimitri Obolensky,

The Byzantine Commonwealth: Eastern Europe, 500–1453 (London, 1971), pp. 374–75; Ruth Macrides, 'Constantinople: The Crusaders' Gaze', in *Travel in the Byzantine World*, ed. Ruth Macrides (Aldershot, 2002), pp. 193–212.

8. Choniates p. 117; Villehardouin, p. 66; Robert of Clari, p. 69; Alexander Van Millingen, *Byzantine Constantinople: The Walls of the City and Adjoining Historical Sites* (London, 1899), p. 229.
9. John Skylitzes, *Synopsis Historiarum*, ed. J. Thurn (Berlin, 1973), pp. 431–32; Villehardouin, p. 59; Odo of Deuil, p. 69.
10. Choniates, p. 303; David Jacoby, 'La population de Constantinople à l'époque Byzantine: une problème de démographie urbaine', *Byzantion*, 31 (1961), pp. 81–109; Ciggaar, *Western Travellers*, p. 47; Andrew Scharf, *Byzantine Jewry from Justinian to the Fourth Crusade* (London, 1971), p. 117; Stephen W. Reinert, 'The Muslim Presence in Constantinople, Ninth–Fifteenth Centuries: Some Preliminary Observations', in *Studies on the Internal Diaspora of the Byzantine Empire*, ed. H. Ahrweiler and A. E. Laiou (Washington, DC, 1998), pp. 125–50.
11. Robert of Clari, p. 101; Fulcher of Chartres, p. 62; Liudprand, p. 12.
12. Benjamin of Tudela, *The Itinerary*, trans. M. N. Adler (London, 1907), pp. 12–13; Miller, *Imperial Constantinople*, pp. 50–54; H. Antoniadis-Bibicou, *Recherches sur les douanes à Byzance: l'Octava, le Kommerkion et les commerciaires* (Paris, 1963), pp. 97–155.
13. Choniates, p. 68.
14. Otto Demus, 'Zur Pala d'Oro', *Jahrbuch der Österreichischen Byzantinischen Gesellschaft*, 16 (1967), pp. 263–79; G. Matthiae, *Le porte bronzee bizantine in Italia* (Rome, 1971).
15. *Ordinances of Leo VI, c. 895, from the Book of the Eparch*, in E. H. Freshfield, *Roman Law in the Later Roman Empire* (Cambridge, 1938), pp. 3–50, at 10–35; Miller, *Imperial Constantinople*, pp. 54–60; Lopez, 'Silk Industry', pp. 6–7.
16. Robert of Clari, pp. 108–9.
17. Procopius, *The Buildings*, trans. H. B. Dewing, Loeb Classical Library (London, 1971), pp. 32–37; Robert of Clari, p. 107; Pero Tafur, *Travels and Adventures, 1435–1439* (London, 1926), pp. 140–41; Cyril Mango, 'The Columns of Justinian and his Successors', *Art Bulletin*, 41 (1959), pp. 1–16 .
18. Constantine VII, *De ceremoniis aulae Byzantinae*, ed. J. Reisky, 2 vols (Bonn, 1829–30), i, pp. 364–69; Anna Comnena, pp. 502–4; Choniates, pp. 160, 172, 285, 305, 358–62; L. Vlad Borelli and A. Guidi Toniato, 'The Origins and Documentary Sources of the Horses of San Marco', in *The Horses of San Marco*, ed. Guido Perocco, trans. J. and V. Wilton-Ely (London, 1979), pp. 127–36, at 127–28; Sarah Guberti Bassett, 'The Antiquities in the Hippodrome of Constantinople', *Dumbarton Oaks Papers*, 45 (1991), pp. 87–96.
19. Choniates, p. 323; Odo of Deuil, p. 65; Fulcher of Chartres, p. 62; Robert of Clari, p. 105; Michael Angold, 'Inventory of the So-Called Palace of Botaneiates', *The Byzantine Aristocracy, IX-XIII Centuries*, ed. Michael Angold (Oxford, 1984), pp. 254–66.
20. Theophanes Continuatus, *Chronographia*, ed. I. Bekker (Bonn, 1838), pp. 144–45,

337–38; Psellos, p. 252; Choniates, p. 117; Anna Comnena, pp. 105, 219; Cyril Mango, *The Brazen House: A Study of the Vestibule of the Imperial Palace at Constantinople* (Copenhagen, 1959), pp. 12–13.

21. Anna Comnena, p. 105; Choniates, p. 117; Kinnamos, pp. 131–32; Odo of Deuil, p. 65; Robert of Clari, p. 105; Benjamin of Tudela, *Itinerary*, p. 13.
22. Psellos, pp. 144–45, 301; Anna Comnena, p. 86; Robert of Clari, p. 110; Morris, *Monks and Laymen*, pp. 55, 95, 172.
23. Procopius, *Buildings*, pp. 10–33; Choniates, p. 132; Tafur, *Travels and Adventures*, p. 139; Paul the Silentiary in W. R. Lethaby and Harold Swainson, *The Church of Saint Sophia, Constantinople: A Study of a Byzantine Building* (London and New York, 1894), pp. 35–60; *The Russian Primary Chronicle: The Laurentian Text*, ed. and trans. S. H. Cross and O. P. Sherbowitz-Wetzor (Cambridge, Massachusetts, 1953), pp. 110–11; Anthony, Archbishop of Novgorod, *Description des lieux-saints de Constantinople*, in *Itinéraires russes en orient*, ed. B. de Khitrowo (Geneva, 1889), pp. 85–111, at 97.
24. Emile Legrand, 'Description des oeuvres d'art et de l'église des Saints Apôtres de Constantinople: poème en vers iambiques par Constantin le Rhodien', *Revue des Etudes Grecques*, 9 (1896), pp. 32–65; Nicolas Mesarites, 'Description of the Church of the Holy Apostles at Constantinople', ed. and trans. Glanville Downey, in *Transactions of the American Philosophical Society*, 47 (1957), pp. 855–924, at 862, 869–89, 891–3; Anthony of Novgorod, pp. 101–2.
25. Procopius, *Buildings*, pp. 48–55; Psellos, pp. 250–52; Choniates, p. 183; Anthony of Novgorod, p. 100.
26. Francis Dvornik, *The Idea of Apostolicity in Byzantium and the Legend of the Apostle Andrew* (Cambridge, Massachusetts, 1958), pp. 138–80.
27. *Chronicon Paschale, 284–628 AD*, trans. Michael Whitby and Mary Whitby (Liverpool, 1989), pp. 169, 178, 180; N. H. Baynes, 'The Supernatural Defenders of Constantinople', in N. H. Baynes, *Byzantine Studies and Other Essays* (London, 1955), pp. 248–60; Robert Lee Wolff, 'Footnote to an Incident of the Latin Occupation of Constantinople: The Church and the Icon of the Hodegetria', *Speculum*, 6 (1948), pp. 319–28.
28. Anthony of Novgorod, pp. 97–100; Robert of Clari, pp. 102–5; Ciggaar, *Western Travellers*, pp. 47–49.
29. Legrand, 'Description des oeuvres d'art', p. 38; Robert of Clari, p. 108; Choniates, p. 125.
30. Procopius, *Buildings*, pp. 26–27; Robert of Clari, p. 106; Cyril Mango and John Parker, 'A Twelfth-Century Description of St Sophia', *Dumbarton Oaks Papers*, 14 (1960), pp. 233–45.
31. Pero Tafur, *Travels and Adventures*, p. 143; Robert of Clari, pp. 110–11; Gunther of Pairis, pp. 116–17.
32. Matthew 22: 21; I Peter 2:17. Most English versions of the Bible translate St Peter's Greek word *Basileus* as 'king' rather than 'emperor'. However, *Basileus* was the title used by the Byzantine emperors, and the Byzantines certainly considered that this was the office that was referred to here.

33. Eusebius of Caesarea, *Tricennial Oration*, in H. A. Drake, *In Praise of Constantine: A Historical Study and New Translation of Eusebius's Tricennial Orations* (Berkeley and Los Angeles, 1976), pp. 83–127, at 87–88, 120; Ernest Barker, *Social and Political Thought in Byzantium from Justinian I to the Last Palaeologus* (Oxford, 1957), pp. 194–96; Steven Runciman, *The Byzantine Theocracy* (Cambridge, 1977), pp. 5–25; Paul J. Alexander, 'The Strength of Empire and Capital as Seen Through Byzantine Eyes', *Speculum*, 37 (1962), pp. 339–57, at 341–47; D. M. Nicol, 'Byzantine Political Thought', in *The Cambridge History of Medieval Political Thought*, ed. J. H. Burns (Cambridge, 1988), pp. 51–79, at 52–53.
34. Anna Comnena, p. 62; Constantine VII Porphyrogenitos, *De administrando imperio*, ed. G. Moravcsik, trans. R. J. H. Jenkins (Washington, DC, 1967), p. 113. Philotheos is cited in Nicol, 'Byzantine Political Thought', p. 60.
35. On Constantinople as New Rome: Anna Comnena, p. 430. As second Jerusalem: *The Life of Saint Daniel the Stylite*, in *Three Byzantine Saints*, trans. Elizabeth Dawes and Norman H. Baynes (2nd edn, Oxford 1977), p. 13; Choniates, p. 326; John Mauropous in A. P. Kazhdan and Ann Wharton Epstein, *Change in Byzantine Culture in the Eleventh and Twelfth Centuries* (Berkeley and Los Angeles, California, 1985), p. 255.
36. Obolensky, *The Byzantine Commonwealth*, p. 104.

Notes to Chapter 2: The Rulers of the Empire

1. Eusebius of Caesarea, *Tricennial Oration*, in H. A. Drake, *In Praise of Constantine: A Historical Study and New Translation of Eusebius's Tricennial Orations* (Berkeley and Los Angeles, 1976), pp. 83–127, at 87; Paul J. Alexander, 'The Strength of Empire and Capital as Seen Through Byzantine Eyes', *Speculum*, 37 (1962), pp. 339–57, at 348–54; Steven Runciman, *The Byzantine Theocracy* (Cambridge, 1977), pp. 5–25; D. M. Nicol, 'Byzantine Political Thought', in *The Cambridge History of Medieval Political Thought c. 350 – c. 1450*, ed. J. H. Burns (Cambridge, 1988), pp. 51–79, at 52–53; J. Chrysostomides, 'Byzantine Concepts of War and Peace', in *War, Peace and World Orders in European History*, ed. Anja V. Hartmann and Beatrice Heuser (London and New York, 2001), pp. 91–101, at 91–92.
2. Bibliothèque Nationale, Paris, MS Coislin 79, fol. 2, reproduced on the cover of this book. On the imperial civil service in general see Dean A. Miller, *Imperial Constantinople* (New York, 1969), pp. 79–114; J. B. Bury, *The Imperial Administrative System in the Ninth Century* (London, 1911), pp. 7–20.
3. Psellos, pp. 43–44.
4. Psellos, p. 28; Shaun Tougher, 'Byzantine Eunuchs: An Overview, with Special Reference to their Creation and Origin', in *Women, Men and Eunuchs: Gender in Byzantium*, ed. Liz James (London, 1997), pp. 168–84, at 170–72.
5. *The Theodosian Code and Novels and the Sirmondian Constitutions*, trans. Clyde Pharr (Princeton, New Jersey, 1952), 14.1.1; N. G. Wilson, *Scholars of Byzantium* (2nd edn, London, 1996), p. 3.

6. Wilson, *Scholars of Byzantium*, pp. 2–4; C. N. Constantinides, *Higher Education in Byzantium in the Thirteenth and Early Fourteenth Centuries, 1204 – c. 1310* (Nicosia, 1982), pp. 1–2; Cyril Mango, *Byzantium: The Empire of the New Rome* (London, 1980), pp. 125–48.
7. Psellos, pp. 178–79, 334; J. M. Hussey, *Church and Learning in the Byzantine Empire, 867–1185* (Oxford, 1937), pp. 37–47; Wilson, *Scholars of Byzantium*, pp. 156–66.
8. Choniates, pp. xi–xii.
9. Constantinides, *Higher Education*, pp. 9–10, 31–32, 66–89; Wilson, *Scholars of Byzantium*, pp. 230–41, 256–64.
10. Mango, *Byzantium*, p. 147.
11. *Iliad*, iii, lines 156–57; Psellos, p. 185.
12. Paul Lemerle, '"Roga" et rent d'état aux X-XIe siècles', *Revue des Etudes Byzantines*, 25 (1967), pp. 77–100, at 84–87; Niketas Stethatos, *Un grand mystique byzantin: vie de Syméon le Nouveau Théologian (949–1022)*, ed. and trans. I. Hausherr (Rome, 1928), p. 4.
13. Psellos, p. 28.
14. Psellos, p. 351; Choniates, p. 311; Anna Comnena, pp. 174–80.
15. Bury, *Imperial Administrative System*, pp. 131–79; Anna Comnena, pp. 111–12; N. Oikonomides, *Les listes de préséance byzantines des IXe et Xe siècles* (Paris, 1972), p. 297.
16. Liudprand, pp. 155–56; Bury, *Imperial Administrative System*, pp. 20–22.
17. Psellos, pp. 263–64; Choniates, p. 116; George Akropolites, *Historia*, ed. A. Heisenberg and P. Wirth, 2 vols (Stuttgart, 1978), p. 124; Ruth Macrides, 'The Historian in the History', *Philellin: Studies in Honour of Robert Browning*, ed. C. N. Constantinides et al. (Venice, 1996), pp. 205–24, at 221–22.
18. Psellos, pp. 170–71; Michael Attaleiates, *Historia*, ed. W. Brunet de Presle and I. Bekker (Bonn, 1853), p. 175; Choniates, pp. 244, 249–50, 265–66.
19. Choniates, pp. xii, xiii, 221; Hussey, *Church and Learning*, pp. 44–47. The eunuch Eustathios, who held the office of *Kanikleiou*, later became admiral of the fleet: Anna Comnena, p. 363.
20. Theophanes Continuatus, *Chronographia*, ed. I. Bekker (Bonn, 1838), pp. 95–96; Choniates, p. 37; Marius Canard, 'Les relations politiques et sociales entre Byzance et les arabes', *Dumbarton Oaks Papers*, 18 (1964), pp. 35–56, at 41; Nike Koutrakou, '*Logos* and *Pathos* between Peace and War: Rhetoric as a Tool of Diplomacy in the Middle Byzantine Period', *Thesaurismata*, 25 (1995), pp. 7–20, at 9–10.
21. Psellos, pp. 335–36; John VI Cantacuzenus, *Historiarum libri IV*, ed. L. Schopen, 3 vols (Bonn, 1827–32), iii, p. 285; Choniates, p. 225; Akropolites, p. 127; Macrides, 'The Historian in the History', pp. 222–23.
22. Psellos, p. 353; F. Miklosich and W. Müller, *Acta et diplomata Graeca medii aevi sacra et profana*, 6 vols (Vienna, 1860–90), iii, p. 46.
23. Psellos, p. 253; H. Bibicou, 'Une page d'histoire diplomatique de Byzance au XIe siècle: Michel VII Doukas, Robert Guiscard, et la pension des dignitaires', *Byzantion*, 29–30 (1959), pp. 43–75, at 44.

24. Leo VI, *Tactica sive de re militari liber*, in *Patrologia Graeca*, vol. 107, cols 669–1120; Constantine VII Porphyrogenitos, *De administrando imperio*, ed. G. Moravcsik, trans. R. J. H. Jenkins (Washington, DC, 1967); idem, *De ceremoniis aulae Byzantinae*, ed. J. Reisky, 2 vols (Bonn, 1829–30); idem, *Three Treatises on Imperial Military Expeditions*, ed. and trans. John Haldon (Vienna, 1990); *Three Byzantine Military Treatises*, ed. and trans. George T. Dennis (Washington, DC, 1985).
25. Charles M. Brand, 'A Byzantine Plan for the Fourth Crusade', *Speculum*, 43 (1968), pp. 462–75, at 465; Michael Italikos, *Lettres et discours*, ed. Paul Gautier (Paris, 1972), pp. 245–70; Paul Magdalino, *The Empire of Manuel I Comnenus, 1143–1180* (Cambridge, 1993), pp. 434–50.
26. George Tornikios, *Discourse on the Death of the Porphyrogenita Anna, the Kaisarissa*, in George and Leo Tornikios, *Lettres et discours*, ed. J. Darrouzès (Paris, 1970), pp. 220–323, at 244–45, 262–63; Anna Comnena, p. 17; J. Chrysostomides, 'A Byzantine Historian: Anna Comnena', in *Medieval Historical Writing in the Christian and Islamic Worlds*, ed. D. O. Morgan (London, 1982), pp. 30–46, at 32–33.
27. Anna Comnena, p. 460; Psellos, pp. 167–68.
28. See, however, the recent work of Anthony Kaldellis, *The Argument of Psellos's Chronographia* (Leiden, 1999), where Psellos is presented as a critic of official ideology.
29. Liudprand, pp. 199–200.
30. Kinnamos, pp. 165–66; Philotheos in Nicol, 'Byzantine Political Thought', p. 60.
31. Paul Lemerle, 'Thomas le Slave', *Travaux et mémoires*, 1 (1965), pp. 255–97, at 255; Liudprand, p. 178.
32. J. Zepos and P. Zepos, *Jus Graecoromanum*, 8 vols (Athens, 1931), ii, pp. 240–42; translation in Ernest Barker, *Social and Political Thought in Byzantium from Justinian I to the Last Palaeologus* (Oxford, 1957), p. 89. In general see Dimitri Obolensky, 'The Principles and Methods of Byzantine Diplomacy', in Dimitri Obolensky, *Byzantium and the Slavs: Collected Studies* (London, 1971), no. I, pp. 45–61, at 52–56; Dimitri Obolensky, *The Byzantine Commonwealth: Eastern Europe, 500–1453* (London, 1971), p. 357.
33. Miklosich and Müller, *Acta et diplomata*, ii, pp. 190–92; translation in Barker, *Social and Political Thought*, pp. 194–96; George Ostrogorsky, *History of the Byzantine State*, trans. J. M. Hussey (2nd edn, Oxford, 1968), pp. 553–54.
34. Theophanes Continuatus, pp. 291–92, translation in Obolensky, *Byzantine Commonwealth*, p. 135.
35. Obolensky, *Byzantine Commonwealth*, pp. 287–302; André Grabar, 'God and the "Family of Princes" Presided over by the Byzantine Emperor', *Harvard Slavic Studies*, 2 (1954), pp. 117–23; George Ostrogorsky, 'The Byzantine Emperor and the Hierarchical World Order', *Slavonic and East European Review*, 35 (1956–57), pp. 1–14; Jonathan Shepard, '"Father" or "Scorpion"? Style and Substance in Alexios's Diplomacy', in *Alexios I Komnenos*, ed. Margaret Mullett and Dion Smythe (Belfast, 1996), pp. 68–132, at 80–82.

36. Matthew of Edessa, *Chronicle*, in A. E. Dostourian, *Armenia and the Crusades* (Lanham, Maryland, 1993), pp. 19–280, at 28–33; Paul E. Walker, 'The "Crusade" of John Tzimisces in the Light of New Arab Evidence', *Byzantion*, 47 (1977), pp. 301–27; Mark Whittow, *The Making of Orthodox Byzantium, 600–1025* (London, 1996), pp. 355–56; Ostrogorsky, *History*, pp. 297–98; George T. Dennis, 'Defenders of the Christian People: Holy War in Byzantium', *The Crusades from the Perspective of Byzantium and the Muslim World*, ed. A. E. Laiou and R. P. Mottahedeh (Washington, DC, 2001), pp. 31–39, at 34–37.
37. Abbas Hamdani, 'Byzantine-Fatimid Relations before the Battle of Mantzikert', *Byzantine Studies*, 1 (1974), pp. 169–79, at 173; Steven Runciman, 'The Byzantine "Protectorate" in the Holy Land in the Eleventh Century', *Byzantion*, 18 (1946–48), pp. 207–15; Stephen W. Reinert, 'The Muslim Presence in Constantinople, Ninth–Fifteenth Centuries: Some Preliminary Observations', in *Studies on the Internal Diaspora of the Byzantine Empire*, ed. H. Ahrweiler and A. E. Laiou (Washington, DC, 1998), pp. 125–50, at 135–40.
38. Bar Hebraeus, *Chronography*, trans. Ernest A. Wallis-Budge, 2 vols (London, 1932), i, p. 195; William of Tyre, i, pp. 406–7.
39. Theophanes Continuatus, pp. 162–65; Obolensky, *Byzantine Commonwealth*, pp. 117–18.
40. Ibn al-Qalanisi, *The Damascus Chronicle of the Crusades*, trans. H. A. R. Gibb (London, 1932), pp. 354–55; Chrysostomides, 'Byzantine Concepts of War and Peace', p. 93.
41. Psellos, p. 170.
42. Benjamin of Tudela, *The Itinerary*, trans. M. N. Adler (London, 1907), p. 13; Michael F. Hendy, *Studies in the Byzantine Monetary Economy, c. 300–1450* (Cambridge, 1985), pp. 237–42; Alan Harvey, *Economic Expansion in the Byzantine Empire, 900–1200* (Cambridge, 1989), pp. 103–5; Ernst Stein, *Studien zur Geschichte des Byzantinischen Reiches vornehmlich unter den Kaisern Justinus II und Tiberius Constantinus* (Stuttgart, 1919), pp. 142–43; Ostrogorsky, *History of the Byzantine State*, p. 485.
43. Psellos, p. 53; Attaleiates, p. 84; John Skylitzes, *Synopsis Historiarum*, ed. J. Thurn (Berlin, 1973), p. 467; Paul Maas, 'Die Musen des Kaisers Alexios I', *Byzantinische Zeitschrift*, 22 (1913), pp. 348–69, at 357; Chrysostomides, 'Byzantine Concepts of War and Peace', p. 94.
44. Constantine VII, *De ceremoniis*, i, p. 576; Liudprand, p. 198; Attaleiates, pp. 156–57; Fulcher of Chartres, p. 64; *Gesta Francorum*, p. 9; Whittow, *Making of Orthodox Byzantium*, pp. 169–70.
45. Liudprand, p. 202; Anna Comnena, p. 366; Obolensky, *Byzantine Commonwealth*, p. 173.
46. Kinnamos, pp. 156–58; Choniates, pp. 67–68.
47. Liudprand, p. 153.
48. Anna Comnena, p. 128; Constantine VII, *Three Treatises*, pp. 109–10; Robin Cormack, 'But is it Art?', in *Byzantine Diplomacy*, ed. Jonathan Shepard and Simon Franklin (Aldershot, 1992), pp. 219–36, at 230–31; K. N. Ciggaar, 'England

and Byzantium on the Eve of the Norman Conquest', *Anglo-Norman Studies*, 5 (1982), pp. 78–96, at 90–95; Anna Muthesius, 'Silken Diplomacy', in *Byzantine Diplomacy*, ed. Jonathan Shepard and Simon Franklin (Aldershot, 1992), pp. 237–48.

49. Attaleiates, pp. 30–31.
50. *Ordinances of Leo VI, c. 895, from the Book of the Eparch*, in E. H. Freshfield, *Roman Law in the Later Roman Empire* (Cambridge, 1938), pp. 3–50, at 17; Liudprand, pp. 202–3; Constantine VII, *De administrando imperio*, pp. 66–69; Pachymeres, i, pp. 61–63; Muthesius, 'Silken Diplomacy', p. 246.
51. Constantine VII, *De ceremoniis*, i, pp. 3–4; Kinnamos, p. 157; Liudprand, p. 153; Jonathan Shepard, 'Byzantine Diplomacy, 800–1204: Means and Ends', in *Byzantine Diplomacy*, ed. Jonathan Shepard and Simon Franklin (Aldershot, 1992), pp. 41–71, at 62–63; Chrysostomides, 'Byzantine Concepts of War and Peace', p. 98.
52. Theophylact of Ochrid, *Discours, traités, poésies*, ed. and trans. P. Gautier (Thessaloniki, 1980), pp. 222–25; Jonathan Shepard, 'Information, Disinformation and Delay in Byzantine Diplomacy', *Byzantinische Forschungen*, 10 (1985), pp. 233–93, at 236–37.
53. Constantine VII, *De administrando imperio*, pp. 48–55; Choniates, p. 113.
54. Anna Comnena, p. 89; Attaleiates, p. 266; Shepard, '"Father" or "Scorpion"', pp. 105–8.
55. Obolensky, *Byzantine Commonwealth*, pp. 262–63.
56. A. M. H. Shboul, 'Arab Attitudes towards Byzantium: Official, Learned, Popular', in *Kathegetria: Essays Presented to Joan Hussey for her 80th Birthday*, ed. J. Chrysostomides (Camberley, 1988), pp. 111–28; Runciman, 'Byzantine "Protectorate"', pp. 211–13; Chrysostomides, 'Byzantine Concepts of War and Peace', pp. 99–100.
57. R. J. H. Jenkins, *Byzantium: The Imperial Centuries, 610–1071* (London, 1966), p. 334; D. M. Nicol, 'The Byzantine View of Western Europe', *Greek, Roman and Byzantine Studies*, 8 (1967), pp. 315–39, at 315, 329; Paul Magdalino, 'Byzantine Snobbery', *The Byzantine Aristocracy*, ed. Michael Angold (Oxford, 1984), pp. 58–78.
58. Anna Comnena, pp. 68, 212; Kinnamos, pp. 67, 226.
59. Nicol, 'Byzantine View', p. 317; Jonathan Harris, 'Distortion, Divine Providence and Genre in Niketas Choniates's Account of the Collapse of Byzantium 1180–1204', *Journal of Medieval History*, 26 (2000), pp. 19–31, at 27.
60. Anna Comnena, p. 301.
61. Nicholas Mystikos, *Letters*, ed. and trans. R. J. H. Jenkins and L. G. Westerink (Washington, DC, 1973), p. 14; Chrysostomides, 'Byzantine Concepts of War and Peace', pp. 99–100; Canard, 'Les relations politiques', pp. 40–41; Elizabeth M. Jeffreys, 'The Image of Arabs in Byzantine Literature', *The Seventeenth International Byzantine Congress: Major Papers* (New Rochelle, New York, 1986), pp. 305–23.
62. Theophanes Continuatus, pp. 185–90; Baha al-Din ibn Shaddad, *The Rare and*

Excellent History of Saladin, trans. D. S. Richards (Aldershot, 2001), p. 121; Obolensky, *Byzantine Commonwealth*, pp. 185–89.

63. Anna Comnena, pp. 405, 477; Leo VI, *Tactica*, col. 1017.
64. Niccolò Machiavelli, *The Prince*, trans. George Bull (2nd edn, Harmondsworth, 1999), p. 50.
65. Nicholas Mesarites, *Description of the Church of the Holy Apostles at Constantinople*, ed. and trans. Glanville Downey, in *Transactions of the American Philosophical Society*, 47 (1957), pp. 855–924, at 866.
66. Psellos, p. 253; Anna Comnena, pp. 77, 183–84.
67. Odo of Deuil, p. 57; *The Russian Primary Chronicle: Laurentian Text*, ed. and trans. S. H. Cross and O. P. Sherbowitz-Wetzor (Cambridge, Massachusetts, 1953), p. 88; Widukind of Corvey, *Rerum gestarum Saxonicarum libri tres*, ed. Paul Hirsch, MGH, Scriptores Rerum Germanicarum, 60 (Hanover, 1935), p. 148; Thietmar of Merseburg, *Chronicon*, ed. Robert Holtzmann, MGH, Scriptores Rerum Germanicarum, new series, 9 (Berlin, 1955), p. 54; Shepard, 'Information, Disinformation', pp. 235–37.

Notes to Chapter 3: The Search for Security

1. Psellos, p. 159.
2. Michael Attaleiates, *Historia*, ed. W. Brunet de Presle and I. Bekker (Bonn, 1853), p. 160.
3. Anna Comnena, p. 198. On Mantzikert and its aftermath, see J. C. Cheynet, 'Mantzikert: un désastre militaire?', *Byzantion*, 50 (1980), pp. 410–38; Michael Angold, *The Byzantine Empire, 1025–1204: A Political History* (2nd edn, Harlow, 1997), pp. 44–48, 117–20.
4. Anna Comnena, pp. 150–53.
5. John Skylitzes, *Synopsis Historiarum*, ed. J. Thurn (Berlin, 1973), pp. 264–65; Constantine VII Porphyrogenitos, *De administrando imperio*, ed. G. Moravcsik, trans. R. Jenkins (Washington, DC, 1967), pp. 156–57; Dimitri Obolensky, *The Byzantine Commonwealth: Eastern Europe, 500–1453* (London, 1971), pp. 151–55.
6. For a detailed account of Byzantine embassies to western Europe in this period, see T. C. Lounghis, *Les ambassades Byzantines en occident depuis la fondation des états barbares, jusqu'aux croisades (407–1096)* (Athens, 1980), pp. 241–54.
7. Attaleiates, pp. 79–82; Mark Whittow, *The Making of Orthodox Byzantium, 600–1025* (London, 1996), pp. 120–21, 183–88; Angold, *Byzantine Empire*, pp. 62–63.
8. Anna Comnena, p. 252.
9. Attaleiates, p. 157.
10. Rodulfus Glaber, *Historiarum libri quinque*, ed. and trans. John France (Oxford, 1989), pp. 202–5; William of Jumièges, *Gesta Normanorum ducum*, trans. Elizabeth M. C. van Houts, 2 vols (Oxford, 1992–95), ii, pp. 82–85; *Anglo-Saxon Chronicle*, trans. D. Whitelock, D. C. Douglas and S. I. Tucker (London, 1961), p. 124; Steven Runciman, 'The Pilgrimages to Palestine before 1095',

in *A History of the Crusades*, ed. K. M. Setton, 6 vols (Madison, Wisconsin, 1969–89), i, pp. 68–78, at 76–77; K. N. Ciggaar, *Western Travellers to Constantinople: The West and Byzantium, 962–1204: Cultural and Political Relations* (Leiden, 1996), pp. 45–77.

11. Glaber, *Historiarum*, pp. 202–3; *Historia translationis Sancti Mamentis*, in *Acta Sanctorum Bollandiana*, 17 August, pp. 440–46, at 443; *Gesta episcoporum Tullensium*, ed. Georg Waitz, MGH, Scriptores, 8 (Hanover, 1848), pp. 631–48, at 647; William of Jumièges, ii, pp. 82–85.
12. Glaber, *Historiarum*, pp. 202–3; Anna Comnena, pp. 229, 232, 252.
13. William of Poitiers, *Gesta Guillelmi*, ed. and trans. R. H. C. Davis and Marjorie Chibnall (Oxford, 1998), pp. 96–97; Einar Joranson, 'The Problem of the Spurious Letter of Emperor Alexios to the Count of Flanders', *American Historical Review*, 55 (1949–50), pp. 811–32; M. de Waha, 'La lettre d'Alexis I Comnène à Robert I le Frison: une révision', *Byzantion*, 47 (1977), pp. 113–25.
14. William of Apulia, *Le geste de Robert Guiscard*, ed. and trans. Marguerite Mathieu (Palermo, 1961), pp. 134–36; *Chronicon monasterii de Abingdon*, ed. J. Stevenson, 2 vols (London, 1858), ii, pp. 46–47; *Cartulary of Holy Trinity Aldgate*, ed. Gerald A. J. Hodgett (London, 1971), p. 3; Jonathan Shepard, 'The Uses of the Franks in Eleventh-Century Byzantium', *Anglo-Norman Studies*, 15 (1993), pp. 275–305, at 289–90.
15. Orderic Vitalis, iv, p. 16; Geoffrey of Malaterra, *Historia Sicula*, in *Rerum Italicarum Scriptores*, ed. L. A. Muratori, 25 vols (Milan, 1724), v, pp. 544–602, at 584; Anna Comnena, pp. 144–48; E. M. C. van Houts, 'Normandy and Byzantium', *Byzantion*, 55 (1985), pp. 544–59; Shepard, 'Uses of the Franks', pp. 283–88. On the Varangian guard, see S. Blöndal, *The Varangians of Byzantium* (Cambridge, 1978).
16. Nikephoros Bryennios, *Historiarum libri quattuor*, ed. and trans. Paul Gautier (Brussels, 1975), pp. 146–49; Anna Comnena, pp. 32–37; Shepard, 'Uses of the Franks', pp. 297–300.
17. Anna Comnena, p. 96; Orderic Vitalis, iv, pp. 16–17; Attaleiates, pp. 46–47; Shepard, 'Uses of the Franks', pp. 290–92. For critical views of the policy of employing mercenaries, see R. J. H. Jenkins, *Byzantium: The Imperial Centuries, 610–1071* (London, 1966), p. 365; George Ostrogorsky, *History of the Byzantine State*, trans. J. M. Hussey (2nd edn, Oxford, 1968), p. 344.
18. H. Bibicou, 'Une page d'histoire diplomatique de Byzance au XIe siècle: Michel VII Doukas, Robert Guiscard, et la pension des dignitaires', *Byzantion*, 29–30 (1959), pp. 43–75, at 44–48; William B. McQueen, 'Relations between the Normans and Byzantium, 1071–1112', *Byzantion*, 56 (1986), pp. 427–76, at 429–32.
19. Anna Comnena, pp. 53, 57–58; Constantine VII, *De administrando imperio*, pp. 70–75.
20. Obolensky, *Byzantine Commonwealth*, pp. 158, 253.
21. Anna Comnena, pp. 126–28.
22. G. Tafel and G. Thomas, *Urkunden zur älteren Handels- und Staatsgeschichte der Republik Venedig*, 3 vols (Vienna, 1856–57), i, pp. 51–53; Anna Comnena,

pp. 137, 191; D. M. Nicol, *Byzantium and Venice: A Study in Diplomatic and Cultural Relations* (Cambridge, 1988), pp. 59–63.

23. Anna Comnena, pp. 138, 189–90; Nicol, *Byzantium and Venice*, pp. 57–59; Ostrogorsky, *History*, p. 359.
24. Tafel and Thomas, i, pp. 36–39.
25. Kinnamos, p. 210; Obolensky, *Byzantine Commonwealth*, pp. 244–47.
26. Liudprand, p. 199. On the background to Byzantine relations with Rome, see: J. M. Hussey, *The Orthodox Church in the Byzantine Empire* (Oxford, 1986), pp. 72–79; Steven Runciman, *The Eastern Schism* (Cambridge, 1955), pp. 1–27; F. Dvornik, *Byzantium and the Roman Primacy*, trans. Edwin A. Quain (New York, 1979, 2nd edn), pp. 27–123.
27. *Liber pontificalis: de gestis Romanorum pontificum*, ed. L. Duchesne, 3 vols (2nd edn, Paris, 1955–57), ii, p. 259.
28. Liudprand, pp. 57–58; *Chronica monasterii Casinensis*, ed. Hartmut Hoffmann, MGH, Scriptores, 34 (Hanover, 1980), pp. 133–35; Constantine VII, *De administrando imperio*, p. 129.
29. Nicholas Mystikos, *Letters*, ed. and trans. R. J. H. Jenkins and L. G. Westerink (Washington, DC, 1973), pp. 286–93; *Liber Pontificalis*, ii, pp. 147–48. Anna Comnena, p. 61, described the papacy as 'a noble office'.
30. William of Apulia, pp. 135–36, 143–47; Heinrich Tritz, 'Die hagiographischen Quellen zur Geschichte Papst Leo IX', *Studi Gregoriani*, 4 (1952), pp. 191–364, at 361.
31. Matthew 16: 19–20.
32. Humbert of Silva Candida, *De Sancta Romana Ecclesia*, in P. E. Schramm, *Kaiser, Rom und Renovatio*, 2 vols (Leipzig and Berlin, 1929), ii, pp. 128–33, at 128; Walter Ullmann, 'Cardinal Humbert and the *Ecclesia Romana*', *Studi Gregoriani*, 4 (1952), pp. 111–27, at 112.
33. *Patrologia Graeca*, vol. 120, cols 835–44; *Patrologia Latina*, vol. 143, col. 774; Runciman, *Eastern Schism*, pp. 40–43; R. Mayne, 'East and West in 1054', *Cambridge Historical Journal*, 11 (1954), pp. 133–48, at 134; D. M. Nicol, 'Byzantium and the Papacy in the Eleventh Century', *Journal of Ecclesiastical History*, 13 (1962), pp. 1–20; Hussey, *Orthodox Church in the Byzantine Empire*, pp. 132–33.
34. Liudprand, pp. 199–200.
35. Runciman, *Eastern Schism*, p. 43; Hussey, *Orthodox Church in the Byzantine Empire*, p. 133.
36. *Patrologia Latina*, vol. 143, cols 773–74.
37. Humbert of Silva-Candida, *Brevis et succincta commemoratio*, in *Patrologia Latina*, vol. 143, cols 1001–4; Cornelius Will, *Acta et scripta quae de controversiis ecclesiae Graecae et Latinae saeculo undecesimo composita extant* (Leipzig and Marburg, 1861), pp. 155–68.
38. Humbert, *Brevis et succincta commemoratio*, col. 1003; Hussey, *Orthodox Church in the Byzantine Empire*, pp. 72–80, 135–36; Mayne, 'East and West in 1054', p. 146; Runciman, *Eastern Schism*, pp. 22–27, 55–58; Nicol, 'Byzantium and the Papacy', pp. 11–12.

39. Michael Psellos, *Epitafios logos eis ton patriarchen Michael Keroullarion*, in C. N. Sathas, *Mesaionike bibliotheke*, 7 vols (Athens, Venice and Paris, 1872–94), iv, pp. 303–87, at 348–49.
40. Humbert, *Brevis et succincta commemoratio*, col. 1001; idem, *Rationes de Sancti Spiritus processione a Patre et Filio*, in Anton Michel, *Humbert und Kerullarios*, 2 vols (Paderborn, 1924–30), i, pp. 97–111.
41. Bonizo of Sutri, *Liber ad amicum*, in *Monumenta Gregoriana*, ed. P. Jaffé (Berlin, 1865), pp. 577–689, at 642–43; Gregory VII, *Registrum libri I-IV*, ed. Erich Caspar, MGH, Epistolae Selectae, 2 (Berlin, 1955), pp. 515–16; Anna Comnena, p. 162.
42. Gregory VII, *Registrum*, pp. 29–30.
43. Gregory VII, *Registrum*, pp. 75–76; H. E. J. Cowdrey, 'The Gregorian Papacy, Byzantium and the First Crusade', *Byzantinische Forschungen*, 13 (1988), pp. 145–69; idem, 'Pope Gregory VII's "Crusading" Plans of 1074', in *Outremer: Studies in the History of the Crusading Kingdom of Jerusalem Presented to Joshua Prawer*, ed. B. Z. Kedar, H. E. Mayer and R. C. Smail (Jerusalem, 1982), pp. 27–40.
44. Cowdrey, 'Gregorian Papacy', pp. 156–57.
45. Anna Comnena, p. 126.
46. Walther Holtzmann, 'Die Unionverhandlungen zwischen Kaiser Alexios I und Papst Urban II im Jahre 1089', *Byzantinische Zeitschrift*, 28 (1928), pp. 38–67, at 60–62; Runciman, *Eastern Schism*, pp. 61–62; Cowdrey, 'Gregorian Papacy', pp. 162–63.
47. This is the view of Steven Runciman, *A History of the Crusades*, 3 vols (Cambridge, 1951–54), i, p. 104; Ostrogorsky, *History*, p. 362.
48. R. D. Thomas, 'Anna Comnena's Account of the First Crusade: History and Politics in the Reigns of the Emperors Alexius I and Manuel I Comnenus', *Byzantine and Modern Greek Studies*, 15 (1991), pp. 269–312, at 274–76; John France, 'Anna Comnena, the Alexiad and the First Crusade', *Reading Medieval Studies*, 10 (1984), pp. 20–38, at 21; Jonathan Shepard, 'Cross Purposes: Alexios Comnenus and the First Crusade', *The First Crusade: Origins and Impact*, ed. Jonathan Phillips (Manchester, 1997), pp. 107–29, at 109.
49. Theodore Skoutariotes, *Synopsis chronike*, in C. N. Sathas, *Mesaionike bibliotheke*, 7 vols (Athens, Venice and Paris, 1872–94), vii, pp. 1–556, at 184–85; Peter Charanis, 'Byzantium, the West and the Origin of the First Crusade', *Byzantion*, 19 (1949), pp. 17–36, at 33–34.
50. Ekkehard of Aura, *Chronicon universale*, MGH, Scriptores, 6 (Hanover, 1844), pp. 33–245, at 213; Bernold of St Blaise, *Chronicon*, MGH, Scriptores, 5 (Hanover, 1844), pp. 385–467, at 462; Charanis, 'Byzantium, the West and the Origins of the First Crusade', pp. 27–29; Anna Comnena, p. 127; Guibert of Nogent, *The Deeds of God through the Franks*, trans. Robert Levine (Woodbridge, 1997), p. 40.
51. Ekkehard, p. 213; Charanis, 'Byzantium, the West, and the Origins of the First Crusade', pp. 27–28.
52. Bibicou, 'Une page d'histoire', pp. 44–48.

53. Joranson, 'Spurious Letter', pp. 814–15.
54. Gregory VII, *Registrum*, pp. 201–8.
55. Fulcher of Chartres, pp. 50–53; Robert of Rheims, *Historia Iherosolimitana*, in *RHC Oc*, iii, pp. 715–882, at 727–30; Baldric of Dol, *Historia Jerosolimitana*, in *RHC Oc*, iv, pp. 9–111, at 12–16; Guibert of Nogent, pp. 42–45.
56. Guibert of Nogent, p. 44. Cf Bernold of St Blaise, p. 464: 'His temporibus maxima multitudine de Italia et omni Gallia et Germania Ierosolimam contra paganos ... ire cepit'; H. E. J. Cowdrey, 'Pope Urban II's Preaching of the First Crusade', *History*, 55 (1970), pp 177–88, at 181–82; Jean Richard, *The Crusades, c. 1071 – c. 1291* (Cambridge, 1999), pp. 19–27.
57. Bernold of St Blaise, p. 464.

Notes to Chapter 4: The Passage of the First Crusade

1. Guibert of Nogent, *The Deeds of God through the Franks*, trans. Robert Levine (Woodbridge, 1997), p. 43.
2. Jonathan Riley-Smith, *The Crusades: A Short History* (New Haven and London, 1987), pp. 18–36; Jean Richard, *The Crusades, c. 1071 – c. 1291*, trans. Jean Birrell (Cambridge, 1999), pp. 27–35.
3. See, however: Jonathan Shepard, '"Father" or "Scorpion"? Style and Substance in Alexios's Diplomacy', in *Alexios I Komnenos*, ed. Margaret Mullett and Dion Smythe (Belfast, 1996), pp. 68–132, where it is argued that Alexios's policy towards the crusaders was innovative.
4. John Zonaras, *Epitome historiarum*, ed. L. Dindorf, 6 vols (Leipzig, 1868–75), iv, pp. 242–43. On Zonaras see Ruth Macrides, 'The Pen and the Sword: Who Wrote the *Alexiad*?', in *Anna Komnene and her Times*, ed. Thalia Gouma-Peterson (New York and London, 2000), pp. 63–81, at 72–75.
5. Choniates, pp. 5–9; Zonaras, pp. 254–60; George Tornikios, *Discourse on the Death of the Porphyrogenita Anna, the Kaisarissa*, in George and Leo Tornikios, *Lettres et discours*, ed. J. Darrouzès (Paris, 1970), pp. 220–323, at 283–301.
6. Anna Comnena, pp. 308–68, 411; J. Chrysostomides, 'A Byzantine Historian: Anna Comnena', *Medieval Historical Writings in the Christian and Islamic Worlds*, ed. D. O. Morgan (London, 1982), pp. 30–46, at 40–42; Ruth Macrides, 'The Historian in the History', *Philellin: Studies in Honour of Robert Browning*, ed. C. N. Constantinides et al. (Venice, 1996), pp. 205–24, at 217–20.
7. Paul Magdalino, 'The Pen of the Aunt: Echoes of the Mid Twelfth Century in the *Alexiad*', in *Anna Komnene and her Times*, ed. Thalia Gouma-Peterson (New York and London, 2000), pp. 15–43, at 24–29; Jonathan Shepard, 'Cross Purposes: Alexios Comnenus and the First Crusade', *The First Crusade: Origins and Impact*, ed. Jonathan Phillips (Manchester, 1997), pp. 107–29, at 109; R. D. Thomas, 'Anna Comnena's Account of the First Crusade', *Byzantine and Modern Greek Studies*, 15 (1991), pp. 269–312, at 293–96; John France, 'Anna Comnena, the *Alexiad* and the First Crusade', *Reading Medieval Studies*, 10 (1984), pp. 20–38, at 31.

8. Anna Comnena, pp. 321–22, 340–41, 460; Chrysostomides, 'Byzantine Historian', pp. 32–33; Macrides, 'Pen and the Sword', pp. 70–71.
9. Anna Comnena, pp. 311, 313, 319, 326–27; Fulcher of Chartres, p. 62.
10. Anna Comnena, p. 439.
11. *Three Byzantine Military Treatises*, ed. and trans. George Dennis (Washington, DC, 1985), pp. 124–25.
12. Anna Comnena, pp. 310–11, 319, 323.
13. Anna Comnena, pp. 311–13.
14. *Gesta Francorum*, pp. 2–5; Colin Morris, 'Peter the Hermit and the Chroniclers', in *The First Crusade: Origins and Impact*, ed. Jonathan Phillips (Manchester, 1997), pp. 21–34, at 23–24.
15. Anna Comnena, pp. 318–19, 325. Cf. *Gesta Francorum*, p. 6.
16. Anna Comnena, pp. 313–15, 319; Albert of Aachen, *Historia Hierosolymitana*, *RHC Oc*, iv, pp. 265–713, at 304.
17. Anna Comnena, pp. 315, 319, 323.
18. Anna Comnena, pp. 323, 328. Cf. Heinrich Hagenmeyer, *Epistulae et chartae ad historiam primi belli sacri spectantes: die Kreuzzugsbriefe aus den Jahre 1088–1100* (Innsbruck, 1901), p. 138; Fulcher of Chartres, p. 62. The adoption is mentioned by Ekkehard of Aura, *Chronicon universale*, MGH, Scriptores, 6 (Hanover, 1844), pp. 33–245, at 220.
19. Michael Attaleiates, *Historia*, ed. I. Bekker (Bonn, 1853), pp. 158–59; H. Bibicou, 'Une page d'histoire diplomatique de Byzance au XIe siècle: Michel VII Doukas, Robert Guiscard, et la pension des dignitaires', *Byzantion*, 29–30 (1959), pp. 43–75, at 47; Anna Comnena, pp. 127, 229; Dimitri Obolensky, *The Byzantine Commonwealth: Eastern Europe, 500–1453* (London, 1971), pp. 118, 245.
20. Anna Comnena, pp. 334–40, 346–48, 356; Albert of Aachen, p. 564; Ralph-Johannes Lilie, *Byzantium and the Crusader States, 1095–1204*, trans. J. C. Morris and J. E. Ridings (Oxford, 1993), pp. 67–68.
21. Anna Comnena, pp. 328–29, 439.
22. Guibert of Nogent, pp. 28, 43, 73.
23. *Gesta Francorum*, pp. 8–9; Raymond of Aguilers, *Historia Francorum qui ceperunt Iherusalem*, trans. J. H. Hill and L. Hill (Philadelphia, 1968), pp. 18–21; Peter Tudebode, *Historia de Hierosolymitano itinere*, trans. J. H. Hill and L. L. Hill (Philadelphia, 1974), pp. 27–28; Albert of Aachen, pp. 305–6.
24. Anna Comnena, pp. 339–40; *Gesta Francorum*, p. 17; Raymond of Aguilers, pp. 26–27.
25. C. Cahen, 'La chronique abrégée d'Al-Azimi', *Journal Asiatique*, 230 (1938), pp. 353–448, at 370; Ibn al-Qalanisi, *The Damascus Chronicle of the Crusades*, trans. H. A. R. Gibb (London, 1932), p. 42; Carole Hillenbrand, *The Crusades: Islamic Perspectives* (Edinburgh, 1999), p. 44; Orderic Vitalis, v, p. 335. Alexios's letters warning the Fatimids of the approach of the Franks may have been those which were found in the Egyptian camp after the crusader victory at Ascalon in August 1099: Raymond of Aguilers, p. 90; Lilie, *Byzantium and the Crusader States*, pp. 235–36.

26. Bibicou, 'Une page d'histoire', p. 45.
27. Raymond of Aguilers, 23–24; *Gesta Francorum*, pp. 6–7, 11–12; Albert of Aachen, pp. 305–12; Anna Comnena, pp. 319–23, 340–41; J. H. Hill and L. L. Hill, 'The Convention of Alexios Comnenus and Raymond of Saint-Gilles', *American Historical Review*, 58 (1952–53), pp. 322–27.
28. Anna Comnena, pp. 325, 341.
29. Raymond of Aguilers, p. 24; Albert of Aachen, p. 311; Anna Comnena, p. 328; William of Jumièges, *Gesta Normanorum ducum*, trans. Elizabeth M. C. van Houts, 2 vols (Oxford, 1992–95), ii, pp. 82–85.
30. Anna Comnena, p. 326.
31. Peter Tudebode, p. 29; Raymond of Aguilers, pp. 23–24; Albert of Aachen, p. 303.
32. Hagenmeyer, *Epistulae*, p. 138; Fulcher of Chartres, p. 62.
33. Fulcher of Chartres, pp. 95–96; Anna Comnena, pp. 329–30, 353–55; *Gesta Francorum*, p. 72; William of Tyre, i, p. 298; Lilie, *Byzantium and the Crusader States*, pp. 66–70.
34. Anna Comnena, pp. 357–58.
35. *Gesta Francorum*, p. 12; August C. Krey, 'A Neglected Passage of the *Gesta* and its Bearing on the Literature of the First Crusade', *The Crusades and Other Historical Essays Presented to Dana C. Munro by his Former Students*, ed. Louis J. Paetow (New York, 1928), pp. 57–78.
36. Anna Comnena, p. 329; *Gesta Francorum*, pp. 13–14. For a detailed discussion of the relations between Bohemond and Alexios, see Jonathan Shepard, 'When Greek Meets Greek: Alexios Comnenus and Bohemond in 1097–98', *Byzantine and Modern Greek Studies*, 12 (1988), pp. 185–277. On the office of Domestic of the East, see Warren Treadgold, *Byzantium and its Army, 284–1081* (Stanford, California, 1995), p. 34.
37. Anna Comnena, p. 341; Kinnamos, pp. 67, 151.
38. Anna Comnena, pp. 340–41.
39. *Gesta Francorum*, p. 12.
40. Hagenmeyer, *Epistulae*, pp. 153–54.
41. Anna Comnena, pp. 330, 341. For discussions of how both sides interpreted the oaths, see Lilie, *Byzantium and the Crusader States*, pp. 24–25; J. H. Pryor, 'The Oaths of the Leaders of the First Crusade to the Emperor Alexios I Comnenus: Fealty, Homage – Pistis, Douleia', *Parergon*, new series, 2 (1984), pp. 111–32.
42. *Gesta Francorum*, pp. 25–26; Peter Tudebode, pp. 40–41; Raymond of Aguilers, pp. 36–37.
43. Anna Comnena, pp. 343, 360; *Gesta Francorum*, pp. 34–35; Guibert of Nogent, pp. 81–82. For a full discussion of the question, see John France, 'The Departure of Tatikios from the Crusader Army', *Bulletin of the Institute of Historical Research*, 44 (1971), pp. 137–47.
44. *Gesta Francorum*, pp. 62–63.
45. Anna Comnena, p. 345.
46. Hagenmeyer, *Epistulae*, pp. 152–53; Herbert Bloch, 'Monte Cassino, Byzantium

and the West in the Earlier Middle Ages', *Dumbarton Oaks Papers*, 3 (1946), pp. 163–224, at 222.

47. Raymond of Aguilers, p. 88; Steven Runciman, *A History of the Crusades*, 3 vols (Cambridge, 1951–54), i, pp. 226–27; Nicholas Hooper, 'Edgar the Aethling: Anglo-Saxon Prince, Rebel and Crusader', *Anglo-Saxon England*, 14 (1985), pp. 197–214, at 208–9.
48. Anna Comnena, pp. 346–50; *Gesta Francorum*, pp. 63–65.
49. Fulcher of Chartres, p. 76; Anna Comnena, p. 351; *Gesta Francorum*, pp. 59–60, 65–66.
50. *Gesta Francorum*, pp. 67–71; Anna Comnena, pp. 351–52; Fulcher of Chartres, pp. 80–81.
51. *Gesta Francorum*, p. 72; William of Tyre, i, p. 298; Lilie, *Byzantium and the Crusader States*, pp. 39–40; Thomas S. Asbridge, *The Creation of the Principality of Antioch, 1098–1130* (Woodbridge, 2000), pp. 34–46.
52. Anna Comnena, p. 352; Lilie, *Byzantium and the Crusader States*, p. 43 n. 182.
53. *Gesta Francorum*, p. 71; William of Tyre, i, pp. 244, 297, 300, 313, 326–28; Raymond of Aguilers, pp. 105–6; Anna Comnena, p. 352.
54. Anna Comnena, p. 355.
55. Anna Comnena, pp. 355–57; Lilie, *Byzantium and the Crusader States*, pp. 66–70.
56. Anna Comnena, pp. 357–58. For a reconstruction of the chronology of Bohemond's establishment of the principality of Antioch, see Lilie, *Byzantium and the Crusader States*, pp. 259–76.

Notes to Chapter 5: Jerusalem and Antioch

1. Jean Richard, *The Crusades, c. 1071 – c. 1291*, trans. Jean Birrell (Cambridge, 1999), pp. 77–87; Jonathan Riley-Smith, *The Crusades: A Short History* (New Haven and London, 1987), pp. 40–43; Ralph-Johannes Lilie, *Byzantium and the Crusader States, 1095–1204*, trans. J. C. Morris and J. C. Ridings (Oxford, 1993), pp. 61–72.
2. Fulcher of Chartres, pp. 89–92; *Gesta Francorum*, pp. 87–92; Anna Comnena, p. 352.
3. Anna Comnena, p. 354; William Saunders, 'The Greek Inscription on the Harran Gate at Edessa: Some Further Evidence', *Byzantinische Forschungen*, 21 (1995), pp. 301–4; Lilie, *Byzantium and the Crusader States*, p. 70.
4. Anna Comnena, pp. 111–12, 120–21, 174–80; Michael Angold, *The Byzantine Empire, 1025–1204: A Political History* (2nd edn, Harlow, 1997), pp. 136–56.
5. Paul Maas, 'Die Musen des Kaisers Alexios I', *Byzantinische Zeitschrift*, 22 (1913), pp. 348–69, at 356–58. The translation is from Paul Magdalino, *The Empire of Manuel I Komnenos, 1143–1180* (Cambridge, 1993), p. 28.
6. Abbas Hamdani, 'Byzantine-Fatimid Relations before the Battle of Mantzikert', *Byzantine Studies*, 1 (1974), pp. 169–79, at 173; Steven Runciman, 'The Byzantine "Protectorate" in the Holy Land in the Eleventh Century', *Byzantion*, 18 (1946–48), pp. 207–15.

7. Angold, *Byzantine Empire*, p. 164; Warren Treadgold, *A History of the Byzantine State and Society* (Stanford, California, 1997), pp. 636–37.
8. Leo the Deacon, *Nikephoros Phokas, "der bleiche Tod der Sarazenen" und Johannes Tzimiskes*, trans. Franz Loretto (Vienna, 1961), p. 72; Liudprand, pp. 186–87.
9. William of Tyre, i, p. 297; Bernard Hamilton, *The Latin Church in the Crusader States* (London, 1980), pp. 16–17.
10. Anna Comnena, pp. 358–59; Lilie, *Byzantium and the Crusader States*, pp. 63–65; Thomas S. Asbridge, *The Creation of the Principality of Antioch, 1098–1130* (Woodbridge, 2000), pp. 47–53.
11. William of Tyre, i, pp. 451, 460; Anna Comnena, pp. 366–68.
12. Anna Comnena, pp. 405–8, 417; Orderic Vitalis, vi, p. 103.
13. Anna Comnena, pp. 424–34. Detailed analysis can be found in Lilie, *Byzantium and the Crusader States*, pp. 75–82; Asbridge, *Creation*, pp. 94–98.
14. Anna Comnena, pp. 424–8, 430.
15. Lilie, *Byzantium and the Crusader States*, pp. 76–77. Asbridge, *Creation*, p. 97 disagrees with this approach.
16. Anna Comnena, pp. 425–26, 432–33.
17. Anna Comnena, pp. 424–25, 430–31; H. Bibicou, 'Une page d'histoire diplomatique de Byzance au XIe siècle: Michel VII Doukas, Robert Guiscard, et la pension des dignitaires', *Byzantion*, 29–30 (1959), pp. 43–75, at 45.
18. Antra R. Gadolin, 'Prince Bohemond's Death and Apotheosis in the Church of San Sabino, Canosa di Puglia', *Byzantion*, 52 (1982), pp. 124–53; Ann Wharton Epstein, 'The Date and Significance of the Cathedral of Canosa in Apulia, Southern Italy', *Dumbarton Oaks Papers*, 37 (1983), pp. 79–90.
19. Anna Comnena, pp. 438–44; Ibn al-Qalanisi, *The Damascus Chronicle of the Crusades*, trans. H. A. R. Gibb (London, 1932), pp. 112–13; Lilie, *Byzantium and the Crusader States*, pp. 83–87; Carole Hillenbrand, *The Crusades: Islamic Perspectives* (Edinburgh, 1999), pp. 68–69.
20. On the earlier years of John's reign, see Kinnamos, pp. 7–21; Choniates, pp. 5–13; Angold, *Byzantine Empire*, pp. 181–90.
21. Lilie, *Byzantium and the Crusader States*, pp. 138–41; Angold, *Byzantine Empire*, p. 189; Magdalino, *Empire of Manuel I*, pp. 36–37.
22. This is the argument of John L. La Monte, 'To What Extent was the Byzantine Empire Suzerain of the Latin Crusading States?', *Byzantion*, 7 (1932), pp. 253–64.
23. William of Tyre, ii, pp. 208, 212.
24. Kinnamos, p. 4; Choniates, pp. xv–xvi; Peter W. Edbury and John Gordon Rowe, *William of Tyre: Historian of the Latin East* (Cambridge, 1988), p. 26; Jonathan Harris, 'Distortion, Divine Providence and Genre in Niketas Choniates's Account of the Collapse of Byzantium 1180–1204', *Journal of Medieval History*, 26 (2000), pp. 19–31, at 20.
25. William of Tyre, i, p. 57.
26. William of Tyre, ii, p. 83; Choniates, pp. 13–14; Kinnamos, pp. 22–23; Lilie, *Byzantium and the Crusader States*, pp. 110–12.

27. William of Tyre, ii, pp. 92–93.
28. Kinnamos, pp. 23–24; Choniates, p. 16.
29. Lilie, *Byzantium and the Crusader States*, pp. 120–25; Jonathan Phillips, *Defenders of the Holy Land: Relations between the Latin East and the West, 1119–1187* (Oxford, 1996), pp. 68–71.
30. Usamah Ibn-Munqidh, *An Arab-Syrian Gentleman and Warrior in the Period of the Crusades*, trans. Philip K. Hitti (2nd edn, New York, 2000), pp. 143–44; S. D. Goitein, 'A Letter from Seleucia (Cilicia) Dated 21 July 1137', *Speculum*, 39 (1964), pp. 298–303, at 300. On the role of the emperor in leading the war against infidels, see George T. Dennis, 'Defenders of the Christian People: Holy War in Byzantium', *The Crusades from the Perspective of Byzantium and the Muslim World*, ed. A. E. Laiou and R. P. Mottahedeh (Washington, DC, 2001), pp. 31–39, at 34–37.
31. William of Tyre, ii, pp. 94–97.
32. Kinnamos, pp. 24–25; Choniates, pp. 17–18.
33. Baha' al-Din Ibn Shaddad, *The Rare and Excellent History of Saladin*, trans. D. S. Richards (Aldershot, 2001), pp. 201–2; George Ostrogorsky, *History of the Byzantine State*, trans. J. M. Hussey (2nd edn, Oxford, 1968), pp. 277–78.
34. William of Tyre, ii, pp. 97–102; Lilie, *Byzantium and the Crusader States*, pp. 128–30.
35. Choniates, p. 18.
36. Kinnamos, pp. 26–27; Choniates, p. 22.
37. When a similar plan was suggested in the fourteenth century, it was roundly condemned as a western innovation: Nikephoros Gregoras, *Rhomäische Geschichte*, J. L. Van Dieten, 4 vols (Stuttgart, 1973–94), i, pp. 184–85.
38. William of Tyre, ii, pp. 123–25; Lilie, *Byzantium and the Crusader States*, pp. 135–38.
39. Choniates, p. 22; William of Tyre, ii, pp. 126–27.
40. Kinnamos, pp. 27–34; Choniates pp. 23–29; William of Tyre, ii, pp. 128–30.
41. Michael Italikos, *Lettres et discours*, ed. and trans. Paul Gautier (Paris, 1972), pp. 243, 259–60.
42. Anna Comnena, pp. 19–20, 448; Paul Magdalino, 'The Pen of the Aunt: Echoes of the Mid Twelfth Century in the *Alexiad*' in *Anna Komnene and her Times*, ed. Thalia Gouma-Peterson (New York and London, 2000), pp. 15–43, at 20–21.
43. Theophanes Continuatus, *Chronographia*, ed. I. Bekker (Bonn, 1838), pp. 164–65.
44. Orderic Vitalis, vi, pp. 502–9.
45. Odo of Deuil, pp. 68–69.
46. Choniates, p. 45.
47. William of Tyre, i, pp. 461, 470–71; Orderic Vitalis, vi, pp. 69–71; Bohemond to Pope Paschal II in Walther Holtzmann, 'Zur Geschichte des Investiturstreites', *Neues Archiv der Gesellschaft für ältere deutsche Geschichtskunde*, 50 (1935), pp. 246–319, at 280–82. Cf. William of Poitiers, *Gesta Guillelmi*, ed. and trans. R. H. C. Davis and Marjorie Chibnall (Oxford, 1998), pp. 70–71, 76–79, 100–1.

48. Holtzmann, 'Zur Geschichte des Investiturstreites', p. 281.
49. *Gesta Francorum*, pp. 5, 7, 11, 12, 17; August C. Krey, 'A Neglected Passage of the *Gesta* and its Bearing on the Literature of the First Crusade', *The Crusades and Other Historical Essays Presented to Dana C. Munro by his Former Students*, ed. Louis J. Paetow (New York, 1928), pp. 57–78; K. B. Wolf, 'Crusade and Narrative: Bohemond and the *Gesta Francorum*', *Journal of Medieval History*, 17 (1991), pp. 207–16; C. Morris, 'The *Gesta Francorum* as Narrative History', *Reading Medieval Studies*, 19 (1993), pp. 55–71.
50. Ekkehard of Aura, *Chronicon universale*, MGH, Scriptores, 6 (Hanover, 1844), pp. 33–245, at 220–21.
51. William of Malmesbury, *Gesta regum Anglorum*, trans. R. A. B. Mynors, R. M. Thomson, and M. Winterbottom, 2 vols (Oxford, 1998–99), i, p. 611; Orderic Vitalis, v, pp. 46–47, 331–32.
52. William of Tyre, ii, pp. 461–62; Guibert of Nogent, *The Deeds of God through the Franks*, trans. Robert Levine (Woodbridge, 1997), pp. 30–31, 38, 60; Odo of Deuil, pp. 56–59, 88–89, 98–99; Benjamin of Tudela, *The Itinerary* (London, 1907), p. 13; Walter Map, *De nugis curialium*, trans. M. R. James, Cymmrodorion Record Society, 9 (London, 1923), p. 95; *Chronicle of the Third Crusade*, trans. H. J. Nicholson (Aldershot, 1997), p. 57.
53. Liudprand, pp. 202–3; Widukind of Corvey, *Rerum gestarum Saxonicarum libri tres*, ed. Paul Hirsch, MGH, Scriptores Rerum Germanicarum, 60 (Hanover, 1935), p. 148; Nicholas I, *Epistolae ad res orientales, praecipue ad causam Ignatii et Photii pertinentes*, MGH: Epistolae Karolini Aevi, 4 (Berlin, 1925), pp. 433–610, at 601; Dimitri Obolensky, *The Byzantine Commonwealth: Eastern Europe, 500–1453* (London, 1971), pp. 117–18.
54. Holtzmann, 'Zur Geschichte des Investiturstreites', p. 281; Guibert of Nogent, p. 31; John H. Van Engen, *Rupert of Deutz* (Berkeley, Los Angeles and London, 1983), p. 362.
55. Anna Comnena, pp. 389–90; Suger, *The Deeds of Louis the Fat*, trans. R. C. Cusimano and John Moorhead (Washington, DC, 1992), pp. 43–46. It has been argued, however, that Bohemond only had papal approval for an expedition to Jerusalem, not for an assault on the Byzantine empire. See J. G. Rowe, 'Paschal II, Bohemond of Antioch and the Byzantines', *Bulletin of the John Rylands Library*, 49 (1966–67), pp. 105–202.
56. *Patrologia Latina*, vol. 179, cols 354–55; Odo of Deuil, pp. 68–71; Lilie, *Byzantium and the Crusader States*, p. 131. Cf Robert of Clari, p. 94; Gunther of Pairis, p. 90.
57. Anna Comnena, p. 330; Heinrich Hagenmeyer, *Epistulae et chartae ad historiam primi belli sacri spectantes: die Kreuzzugsbriefe aus den Jahre 1088–1100* (Innsbruck, 1901), pp. 140–41, 152–53.
58. Anna Comnena, pp. 369–71. Cf. Orderic Vitalis, v, p. 351.
59. H. Bloch, 'Monte Cassino, Byzantium and the West in the Earlier Middle Ages', *Dumbarton Oaks Papers*, 3 (1946), pp. 163–224, at 222–23; A. Theiner and

F. Miklosich, *Monumenta spectantia ad unionem ecclesiarum Graecae et Romanae* (Vienna, 1872), pp. 1–3; Anselm of Havelberg, *Dialogorum Libri III*, in *Spicilegium sive collectio veterum aliquot scriptorum*, ed. L. d'Achery, 3 vols (Paris, 1723), i, pp. 161–207, at 172–91; F. Dvornik, *Byzantium and the Roman Primacy*, trans. Edwin A. Quain (2nd edn, New York, 1979), pp. 145–47; Steven Runciman, *The Eastern Schism* (Cambridge, 1955), pp. 113–18; Norman Russell, 'Anselm of Havelberg and the Union of the Churches: I. The Problem of the Filioque', *Sobornost*, 1 (1979), pp. 19–41, at 21–22.

60. Orderic Vitalis, iv, pp. 14–15.

Notes to Chapter 6: Innovation and Continuity

1. Kinnamos, pp. 144–45, 168, 184, 190, 217; John Phokas, *The Pilgrimage of John Phokas in the Holy Land in the Year 1185 AD*, trans. Aubrey Stewart, Palestine Pilgrim Text Society, 5 (London, 1896), pp. 29, 31.
2. William of Tyre, ii, pp. 452, 461; Robert of Clari, p. 46.
3. Ralph-Johannes Lilie, *Byzantium and the Crusader States, 1096–1204*, trans. J. C. Morris and J. E. Ridings (Oxford, 1993), p. 141; Paul Magdalino, *The Empire of Manuel I Komnenos, 1143–1180* (Cambridge, 1993), pp. 44–46.
4. Kinnamos, pp. 32–33. Lilie, *Byzantium and the Crusader States*, p. 143, regards Kinnamos's version of Manuel's reply as unhistorical.
5. Kinnamos, pp. 35–36; Choniates, p. 31.
6. Paul Magdalino, 'The Pen of the Aunt: Echoes of the Mid-Twelfth Century in the *Alexiad*', *Anna Komnene and her Times* (New York and London, 2000), pp. 15–43, at 16; R. D. Thomas, 'Anna Comnena's Account of the First Crusade', *Byzantine and Modern Greek Studies*, 15 (1991), pp. 269–312, at 304–5.
7. Paul Maas, 'Die Musen des Kaisers Alexios I', *Byzantinische Zeitschrift*, 22 (1913), pp. 348–69, at 356–58; Magdalino, *Empire of Manuel I* , p. 28.
8. Kinnamos, p. 58. For accounts of the second crusade, see Lilie, *Byzantium and the Crusader States*, pp. 145–63; Richard, *The Crusades*, pp. 155–69; Magdalino, *Empire of Manuel I*, pp. 46–53.
9. Otto of Freising, *The Deeds of Frederick Barbarossa*, trans. C. C. Mierow (Toronto, 1953), pp. 69–70; Kinnamos, p. 76; Choniates, pp. 43–45; Odo of Deuil, pp. 11, 83.
10. Eustathios of Thessalonica, *Opuscula*, ed. T. L. F. Tafel (Frankfurt, 1832), p. 199, trans. Michael Angold, *The Byzantine Empire, 1025–1204: A Political History* (2nd edn, Harlow, 1997), p. 198.
11. Kinnamos, pp. 58–61, 67, 71; Elizabeth and Michael Jeffreys, 'The "Wild Beast from the West": Immediate Literary Reactions in Byzantium to the Second Crusade', *The Crusades from the Perspective of Byzantium and the Muslim World*, ed. A. E. Laiou and R. P. Mottahedeh (Washington, DC, 2001), pp. 101–16.
12. Kinnamos, pp. 60–62; Choniates, p. 37; Odo of Deuil, pp. 42–43.
13. Kinnamos, pp. 63–67.

14. Kinnamos, pp. 68–69.
15. Odo of Deuil, pp. 24–29.
16. Odo of Deuil, pp. 40–43.
17. Odo of Deuil, p. 55.
18. Odo of Deuil, p. 83.
19. Odo of Deuil, pp. 89, 109; *Recueil des historiens des Gaules et de la France*, ed. L. Deslisle, 24 vols (Paris, 1869–1904), xv, p. 496.
20. Odo of Deuil, pp. 40–45, 49.
21. *Recueil des historiens des Gaules et de la France*, xvi, pp. 9–10. Manuel also wrote to the pope, promising to assist the enterprise: A. Theiner and F. Miklosich, *Monumenta spectantia ad unionem ecclesiarum Graecae et Romanae* (Vienna, 1872), pp. 6–8.
22. *Recueil des historiens des Gaules et de la France*, xvi, pp. 9–10; Kinnamos, p. 58.
23. Odo of Deuil, pp. 68–71; Choniates, pp. 38–39; Michael the Syrian, *Chronique*, trans. J.-B. Chabot, 4 vols (Paris, 1899–1910), iii, pp. 275–76; W. R. Taylor, 'A New Syriac Fragment Dealing with Incidents in the Second Crusade', *Annual of the American Schools of Oriental Research*, 11 (1929–30), pp. 120–30.
24. William of Tyre, ii, 167–70; John of Salisbury, *Historia pontificalis*, ed. and trans. Marjorie Chibnall (Oxford, 1986), p. 54; Henry of Huntingdon, *Historia Anglorum: The History of the English People*, ed. and trans. Diana Greenway (Oxford, 1996), pp. 750–53; William of Newburgh, *The History of English Affairs: Book I*, ed. P. G. Walsh and M. J. Kennedy (Warminster, 1988), pp. 92–95; Giles Constable, 'The Second Crusade as Seen by Contemporaries', *Traditio*, 9 (1953), pp. 213–79, at 216–22, 272–73; Peter W. Edbury, 'Looking Back on the Second Crusade: Some Late Twelfth-Century English Perspectives', *The Second Crusade and the Cistercians*, ed. Michael Gervers (New York, 1972), pp. 163–69, at 166; Henry Mayr-Harting, 'Odo of Deuil, the Second Crusade and the Monastery of Saint-Denis', *The Culture of Christendom: Essays in Medieval History in Commemoration of Denis L. T. Bethell* (London and Rio Grande, Ohio, 1993), pp. 225–40.
25. Odo of Deuil, pp. 54–57, 68–71.
26. *The Letters of Peter the Venerable*, ed. Giles Constable, 2 vols (Cambridge, Massachusetts, 1967), ii, pp. 394–95; Suger, *Lettres*, in *Oeuvres complètes de Suger*, ed. A. Leroy de La Marche (Paris, 1867), pp. 239–317, at 245, 292–93; Mayr-Harting, 'Odo of Deuil', pp. 234–35; Jonathan Phillips, *Defenders of the Holy Land: Relations between the Latin East and the West, 1119–1187* (Oxford, 1996), pp. 113–18; Timothy Reuter, 'The "Non-Crusade" of 1149–50', in *The Second Crusade: Scope and Consequences*, ed. Jonathan Phillips and Martin Hoch (Manchester, 2001), pp. 150–63.
27. Anna Comnena, pp. 126–28, 160; Otto of Freising, pp. 54–59.
28. Kinnamos, pp. 70–72; Wibald of Corvey, *Epistolae*, in *Bibliotheca rerum Germanicarum*, ed. P. Jaffé, 6 vols (Berlin, 1864–73), i, pp. 76–616, at 376–78; Dana C. Munro, *Letters of the Crusaders Written from the Holy Land* (2nd edn, Philadelphia, 1902), p. 13.

29. Lilie, *Byzantium and the Crusader States*, pp. 164–65, 179–80, 220–21; Phillips, *Defenders of the Holy Land*, pp. 123–25.
30. Theiner and Miklosich, *Monumenta*, pp. 4–6.
31. Anselm of Havelberg, *Dialogorum Libri III*, in *Spicilegium sive collectio veterum aliquot scriptorum*, ed. L. d'Achery, 3 vols (Paris, 1723), i, pp. 161–207, at 172–91; F. Dvornik, *Byzantium and the Roman Primacy*, trans. Edwin A. Quain (2nd edn, New York, 1979), pp. 145–47; Anna Comnena, p. 62; *Sacrorum conciliorum nova et amplissima collectio*, ed. J. D. Mansi, 54 vols (Florence and Venice, 1759–98), xxi, cols 799–802; Angold, *Byzantine Empire*, pp. 166–67; Steven Runciman, *The Eastern Schism* (Cambridge, 1955), pp. 102–23; John Gordon Rowe, 'The Papacy and the Greeks, 1122–1153', *Church History*, 28 (1959), pp. 115–30, 310–27, at 115–22; Norman Russell, 'Anselm of Havelberg and the Union of the Churches, 2, The Question of Authority', *Sobornost*, 2 (1980), pp. 29–40, at 32.
32. J. Chrysostomides, 'Byzantine Concepts of War and Peace', in *War, Peace and World Orders in European History*, ed. Anja V. Hartmann and Beatrice Heuser (London and New York, 2001), pp. 91–101, at 92; George T. Dennis, 'Defenders of the Christian People: Holy War in Byzantium', *The Crusades from the Perspective of Byzantium and the Muslim World*, ed. A. E. Laiou and R. P. Mottahedeh (Washington, DC, 2001), pp. 31–39, at 32–33.
33. *Chronica monasterii Casinensis*, ed. Hartmut Hoffmann, MGH, Scriptores, 34 (Hanover, 1980), pp. 590–91.
34. Anna Comnena, pp. 63–64, 317 n. 37.
35. Choniates, p. 32.
36. Anna Comnena, pp. 178–79; Choniates, pp. 32–33, 87, 119–23; Angold, *Byzantine Empire*, pp. 238–40; Magdalino, *Empire of Manuel I*, pp. 249–61, 366–82.
37. Kinnamos, p. 99; Choniates, p. 62; Alexander Kazhdan, 'Latins and Franks in Byzantium: Perception and Reality from the Eleventh to the Twelfth Century', *The Crusades from the Perspective of Byzantium and the Muslim World*, ed. A. E. Laiou and R. P. Mottahedeh (Washington, DC, 2001), pp. 83–100, at 99; Gerald of Wales, *The Journey through Wales and the Description of Wales*, trans. Lewis Thorpe (Harmondsworth, 1978), p. 234; Magdalino, *Empire of Manuel I*, pp. 90–91.
38. A. A. Vasiliev, 'Henry Plantagenet and Manuel Comnenus', *Byzantinische Zeitschrift*, 29 (1929–30), pp. 233–44, at 237. Manuel wrote letters to the pope around the same time with a similar tone: *Recueil des historiens des Gaules et de la France*, xv, pp. 952–53; Magdalino, *Empire of Manuel I*, p. 96; Lilie, *Byzantium and the Crusader States*, pp. 211–14.
39. Kinnamos, p. 44; *Recueil des historiens des Gaules et de la France*, xv, pp. 952–53; Magdalino, *Empire of Manuel I*, p. 96; Lilie, *Byzantium and the Crusader States*, pp. 211–14.
40. Jacques Joseph Champollion-Figeac, *Lettres de rois, reines et autres personnages des cours de France et d'Angleterre*, 2 vols (Paris, 1839), i, pp. 1–3; William of Tyre, ii, p. 449; Magdalino, *Empire of Manuel I*, p. 100.
41. Antoine Dondaine, 'Hugues Ethérien et le concile de Constantinople de 1166',

Historisches Jahrbuch, 77 (1958), pp. 473–83, at 480–82; J. Darrouzès, 'Les documents byzantins du XIIe siècle sur la primauté romaine', *Revue des études Byzantines*, 23 (1965), pp. 42–88, at 76; Antoine Dondaine, 'Hugues Ethérien et Léon Toscan', *Archives d'histoire doctrinale et littéraire du moyen âge*, 19 (1952), pp. 67–134, at 126–27; Angold, *Byzantine Empire*, pp. 213–14; Magdalino, *Empire of Manuel I*, pp. 90–91.

42. Dondaine, 'Hugues Ethérien', pp. 126–27; trans. Magdalino, *Empire of Manuel I*, p. 91.
43. Kinnamos, pp. 196–97; *Liber pontificalis: de gestis Romanorum pontificum*, ed. L. Duchesne, 3 vols (2nd edn, Paris, 1955–57), ii, p. 415; Magdalino, *Empire of Manuel I*, pp. 83–89.
44. William of Tyre, ii, pp. 196–201.
45. Kinnamos, pp. 96–98, 136; William of Tyre, ii, p. 224; Lilie, *Byzantium and the Crusader States*, pp. 163–65.
46. Kinnamos, pp. 136–37; William of Tyre, ii, pp. 253–54.
47. William of Tyre, ii, pp. 253–54; Kinnamos, pp. 136–37.
48. William of Tyre, ii, pp. 254, 276; J. G. Rowe, 'Hadrian IV, the Byzantine Empire and the Latin Orient', *Essays in Medieval History Presented to Bertie Wilkinson*, ed. T. A. Sandquist and M. R. Powicke (Toronto, 1969), pp. 3–16.
49. William of Tyre, ii, p. 277; Kinnamos, pp. 138–39; Choniates, pp. 61–62; Magdalino, 'Pen of the Aunt', p. 19.
50. Kinnamos, pp. 138–39, 141–42; Lilie, *Byzantium and the Crusader States*, pp. 117–18; Magdalino, *Empire of Manuel I*, p. 67.
51. Kinnamos, pp. 142–43; Choniates, pp. 61–62; William of Tyre, ii, pp. 279–81.
52. William of Tyre, ii, pp. 280–81; Kinnamos, pp. 143–44; Ibn al-Qalanisi, *The Damascus Chronicle of the Crusades*, trans. H. A. R. Gibb (London, 1932), pp. 354–55. Sirappie der Nersessian, 'The Armenian Chronicle of the Constable Sinpad or of the "Royal Historian"', *Dumbarton Oaks Papers*, 13 (1959), pp. 143–68, at 149.
53. Anna Comnena, pp. 370–71; *Chronique d'Ernoul et de Bernard le Trésorier*, ed. Louis de Mas Latrie (Paris, 1871), pp. 57–59; Lilie, *Byzantium and the Crusader States*, p. 219; Bernard Hamilton, 'Manuel I Comnenus and Baldwin IV of Jerusalem', *Kathegetria: Essays Presented to Joan Hussey for her Eightieth Birthday*, ed. J. Chrysostomides (Camberley, 1988), pp. 353–75, at 372.
54. Kinnamos, pp. 158–60; Choniates, pp. 65–66; Michael the Syrian, iii, p. 326; Bernard Hamilton, 'Three Patriarchs at Antioch, 1165–70', *Dei gesta per Francos: Etudes sur les croisades dédiées à Jean Richard*, ed. M. Balard, B. Z. Kedar and J. Riley-Smith (Aldershot, 2001), pp. 199–207, at 199–200.
55. Michael the Syrian, iii, pp. 336–39; Hamilton, 'Three Patriarchs', pp. 204–6.
56. William of Tyre, ii, pp. 264–65, 273–75; Lilie, *Byzantium and the Crusader States*, pp. 175–76; Phillips, *Defenders of the Holy Land*, pp. 132–34.
57. Kinnamos, pp. 140–43, 179; William of Tyre, ii, pp. 277–79.
58. Kinnamos, pp. 178–79; William of Tyre, ii, pp. 344–45.
59. William of Tyre, ii, pp. 377–83; Kinnamos, p. 209; Steven Runciman, 'The Visit of King Amalric I to Constantinople in 1171', *Outremer: Studies in the History*

of the Crusading Kingdom of Jerusalem Presented to Joshua Prawer, ed. B. Z. Kedar, H. E. Meyer and R. C. Smail (Jerusalem, 1982), pp. 153–58.

60. William of Tyre, ii, pp. 347–48, 362–70; Kinnamos, pp. 208–9; Choniates, p. 91–96; Lilie, *Byzantium and the Crusader States*, pp. 198–202.
61. William of Tyre, ii, pp. 420–24; Kinnamos, p. 224; Lilie, *Byzantium and the Crusader States*, pp. 215–16, 309–20; Hamilton, 'Manuel I and Baldwin IV', pp. 365–66.
62. John Phokas, pp. 19, 27, 30–31; Hamilton, 'Manuel I and Baldwin IV', p. 368; Andrew Jotischky, 'Manuel Comnenus and the Reunion of the Churches: The Evidence of the Conciliar Mosaics in the Church of the Nativity in Bethlehem', *Levant*, 26 (1994), pp. 207–24; Jaroslav Folda, *The Art of the Crusaders in the Holy Land, 1098–1187* (Cambridge, 1994), pp. 347–64.

Notes to Chapter 7: Andronicus

1. C. M. Brand, 'The Byzantines and Saladin, 1185–1192: Opponents of the Third Crusade', *Speculum*, 37 (1962), pp. 167–81, at 167–68; C. M. Brand, *Byzantium Confronts the West, 1180–1204* (Cambridge, Massachusetts, 1968), pp. 34–35, 41–43; George Ostrogorsky, *History of the Byzantine State*, trans. J. M. Hussey (2nd edn, Oxford, 1968), p. 395; Ralph-Johannes Lilie, *Byzantium and the Crusader States, 1096–1204*, trans. J. C. Morris and J. E. Ridings (Oxford, 1993), pp. 222–23; Jean Richard, *The Crusades, c. 1071 – c. 1291*, trans. Jean Birrell (Cambridge, 1999), p. 182.
2. *Chronicon monasterii de Abingdon*, ed. J. Stevenson, 2 vols (London, 1858), ii, pp. 46–47; Jonathan Shepard, 'The Uses of the Franks in Eleventh-Century Byzantium', *Anglo-Norman Studies*, 15 (1993), pp. 275–305; Alexander Kazhdan, 'Latins and Franks in Byzantium: Perception and Reality from the Eleventh to the Twelfth Century', *The Crusades from the Perspective of Byzantium and the Muslim World*, ed. A. E. Laiou and R. P. Mottahedeh (Washington, DC, 2001), pp. 83–100, at 93–99.
3. Anna Comnena, p. 434.
4. Kekaumenos, *Strategon et incerti scriptoris de officis regiis libellus*, ed. B. Wassiliewsky and V. Jernstedt (St Petersburg, 1896), p. 95; D. M. Nicol, 'The Byzantine View of Western Europe', *Greek, Roman and Byzantine Studies*, 8 (1967), pp. 315–39, at 328–29.
5. Anna Comnena, p. 96; Choniates, pp. 140, 210; Shepard, 'Uses of the Franks', pp. 290–92; Jonathan Harris, 'Distortion, Divine Providence and Genre in Niketas Choniates's Account of the Collapse of Byzantium 1180–1204', *Journal of Medieval History*, 26 (2000), pp. 19–31, at 27.
6. Antoine Dondaine, 'Hugues Ethérien et le concile de Constantinople de 1166', *Historisches Jahrbuch*, 77 (1958), pp. 473–83, at 481; Michael Angold, *The Byzantine Empire, 1025–1204: A Political History* (2nd edn, Harlow, 1997), p. 240.
7. Choniates, pp. 115–16; George and Demetrius Tornikios, *Lettres et discours*, ed. Jean Darrouzès (Paris, 1970), pp. 129, 234–35.

8. Robert of Auxerre, *Chronicon*, ed. O. Holder-Egger, MGH, Scriptores, 26 (Hanover, 1882), pp. 219–79, at 246; William of Tyre, ii, p. 461; Robert of Clari, p. 46.
9. Angold, *Byzantine Empire*, pp. 233–40; Paul Magdalino, *The Empire of Manuel I Komnenos, 1143–1180* (Cambridge, 1993), pp. 222–23; Kazhdan, 'Latins and Franks', pp. 95–96.
10. Psellos, pp. 263–64.
11. G. Tafel and G. Thomas, *Urkunden zur älteren Handels- und Staatsgeschichte der Republik Venedig*, 3 vols (Vienna, 1856–57), i, pp. 51–53; Anna Comnena, pp. 137, 191; D. M. Nicol, *Byzantium and Venice: A Study in Diplomatic and Cultural Relations* (Cambridge, 1988), pp. 59–63.
12. Kinnamos, p. 210; Nicol, *Byzantium and Venice*, pp. 77–81.
13. Gerald W. Day, *Genoa's Response to Byzantium, 1155–1204* (Urbana and Chicago, 1988), pp. 8, 25–27; Nicol, *Byzantium and Venice*, pp. 75–76; Jonathan Riley-Smith, 'Government in Latin Syria and the Commercial Privileges of Foreign Merchants', *Relations between East and West in the Middle Ages*, ed. Derek Baker (Edinburgh, 1973), pp. 109–32; Angold, *Byzantine Empire*, pp. 226–33.
14. Eustathios of Thessalonica, *The Capture of Thessaloniki*, trans. J. R. Melville-Jones (Canberra, 1988), pp. 33–35; Kinnamos, p. 210; Choniates, p. 97.
15. Caffaro et al., *Annali genovesi*, ed. Luigi T. Belgrano and Cesare Imperiale di Sant'Angelo, 5 vols (Rome, 1890–1929), i, p. 68; Day, *Genoa's Response*, pp. 26–28. For negative western attitudes to the Italian maritime republics, see *Chronique d'Ernoul and de Bernard le trésorier*, ed. M. L. de Mas Latrie (Paris, 1971), pp. 345–46; Gunther of Pairis, pp. 90–91; Donald E. Queller and Irene B. Katele, 'Attitudes towards the Venetians in the Fourth Crusade: The Western Sources', *International History Review*, 4 (1982), pp. 1–36, at 27.
16. *Historia ducum Veneticorum*, ed. H. Simonsfeld, MGH, Scriptores, 14 (Hanover, 1883), pp. 72–97, at 78–80; Kinnamos, pp. 211–12; Choniates, pp. 97–98; Brand, *Byzantium Confronts*, p. 67; Magdalino, *Empire of Manuel I* , pp. 93–94; Nicol, *Byzantium and Venice*, pp. 97–103.
17. Choniates, pp. 50–51.
18. Kinnamos, pp. 212–14; Choniates, pp. 97–98; Brand, *Byzantium Confronts*, pp. 195–221.
19. Andrea Dandolo, *Chronica Venetum*, ed. E. Pastorello, Rerum Italicarum Scriptores, new series, 12/1 (Bologna, 1938), p. 260.
20. Choniates, pp. 127–36; Eustathios of Thessalonica, *Capture*, pp. 18–27.
21. William of Tyre, ii, pp. 462–63; Continuator of Sigebert of Gembloux, *Continuatio Aquicinctina*, ed. L. Conrad Bethmann, MGH, Scriptores, 6 (Hanover, 1844), pp. 405–38, at 421; Brand, *Byzantium Confronts*, pp. 33–34.
22. Choniates, pp. 131–32; Eustathios of Thessalonica, *Capture*, pp. 20–27.
23. Kinnamos, pp. 99–103, 175–77, 185, 188–89; William of Tyre, ii, pp. 345–46; Choniates, pp. 59–61, 73–75, 79–81, 128–29.
24. Choniates, pp. 137–41.
25. Choniates, p. 143.
26. Choniates, pp. 144–45, 148–53; Eustathios of Thessalonica, *Capture*, pp. 50–57.

27. Choniates, pp. 31, 148, 150, 162–63, 185; Eustathios of Thessalonica, *Capture*, pp. 44–55; Brand, *Byzantium Confronts*, pp. 57–61.
28. Choniates, pp. 158–60.
29. Choniates, pp. 140, 177.
30. Anna Comnena, pp. 97–98.
31. William of Tyre, ii, pp. 464–67; Eustathios of Thessalonica, *Capture*, pp. 33–35; Choniates, pp. 140–41; Brand, *Byzantium Confronts*, pp. 41–43.
32. William of Tyre, ii, pp. 461–62, 465; Robert of Torigny, *Chronicle*, in *Chronicles of the Reigns of Stephen, Henry II and Richard I*, ed. Richard Howlett, 4 vols (London, 1884–89), iv, pp. 301–2, 307; Bernardo Maragone, *Annales Pisani*, ed. M. L. Gentile, Rerum Italicarum Scriptores, new series, 6.2 (Bologna, 1936), p. 73; Gunther of Pairis, p. 84.
33. *Historia ducum Veneticorum*, pp. 89–90, 92; Brand, *Byzantium Confronts*, p. 196; Nicol, *Byzantium and Venice*, pp. 108–9.
34. Brand, 'Byzantines and Saladin', pp. 167–68; Brand, *Byzantium Confronts*, pp. 34–35, 41–43; Ostrogorsky, *History*, p. 395; Lilie, *Byzantium and the Crusader States*, pp. 222–23.
35. Magnus of Reichersberg, *Chronicon*, ed. W. Wattenbach, MGH, Scriptores, 17 (Hanover, 1861), pp. 439–534, at 511–12; Brand, 'Byzantines and Saladin', pp. 168–69.
36. Raymond of Aguilers, *Historia Francorum qui ceperunt Iherusalem*, trans. J. H. Hill and L. Hill (Philadelphia, 1968), p. 90; Abbas Hamdani, 'Byzantine-Fatimid Relations before the Battle of Mantzikert', *Byzantine Studies*, 1 (1974), pp. 169–79, at 169–73; Carole Hillenbrand, *The Crusades: Islamic Perspectives* (Edinburgh, 1999), pp. 44, 69; Lilie, *Byzantium and the Crusader States*, pp. 235–36.
37. William of Tyre, ii, pp. 280–81; Kinnamos, pp. 143–44; Ibn al-Qalanisi, *The Damascus Chronicle of the Crusades*, trans. H. A. R. Gibb (London, 1932), pp. 354–55; Makrizi, *Histoire d'Egypte*, trans. E. Blochet, *Revue de l'Orient Latin*, 8 (1900–1), pp. 165–212, 501–53, at 539; Brand, *Byzantium Confronts*, p. 34.
38. Brand, 'Byzantines and Saladin', pp. 167–81; Richard, *Crusades*, pp. 198–99.
39. Magnus of Reichersberg, p. 511.
40. This is the interpretation preferred by Lilie, *Byzantium and the Crusader States*, pp. 230–32.
41. William of Tyre, ii, pp. 452–53; Lilie, *Byzantium and the Crusader States*, pp. 223–27; Bernard Hamilton, *The Leper King and his Heirs* (Cambridge, 2000), pp. 173–74.
42. Choniates, p. 183; Eustathios of Thessalonica, *Capture*, pp. 54–55.
43. Choniates, pp. 187–95; Robert of Clari, pp. 50–56.

Notes to Chapter 8: Iron not Gold

1. Ansbert, *Historia de expeditione Friderici Imperatoris*, in *Quellen zur Geschichte des Kreuzzuges Kaiser Friedrichs I*, ed. A. Chroust, MGH, Scriptores Rerum Germanicarum, 5 (Berlin, 1928), pp. 1–115, at 6–10.

2. Magnus of Reichersberg, *Chronicon*, ed. W. Wattenbach, MGH, Scriptores, 17 (Hanover, 1861), pp. 439–534, at 511.
3. Choniates, pp. 204–5, 291; Robert of Clari, p. 56; Villehardouin, p. 44.
4. Francesco Gabrielli, *Arab Historians of the Crusades*, trans. E. J. Costello (London, 1969), pp. 115–16.
5. C. M. Brand, 'The Byzantines and Saladin, 1185–1192: Opponents of the Third Crusade', *Speculum*, 37 (1962), pp. 167–81, at 170–72; C. M. Brand, *Byzantium Confronts the West, 1180–1204* (Cambridge, Massachusetts, 1968), p. 177; George Ostrogorsky, *History of the Byzantine State*, trans. J. M. Hussey (2nd edn, Oxford, 1968), pp. 406–7; Ralph-Johannes Lilie, *Byzantium and the Crusader States, 1096–1204*, trans. J. C. Morris and J. E. Ridings (Oxford, 1993), pp. 239–41; Jonathan Riley-Smith, *The Crusades: A Short History* (New Haven and London, 1987), pp. 111–12.
6. Eustathios of Thessalonica, *The Capture of Thessaloniki*, trans. J. R. Melville-Jones (Canberra, 1988), pp. 113–41; Choniates, pp. 165–70.
7. Choniates, p. 167. The translation is that in *Cambridge Medieval History*, iv, pt 2, ed. J. M. Hussey (Cambridge, 1967), p. 81.
8. Magnus of Reichersberg, p. 511; Brand, 'Byzantines and Saladin', pp. 169–70.
9. Magnus of Reichersberg, p. 512; Dana C. Munro, *Letters of the Crusaders Written from the Holy Land* (2nd edn, Philadelphia, 1902), p. 21; Roger of Hoveden, *Chronica*, ed. William Stubbs, 4 vols (London, 1868–71), ii, pp. 355–56; Roger of Wendover, *Liber qui dicitur flores historiarum*, 3 vols (London, 1886–89), i, p. 154; Benedict of Peterborough, *Gesta Regis Henrici Secundi*, ed. William Stubbs, 2 vols (London, 1867), ii, pp. 51–53.
10. Choniates, pp. 210–16, 231; Robert of Clari, pp. 59–62; F. Miklosich and W. Müller, *Acta et diplomata Graeca medii aevi sacra et profana*, 6 vols (Vienna, 1860–90), iii, p. 40; Brand, *Byzantium Confronts*, pp. 66–67, 207–13; Michael Angold, *The Byzantine Empire, 1025–1204: A Political History* (2nd edn, Harlow, 1997), pp. 321–22.
11. Choniates, p. 225.
12. Abu Shama, *Le livre des deux jardins: histoire des deux règnes, celui de Nour ed-Dîn et celui de Salah ed-Dîn*, in *RHC Or*, iv, pp. 3–522, at 389, 470–3, 508–10; Baha al-Din ibn Shaddad, *The Rare and Excellent History of Saladin*, trans. D. S. Richards (Aldershot, 2001), pp. 121–2, 201–2.
13. Bar Hebraeus, *Chronography*, trans. Ernest A. Wallis-Budge, 2 vols (London, 1932), i, p. 327; Bernard Hamilton, 'Manuel I Comnenus and Baldwin IV of Jerusalem', *Kathegetria: Essays Presented to Joan Hussey for her 80th Birthday*, ed. J. Chrysostomides (Camberley, 1988), pp. 353–75, at 368.
14. *Chronicle of the Third Crusade*, trans. Helen J. Nicholson (Aldershot, 1997), p. 58; Ansbert, p. 39; Magnus of Reichersberg, p. 512; Roger of Wendover, i, p. 153; Abu Shama, pp. 470–1, 508; Baha al-Din, p. 121; Stephen W. Reinert, 'The Muslim Presence in Constantinople, Ninth–Fifteenth Centuries: Some Preliminary Observations', in *Studies on the Internal Diaspora of the Byzantine Empire*, ed. H. Ahrweiler and A. E. Laiou (Washington, DC, 1998), pp. 125–50,

at 140–42; Abbas Hamdani, 'Byzantine-Fatimid Relations before the Battle of Mantzikert', *Byzantine Studies*, 1 (1974), pp. 169–79, at 173, 175.

15. Roger of Wendover, i, p. 153.
16. Kinnamos, pp. 61, 154, 165–67; Choniates, pp. 37, 113.
17. Choniates, p. 222; Magnus of Reichersberg, p. 509; M. Pavlova, 'The Role of the Serbs in the Third Crusade' (in Czech with French summary), *Byzantinoslavica*, 5 (1933–34), pp. 235–303; Ostrogorsky, *History of the Byzantine State*, p. 406; Lilie, *Byzantium and the Crusader States*, p. 242.
18. Choniates, p. 221; Ansbert, pp. 14–15; *Historia Peregrinorum*, in *Quellen zur Geschichte des Kreuzzuges Kaiser Friedrichs I*, ed. A. Chroust, MGH, Scriptores Rerum Germanicarum, 5 (Berlin, 1928), pp. 116–72, at 127–29; Brand, *Byzantium Confronts*, pp. 176–77.
19. Ansbert, pp. 27–28, 37–39; *Historia Peregrinorum*, pp. 129–30, 133–34; Magnus of Reichersberg, pp. 509–10. Cf. *Gesta Francorum*, pp. 8–9.
20. Magnus of Reichersberg, p. 510.
21. Ansbert, pp. 49–50; *Historia Peregrinorum*, pp. 140–41. Cf. Odo of Deuil, pp. 26–27.
22. Munro, *Letters*, pp. 21–22.
23. Ansbert, pp. 38–39, 48–49; *Historia Peregrinorum*, p. 143; Magnus of Reichersberg, p. 510.
24. Ansbert, pp. 54–55; *Historia Peregrinorum*, pp. 143, 148; Brand, *Byzantium Confronts*, p. 182. The story of the poisoned wine may have had its origin in the fate of some Normans who died from drinking unfermented wine at Thessalonica in 1185: Eustathios of Thessalonica, *Capture*, p. 149.
25. Ansbert, p. 44; Choniates, pp. 224–25; Brand, *Byzantium Confronts*, pp. 180–81. Cf. Anna Comnena, pp. 320–23; Kinnamos, p. 65.
26. Ansbert, pp. 52–53; *Historia Peregrinorum*, pp. 144–45; Brand, *Byzantium Confronts*, pp. 183–84.
27. Munro, *Letters*, p. 20; Ansbert, pp. 40–43.
28. Ansbert, pp. 64–66; *Historia Peregrinorum*, p. 150; Baha al-Din, p. 114; Choniates, p. 226; Karl Hampe, 'Ein ungedruckter Bericht über den Vertrag von Adrianopel zwischen Friedrich I. und Isaak Angelos vom Febr. 1190', *Neues Archiv der Gesellschaft für ältere deutsche Geschichtskunde*, 23 (1898), pp. 398–400; Brand, *Byzantium Confronts*, pp. 185–87.
29. Abu Shama, p. 389; Baha al-Din, p. 122; Imad ad-Din al-Isfahani, *Conquête de la Syrie et de la Palestine par Saladin*, trans. Henri Massé (Paris, 1972), pp. 244–45; Brand, 'Byzantines and Saladin', pp. 176–77.
30. Ibn al-Qalanisi, *The Damascus Chronicle of the Crusades*, trans. H. A. R. Gibb (London, 1932), pp. 112–13; Carole Hillenbrand, *The Crusades: Islamic Perspectives* (Edinburgh, 1999), p. 69.
31. Baha al-Din, p. 114; Abu Shama, p. 508; Lilie, *Byzantium and the Crusader States*, p. 242.
32. Baha al-Din, p. 122.
33. Ansbert, pp. 72–88.

34. Eustathios of Thessalonica, *Capture*, p. 3; Niketas Choniates, *Orationes et Epistulae*, ed. J. A. Van Dieten (Berlin and New York, 1972), pp. 3, 89. Cf *Iliad*, bk. i, line 131; Brand, *Byzantium Confronts*, p. 113.
35. Choniates, p. 233.
36. Ostrogorsky, *History*, p. 353; D. M. Nicol, 'The Byzantine View of Western Europe', *Greek, Roman and Byzantine Studies*, 8 (1967), pp. 315–39, at 330; Brand, *Byzantium Confronts*, p. 177; Brand, 'Byzantines and Saladin', p. 180; Lilie, *Byzantium and the Crusader States*, p. 284.
37. Choniates, pp. 164, 167–69, 201, 210–12; Jonathan Harris, 'Distortion, Divine Providence and Genre in Niketas Choniates's Account of the Collapse of Byzantium 1180–1204', *Journal of Medieval History*, 26 (2000), pp. 19–31, at 27–28.
38. Choniates, pp. 23, 35–39. Cf. Odo of Deuil, pp. 40–41, 109; *Eulogium historiarum*, ed. F. S. Haydon, 3 vols (London, 1858–63), i, p. 386.
39. Choniates, pp. xiii, 224.
40. Choniates, pp. 221–25.
41. Choniates, pp. 227–29.
42. Choniates, pp. 225–26. Cf. Ansbert, pp. 48–49; Anna Comnena, pp. 325–26. Cf. Odo of Deuil, pp. 24–27.
43. Choniates, p. 262.
44. Peter Edbury, *The Kingdom of Cyprus and the Crusades, 1191–1374* (Cambridge, 1991), pp. 1–12.
45. For Richard's letter, see *The Conquest of Jerusalem and the Third Crusade: Sources in Translation*, ed. Peter W. Edbury (Aldershot, 1998), pp. 178–79.
46. *Chronicle of the Third Crusade*, pp. 178–79; Ambroise, *The Crusade of Richard the Lion-Heart*, trans. Merton Jerome Hubert (New York, 1941), pp. 82–83; *Old French Continuation of William of Tyre*, trans. Peter W. Edbury in *The Conquest of Jerusalem and the Third Crusade: Sources in Translation* (Aldershot, 1998), pp. 1–145, at 100–2; Benedict of Peterborough, i, pp. 261–62; *L'estoire de Eracles empereur et la conqueste de la terre d'outremer*, in *RHC Oc*, ii, pp. 1–487 at 165.
47. *Chronicle of the Third Crusade*, pp. 179, 195; Ambroise, p. 82; Richard of Devizes, *The Chronicle of the Time of Richard the First*, ed. John T. Appleby (London, 1963), p. 38. On this argument, see James A. Brundage, 'Richard the Lionheart and Byzantium', *Studies in Medieval Culture*, 6–7 (1976), pp. 63–70.
48. Neophytos, *De calamitatibus Cypri*, in *Chronicles and Memorials of the Reign of Richard I*, ed. William Stubbs, 2 vols (London, 1864–65), i, pp. clxxxiv-clxxxix; Choniates, pp. 204, 254–55.
49. *Die Register Innocenz III*, ed. O. Hageneder et al., 7 vols (Graz and Cologne, 1964–99), ii, pp. 459–62; Baha al-Din, pp. 201–2; Abu Shama, p. 510; Edbury, *Kingdom of Cyprus*, pp. 10–11.

Notes to Chapter 9: The Fall of Constantinople

1. Baha al-Din Ibn Shaddad, *The Rare and Excellent History of Saladin*, trans. D. S. Richards (Aldershot, 2001), p. 122.

2. George and Leo Tornikios, *Lettres et discours*, ed. J. Darrouzès (Paris, 1970), pp. 340–41; Michael Angold, *The Byzantine Empire, 1025–1204: A Political History* (2nd edn, Harlow, 1997), p. 319.
3. Choniates, pp. 247–48; C. M. Brand, *Byzantium Confronts the West, 1180–1204* (Cambridge, Massachusetts, 1968), pp. 112–13.
4. Choniates, pp. 247–48; Robert of Clari, p. 57; Villehardouin, pp. 44,84; Gunther of Pairis, p. 93.
5. *Die Register Innocenz III*, ed. O. Hageneder et al., 7 vols (Graz and Cologne, 1964–99), ii, pp. 390–93; *Gesta Innocentii*, *Patrologia Latina*, vol. 214. cols xvii-ccxxviii, at cxix-cxx; Brand, *Byzantium Confronts*, pp. 225–27; A. Papadakis and Alice Mary Talbot, 'John X Camaterus Confronts Innocent III: An Unpublished Correspondence', *Byzantinoslavica*, 33 (1972), pp. 26–41.
6. Choniates, pp. 252, 265, 322.
7. Richard of Devizes, *The Chronicle of the Time of Richard the First*, ed. John T. Appleby (London, 1963), p. 9; *Chronicle of the Third Crusade*, trans. H. J. Nicholson (Aldershot, 1997), p. 278; *The Conquest of Jerusalem and the Third Crusade: Sources in Translation*, ed. Peter W. Edbury (Aldershot, 1998), p. 181; Fred A. Cazel, 'Financing the Crusades', in *A History of the Crusades*, ed. K. M. Setton, 6 vols (Madison, Wisconsin, 1969–89), vi, pp. 116–49.
8. Angold, *Byzantine Empire*, pp. 295–315; Brand, *Byzantium Confronts*, pp. 85–86.
9. Eustathios of Thessalonica, *The Capture of Thessaloniki*, trans. J. R. Melville-Jones (Canberra, 1988), pp. 57–61; Choniates, pp. 164, 231–33, 253–54.
10. Abu Shama, *Le livre des deux jardins: histoire des deux règnes, celui de Nour ed-Dîn et celui de Salah ed-Dîn*, in *RHC Or*, iv, pp. 3–522, at 510.
11. Choniates, pp. 261–62; *Old French Continuation of William of Tyre*, trans. Peter W. Edbury in *The Conquest of Jerusalem and the Third Crusade: Sources in Translation* (Aldershot, 1998), pp. 1–145 at 137–39; Otto of St Blaise, *Chronica*, ed. Adolf Hofmeister, MGH, Scriptores Rerum Germanicarum, 47 (Hanover and Leipzig, 1912), pp. 69–70; Brand, *Byzantium Confronts*, pp. 189–94.
12. Choniates, pp. 62–63.
13. *Die Register Innocenz III*, ii, pp. 394–97, at 395; *Gesta Innocentii*, col. cxx.
14. *Die Register Innocenz III*, i, pp. 526–28, at 526: 'cum tam ex vicinitate locorum quam habundantia divitiarum tuarum et potentia, qua inimicos crucis munere divino precellis, id potueris commodius et expeditius aliis principibus adimplere'.
15. *Die Register Innocenz III*, v, pp. 239–43; Alfred J. Andrea, *Contemporary Sources for the Fourth Crusade* (Leiden, 2000), pp. 35–39, at 38.
16. *Die Register Innocenz III*, vi, pp. 166–68, at 167; Andrea, *Contemporary Sources*, pp. 67–68. For a discussion of this letter, see Alfred J. Andrea and John C. Moore, 'The Date of Reg. 6: 102: Pope Innocent III's Letter of Advice to the Crusaders', in *Medieval and Renaissance Venice*, ed. Ellen E. Kittell and Thomas F. Madden (Urbana and Chicago, 1999), pp. 109–23.
17. *Die Register Innocenz III*, vi, pp. 163–65, 167; Andrea, *Contemporary Sources*, pp. 62–63, 67–68.

18. Gunther of Pairis, p. 84.
19. Villehardouin, pp. 37–38.
20. Robert of Clari, pp. 59–66; Robert of Torigny, *Chronicle*, in *Chronicles of the Reigns of Stephen, Henry II and Richard I*, ed. Richard Howlett, 4 vols (London, 1884–89), iv, pp. 81–315, at 285; *Gesta Innocentii*, col. cxxxii; Henri Grégoire, 'The Question of the Diversion of the Fourth Crusade, or an Old Controversy Solved by a Latin Adverb', *Byzantion*, 15 (1940–41), pp. 158–66; Jaroslav Folda, 'The Fourth Crusade, 1201–1203: Some Reconsiderations', *Byzantinoslavica*, 26 (1965), pp. 277–90; Queller and Madden, *The Fourth Crusade*, p. 35; Alexander Kazhdan, 'Latins and Franks in Byzantium: Perception and Reality from the Eleventh to the Twelfth Century', *The Crusades from the Perspective of Byzantium and the Muslim World*, ed. A. E. Laiou and R. P. Mottahedeh (Washington, DC, 2001), pp. 83–100, at 96; Paul Magdalino, *The Empire of Manuel I Komnenos, 1143–1180* (Cambridge, 1993), p. 100.
21. Villehardouin, pp. 105–7; Robert of Clari, p. 124; Gunther of Pairis, pp. 107–8; Peter Lock, *The Franks in the Aegean, 1204–1500* (London, 1995), pp. 43–50.
22. *Die Register Innocenz III*, vi, pp. 358–61, at 359; Andrea, *Contemporary Sources*, pp. 80–84, at 81.
23. Choniates, pp. 294–95; Villehardouin, pp. 44–45; Jared Gordon, 'The Novgorod Account of the Fourth Crusade', *Byzantion*, 43 (1973), pp. 297–311, at 306; Folda, 'Fourth Crusade', p. 288.
24. *Die Register Innocenz III*, v, pp. 239–43, at 240; Andrea, *Contemporary Sources*, pp. 35–36.
25. Villehardouin, p. 45; Robert of Clari, pp. 45–46; Donald E. Queller and Thomas F. Madden, *The Fourth Crusade: The Conquest of Constantinople* (2nd edn, Philadelphia, 1997), pp. 34–39.
26. Villehardouin, p. 35; Robert of Clari, p. 36.
27. Villehardouin, pp. 33, 43; Robert of Clari, pp. 40–41.
28. Robert of Clari, p. 45; Gunther of Pairis, p. 78.
29. Villehardouin, p. 50
30. Villehardouin, p. 35.
31. Villehardouin, pp. 51, 55–56; Robert of Clari, p. 44; *Devastatio Constantinopolitana* in Andrea, *Contemporary Sources*, pp. 205–221, at 216. On the numbers who left, see D. E. Queller, T. K. Compton and D. A. Campbell, 'The Fourth Crusade: The Neglected Majority', *Speculum*, 49 (1974), pp. 441–65.
32. Villehardouin, pp. 51–2; Robert of Clari, pp. 59, 66.
33. Villehardouin, pp. 54, 57–59; Robert of Clari, pp. 58, 66–67.
34. Choniates, pp. 297–98.
35. Villehardouin, pp. 62–63.
36. Hugh of St-Pol, *Report to the West*, in Andrea, *Contemporary Sources*, pp. 177–201, at 190; Robert of Clari, p. 67.
37. Choniates, p. 297; Queller and Madden, *The Fourth Crusade*, pp. 111–18.
38. Villehardouin, p. 67; Choniates, pp. 298–99; Queller and Madden, *The Fourth Crusade*, pp. 119–30.

39. Villehardouin, pp. 70–73; Robert of Clari, pp. 75–78; Choniates, pp. 298–302.
40. Villehardouin, pp. 74–75; Choniates, pp. 304–5.
41. Villehardouin, pp. 74–76; Hugh of St-Pol, *Report to the West*, pp. 200–1.
42. C. M. Brand, 'A Byzantine Plan for the Fourth Crusade', *Speculum*, 43 (1968), pp. 462–75, at 467.
43. Choniates, p. 302.
44. Villehardouin, pp. 76–79; Robert of Clari, pp. 81–82; Choniates, pp. 302, 304.
45. Villehardouin, p. 77.
46. Villehardouin, pp. 79–80; Choniates, pp. 302–4.
47. Villehardouin, p. 81; Robert of Clari, pp. 82–3; *Die Register Innocenz III*, vii, p. 254; Andrea, *Contemporary Sources*, p. 101.
48. Villehardouin, pp. 82–83.
49. Choniates, pp. 306–7.
50. Choniates, pp. 307–9, Villehardouin, p. 84.
51. Robert of Clari, pp. 88–91; Choniates, p. 312; Villehardouin, pp. 85–86; Psellos, p. 36; Robert Lee Wolff, 'Footnote to an Incident of the Latin Occupation of Constantinople: The Church and the Icon of the Hodegetria', *Traditio*, 6 (1948), pp. 319–28.
52. Villehardouin, pp. 84–85; Gunther of Pairis, p. 90; Robert of Clari, pp. 85–86, 94.
53. Gunther of Pairis, p. 107; Robert of Clari, p. 100–1.
54. Choniates, p. 323; Villehardouin, p. 92; Robert of Clari, pp. 101–2; Christopher G. Ferrard, 'The Amount of Constantinopolitan Booty in 1204', *Studi Veneziani*, 13 (1971), pp. 95–104, at 98.
55. Villehardouin, pp. 91–92; Gunther of Pairis, p. 185; Choniates, p. 313; T. F. Madden, 'The Fires of the Fourth Crusade in Constantinople, 1203–1204: A Damage Assessment', *Byzantinische Zeitschrift*, 84–85 (1991–92), pp. 72–93, at 88–89.

Notes to Chapter 10: Recovery

1. *Die Register Innocenz III*, ed. O. Hageneder et al., 7 vols (Graz and Cologne, 1964–99), vii, p. 264; Alfred J. Andrea, *Contemporary Sources for the Fourth Crusade* (Leiden, 2000), p. 117.
2. G. L. Tafel and G. M. Thomas, *Urkunden zur älteren Handels- und Staatsgeschichte der Republik Venedig*, 3 vols (Vienna, 1856–57), i, pp. 444–52; Antonio Carile, 'Partitio terrarum imperii Romaniae', *Studi Veneziani*, 7 (1965), pp. 125–305, at 217–22; Villehardouin, p. 88; Robert of Clari, pp. 91–92.
3. Villehardouin, pp. 94–97; Robert of Clari, pp. 116–18; Choniates, p. 329; D. E. Queller and T. F. Madden, *The Fourth Crusade: The Conquest of Constantinople* (2nd edn, Philadelphia, 1997), pp. 200–3; J. M. Hussey, *The Orthodox Church in the Byzantine Empire* (Oxford, 1986), p. 184; Peter Lock, *The Franks in the Aegean, 1204–1500* (London, 1995), pp. 40–45.
4. Villehardouin, pp. 112–14; Lock, *Franks in the Aegean*, pp. 45–51, 142–55; D. M. Nicol, *Byzantium and Venice: A Study in Diplomatic and Cultural*

Relations (Cambridge, 1988), pp. 148–65; David Jacoby, 'The Latin Empire of Constantinople and the Frankish States of Greece', in *The New Cambridge Medieval History, v, c. 1198 – c. 1300*, ed. David Abulafia (Cambridge, 1999), pp. 525–42, at 528–33; R. L. Wolff, 'The Latin Empire of Constantinople, 1204–1261', in *A History of the Crusades*, ed. K. M. Setton, 6 vols (Madison, Wisconsin, 1969–89), ii, pp. 187–233, at 190–95.

5. Gunther of Pairis, pp. 107–8, 114–17; Robert of Clari, pp. 117, 124; Villehardouin, pp. 108–9.
6. Choniates, pp. 326, 329–30; Robert of Clari, pp. 118–19; David Jacoby, 'The Encounter of Two Societies: Western Conquerors and the Byzantines in the Peloponnesos after the Fourth Crusade', *American Historical Review*, 78 (1973), pp. 873–906, at 885–89; Lock, *Franks in the Aegean*, pp. 193–216.
7. On the establishment of the three successor states, see Michael Angold, *A Byzantine Government in Exile. Government and Society under the Laskarids of Nicaea, 1204–1261* (Oxford, 1975), pp. 2–33; idem, 'Byzantium in Exile', in *The New Cambridge Modern History, v, c. 1198 – c. 1300*, ed. David Abulafia (Cambridge, 1999), pp. 543–68; D. M. Nicol, *The Despotate of Epiros I, 1204–1267* (Oxford, 1957), p. 16; A. A. Vasiliev, 'The Foundation of the Empire of Trebizond', *Speculum*, 11 (1936), pp. 3–37, at 17–20.
8. Demetrius Chomatianos, *Juris ecclesiastici Graecorum selecta paralipomena*, in *Analecta sacra et classica spicilegio solesmensi*, ed. J. B. Pitra, 8 vols (Paris, 1876–91), vi, cols 90, 99; N. G. Wilson, *Scholars of Byzantium* (2nd edn, London, 1996), pp. 218–22; C. N. Constantinides, *Higher Education in Byzantium in the Thirteenth and Early Fourteenth Centuries, 1204 – c. 1310* (Nicosia, 1982), pp. 5–27; Clive Foss, *Nicaea: A Byzantine Capital and its Praises* (Brookline, Massachusetts, 1996), pp. 123–63.
9. August Heisenberg, 'Neue Quellen zur Geschichte des lateinischen Kaisertum und der Kircheunion II: die Unionsverhandlungen vom 30. August 1206 Patriarchenwahl und Kaiserkrönung in Nikaia 1208', *Sitzungsberichte der Bayerischen Akademie der Wissenschaften, Philosophisch-philologische und Historische Klasse. Jahrgang 1920, 10*, pp. 3–56, at 5–12; Angold, 'Byzantium in Exile', p. 545; Nicol, *Despotate of Epiros*, pp. 64–71; Vasiliev, 'Foundation', pp. 30–37; V. Grumel, 'L'authenticité de la lettre de Jean Vatatzes, empereur de Nicée, au pape Grégoire IX', *Echos d'Orient*, 29 (1930), pp. 450–58; John S. Langdon, 'Byzantium in Anatolian Exile: Imperial Vicegerency Reaffirmed during Byzantine-Papal Discussions at Nicaea and Nymphaion, 1234', *Byzantinische Forschungen*, 20 (1994), pp. 197–233, at 217–21.
10. Choniates, pp. 225–26, 262, 322; Ernest Barker, *Social and Political Thought in Byzantium from Justinian I to the Last Palaeologus* (Oxford, 1957), p. 156; Michael Acominatos Choniates, *Ta sozomena*, ed. S. P. Lambros, 2 vols (Athens, 1879–80), i, p. 183; Michael Angold, *The Byzantine Empire, 1025–1204: A Political History* (2nd edn, Harlow, 1997), p. 314; Jonathan Harris, 'Distortion, Divine Providence and Genre in Niketas Choniates's Account of the Collapse of Byzantium 1180–1204', *Journal of Medieval History*, 26 (2000), pp. 19–31, at

30–31; Angold, *Byzantine Government*, pp. 29–32; Constantinides, *Higher Education*, pp. 20–21.

11. Choniates, pp. xiv–xv, 324–25; Nicholas Mesarites, *Der Epitaphios des Nikolaos Mesarites auf seinem Bruder Johannes*, ed. August Heisenberg, 'Neue Quellen zur Geschichte des lateinischen Kaisertum und der Kircheunion, I', *Sitzungsberichte der Bayerischen Akademie der Wissenschaften, Philosophisch-philologische und Historische Klasse. Jahrgang 1922, v*, pp. 3–75, at 46–47; translation in C. M. Brand, *Byzantium Confronts the West, 1180–1204* (Cambridge, Massachusetts, 1968), p. 269.
12. Choniates, pp. 315, 357; J. Darrouzès, 'Le mémoire de Constantin Stilbès contre les Latins', *Revue des Etudes Byzantines*, 21 (1963), pp. 50–100, at 81–82.
13. Robert of Clari, p. 92.
14. Andrea, *Contemporary Sources*, p. 166.
15. Gunther of Pairis, pp. 109–12.
16. Choniates, p. 316; Mesarites, *Epitaphios*, pp. 46–47; translation in Brand, *Byzantium Confronts*, p. 269.
17. Mesarites, *Epitaphios*, pp. 52–61; Heisenberg, *Neue Quellen II*, pp. 15–25; Joseph Gill, *Byzantium and the Papacy, 1198–1400* (New Brunswick, New Jersey, 1979), pp. 32–34; Hussey, *Orthodox Church*, pp. 189–92.
18. Mesarites, *Epitaphios*, pp. 63–66; George Akropolites, *Historia*, ed. A. Heisenberg and P. Wirth, 2 vols (Stuttgart, 1978), i, pp. 29–30. A favourable view of papal attempts to secure compliance from the Greeks can be found in Gill, *Byzantium and the Papacy*, pp. 39–40; Joseph Gill, 'Innocent III and the Greeks: Aggressor or Apostle?', in *Relations between East and West in the Middle Ages*, ed. Derek Baker (Edinburgh, 1973), pp. 95–108.
19. On the weakness of the Latin empire, see: Lock, *Franks in the Aegean*, pp. 53–54; Jacoby, 'Latin Empire', pp. 528–29; Wolff, 'Latin Empire', pp. 199–202.
20. Choniates, pp. 357–62; L. Vlad Borelli and A. Guidi Toniato, 'The Origins and Documentary Sources of the Horses of San Marco', in *The Horses of San Marco*, ed. Guido Perocco, trans. J. and V. Wilton-Ely (London, 1979), pp. 127–36; R. L. Wolff, 'Hopf's So-Called "Fragmentum" of Marino Sanudo Torsello', *The Joshua Starr Memorial Volume* (New York, 1953), pp. 149–59, at 150–51.
21. Gunther of Pairis, pp 125–27; *The Deeds of the Bishops of Halberstadt*, in Andrea, *Contemporary Sources*, pp. 239–64, at 262; Francis Wormald, 'The Rood of Bromholm', *Journal of the Warburg and Courtauld Institutes*, 1 (1937–38), pp. 31–45.
22. Anonymous of Soissons, *Concerning the Land of Jerusalem and the Means by which Relics were Carried to this Church from the City of Constantinople*, in Andrea, *Contemporary Sources*, pp. 223–38, at 236; Robert Lee Wolff, 'Mortgage and Redemption of an Emperor's Son: Castile and the Latin Empire of Constantinople', *Speculum*, 29 (1954), pp. 45–84, at 52–53.
23. *Die Register Innocenz III*, vii, pp. 262–64, at 263; Andrea, *Contemporary Sources*, pp. 113–15, at 114.

24. Robert of Auxerre, *Chronicon*, ed. O. Holder-Egger, MGH, Scriptores, 26 (Hanover, 1882), pp. 219–79, at 269; Villehardouin, p. 110; Matthew Paris, *Chronica majora*, ed. Henry R. Luard, 7 vols (London, 1872–83), iii, pp. 469–70.
25. Matthew Paris, iii, p. 620; John of Joinville, *The Life of Saint Louis*, in *Chronicles of the Crusades*, trans. M. R. B. Shaw (Harmondsworth, 1963), pp. 161–362, at 199; Malcolm Barber, 'Western Attitudes to Frankish Greece in the Thirteenth Century', in *Latins and Greeks in the Eastern Mediterranean after 1204*, ed. B. Arbel, B. Hamilton and D. Jacoby (London, 1989), pp. 111–28, at 116–18; Christopher Tyerman, 'Some English Evidence of Attitudes to Crusading in the Thirteenth Century', in *Thirteenth-Century England, 1, Proceedings of the Newcastle-Upon-Tyne Conference*, ed. P. R. Coss and S. D. Lloyd (Woodbridge, 1986), pp. 168–74 at 171; A. Palmer Throop, *Criticism of the Crusade: A Study of Public Opinion and Crusade Propaganda* (Amsterdam, 1940), pp. 30–31.
26. A detailed account of these events can be found in Nicol, *Despotate of Epiros*, pp. 47–75, 102–12.
27. Nikephoros Gregoras, *Rhomäische Geschichte*, trans. J. L. Van Dieten, 4 vols (Stuttgart, 1973–94), i, pp. 84–85; George Ostrogorsky, *History of the Byzantine State*, trans. J. M. Hussey (2nd edn, Oxford, 1968), pp. 442–43; Angold, 'Byzantium in Exile', pp. 550–51.
28. *The Rothelin Continuation of the History of William of Tyre*, trans. Janet Shirley, in *Crusader Syria in the Thirteenth Century* (Aldershot, 1999), pp. 13–120, at 59; Matthew Paris, *Chronica majora*, iv, pp. 299, 357, 453; Pachymeres, i, pp. 244–45; N. Festa, 'Le lettere greche di Federigo II', *Archivio Storico Italiano*, 13 (1894), pp. 1–34, at 22.
29. The complex events of the period 1222–54 are discussed in detail in Ostrogorsky, *History*, pp. 434–44; Warren Treadgold, *A History of the Byzantine State and Society* (Stanford, California, 1997), pp. 723–30.
30. On the Battle of Pelagonia and its effects, see D. J. Geanakoplos, 'Greco-Latin Relations on the Eve of Restoration: The Battle of Pelagonia, 1259', *Dumbarton Oaks Papers*, 7 (1953), pp. 101–41; D. J. Geanakoplos, *Emperor Michael Palaeologus and the West, 1258–1282: A Study in Byzantine Latin Relations* (Cambridge, Massachusetts, 1959), pp. 63–74.
31. For details of the treaty with Genoa, see Camillo Manfroni, 'Le relazioni fra Genova, l'impero bizantino e i Turchi', *Atti della Società Ligure di Storia Patria*, 28 (1896), 574–858; Geanakoplos, *Emperor Michael Palaeologus*, pp. 87–89.
32. Michael VIII Palaeologus, *Autobiography with the Charter of the Monastery of Demetrios in Constantinople*, trans. A. Pelendrides (London, 1998), pp. 60–61; Akropolites, *Historia*, i, pp. 186–88; Pachymeres, i, pp. 190–218; Geanakoplos, *Emperor Michael Palaeologus*, pp. 119–22.
33. Pachymeres, ii, pp. 652–57. Cf. Dimitri Obolensky, *The Byzantine Commonwealth: Eastern Europe, 500–1453* (London, 1971), pp. 287–302; André Grabar, 'God and the "Family of Princes" Presided over by the Byzantine Emperor', *Harvard Slavic Studies*, 2 (1954), pp. 117–23; George Ostrogorsky, 'The Byzantine

Emperor and the Hierarchical World Order', *Slavonic and East European Review*, 35 (1956–57), pp. 1–14.

34. Pseudo-Codinus, *Traité des offices*, ed. J. Verpeaux (Paris, 1966), p. 235; Pachymeres, i, pp. 120–25.
35. For a more detailed account of these events, see Jean Richard, *The Crusades, c. 1071–c. 1291*, trans. Jean Birrell (Cambridge, 1999), pp. 294–356, 408–20; Jonathan Riley-Smith, *The Crusades: A Short History* (New Haven and London, 1987), pp. 141–61.
36. *Rothelin Continuation of the History of William of Tyre*, p. 109; *The Mission of Friar William of Rubruck: His Journey to the Court of the Great Khan Möngke, 1253–1255*, trans. Peter Jackson (London, 1990), pp. 65, 175; John S. Langdon, 'Byzantium's Initial Encounter with the Chinggisids: An Introduction to Byzantino-Mongolica', *Viator*, 29 (1998), pp. 95–140, at 125–30.
37. H. F. Delaborde, 'Lettre des Chrétiens de Terre-Sainte à Charles d'Anjou (22 avril 1260)', *Revue de l'Orient Latin*, 2 (1894), pp. 206–15, at 213; Bernard Hamilton, *The Latin Church in the Crusader States* (London, 1980), pp. 235–36.
38. P. M. Holt, *Early Mamluk Diplomacy, 1260–1290: Treaties of Baybars and Qalawun with Christian Rulers* (Leiden, 1995), p. 118.
39. Pachymeres, i, pp. 234–35; Steven Runciman, 'The Ladies of the Mongols', in *Eis mnêmên K. I. Amantou* (Athens, 1960), pp. 46–53, at 46–49.
40. Marius Canard, 'Le traité de 1281 entre Michel Paléologue et le sultan Qalâ'un', *Byzantion*, 10 (1935), pp. 669–80; Holt, *Early Mamluk Diplomacy*, pp. 122–40; J. J. Saunders, 'The Mongol Defeat at Ain Jalut and the Restoration of the Greek Empire', in J. J. Saunders, *Muslims and Mongols: Essays on Medieval Asia*, ed. G. W. Rice (Christchurch, 1977), pp. 67–76; David O. Morgan, 'The Mongols and the Eastern Mediterranean' , in *Latins and Greeks in the Eastern Mediterranean after 1204*, ed. B. Arbel, B. Hamilton and D. Jacoby (London, 1989), pp. 198–211, at 204–5.
41. Gregoras, iii, pp. 203–4; Michael F. Hendy, *Studies in the Byzantine Monetary Economy, c. 300–1450* (Cambridge, 1985), pp. 513–36.
42. *Die Register Innocenz III*, vii, p. 263; Andrea, *Contemporary Sources*, p. 114; Matthew Paris, *Chronica majora*, iii, p. 386.
43. *Les registres d'Urbain IV, 1261–1264*, ed. Jean Guiraud, 4 vols (Paris, 1900–58), ii, pp. 292–93; K. M. Setton, *The Papacy and the Levant, 1204–1571*, 4 vols (Philadelphia, 1976–84), i, pp. 98–100.
44. Geanakoplos, *Emperor Michael Palaeologus*, pp. 197–200; Setton, *Papacy and Levant*, i, pp. 104–5.
45. Hussey, *Orthodox Church*, pp. 211–19; Gill, *Byzantium and the Papacy*, pp. 62–96.
46. *Les registres de Grégoire X, 1272–1276*, ed. Jean Guiraud (Paris, 1892), pp. 119–22; Geanakoplos, *Emperor Michael Palaeologus*, pp. 242–43; Norman Housley, *The Later Crusades: From Lyons to Alcazar, 1274–1580* (Oxford, 1992), pp. 11–14.

47. Pachymeres, i, pp. 473–511; Setton, *Papacy and the Levant*, i, pp. 112–17; Hussey, *Orthodox Church*, pp. 220–35; Geanakoplos, *Emperor Michael Palaeologus*, pp. 258–64.
48. Pachymeres, i, pp. 509–11.
49. Léopold Delisle, *Notice sur cinq manuscrits de la Bibliothèque Nationale et sur un manuscrit de la Bibliothèque de Bordeaux, contenant des recueils épistolaires de Bérard de Naples* (Paris, 1877), p. 82; V. Laurent, 'Le rapport de Georges le Métochite Apocrisiaire de Michel Paléologue auprès du Pape Grégoire X (1275/76)', *Revue historique du Sud-Est Européen*, 23 (1946), pp. 233–47, at 242; Geanakoplos, *Emperor Michael Palaeologus*, pp. 285–86; Hussey, *Orthodox Church*, pp. 235–42.
50. Barlaam of Calabria, *Oratio pro unione*, in *Patrologia Graeca*, vol. 151, cols 1331–42, at 1336; Thomas Kaeppeli, 'Deux nouveaux ouvrages de Fr. Philippe Incontri de Péra OP', *Archivum Fratrum Praedicatorum*, 23 (1953), pp. 163–83, at 179.
51. Laurent, 'Rapport', p. 247; Pachymeres, ii, pp. 486–87.
52. Pachymeres, ii, pp. 616–17.
53. Gregoras, *Rhomäische Geschichte*, i, p. 128.
54. Pachymeres, ii, pp. 486–87, 502–5, 580–81, 624–27; D. M. Nicol, 'The Greeks and the Union of the Churches: The Report of Ogerius, Protonotarius of Michael VIII Palaiologos, in 1280', in D. M. Nicol, *Byzantium: Its Ecclesiastical History and Relations with the Western World* (London, 1972), no. VII, pp. 1–16, at 11.
55. *Les registres de Martin IV, 1281–1285*, ed. M. Olivier-Martin (Paris, 1901), p. 100; Geanakoplos, *Emperor Michael Palaeologus*, pp. 340–42.
56. Marino Sanudo, *Istoria del regno di Romania*, in *Chroniques Gréco-Romanes*, ed. C. Hopf (Berlin, 1873), pp. 99–174 at 133; Steven Runciman, *The Sicilian Vespers* (Cambridge, 1958), pp. 222–35; Donald M. Nicol, *The Last Centuries of Byzantium* (2nd edn, Cambridge, 1993), pp. 69–71; Geanakoplos, *Emperor Michael Palaeologus*, pp. 344–51. Cf. Anna Comnena, pp. 160–62.
57. Gill, *Byzantium and the Papacy*, pp. 182–85.
58. *Registrum Clementis Papae V*, 8 vols (Rome, 1885–1948), ii, p. 56 (annus secundus); *Lettres communes des papes d'Avignon: Jean XXII (1316–1334)*, ed. G. Mollat, 15 vols (Paris, 1904–40), iv, p. 213; *Les registres de Nicolas IV*, ed. Ernest Langlois, 2 vols (Paris, 1905), ii, p. 904; P. Eugene Kamar, 'Projet de Ramon Lull, "De acquisitione Sanctae Terrae"', in *Studia orientalia Christiana: Collectanea, 6* (Cairo, 1961), pp. 3–131, at 108–9; Pierre Dubois, *The Recovery of the Holy Land*, trans. Walther I. Brandt (New York, 1956), pp. 156, 172; A. E. Laiou, *Constantinople and the Latins* (Cambridge, Massachusetts, 1972), pp. 43–56; Housley, *Later Crusades*, pp. 53–55; Antony Leopold, *How to Recover the Holy Land: The Crusade Proposals of the Late Thirteenth and Early Fourteenth Centuries* (Aldershot, 2000), pp. 138–43.
59. Pachymeres, iii, 92–95, 98–99.

Notes to Chapter 11: Survival

1. Michael Kritoboulos, *History of Mehmed the Conqueror*, trans. C. T. Rigg (Princeton, 1954), p. 11.
2. On these aspects, see Timothy Ware, *The Orthodox Church* (3rd edn, Harmondsworth, 1993); Jonathan Harris, *Greek Emigrés in the West, 1400–1520* (Camberley, 1995).

Bibliography

PRIMARY SOURCES

Abu Shama, *Le livre des deux jardins: histoire des deux règnes, celui de Nour ed-Dîn et celui de Salah ed-Dîn*, in *RHC Or*, iv, pp. 3–522.

Akropolites, George, *Historia*, ed. A. Heisenberg and P. Wirth, 2 vols (Stuttgart, 1978).

Al-Azimi, ed. C. Cahen, 'La chronique abrégée d'Al-Azimi', *Journal Asiatique*, 230 (1938), pp. 353–448.

Albert of Aachen, *Historia Hierosolymitana*, *RHC Oc*, iv, pp. 265–713.

Ambroise, *The Crusade of Richard the Lion-Heart*, trans. Merton Jerome Hubert (New York, 1941).

Anglo-Saxon Chronicle, trans. D. Whitelock, D. C. Douglas and S. I. Tucker (London, 1961).

Anonymous of Soissons, *Concerning the Land of Jerusalem and the Means by which Relics were Carried to this Church from the City of Constantinople*, in Alfred J. Andrea, *Contemporary Sources for the Fourth Crusade* (Leiden, 2000), pp. 223–38.

Ansbert, *Historia de expeditione Friderici Imperatoris*, in *Quellen zur Geschichte des Kreuzzuges Kaiser Friedrichs I*, ed. A. Chroust, MGH, Scriptores Rerum Germanicarum, 5 (Berlin, 1928), pp. 1–115.

Anselm of Havelberg, *Dialogorum libri III*, in *Spicilegium sive collectio veterum aliquot scriptorum*, ed. L. d'Achery, 3 vols (Paris, 1723), i, pp. 161–207.

Anthony, Archbishop of Novgorod, *Description des lieux-saints de Constantinople*, in *Itinéraires russes en orient*, ed. B. de Khitrowo (Geneva, 1889), pp. 85–111.

Attaleiates, Michael, *Historia*, ed. W. Brunet de Presle and I. Bekker (Bonn, 1853).

Baha al-Din ibn Shaddad, *The Rare and Excellent History of Saladin*, trans. D. S. Richards (Aldershot, 2001).

Baldric of Dol, *Historia Jerosolimitana*, in *RHC Oc*, iv, pp. 9–111.

Bar Hebraeus, *Chronography*, trans. Ernest A. Wallis-Budge, 2 vols (London, 1932).

Barker, Ernest, *Social and Political Thought in Byzantium from Justinian I to the Last Palaeologus* (Oxford, 1957).

Barlaam of Calabria, *Oratio pro unione*, in *Patrologia Graeca*, vol. 151, cols 1331–42.

Benedict of Peterborough, *Gesta Regis Henrici Secundi*, ed. William Stubbs, 2 vols (London, 1867).

Benjamin of Tudela, *The Itinerary*, trans. M. N. Adler (London, 1907).

Bernold of St Blaise, *Chronicon*, MGH, Scriptores, 5 (Hanover, 1844), pp. 385–467.

Bonizo of Sutri, *Liber ad amicum*, in *Monumenta Gregoriana*, ed. P. Jaffé (Berlin, 1865), pp. 577–689.

Bryennios, Nikephoros, *Historiarum libri quattuor*, ed. and trans. Paul Gautier (Brussels, 1975).

Caffaro et al., *Annali genovesi*, ed. Luigi T. Belgrano and Cesare Imperiale di Sant'Angelo, 5 vols (Rome, 1890–1929).

Carile, Antonio, 'Partitio terrarum imperii Romaniae', *Studi Veneziani*, 7 (1965), pp. 125–305.

Cartulary of Holy Trinity Aldgate, ed. Gerald A. J. Hodgett (London, 1971).

Chomatianos, Demetrius, *Juris ecclesiastici Graecorum selecta paralipomena* in *Analecta sacra et classica spicilegio solesmensi*, ed. J. B. Pitra, 8 vols (Paris, 1876–91).

Choniates, Michael Acominatos, *Ta sozomena*, ed. S. P. Lambros, 2 vols (Athens, 1879–80).

Choniates, Niketas, *O City of Byzantium: Annals of Niketas Choniates*, trans. H. J. Magoulias (Detroit, 1984).

—, *Orationes et epistulae*, ed. J. A. Van Dieten (Berlin and New York, 1972).

Chronica monasterii Casinensis, ed. Hartmut Hoffmann, MGH, Scriptores, 34 (Hanover, 1980).

Chronicle of the Third Crusade, trans. H. J. Nicholson (Aldershot, 1997).

Chronicon monasterii de Abingdon, ed. J. Stevenson, 2 vols (London, 1858).

Comnena, Anna, *The Alexiad*, trans. E. R. A. Sewter (Harmondsworth, 1969).

Constantine VII Porphyrogenitos, *De administrando imperio*, ed. G. Moravcsik, trans. R. J. H. Jenkins (Washington, DC, 1967).

—, *De ceremoniis aulae Byzantinae*, ed. J. Reisky, 2 vols (Bonn, 1829–30).

—, *Three Treatises on Imperial Military Expeditions*, ed. and trans. John Haldon (Vienna, 1990).

Continuator of Sigebert of Gembloux, *Continuatio Aquicinctina*, ed. L. Conrad Bethmann, MGH, Scriptores, 6 (Hanover, 1844), pp. 405–38.

Dandolo, Andrea, *Chronica Venetum*, ed. E. Pastorello, Rerum Italicarum Scriptores, new series 12/1 (Bologna, 1938).

Darrouzès, J., 'Le mémoire de Constantin Stilbès contre les Latins', *Revue des Etudes Byzantines*, 21 (1963), pp. 50–100.

The Deeds of the Bishops of Halberstadt, in Alfred J. Andrea, *Contemporary Sources for the Fourth Crusade* (Leiden, 2000), pp. 239–64.

Delaborde, H. F., 'Lettre des Chrétiens de Terre-Sainte à Charles d'Anjou (22 avril 1260)', *Revue de l'Orient Latin*, 2 (1894), pp. 206–15.

Delisle, Léopold, *Notice sur cinq manuscrits de la Bibliothèque Nationale et sur un manuscrit de la Bibliothèque de Bordeaux, contenant des recueils épistolaires de Bérard de Naples* (Paris, 1877).

Devastatio Constantinopolitana, in Alfred J. Andrea, *Contemporary Sources for the Fourth Crusade* (Leiden, 2000), pp. 205–221.

Dubois, Pierre, *The Recovery of the Holy Land*, trans. Walther I. Brandt (New York, 1956).

Ekkehard of Aura, *Chronicon universale*, MGH, Scriptores, 6 (Hanover, 1844), pp. 33–245.

Eparch, Book of the, in E. H. Freshfield, *Roman Law in the Later Roman Empire* (Cambridge, 1938), pp. 3–50.

Ernoul, *Chronique d'Ernoul et de Bernard le Trésorier*, ed. Louis de Mas Latrie (Paris, 1871).

L'estoire de Eracles empereur et la conqueste de la terre d'Outremer, in *RHC Oc*, ii, pp. 1–487.

Eulogium historiarum, ed. F. S. Haydon, 3 vols (London, 1858–63).

Eusebius of Caesarea, *Tricennial Oration*, in H. A. Drake, *In Praise of Constantine: A Historical Study and New Translation of Eusebius's Tricennial Orations* (Berkeley and Los Angeles, 1976), pp. 83–127.

Eustathios of Thessalonica, *The Capture of Thessaloniki*, trans. J. R. Melville-Jones (Canberra, 1988).

—, *Opuscula*, ed. T. L. F. Tafel (Frankfurt, 1832).

Festa, N., 'Le lettere greche di Federigo II', *Archivio Storico Italiano*, 13 (1894), pp. 1–34.

Fulcher of Chartres, *Chronicle*, trans. M. E. McGinty, in *The First Crusade: The Chronicle of Fulcher of Chartres and Other Source Materials*, ed. E. Peters (2nd edn, Philadelphia, 1998), pp. 47–101.

Gabrielli, Francesco, *Arab Historians of the Crusades*, trans. E. J. Costello (London, 1969).

Geoffrey of Malaterra, *Historia Sicula*, in *Rerum Italicarum Scriptores*, ed. L. A. Muratori, 25 vols (Milan, 1724), v, pp. 544–602.

Gesta episcoporum Tullensium, ed. Georg Waitz, MGH, Scriptores, 8 (Hanover, 1848), pp. 631–48.

Gesta Francorum et aliorum Hierosolimitanorum, trans. R. Hill (Oxford, 1962).

Gesta Innocentii, in *Patrologia Latina*, vol. 214, cols xvii-ccxxviii.

Goitein, S. D., 'A Letter from Seleucia (Cilicia) Dated 21 July 1137', *Speculum*, 39 (1964), pp. 298–303.

Gordon, Jared, 'The Novgorod Account of the Fourth Crusade', *Byzantion*, 43 (1973), 297–311.

Gregoras, Nikephoros, *Rhomäische Geschichte*, J. L. Van Dieten, 4 vols (Stuttgart, 1973–94).

Gregory VII, *Registrum libri I-IV*, ed. Erich Caspar, MGH, Epistolae Selectae, 2 (Berlin, 1955).

Guibert of Nogent, *The Deeds of God through the Franks*, trans. Robert Levine (Woodbridge, 1997).

Gunther of Pairis, *The Capture of Constantinople*, trans. A. J. Andrea (Philadelphia, 1997).

Hagenmeyer, Heinrich, *Epistulae et chartae ad historiam primi belli sacri spectantes: die Kreuzzugsbriefe aus den Jahre 1088–1100* (Innsbruck, 1901).

Hampe, Karl, 'Ein ungedruckter Bericht über den Vertrag von Adrianopel zwischen Friedrich I. und Isaak Angelos vom Febr. 1190', *Neues Archiv der Gesellschaft für ältere deutsche Geschichtskunde*, 23 (1898), pp. 398–400.

Historia ducum Veneticorum, ed. H. Simonsfeld, MGH, Scriptores, 14 (Hanover, 1883), pp. 72–97.

Historia peregrinorum, in *Quellen zur Geschichte des Kreuzzuges Kaiser Friedrichs I*, ed. A. Chroust, MGH, Scriptores Rerum Germanicarum, 5 (Berlin, 1928), pp. 116–72.

Historia translationis Sancti Mamentis, in *Acta Sanctorum Bollandiana*, 17 August, pp. 440–46.

Hugh of St-Pol, *Report to the West*, in Alfred J. Andrea, *Contemporary Sources for the Fourth Crusade* (Leiden, 2000), pp. 177–201.

Humbert of Silva-Candida, *Brevis et succincta commemoratio*, in *Patrologia Latina*, vol. 143, cols 1001–4.

—, *Rationes de Sancti Spiritus processione a Patre et Filio*, in Anton Michel, *Humbert und Kerullarios*, 2 vols (Paderborn, 1924–30), i, pp. 97–111.

—, *De Sancta Romana Ecclesia*, in P. E. Schramm, *Kaiser, Rom und Renovatio*, 2 vols (Leipzig and Berlin, 1929), ii, pp. 128–33.

Ibn al-Qalanisi, *The Damascus Chronicle of the Crusades*, trans. H. A. R. Gibb (London, 1932).

Imad ad-Din al-Isfahani, *Conquête de la Syrie et de la Palestine par Saladin*, trans. Henri Massé (Paris, 1972).

Italikos, Michael, *Lettres et discours*, ed. Paul Gautier (Paris, 1972).

Joinville, John of, *The Life of Saint Louis*, in *Chronicles of the Crusades*, trans. M. R. B. Shaw (Harmondsworth, 1963), pp. 161–362.

Kekaumenos, *Strategon et incerti scriptoris de officis regiis libellus*, ed. B. Wassiliewsky and V. Jernstedt (St Petersburg, 1896).

Kinnamos, John, *The Deeds of John and Manuel Comnenus*, trans. C. M. Brand (New York, 1976).

Legrand, Emile, 'Description des oeuvres d'art et de l'église des Saints Apôtres de Constantinople: poème en vers iambiques par Constantin le Rhodien', *Revue des Etudes Grecques*, 9 (1896), pp. 32–65.

Leo VI, *Tactica sive de re militari liber*, in *Patrologia Graeca*, vol. 107, cols 669–1120.

Leo the Deacon, *Nikephoros Phokas, 'der bleiche Tod der Sarazenen' und Johannes Tzimiskes*, trans. Franz Loretto (Vienna, 1961).

Lettres communes des papes d'Avignon: Jean XXII (1316–1334), ed. G. Mollat, 15 vols (Paris, 1904–40).

Liber pontificalis: de gestis Romanorum pontificum, ed. L. Duchesne, 3 vols (2nd edn, Paris, 1955–57).

Lull, Ramon, *De acquisitione Sanctae Terrae*, trans. P. Eugene Kamar in *Studia orientalia Christiana: Collectanea 6* (Cairo, 1961), pp. 3–131.

Maas, Paul, 'Die Musen des Kaisers Alexios I', *Byzantinische Zeitschrift*, 22 (1913), pp. 348–69.

Magnus of Reichersberg, *Chronicon*, ed. W. Wattenbach, MGH, Scriptores, 17 (Hanover, 1861), pp. 439–534.

Makrizi, *Histoire d'Egypte*, trans. E. Blochet, *Revue de l'Orient Latin*, 8 (1900–1), pp. 165–212, 501–53.

Maragone, Bernardo, *Annales Pisani*, ed. M. L. Gentile, Rerum Italicarum Scriptores, new series 6.2 (Bologna, 1936).

Matthew of Edessa, *Chronicle*, in A. E. Dostourian, *Armenia and the Crusades* (Lanham, Maryland, 1993).

Matthew Paris, *Chronica majora*, ed. Henry R. Luard, 7 vols (London, 1872–83).

Mesarites, Nicholas, *Description of the Church of the Holy Apostles at Constantinople*, ed. and trans. Glanville Downey, in *Transactions of the American Philosophical Society*, 47 (1957), pp. 855–924.

—, *Der Epitaphios des Nikolaos Mesarites auf seinem Bruder Johannes*, ed. August Heisenberg, 'Neue Quellen zur Geschichte des lateinischen Kaisertum und der Kircheunion, I', *Sitzungsberichte der Bayerischen Akademie der Wissenschaften, Philosophisch-philologische und Historische Klasse. Jahrgang 1922, v*, pp. 3–75; reprinted in Heisenberg, *Quellen und Studien zur spätbyzantinischen Geschichte* (London, 1973), no. II.

Michael VIII Palaeologus, *Autobiography with the Charter of the Monastery of Demetrios in Constantinople*, trans. A. Pelendrides (London, 1998).

Miklosich, F., and Müller, W., *Acta et diplomata Graeca medii aevi sacra et profana*, 6 vols (Vienna, 1860–90).

Munro, Dana C., *Letters of the Crusaders Written from the Holy Land* (2nd edn, Philadelphia, 1902).

Neophytos, *De calamitatibus Cypri*, in *Chronicles and Memorials of the Reign of Richard I*, ed. William Stubbs, 2 vols (London, 1864–65), i, pp. clxxxiv-clxxxix.

Nicholas Mystikos, *Letters*, ed. and trans. R. J. H. Jenkins and L. G. Westerink (Washington, DC, 1973).

Odo of Deuil, *De profectione Ludovici VII in orientem*, ed. and trans. V. G. Berry (New York, 1948).

Old French Continuation of William of Tyre, trans. Peter W. Edbury in *The Conquest of Jerusalem and the Third Crusade: Sources in Translation* (Aldershot, 1998), pp. 1–145.

Orderic Vitalis, *The Ecclesiastical History*, ed. and trans. Marjorie Chibnall, 6 vols (Oxford, 1969–80).

Otto of Freising, *The Deeds of Frederick Barbarossa*, trans. C. C. Mierow (Toronto, 1953).

Otto of St Blaise, *Chronica*, ed. Adolf Hofmeister, MGH, Scriptores Rerum Germanicarum, 47 (Hanover and Leipzig, 1912).

Pachymeres, George, *Relations historiques*, ed. A. Failler, 5 vols (Paris, 1984–2000).

Papadakis, A., and Talbot, Alice Mary, 'John X Camaterus Confronts Innocent III: An Unpublished Correspondence', *Byzantinoslavica*, 33 (1972), pp. 26–41.

Peter Tudebode, *Historia de Hierosolymitano itinere*, trans. J. H. Hill and L. L. Hill (Philadelphia, 1974).

Phokas, John, *The Pilgrimage of John Phocas in the Holy Land in the year 1185 AD*, trans. Aubrey Stewart, Palestine Pilgrim Text Society, 5 (London, 1896).

Procopius, *The Buildings*, trans. H. B. Dewing, Loeb Classical Library (London, 1971).

Psellos, Michael, *Epitafios logos eis ton patriarchen Michael Keroullarion*, in C. N. Sathas, *Mesaionike bibliotheke*, 7 vols (Athens, Venice and Paris, 1872–94), iv, pp. 303–87.

—, *Fourteen Byzantine Rulers*, trans. E. R. A. Sewter (2nd edn, Harmondsworth, 1966).

Pseudo-Codinus, *Traité des offices*, ed. J. Verpeaux (Paris, 1966).

Raymond of Aguilers, *Historia Francorum qui ceperunt Iherusalem*, trans. J. H. Hill and L. Hill (Philadelphia, 1968).

Recueil des historiens des Gaules et de la France, ed. L. Deslisle, 24 vols (Paris, 1869–1904).

Die Register Innocenz III, ed. O. Hageneder et al., 7 vols (Graz and Cologne, 1964–99); translations of relevant letters in Alfred J. Andrea, *Contemporary Sources for the Fourth Crusade* (Leiden, 2000), pp. 7–176.

Les registres de Grégoire X, 1272–1276, ed. Jean Guiraud (Paris, 1892).

Les registres de Martin IV, 1281–1285, ed. M. Olivier-Martin (Paris, 1901).

Les registres de Nicolas IV, ed. Ernest Langlois, 2 vols (Paris, 1905).

Les registres d'Urbain IV, 1261–1264, ed. Jean Guiraud, 4 vols (Paris, 1900–58).

Registrum Clementis Papae V, 8 vols (Rome, 1885–1948).

Richard of Devizes, *The Chronicle of the Time of Richard the First*, ed. John T. Appleby (London, 1963).

Robert of Auxerre, *Chronicon*, ed. O. Holder-Egger, MGH, Scriptores, 26 (Hanover, 1882), pp. 219–79.

Robert of Clari, *The Conquest of Constantinople*, trans. E. H. McNeal (Toronto, 1996).

Robert of Rheims, *Historia Iherosolimitana*, in *RHC Oc*, iii, pp. 715–882.

Robert of Torigny, *Chronicle*, in *Chronicles of the Reigns of Stephen, Henry II and Richard I*, ed. Richard Howlett, 4 vols (London, 1884–89), iv, pp. 81–315.

Rodulfus Glaber, *Historiarum libri quinque*, ed. and trans. John France (Oxford, 1989).

Roger of Hoveden, *Chronica*, ed. William Stubbs, 4 vols (London, 1868–71).

Roger of Wendover, *Liber qui dicitur flores historiarum*, 3 vols (London, 1886–89).

The Rothelin Continuation of the History of William of Tyre, trans. Janet Shirley, in *Crusader Syria in the Thirteenth Century* (Aldershot, 1999), pp. 13–120.

Rubruck, William, *The Mission of Friar William of Rubruck: His Journey to the Court of the Great Khan Möngke, 1253–1255*, trans. Peter Jackson (London, 1990).

The Russian Primary Chronicle: the Laurentian Text, ed. and trans. S. H. Cross and O. P. Sherbowitz-Wetzor (Cambridge, Massachusetts, 1953).

Sanudo, Marino, *Istoria del regno di Romania*, in *Chroniques Gréco-Romanes*, ed. C. Hopf (Berlin, 1873), pp. 99–174.

Skoutariotes, Theodore, *Synopsis chronike*, in C. N. Sathas, *Mesaionike bibliotheke*, 7 vols (Athens, Venice and Paris, 1872–94), vii, pp. 1–556.

Skylitzes, John, *Synopsis historiarum*, ed. J. Thurn (Berlin, 1973).

Stethatos, Niketas, *Un grand mystique byzantin: vie de Syméon le Nouveau Théologian (949–1022)*, ed. and trans. I. Hausherr (Rome, 1928).

Suger, *The Deeds of Louis the Fat*, trans. R. C. Cusimano and John Moorhead (Washington, DC, 1992).

—, *Lettres*, in *Oeuvres complètes de Suger*, ed. A. Leroy de La Marche (Paris, 1867), pp. 239–317.

Tafel, G. L. F. and Thomas, G. M., *Urkunden zur älteren Handels- und Staatsgeschichte der Republik Venedig*, 3 vols (Vienna, 1856–57).

Tafur, Pero, *Travels and Adventures, 1435–1439* (London, 1926).

Theiner, A., and Miklosich, F., *Monumenta spectantia ad unionem ecclesiarum Graecae et Romanae* (Vienna, 1872).

Theophanes Continuatus, *Chronographia*, ed. I. Bekker (Bonn, 1838).

Theophylact of Ochrid, *Discours, traités, poésies*, ed. and trans. P. Gautier (Thessaloniki, 1980).

Three Byzantine Military Treatises, ed. and trans. George T. Dennis (Washington, DC, 1985).

Tornikios, George and Leo, *Lettres et discours*, ed. J. Darrouzès (Paris, 1970).

Tritz, Heinrich, 'Die hagiographischen Quellen zur Geschichte Papst Leo IX', *Studi Gregoriani*, 4 (1952), pp. 191–364.

Usamah ibn-Munqidh, *An Arab-Syrian Gentleman and Warrior in the Period of the Crusades*, trans. Philip K. Hitti (2nd edn, New York, 2000).

Villehardouin, Geoffrey of, *The Conquest of Constantinople*, in *Chronicles of the Crusades*, trans. M. R. B. Shaw (Harmondsworth, 1963), pp. 29–160.

Walter Map, *De nugis curialium*, trans. M. R. James, Cymmrodorion Record Society, 9 (London, 1923).

Wibald of Corvey, *Epistolae*, in *Bibliotheca rerum Germanicarum*, ed. P. Jaffé, 6 vols (Berlin, 1864–73), i, pp. 76–616.

Widukind of Corvey, *Rerum gestarum Saxonicarum libri tres*, ed. Paul Hirsch, MGH, Scriptores Rerum Germanicarum, 60 (Hanover, 1935).

Will, Cornelius, *Acta et scripta quae de controversiis ecclesiae Graecae et Latinae saeculo undecesimo composita extant* (Leipzig and Marburg, 1861).

William of Apulia, *Le geste de Robert Guiscard*, ed. and trans. Marguerite Mathieu (Palermo, 1961).

William of Jumièges, *Gesta Normanorum ducum*, trans. Elizabeth M. C. van Houts, 2 vols (Oxford, 1992–95).

William of Malmesbury, *Gesta regum Anglorum*, trans. R. A. B. Mynors, R. M. Thomson and M. Winterbottom, 2 vols (Oxford, 1998–99).

William of Poitiers, *Gesta Guillelmi*, ed. and trans. R. H. C. Davis and Marjorie Chibnall (Oxford, 1998).

William of Tyre, *A History of Deeds Done Beyond the Sea*, trans. E. A. Babcock and A. C. Krey, 2 vols (New York, 1943).

Zepos, J. and Zepos, P., *Jus Graecoromanum*, 8 vols (Athens, 1931).

Zonaras, John, *Epitome historiarum*, ed. L. Dindorf, 6 vols (Leipzig, 1868–75).

SECONDARY WORKS

Andrea, Alfred J., and Moore, John C., 'The Date of Reg. 6: 102: Pope Innocent III's Letter of Advice to the Crusaders', *Medieval and Renaissance Venice*, ed. Ellen E. Kittell and Thomas F. Madden (Urbana and Chicago, 1999), pp. 109–23.

Angold, Michael, *The Byzantine Empire, 1025–1204: A Political History* (2nd edn, Harlow, 1997).

—, *A Byzantine Government in Exile: Government and Society under the Laskarids of Nicaea, 1204–1261* (Oxford, 1975).

—, 'Byzantium in Exile', *The New Cambridge Modern History, v, c. 1198 – c. 1300*, ed. David Abulafia (Cambridge, 1999), pp. 543–68.

—, 'The Road to 1204: The Byzantine Background to the Fourth Crusade', *Journal of Medieval History*, 25 (1999), pp. 257–78.

Asbridge, Thomas S., *The Creation of the Principality of Antioch, 1098–1130* (Woodbridge, 2000).

Barber, Malcolm, 'Western Attitudes to Frankish Greece in the Thirteenth Century', *Latins and Greeks in the Eastern Mediterranean after 1204*, ed. B. Arbel, B. Hamilton and D. Jacoby (London, 1989), pp. 111–28.

Bassett, Sarah Guberti, 'The Antiquities in the Hippodrome of Constantinople', *Dumbarton Oaks Papers*, 45 (1991), pp. 87–96.

Baynes, Norman, 'The Supernatural Defenders of Constantinople', in N. H. Baynes, *Byzantine Studies and Other Essays* (London, 1955), pp. 248–60.

Bibicou, H., 'Une page d'histoire diplomatique de Byzance au XIe siècle: Michel VII Doukas, Robert Guiscard, et la pension des dignitaires', *Byzantion*, 29–30 (1959), pp. 43–75.

Bloch, Herbert, 'Monte Cassino, Byzantium and the West in the Earlier Middle Ages', *Dumbarton Oaks Papers*, 3 (1946), pp. 163–224.

Blöndal, S., *The Varangians of Byzantium* (Cambridge, 1978).

Borelli, L. Vlad, and Toniato, A. Guido, 'The Origins and Documentary Sources of the Horses of San Marco', *The Horses of San Marco*, ed. Guido Perocco, trans. J. and V. Wilton-Ely (London, 1979), pp. 127–36.

Brand, C. M., 'A Byzantine Plan for the Fourth Crusade', *Speculum*, 43 (1968), pp. 462–75.

—, 'The Byzantines and Saladin, 1185–1192: Opponents of the Third Crusade', *Speculum*, 37 (1962), pp. 167–81.

—, *Byzantium Confronts the West, 1180–1204* (Cambridge, Massachusetts, 1968).

—, 'The Fourth Crusade: Some Recent Interpretations', *Medievalia et Humanistica*, 12 (1984), pp. 33–45.

Browning, Robert, 'Byzantine Thessalonike: A Unique City?', *Dialogos: Hellenic Studies Review*, 2 (1995), pp. 91–104.

Brundage, James A., 'Richard the Lionheart and Byzantium', *Studies in Medieval Culture*, 6–7 (1976), pp. 63–70; reprinted in Brundage, *The Crusades, Holy War and Canon Law* (Aldershot, 1991), no. IV.

Bryer, A. A. M., 'The First Encounter with the West, AD 1050–1204', *Byzantium: An Introduction*, ed. Philip Whitting (2nd edn, London, 1981), pp. 85–110.

Bury, J. B., *The Imperial Administrative System in the Ninth Century* (London, 1911).

Canard, Marius, 'Les relations politiques et sociales entre Byzance et les arabes', *Dumbarton Oaks Papers*, 18 (1964), pp. 35–56.

—, 'Le traité de 1281 entre Michel Paléologue et le sultan Qalâ'un', *Byzantion*, 10 (1935), pp. 669–80.

Cazel, Fred A., 'Financing the Crusades', *A History of the Crusades*, ed. K. M. Setton, 6 vols (Madison, Wisconsin, 1969–89), vi, pp. 116–49.

Charanis, Peter, 'Byzantium, the West and the Origin of the First Crusade', *Byzantion*, 19 (1949), pp. 17–36; reprinted in Peter Charanis, *Social, Economic and Political Life in the Byzantine Empire* (London, 1973), no. XIV.

Cheynet, J. C., 'Mantzikert: un désastre militaire?', *Byzantion*, 50 (1980), pp. 410–38.

Chrysostomides, J., 'Byzantine Concepts of War and Peace', *War, Peace and World Orders in European History*, ed. Anja V. Hartmann and Beatrice Heuser (London and New York, 2001), pp. 91–101.

—, 'A Byzantine Historian: Anna Comnena', *Medieval Historical Writings in the Christian and Islamic Worlds*, ed. D. O. Morgan (London, 1982), pp. 30–46.

Ciggaar, Krijnie N., 'England and Byzantium on the Eve of the Norman Conquest', *Anglo-Norman Studies*, 5 (1982), pp. 78–96.

—, *Western Travellers to Constantinople: The West and Byzantium, 962–1204. Cultural and Political Relations* (Leiden, 1996).

Constable, G., 'The Second Crusade as Seen by Contemporaries', *Traditio*, 9 (1953), pp. 213–79.

Constantinides, C. N., *Higher Education in Byzantium in the Thirteenth and Early Fourteenth Centuries, 1204 – c. 1310* (Nicosia, 1982).

Cowdrey, H. E. J., 'The Gregorian Papacy, Byzantium, and the First Crusade', *Byzantinische Forschungen*, 13 (1988), pp. 145–69.

—, 'Pope Gregory VII's "Crusading" Plans of 1074', *Outremer: Studies in the History of the Crusading Kingdom of Jerusalem Presented to Joshua Prawer*, ed. B. Z. Kedar, H. E. Mayer and R. C. Smail (Jerusalem, 1982), pp. 27–40.

—, 'Pope Urban II's Preaching of the First Crusade', *History*, 55 (1970), pp 177–88.

Darrouzès, J., 'Les documents byzantins du XIIe siècle sur la primauté romaine', *Revue des Etudes Byzantines*, 23 (1965), pp. 42–88.

Day, Gerald W., *Genoa's Response to Byzantium, 1155–1204* (Urbana and Chicago, 1988).

Dennis, George T., 'Defenders of the Christian People: Holy War in Byzantium', *The Crusades from the Perspective of Byzantium and the Muslim World*, ed. A. E. Laiou and R. P. Mottahedeh (Washington, DC, 2001), pp. 31–39.

Dondaine, Antoine, 'Hugues Ethérien et le concile de Constantinople de 1166', *Historisches Jahrbuch*, 77 (1958), pp. 473–83.

—, 'Hugues Ethérien et Léon Toscan', *Archives d'histoire doctrinale et littéraire du moyen âge*, 19 (1952), pp. 67–134.

Dvornik, F., *Byzantium and the Roman Primacy*, trans. Edwin A. Quain (2nd edn, New York, 1979).

Edbury, Peter W., *The Kingdom of Cyprus and the Crusades, 1191–1374* (Cambridge, 1991).

—, 'Looking Back on the Second Crusade: Some Late Twelfth-Century English Perspectives', *The Second Crusade and the Cistercians*, ed. M. Gervers (New York, 1992), pp. 163–69.

Edbury, Peter W., and Rowe, John Gordon, *William of Tyre: Historian of the Latin East* (Cambridge, 1988).

Epstein, Ann Wharton, 'The Date and Significance of the Cathedral of Canosa in Apulia, Southern Italy', *Dumbarton Oaks Papers*, 37 (1983), pp. 79–90.

Ferrard, Christopher G., 'The Amount of Constantinopolitan Booty in 1204', *Studi Veneziani*, 13 (1971), pp. 95–104.

Folda, Jaroslav, *The Art of the Crusaders in the Holy Land, 1098–1187* (Cambridge, 1994).

—, 'The Fourth Crusade, 1201–1204: Some Reconsiderations', *Byzantinoslavica*, 26 (1965), pp. 277–90.

Foss, Clive, *Byzantine and Turkish Sardis* (Cambridge, Massachusetts, 1976).

—, *Nicaea: A Byzantine Capital and its Praises* (Brookline, Massachusetts, 1996).

France, John, 'Anna Comnena, the *Alexiad* and the First Crusade', *Reading Medieval Studies*, 10 (1984), pp. 20–38.

—, 'The Departure of Tatikios from the Crusader Army', *Bulletin of the Institute of Historical Research*, 44 (1971), pp. 137–47.

Gadolin, Antra R., 'Prince Bohemond's Death and Apotheosis in the Church of San Sabino, Canosa di Puglia', *Byzantion*, 52 (1982), pp. 124–53.

Geanakoplos, D. J., *Emperor Michael Palaeologus and the West, 1258–1282: A Study in Byzantine Latin Relations* (Cambridge, Massachusetts, 1959).

—, 'Greco-Latin Relations on the Eve of Restoration: The Battle of Pelagonia, 1259', *Dumbarton Oaks Papers*, 7 (1953), pp. 101–41.

Gibbon, Edward, *The History of the Decline and Fall of the Roman Empire*, ed. J. B. Bury, 7 vols (London, 1926–27).

Gill, Joseph, *Byzantium and the Papacy, 1198–1400* (New Brunswick, New Jersey, 1979).

—, 'Innocent III and the Greeks: Aggressor or Apostle?', *Relations between East and West in the Middle Ages*, ed. Derek Baker (Edinburgh, 1973), pp. 95–108.

Godfrey, J., *1204: The Unholy Crusade* (Oxford, 1980).

Grabar, André, 'God and the "Family of Princes" Presided over by the Byzantine Emperor', *Harvard Slavic Studies*, 2 (1954), pp. 117–23.

Grégoire, Henri, 'The Question of the Diversion of the Fourth Crusade, or an Old Controversy Solved by a Latin Adverb', *Byzantion*, 15 (1940–41), pp. 158–66.

Grumel, V., 'L'authenticité de la lettre de Jean Vatatzes, empereur de Nicée, au pape Grégoire IX', *Echos d'Orient*, 29 (1930), pp. 450–58.

Hamdani, Abbas, 'Byzantine-Fatimid Relations before the Battle of Mantzikert', *Byzantine Studies*, 1 (1974), pp. 169–79.

Hamilton, Bernard, *The Latin Church in the Crusader States* (London, 1980).

—, *The Leper King and his Heirs* (Cambridge, 2000).

—, 'Manuel I Comnenus and Baldwin IV of Jerusalem', *Kathegetria: Essays Presented to Joan Hussey for her 80th Birthday*, ed. J. Chrysostomides (Camberley, 1988), pp. 353–75.

—, 'Three Patriarchs at Antioch, 1165–70', *Dei gesta per Francos: études sur les croisades dédiées à Jean Richard*, ed. M. Balard, B. Z. Kedar and J. Riley-Smith (Aldershot, 2001), pp. 199–207.

Harris, Jonathan, 'Distortion, Divine Providence and Genre in Niketas Choniates's Account of the Collapse of Byzantium, 1180–1204', *Journal of Medieval History*, 26 (2000), pp. 19–31.

—, *Greek Emigrés in the West, 1400–1520* (Camberley, 1995).

Harvey, Alan, *Economic Expansion in the Byzantine Empire, 900–1200* (Cambridge, 1990).

Heisenberg, August, 'Neue Quellen zur Geschichte des lateinischen Kaisertum und der Kircheunion II: die Unionsverhandlungen vom 30. August 1206 Patriarchenwahl und Kaiserkrönung in Nikaia 1208', *Sitzungsberichte der Bayerischen Akademie der Wissenschaften, Philosophisch-philologische und Historische Klasse. Jahrgang 1920, X*, pp. 3–56; reprinted in Heisenberg, *Quellen und Studien zur spätbyzantinischen Geschichte* (London, 1973), no. II.

Hendy, Michael F., *Studies in the Byzantine Monetary Economy, c. 300–1450* (Cambridge, 1985).

Hill, J. H. and Hill, L. L., 'The Convention of Alexius I and Raymond of Saint-Gilles', *American Historical Review*, 58 (1952–3), pp. 322–27.

Hillenbrand, Carole, *The Crusades: Islamic Perspectives* (Edinburgh, 1999).

Holt, P. M., *Early Mamluk Diplomacy, 1260–1290: Treaties of Baybars and Qalawun with Christian Rulers* (Leiden, 1995).

Holtzmann, Walther, 'Die Unionverhandlungen zwischen Kaiser Alexios I. und Papst Urban II. im Jahre 1089', *Byzantinische Zeitschrift*, 28 (1928), pp. 38–67.

—, 'Zur Geschichte des Investiturstreites', *Neues Archiv der Gesellschaft für ältere deutsche Geschichtskunde*, 50 (1935), pp. 246–319.

Housley, Norman, *The Later Crusades, 1274–1580* (Oxford, 1992).

Houts, E. M. C. van, 'Normandy and Byzantium', *Byzantion*, 55 (1985), pp. 544–59.

Hussey, J. M., *Church and Learning in the Byzantine Empire, 867–1185* (Oxford, 1937).

—, *The Orthodox Church in the Byzantine Empire* (Oxford, 1986).

Jacoby, David, 'The Encounter of Two Societies: Western Conquerors and the Byzantines in the Peloponnesos after the Fourth Crusade', *American Historical Review*, 78 (1973), pp. 873–906.

—, 'The Latin Empire of Constantinople and the Frankish States of Greece', *The New Cambridge Medieval History, v, c. 1198 – c. 1300*, ed. David Abulafia (Cambridge, 1999), pp. 525–42.

Jeffreys, Elizabeth M., 'The Image of Arabs in Byzantine Literature', *The Seventeenth International Byzantine Congress: Major Papers* (New Rochelle, New York, 1986), pp. 305–23.

Jeffreys, Elizabeth M. and Michael, 'The "Wild Beast from the West": Immediate Literary Reactions in Byzantium to the Second Crusade', *The Crusades from the Perspective of Byzantium and the Muslim World*, ed. A. E. Laiou and R. P. Mottahedeh (Washington, DC, 2001), pp. 101–16.

Jenkins, R. J. H., *Byzantium: The Imperial Centuries, 610–1071* (London, 1966).

Joranson, Einar, 'The Problem of the Spurious Letter of Emperor Alexius to the Count of Flanders', *American Historical Review*, 55 (1949–50), pp. 811–32.

Jotischky, Andrew, 'Manuel Comnenus and the Reunion of the Churches: The Evidence of the Conciliar Mosaics in the Church of the Nativity in Bethlehem', *Levant*, 26 (1994), pp. 207–24.

Kaeppeli, Thomas, 'Deux nouveaux ouvrages de Fr. Philippe Incontri de Péra OP', *Archivum Fratrum Praedicatorum*, 23 (1953), pp. 163–83.

Kazhdan, Alexander P., 'Latins and Franks in Byzantium: Perception and Reality from the Eleventh to the Twelfth Century', *The Crusades from the Perspective of Byzantium and the Muslim World*, ed. A. E. Laiou and R. P. Mottahedeh (Washington, DC, 2001), pp. 83–100.

Kazhdan, Alexander P., and Epstein, Ann Wharton, *Change in Byzantine Culture in the Eleventh and Twelfth Centuries* (Berkeley and Los Angeles, California, 1985).

Koutrakou, Nike, '*Logos* and *Pathos* between Peace and War: Rhetoric as a Tool of Diplomacy in the Middle Byzantine Period', *Thesaurismata*, 25 (1995), pp. 7–20.

Krey, August C., 'A Neglected Passage of the *Gesta* and its Bearing on the Literature of the First Crusade', *The Crusades and Other Historical Essays Presented to Dana C. Munro by his Former Students*, ed. Louis J. Paetow (New York, 1928), pp. 57–78.

Laiou, A. E., *Constantinople and the Latins: The Foreign Policy of Andronicus II, 1282–1328* (Cambridge, Massachusetts, 1972).

La Monte, John L., 'To What Extent was the Byzantine Empire Suzerain of the Latin Crusading States?', *Byzantion*, 7 (1932), pp. 253–64.

Langdon, John S., 'Byzantium's Initial Encounter with the Chinggisids: An Introduction to Byzantino-Mongolica', *Viator*, 29 (1998), pp. 95–140.

—, 'Byzantium in Anatolian Exile: Imperial Vicegerency Reaffirmed during Byzantine-Papal Discussions at Nicaea and Nymphaion, 1234', *Byzantinische Forschungen*, 20 (1994), pp. 197–233.

Laurent, V., 'Le rapport de Georges le Métochite Apocrisiaire de Michel Paléologue auprès du Pape Grégoire X (1275/76)', *Revue historique du Sud-Est Européen*, 23 (1946), pp. 233–47.

Leopold, Antony, *How to Recover the Holy Land: The Crusade Proposals of the Late Thirteenth and Early Fourteenth Centuries* (Aldershot, 2000).

Lilie, Ralph-Johannes, *Byzantium and the Crusader States, 1095–1204*, trans. J. C. Morris and J. C. Ridings (Oxford, 1993).

Lock, Peter, *The Franks in the Aegean, 1204–1500* (London, 1995).

Lopez, R. S., 'Silk Industry in the Byzantine Empire', *Speculum*, 20 (1945), pp. 1–42.

Lounghis, T. C., *Les ambassades Byzantines en occident depuis la fondation des états barbares, jusqu'aux croisades, 407–1096* (Athens, 1980).

Macrides, Ruth, 'Constantinople: The Crusaders' Gaze', *Travel in the Byzantine World*, ed. Ruth Macrides (Aldershot, 2002), pp. 193–212.

—, 'The Historian in the History', *Philellin: Studies in Honour of Robert Browning*, ed. C. N. Constantinides et al. (Venice, 1996), pp. 205–24.

—, 'The Pen and the Sword: Who Wrote the *Alexiad*?', *Anna Komnene and her Times*, ed. Thalia Gouma-Peterson (New York and London, 2000), pp. 63–81.

Madden, T. F., 'The Fires of the Fourth Crusade in Constantinople, 1203–1204: A Damage Assessment', *Byzantinische Zeitschrift*, 84–85 (1991–92), pp. 72–93.

Magdalino, Paul, 'Byzantine Snobbery', *The Byzantine Aristocracy*, ed. Michael Angold (Oxford, 1984), pp. 58–78.

—, *The Empire of Manuel I Komnenos, 1143–1180* (Cambridge, 1993).

—, 'The Pen of the Aunt: Echoes of the Mid-Twelfth Century in the *Alexiad*', in *Anna Komnene and her Times*, ed. Thalia Gouma-Peterson (New York and London, 2000), pp. 15–43.

Manfroni, Camillo, 'Le relazioni fra Genova, l'impero bizantino e i Turchi', *Atti della Società Ligure di Storia Patria*, 28 (1896), 574–858.

Mango, Cyril, *Byzantium: The Empire of New Rome* (London, 1980).

Mayne, Richard, 'East and West in 1054', *Cambridge Historical Journal*, 11 (1954), pp. 133–48.

Mayr-Harting, Henry, 'Odo of Deuil, the Second Crusade, and the Monastery of Saint-Denis', *The Culture of Christendom: Essays in Medieval History in Memory of Denis L. T. Bethell*, ed. M. A. Meyer (London and Rio Grande, Ohio, 1993), pp. 225–41.

McQueen, William B., 'Relations between the Normans and Byzantium, 1071–1112', *Byzantion*, 56 (1986), pp. 427–76.

Meyer, H. E., *The Crusades* (2nd edn, Oxford, 1988).

Miller, Dean A., *Imperial Constantinople* (New York, 1969).

Morgan, David O., 'The Mongols and the Eastern Mediterranean', *Latins and Greeks in the Eastern Mediterranean after 1204*, ed. B. Arbel, B. Hamilton and D. Jacoby (London, 1989), pp. 198–211.

Morris, Colin, 'The *Gesta Francorum* as Narrative History', *Reading Medieval Studies*, 19 (1993), pp. 55–71.

—, 'Peter the Hermit and the Chroniclers', *The First Crusade: Origins and Impact*, ed. Jonathan Phillips (Manchester, 1997), pp. 21–34.

Morris, Rosemary, *Monks and Laymen in Byzantium, 843–1118* (Cambridge, 1995).

Muthesius, Anna, 'Silken Diplomacy', *Byzantine Diplomacy*, ed. Jonathan Shepard and Simon Franklin (Aldershot, 1992), pp. 237–48.

Nicol, D. M., 'Byzantine Political Thought', *The Cambridge History of Medieval Political Thought c. 350 – c. 1450*, ed. J. H. Burns (Cambridge, 1988), pp. 51–79.

—, 'The Byzantine View of Western Europe', *Greek, Roman and Byzantine Studies*, 8 (1967), pp. 315–39.

—, 'Byzantium and the Papacy in the Eleventh Century', *Journal of Ecclesiastical History*, 13 (1962), pp. 1–20.

—, *Byzantium and Venice: A Study in Diplomatic and Cultural Relations* (Cambridge, 1988).

—, *The Despotate of Epiros I, 1204–1267* (Oxford, 1957).

—, *The Last Centuries of Byzantium, 1261–1453* (2nd edn, Cambridge, 1993).

—, 'The Greeks and the Union of the Churches: The Report of Ogerius, Protonotarius of Michael VIII Palaiologos, in 1280', in D. M. Nicol, *Byzantium:*

Its Ecclesiastical History and Relations with the Western World (London, 1972), no. VII.

Obolensky, Dimitri, *The Byzantine Commonwealth: Eastern Europe, 500–1453* (London, 1971).

—, 'The Principles and Methods of Byzantine Diplomacy', in Dimitri Obolensky, *Byzantium and the Slavs: Collected Studies* (London, 1971), no. I.

Oikonomides, N., *Les listes de préséance byzantines des IXe et Xe siècles* (Paris, 1972).

Ostrogorsky, George, 'The Byzantine Emperor and the Hierarchical World Order', *Slavonic and East European Review*, 35 (1956–57), pp. 1–14.

—, *History of the Byzantine State*, trans. J. M. Hussey (2nd edn, Oxford, 1968).

Pavlova, M, 'The Role of the Serbs in the Third Crusade' (in Czech with French summary), *Byzantinoslavica*, 5 (1933–34), pp. 235–303.

Pears, Edwin, *The Fall of Constantinople: Being the Story of the Fourth Crusade* (London, 1885).

Phillips, Jonathan, *Defenders of the Holy Land: Relations between the Latin East and the West, 1119–1187* (Oxford, 1996).

Pryor, J. H., 'The Oaths of the Leaders of the First Crusade to the Emperor Alexius I Comnenus: Fealty, Homage – Pistis, Douleia', *Parergon*, new series, 2 (1984), pp. 111–32.

Queller, D. E., *The Latin Conquest of Constantinople* (New York, 1971).

Queller, D. E., Compton, T. K. and Campbell, D. A., 'The Fourth Crusade: The Neglected Majority', *Speculum*, 49 (1974), pp. 441–65.

Queller, D. E. and Katele, Irene B., 'Attitudes towards the Venetians in the Fourth Crusade: the Western Sources', *International History Review*, 4 (1982), pp. 1–36.

Queller, D. E. and Madden, T. F., *The Fourth Crusade: The Conquest of Constantinople* (2nd edn, Philadelphia, 1997).

Queller, D. E. and Stratton, S. J., 'A Century of Controversy on the Fourth Crusade', *Studies in Medieval and Renaissance History*, 6 (1969), pp. 235–77.

Reinert, Stephen W., 'The Muslim Presence in Constantinople, Ninth–Fifteenth Centuries: Some Preliminary Observations', *Studies on the Internal Diaspora of the Byzantine Empire*, ed. H. Ahrweiler and A. E. Laiou (Washington, DC, 1998), pp. 125–50.

Reuter, Timothy, 'The "Non-Crusade" of 1149–50', *The Second Crusade: Scope and Consequences*, ed. Jonathan Phillips and Martin Hoch (Manchester, 2001), pp. 150–63.

Richard, Jean, *The Crusades, c. 1071 – c. 1291*, trans. Jean Birrell (Cambridge, 1999).

Riley-Smith, Jonathan, *The Crusades: A Short History* (New Haven and London, 1987).

Rowe, J. G., 'Hadrian IV, the Byzantine Empire and the Latin Orient', *Essays in Medieval History Presented to Bertie Wilkinson*, ed. T. A. Sandquist and M. R. Powicke (Toronto, 1969), pp. 3–16.

—, 'The Papacy and the Greeks, 1122–1153', *Church History*, 28 (1959), pp. 115–30, 310–27.

—, 'Paschal II, Bohemond of Antioch and the Byzantines', *Bulletin of the John Rylands Library*, 49 (1966–67), pp. 105–202.

Runciman, Steven, 'The Byzantine "Protectorate" in the Holy Land in the Eleventh Century', *Byzantion*, 18 (1946–48), pp. 207–15.

—, *The Byzantine Theocracy* (Cambridge, 1977).

—, *The Eastern Schism* (Cambridge, 1955).

—, *A History of the Crusades*, 3 vols (Cambridge, 1951–54).

—, 'The Ladies of the Mongols', *Eis mnêmên K. I. Amantou* (Athens, 1960), pp. 46–53.

—, 'The Pilgrimages to Palestine before 1095', *A History of the Crusades*, ed. K. M. Setton, 6 vols (Madison, Wisconsin, 1969–89), i, pp. 68–78.

—, 'The Visit of King Amalric I to Constantinople in 1171', *Outremer: Studies in the History of the Crusading Kingdom of Jerusalem Presented to Joshua Prawer*, ed. B. Z. Kedar, H. E. Meyer and R. C. Smail (Jerusalem, 1982), pp. 153–58.

Russell, Norman, 'Anselm of Havelberg and the Union of the Churches, I, The Problem of the Filioque', *Sobornost*, 1 (1979), pp. 19–41.

—, 'Anselm of Havelberg and the Union of the Churches, II, The Question of Authority', *Sobornost*, 2 (1980), pp. 29–40.

Saunders, J. J., 'The Mongol Defeat at Ain Jalut and the Restoration of the Greek Empire', in J. J. Saunders, *Muslims and Mongols: Essays on Medieval Asia*, ed. G. W. Rice (Christchurch, 1977), pp. 67–76.

Saunders, William, 'The Greek Inscription on the Harran Gate at Edessa: Some Further Evidence', *Byzantinische Forschungen*, 21 (1995), pp. 301–4.

Setton, K. M. (ed.), *A History of the Crusades*, 6 vols (Madison, Wisconsin, 1969–89).

—, *The Papacy and the Levant, 1204–1571*, 4 vols (Philadelphia, 1976–84).

Shboul, A. M. H., 'Arab Attitudes Towards Byzantium: Official, Learned, Popular', *Kathegetria: Essays Presented to Joan Hussey for her 80th Birthday*, ed. J. Chrysostomides (Camberley, 1988), pp. 111–28.

Shepard, Jonathan, 'Byzantine Diplomacy, 800–1204: Means and Ends', *Byzantine Diplomacy*, ed. Jonathan Shepard and Simon Franklin (Aldershot, 1992), pp. 41–71.

—, 'Cross-Purposes: Alexius Comnenus and the First Crusade', *The First Crusade Origins and Impact*, ed. J. Phillips (Manchester, 1997), pp. 107–29.

—, '"Father" or "Scorpion"? Style and Substance in Alexios's Diplomacy', *Alexios I Komnenos*, ed. Margaret Mullett and Dion Smythe (Belfast, 1996), pp. 68–132.

—, 'The Uses of the Franks in Eleventh-Century Byzantium', *Anglo-Norman Studies*, 15 (1993), pp. 275–305.

—, 'When Greek Meets Greek: Alexius Comnenus and Bohemond in 1097–98', *Byzantine and Modern Greek Studies*, 12 (1988), pp. 185–277.

Taylor, W. R., 'A New Syriac Fragment Dealing with Incidents in the Second

Crusade', *Annual of the American Schools of Oriental Research*, 11 (1929–30), pp. 120–30.

Thomas, R. D., 'Anna Comnena's Account of the First Crusade', *Byzantine and Modern Greek Studies*, 15 (1991), pp. 269–312.

Throop, A. Palmer, *Criticism of the Crusade: A Study of Public Opinion and Crusade Propaganda* (Amsterdam, 1940).

Treadgold, Warren, *A History of the Byzantine State and Society* (Stanford, California, 1997).

Tyerman, Christopher, 'Some English Evidence of Attitudes to Crusading in the Thirteenth Century', *Thirteenth-Century England, 1; Proceedings of the Newcastle-Upon-Tyne Conference*, ed. P. R. Coss and S. D. Lloyd (Woodbridge, 1986), pp. 168–74.

Vasiliev, A. A., 'The Foundation of the Empire of Trebizond', *Speculum*, 11 (1936), pp. 3–37.

—, *History of the Byzantine Empire, 324–1453* (2nd edn, Madison, Wisconsin, 1952).

—, 'Henry Plantagenet and Manuel Comnenus', *Byzantinische Zeitschrift*, 29 (1929–30), pp. 233–44.

Waha, M. de, 'La lettre d'Alexis I Comnène à Robert I le Frison: une révision', *Byzantion*, 47 (1977), pp. 113–25.

Walker, Paul E., 'The "Crusade" of John Tzimisces in the Light of New Arab Evidence', *Byzantion*, 47 (1977), pp. 301–27.

Whittow, Mark, *The Making of Orthodox Byzantium, 600–1025* (London, 1996).

Wilson, N. G., *Scholars of Byzantium* (2nd edn, London, 1996).

Wolf, K. B., 'Crusade and Narrative: Bohemond and the *Gesta Francorum*', *Journal of Medieval History*, 17 (1991), pp. 207–16.

Wolff, Robert Lee, 'Footnote to an Incident of the Latin Occupation of Constantinople: The Church and the Icon of the Hodegetria', *Traditio*, 6 (1948), pp. 319–28.

—, 'Hopf's So-called "Fragmentum" of Marino Sanudo Torsello', *The Joshua Starr Memorial Volume* (New York, 1953), pp. 149–59.

—, 'The Latin Empire of Constantinople, 1204–1261', *A History of the Crusades*, ed. K. M. Setton, 6 vols (Madison, Wisconsin, 1969–89), ii, pp. 187–233.

—, 'Mortgage and Redemption of an Emperor's Son: Castile and the Latin Empire of Constantinople', *Speculum*, 29 (1954), pp. 45–84.

Wormald, Francis, 'The Rood of Bromholm', *Journal of the Warburg and Courtauld Institutes*, 1 (1937–38), pp. 31–45.

Index